Job Hunting &
Career Change
ALL-IN-ONE

FOR

DUMMIES®

Job Hunting & Career Change
ALL-IN-ONE
FOR
DUMMIES®

By Kate Burton, Joyce Lain Kennedy, Malcolm Kushner, Jeni Mumford, Brinley Platts, Romilla Ready, and Steve Shipside

Edited by Dr Rob Yeung

BICENTENNIAL
1807
WILEY
2007
BICENTENNIAL

John Wiley & Sons, Ltd

Job Hunting & Career Change All-in-One For Dummies®

Published by
John Wiley & Sons, Ltd
The Atrium
Southern Gate
Chichester
West Sussex
PO19 8SQ
England

E-mail (for orders and customer service enquires): cs-books@

Visit our Home Page on www.wiley.com

WILEY

About the Authors

Dr Rob Yeung is a director at business psychology consultancy Talentspace. He is often asked to coach teams and individuals on presentation skills – in particular on developing their presence and charisma when presenting. He travels extensively around the world, running workshops, participating in panel discussions, and giving presentations to audiences of up to many hundreds of people at a time.

He has written for the *Guardian*, *Daily Telegraph*, and *Financial Times* and has contributed to publications ranging from *Men's Health* and *New Woman* to *Accountancy* and the *Sunday Times*. He has published twelve other books on career and management topics including, in 2006, *The Rules of Office Politics* and *The Rules of EQ* (Cyan/Marshall Cavendish) and *Answering Tough Interview Questions For Dummies* (Wiley).

He is often seen on television including CNN and Channel 4's *Big Brother's Little Brother*. He is also the presenter of the highly acclaimed BBC television series *How To Get Your Dream Job*. A chartered psychologist of the British Psychological Society with a PhD in psychology from the University of London, he has also lectured at a number of business schools and universities.

Need one of the UK's leading psychologists to work with you, your team or your organisation? Drop Dr Rob an email at rob@talentspace.co.uk or visit www.talentspace.co.uk.

Kate Burton is an independent executive coach, author, and trainer who enables individuals and organisations to focus their energy with confidence. She is co-author of the best-selling *Neuro-linguistic Programming For Dummies* with Romilla Ready. Her business career began in corporate advertising and marketing with Hewlett-Packard. Since then she has worked with varied businesses across industries and cultures on how they can be great and confident communicators. What she loves most is delivering custom-built coaching and training programmes. She thrives on supporting people in boosting their motivation, self-awareness, and confidence. Her belief is that people all have unique talents, abilities, and core values. The skill is about honouring them to the full.

Joyce Lain Kennedy is the author of the Tribune Media Service's twice-weekly column *CAREERS NOW*, in its 35th year and appearing in more than 100 newspapers and web sites.

Joyce has received more than three million reader letters. In her column, she has answered in excess of 4,800 queries from readers.

She is the author or senior author of seven career books, including *Joyce Lain Kennedy's Career Book* (McGraw-Hill), and *Electronic Job Search Revolution, Electronic Resume Revolution*, and *Hook Up, Get Hired! The Internet Job Search Revolution* (the last three published by John Wiley & Sons). *Resumes For Dummies* is one of a trio of job market books published under Wiley's widely popular *For Dummies* imprint. The others are *Cover Letters For Dummies* and *Job Interviews For Dummies*.

Malcolm Kushner, 'America's Favourite Humour Consultant', is an internationally acclaimed expert on humour and communication and a professional speaker. Since 1982, he has trained thousands of managers, executives, and professionals on how to gain a competitive edge with humour. His clients include IBM, Hewlett-Packard, AT&T, Chevron, Aetna, Motorola, and Bank of America.

A popular speaker, his Leading With Laughter presentation features rare video clips of US presidents using humour intentionally and successfully. He has performed the speech at many corporate and association meetings, as well as at the Smithsonian Institute.

A Phi Beta Kappa graduate of the University of Buffalo, Kushner holds a BA in Speech-Communication. His MA in Speech-Communication is from the University of Southern California, where he taught freshman speech. He also has a JD from the University of California Hastings College of the Law. Prior to becoming a humour consultant, he practiced law with a major San Francisco law firm.

Kushner is the author of *The Light Touch: How To Use Humor for Business Success* and *Vintage Humour for Wine Lovers*. He is also a co-creator of the humour exhibit at the Ronald Reagan Presidential Library.

Frequently interviewed by the media, Kushner has been profiled in *Time Magazine, USA Today, The New York Times*, and numerous other publications. His television and radio appearances include CNN, National Public Radio, CNBC, *Voice of America*, and *The Larry King Show*. His annual 'Cost of Laughing Index' has been featured on *The Tonight Show* and the front page of *The Wall Street Journal*.

Need a great speaker for your next meeting or event? Contact Malcolm at P.O. Box 7509, Santa Cruz, CA 95061, call 001-831-425-4839, or e-mail him at mk@kushnergroup.com. Visit his Web site at www.kushnergroup.com.

Jeni Mumford is a coach and facilitator who applies whole life coaching techniques to her work with people and within businesses. Before her own life-changing decision to become a coach, Jeni benefited from a 16-year career with the Hays group, spanning recruitment, sales operations, project management, and people development, where she was lucky enough to embark on a new challenging job role every 18 months or so. It was this experience of discovering that the grass is green wherever you are – if you take proper care of the lawn – that gave Jeni the conviction and motivation to build her purpose around inspiring people to attract and enjoy their own dream life and work.

In her business Jeni uses best practice coaching techniques together with NLP, and is a licensed facilitator of Tetramap (a holistic model of behaviour) and Goal Mapping (a brain friendly technique for identifying and maximising progress towards goals). She is addicted to learning and this helps her add value to her work with clients. But in her moments of brutal self-honesty Jeni will admit that quite a lot of the credit is down to the succession of cats who have owned her, from whom she has picked up a great deal about how to handle the ups and downs of life.*

One of the things Jeni likes best about being a coach is that she feels she always gets as much if not more out of the experience than her clients and she can't thank them enough for the honour of seeing them move themselves from frustration to power. Honestly, it's enough to make you want to write a book about it. . . .

You can find out more about Jeni and her business at: www.reachforstarfish. com.

Brinley Platts is a leading executive coach, researcher, and consultant to FTSE 100 companies. He is one of the UK's leading authorities on CIO and IT executive careers and works with international companies on the integration of senior executive life and career goals. He is a behavioural scientist by training, and his passion is to enable large organisations to become places where ordinary decent people can grow and express their talents freely to the benefit of all stakeholders. He is a co-founder of the Bring YourSELF To Work campaign, which aims to release the pent-up talent and passion of today's global workforce to create the better world we all desire and want our children to inherit.

This philosophy can be summed up as: play, ponder, and when in doubt, take a long nap in the sun or on a comfy bed.

Romilla Ready is a Master Practitioner of Neuro-linguistic Programming, and is the director of Ready Solutions, which was founded in 1996. She runs professionally developed workshops across a range of areas and has trained clients in the UK and overseas, using her cross-cultural skills to build rapport between different nationalities. Romilla has been interviewed on local radio and has had articles on stress management and applications of NLP published in the press.

Steve Shipside is old enough to remember when 'Give us a job' entered the language, and became a business journalist not so very long after. Since then he has written for newspapers including the *Guardian*, the *Daily Telegraph*, and the *Times*. He has written for a large number of business and technology magazines, including *The New Statesman*, *The Director*, *Management Today*, *Personnel Today*, *Campaign*, *Revolution*, *Wired*, *Business 2.0*, *MacUser*, and the BBC's Web sites. He also survived a three-year stint appearing as the 'IT Industry Commentator' on Sky TV.

He is the author of half a dozen books including *Remote and Virtual Working*, *Travel*, and *e-Marketing*, all three being books from the Capstone/Wiley Express Exec series, as well as co-authoring books ranging from *100 Musts in Paris* to *The 100 Best IT companies in the UK*.

Publisher's Acknowledgements

We're proud of this book; please send us your comments through our Dummies online registration form located at www.dummies.com/register/.

Some of the people who helped bring this book to market include the following:

Acquisitions, Editorial, and Media Development

Project Editor: Steve Edwards

Content Editor: Nicole Burnett

Commissioning Editor: Alison Yates

Compiled by: Donald Strachan

Text Splicer: David Price

Technical Editor: Paul MacKenzie-Cummins

Executive Editor: Jason Dunne

Executive Project Editor: Daniel Mersey

Cover Photos: © Tim Tadder/Corbis

Cartoons: Ed McLachlan

Composition Services

Project Coordinator: Erin Smith

Layout and Graphics: Claudia Bell, Carl Byers, Stephanie D. Jumper, Christine Williams

Proofreader: Laura Albert

Indexer: Ty Koontz

Publishing and Editorial for Consumer Dummies

    Diane Graves Steele, Vice President and Publisher, Consumer Dummies

    Joyce Pepple, Acquisitions Director, Consumer Dummies

    Kristin A. Cocks, Product Development Director, Consumer Dummies

    Michael Spring, Vice President and Publisher, Travel

    Kelly Regan, Editorial Director, Travel

Publishing for Technology Dummies

    Andy Cummings, Vice President and Publisher, Dummies Technology/General User

Composition Services

    Gerry Fahey, Vice President of Production Services

    Debbie Stailey, Director of Composition Services

Contents at a Glance

Table of Contents

Introduction

Welcome to *Job Hunting & Career Change All-in-One For Dummies*, your launch pad to success in preparing for and gaining the kind of job you want. Making decisions about your career can be tough, and many people struggle to know the way forward. That's where this book comes in.

Finding a job is a job in itself, and can be a stressful process to work through. While not rocket science, job hunting can be hard work, and there are skills you need to master to transform yourself into the high-calibre candidate employers want and make your search successful. Preparation is key to achieving this success, and whether you're looking to enter the job market for the first time or you've been in employment for donkey's years and are looking for a change of direction, you need the essential tools in place before starting your search.

Successfully hunting down a job or changing career is as much about knowing what direction you want to be heading in and what you have that employers want as it is about actually selling yourself to them. You need to look at what motivates you and what your priorities are, and to have a positive frame of mind before setting to work on your CV, interview preparation, and presentation skills. With help from this book, you can build your confidence, discover exactly what you want to be doing in your professional life, and equip yourself with the right tools to get there.

About This Book

Job Hunting & Career Change All-in-One For Dummies merges the best of *For Dummies* career books with the best of *For Dummies* self-help books. We draw on advice from several other *For Dummies* books, which you may wish to check out for more in-depth coverage of certain topics (all published by Wiley):

- *Answering Tough Interview Questions For Dummies* (Rob Yeung)
- *CVs For Dummies* (Steve Shipside and Joyce Lain Kennedy)
- *Building Self-Confidence For Dummies* (Kate Burton and Brinley Platts)
- *Life Coaching For Dummies* (Jeni Mumford)
- *Neuro-linguistic Programming For Dummies* (Romilla Ready and Kate Burton)
- *Public Speaking & Presentations For Dummies* (Malcolm Kushner and Rob Yeung)

Conventions Used in This Book

To make your reading experience easier and to alert you to key words or points, we use certain conventions in this book:

- ✔ *Italics* introduce new terms, and underscore key differences between words.
- ✔ **Bold** text is used to display the action part of bulleted and numbered lists.
- ✔ Monofont is used to highlight Web addresses, showing you exactly what to type into your computer.

Foolish Assumptions

This book brings together the elements of knowledge that are essential for preparing yourself for career change or searching for a job. As a consequence, to keep the book down to a reasonable number of pages, we've made a few assumptions about you (we hope you don't mind!). Maybe you're someone who is:

- ✔ Staring at a blank CV as a newcomer to job hunting, or looking to rework your CV to aid a change of career as a seasoned veteran of the job market.
- ✔ Entering the daunting world of job interviews and wanting to prepare yourself for the type of questions you are likely to face.
- ✔ Wanting to develop motivation and confidence in your work environment.
- ✔ Facing the prospect of having to deliver a presentation as part of the recruitment process, but have never had to do this before and you're not sure where to start.

If any (or all) of these assumptions accurately describe you, or if you just want to gain a better awareness and understanding of the things you need to do to get the job you want, you've come to the right place!

How This Book Is Organised

We've divided *Job Hunting & Career Change All-in-One For Dummies* into four separate books. This section explains what you'll find out about in each one of these books. Each book is broken into chapters offering different aspects of job-hunting advice. The table of contents gives you more detail about what's in each chapter, and we've even included a cartoon at the start of each book, just to keep you happy.

Book I: Plotting a Course: Your Job and Career Plans

Knowing what you want from your professional life, and how you want to progress, is the name of the game in this book. Motivating yourself, building up your self confidence, and decision making are key themes here that can help you get your plans underway.

Book II: Showcasing Yourself with a StandOut CV

Book II is your guide to the nitty-gritty of putting together a winning CV. Knowing what to include, what to leave out, what language to use, and how to structure and format your CV are important skills, and this book gives you the right advice on how to proceed. This book also talks you through the more recent changes in the world of recruitment, covering innovations and new practices used on the Internet by employers.

Book III: Succeeding at Interviews

Creating a killer CV and making job applications is one thing, but performing on the day at an interview is another. This book helps you to effectively sell yourself (well, your skills and abilities, anyway) to employers on the day and to prepare yourself for their incisive interviewing, giving a polished performance, and thriving in unusual types of interview and assessment. This book shows you how to make the right impression on the big day.

Book IV: Delivering Perfect Presentations

You may find that you need to deliver a presentation as part of your interview, assessment, or selection process. This book helps you to prepare for such an eventuality, giving you the lowdown on preparation, structure, and organisation, and on other areas such as dealing with any nervousness you might feel on the day, and on how to use body language to your best advantage. This book shows you how to shine in front of a discerning audience!

Icons Used in This Book

To help your navigation through this book, keep an eye out for the icons, the little pictures that sit in the margin. They guide you to particular types of information. This list tells you what the icons in this book mean.

This icon highlights practical advice to get our job hunting and career change methods working for you.

This icon is a friendly reminder of important points that it may be a good idea to take note of.

This icon covers the boring stuff that only anoraks would ever know. You can safely skip paragraphs marked by this icon without missing anything essential, or you can read it and improve your wealth of knowledge even further!

This icon marks things to avoid in your enthusiasm when trying out your job-hunting skills.

This icon calls your attention to anecdotes and examples that you may find useful.

Where to Go from Here

We've made this book into an easy-to-use reference tool that you should be comfortable with, no matter what your level of experience. You can use this book in a couple of ways: as a cover-to-cover read or as a reference for when you run into problems or need inspiration. Feel free to skip straight to the chapters that interest you. You don't have to scour each chapter methodically from beginning to end to find what you want.

What direction you go in depends on your own needs. If you're just starting out and want to assess your current state of play, see Book I. Searching for the right choice of words to give your CV that professional edge? Check out Book II. If you're shuddering with nerves at the thought of having to deliver a presentation to your potential employers, Book IV is the place to be. Facing your first interview in years and not sure what kind of questioning to expect? Head over to Book III. If you're not yet sure where to start, have a good look at the table of contents to get an idea of what you'll read about where in the book. The table of contents is very detailed and gives you an excellent overview of the whole book and the way in which it is structured. Just start where it suits you and come back later for more.

And the very best of luck to you in your search for the perfect job!

Book I
Plotting a Course: Your Job and Career Plans

'If you want to be part of our management team, you've got to be able to do this.'

In this book . . .

This book helps you through the process of setting your employment compass in the right direction. From working out your priorities and knowing where you're going in the world of work, to preparing and motivating yourself to get there, this books helps to get your career plans rolling. What are you waiting for?

Here are the contents of Book I at a glance:

Chapter 1

Assessing Career and Work

. . . .

In This Chapter

▶ Making proactive work choices

▶ Understanding the power of focus and feedback

▶ Looking to the future of your work

. . . .

*Y*ou probably spend a large proportion of your time 'at work'. Or, if you're not currently employed, you may spend a fair bit of time and energy searching for work. If you're retired from a career or job, you may be in the process of redefining what can fill the gap that your work used to fill in your life. But the paid work that you do, or have done in the past, is only one aspect of what constitutes work for you over your lifetime. Your work as a parent, caregiver, volunteer, and even your hobbies or interests are all facets of your natural drive to be involved in purposeful activity for your own or others' benefit.

A helpful definition of 'work' is that it is the context in which you use your skills and talents in some way to give and (often) receive something of value, whether monetary, in kind, for your own satisfaction, or as a duty of care. Having a 'career' on the other hand, means that you also make choices that allow you to build on the skills and abilities you use at work so that you can take on bigger and/or more demanding roles. These roles are usually associated with pay rises and improved benefits because you're stretching the range of what you can offer and as an employee you can command more value in return. Building your career may include self-employment and consultancy work where you create and generate opportunities for yourself in a broader market-place.

Not everyone wants a career in this sense and you may be happy to consider the work that you do as a lower priority in your life than, for example, your family or your commitment to your health. You may work simply to get enough money to fund the lifestyle that you want and so choose to invest most of your energy in areas that are more important to you than work.

This chapter focuses on three main aspects of your work and career – how satisfied you are with what you do; how much you feel your efforts are recognised through pay, promotion, and feedback if you're in a paid job; and the extent to which you have opportunities to develop your skills and potential through your work or career. This chapter guides you through some of your options to improve these three areas and helps you identify aspects of your work and career that are fundamental for you in your life as a whole.

Assessing Your Attitudes to Work

We often hear people complain about 'that Monday morning feeling' when the sound of the alarm bell going off just makes you want to slide back under the duvet and go back to sleep. But work, maybe more than love, does seem to make the world go round. Even if you don't need to work for money, the instinct to focus on purposeful activity is still very strong. What's true for you right now? Do you work to live or live to work? Does your current work need to change to reflect your attitudes in life, or does your attitude to work need a bit of fine-tuning?

Playing your part in different work roles

When people ask 'What do you do?' your answer is probably to give your job title, or to talk about the company you work at or own. How much of your identity is attached to your paid work (or lack of it)? Imagine for a moment that you're actually forbidden from working for pay at all. Think about what your response would be when asked 'What do you do?' How comfortable would you feel answering that question? The degree of discomfort you feel may indicate the strength of your reliance on the work you do for pay as a strong validation of your success and self-worth. Nothing's wrong with that; recognising the other ways in which you use your talents to work is a great way of enhancing your overall skill set and becoming happier with the idea of work.

Balancing your different roles

Consider the three main work roles that you probably play:

- **Pay:** Work that you get paid for – your job or business.
- **People:** Work that you do for the people in your life and world – parenting, caring, voluntary work.
- **Passion:** Work that is linked to your interests and passions – activity in a hobby, learning a new skill, being a member of a club.

These three areas may well overlap for you, or you may see them as sitting in three different compartments of your life. The balance between these three aspects of work is rarely an equal split in terms of time. Most people spend more of their time in paid work, at least for certain periods of their life. But think about the times you don't have paid work – periods of unemployment, maternity or paternity leave, sabbaticals, and retirement. What will define your idea of work then?

Perhaps you don't feel that you've identified 'passion' work yet. If you spend a lot of time and energy on building your career then you may have to put 'passion' work at the bottom of your pile of priorities.

The following activity can help you to see the links and differences in your attitudes to different work areas. Think of the roles that you carry out in the work areas of pay, people, and passion and answer the questions in Table 1-1, which uses Stuart, who runs his own business, as an example. In this example we focus on one role within each work area but of course you may have more than one (such as being a parent and also caring for elderly relatives in the 'people' work area). Choose the roles that are most significant for you.

Book I

Plotting a Course: Your Job and Career Plans

Table 1-1	Identifying Your Role in Different Work Areas		
	Pay	*People*	*Passion*
What is the main role I work at in this area?	Run my business.	Father of John and Sophie.	Member of local art group.
How much time do I spend on this work?	Too much! At least 50 hours during the week and I often work at weekends.	Not nearly enough . . . bedtime stories during the week. Weekends better but often interrupted by paid work issues.	Have missed the last 6 meetings.
What value do I get from this work?	Money, stimulation, sense of self-worth and achievement.	Love, joy, laughter, sense of contribution to my family.	A real buzz from tapping into my creativity and helping to stage exhibitions of our work.
What feelings do I have about this work?	I veer between feeling very motivated and pretty stressed depending on the challenges.	I feel very peaceful and calm in this role and find it helps me get perspective and de-stress.	I have a lot of fun in this role and feel alive and purposeful. My energy levels are higher after a meeting.

(continued)

Table 1-1 *(continued)*

	Pay	People	Passion
What is my current attitude to this work in 10 words or less?	Takes more time and attention relative to the rewards I get.	I always get more out than I put in.	I've been taking this for granted and reducing its impact.
What do I need to change about this work to balance my portfolio?	I can be more disciplined, delegate more, and reduce the time I give to this role. I probably only need to reduce my hours by an hour a day to make a significant difference. And I can cut out weekend working.	Freeing up time from paid work will allow me to will allow me to devote more time to this role. I'd like to commit to organising family suppers at least twice a week.	I can make a regular weekly commitment here by giving it a higher priority in my life. I'll also investigate opening up the club to children occasionally so I can share my interest with John and Sophie.

Your answers to the questions in Table 1-1 highlight the relative importance you place on each area of work, the time you allocate to these areas, and how they feed your most important values. Stuart's completed table shows clearly that the time he allocates to the most pressing one – paid work – drains the value he gets out of the other two. By recognising that, he can see ways to manage his paid work time a little better and focus on the other two areas, which in turn help to re-energise him for his paid work.

Setting Your Work in Context

Adjusting the balance on your work areas helps you to identify ways to ensure that you get what you need from all aspects of the work that you do. The rest of this chapter focuses on improving what most people classify as work: your paid job.

Even if work is just something you do to pay the bills, you probably spend a fair amount of time doing it so considering how work fits into your life and preferences as a whole makes sense. To what extent does your job match your natural abilities, fit with your beliefs about your world, and support the values that you hold most dear? Why should what you do best in terms of skills determine the most natural choice of work for you? Would you get even more personal satisfaction in an environment where you were developing skills that are currently less strong for you? For the work that you choose to do most of the time – whether that be paid or unpaid – this section helps you to find your unique balance between being comfortable using your best skills and stretching yourself to your natural potential.

Making a conscious choice

Think for a moment about how you ended up in the role you currently hold, or the jobs you have formerly performed. What made you choose the work you currently do? Did happy or not-so-happy accidents result in your career choices? Were you influenced by a parent or an older adult? Did you get swept along by an interview process and suddenly find yourself accepting an offer? Would you choose your job again knowing what you now know?

Perhaps you're struggling with work issues, or you're in the wrong job, or you're not using your skills to best advantage, and you can't see how to get to the work that you're meant to do (or even decide what it is). All of that experience, however uncomfortable, is preparing you in just the right way for what's around the corner. Whichever route you take – either being open and flexible to opportunities or planning every move – use the detachment and questioning skills of coaching to ensure that you're heading in the right direction. You may choose to stay where you are for the moment, knowing that you need to gather strength (maybe a strong sense of self-belief and confidence) and resources (skills, knowledge, and experience) to make a change. Making that choice in itself is part of the process of moving forward.

Evaluating your job

You may find that you get so caught up in the detail of your work, for good or ill, that before you know it another year has passed and you wonder what's changed for the better. You can adapt to almost anything and you may find yourself settling for a role that you've long outgrown, or that imposes unhealthy pressure on you, simply because you haven't taken the time to ask yourself some searching questions on a regular basis. A high proportion of workplace stress is caused by the accumulation of lots of small irritations piled on top of each other and left to go unchecked. If you're ambitious and want to progress your career, you need to carefully assess where you are and where you're heading.

You can assess whether your skills and natural preferences are best suited to what you currently do by putting yourself in the role of someone who is evaluating the requirements, ups and downs, and perks and potholes of your job. See how you measure up against this evaluation. Don't think about your official job specification – often the things that aren't written down cause the most frustration or offer the most joy. Try the following activity and feel free to add other questions to tailor it to the context of your own work.

- What is your main purpose for doing the work you do?
- What do you spend 80 per cent of your time doing at work?
- Which of your best skills do you use at work?
- Which of your skills do you never or rarely get the opportunity to use at work?
- What proportion of your time do you spend
  - Feeling stressed?
  - Feeling bored?
  - Feeling stimulated?
  - Enjoying your work?
- To what extent do you feel in control at work?
- How often do you stretch your capabilities?
- How often do you coast along at work?
- How would you describe your working environment on a scale of 1 (= your worst nightmare) to 10 (= your idea of heaven)?
- Finish the following statement: 'I choose the work I currently do because . . .'
- Choose the statement that best describes how you feel about your work:
  - 'I'm living my work dream – I don't even think of it as "work".'
  - 'I feel challenged, stimulated, and valued most of the time, and this carries me through the difficult bits.'
  - 'Some days are better than others and on the whole, I can take it or leave it. Work is not a priority area for me.'
  - 'I often get frustrated, anxious, or bored at work and this affects my enjoyment of the good bits.'
  - 'I have to drag myself in every day; I'm ready to quit.'

As a result of this activity, what have you discovered about your work that needs to change? Perhaps you found that you spend 80 per cent of your time doing tasks that bore you or use skills that you least enjoy? Or you may have discovered that you feel bored half the time and stimulated the other half, and that overall the stimulation outweighs the boredom. Or perhaps you've identified that your attitude to your work is in the middle ground – 'take it or leave it' – and that this means you can put up with day to day irritations because work is a low priority for you. Look for common themes and links in your answers to the activity. Is your main purpose the same as the reason you choose the work you do?

When Stuart completed this evaluation he described the main purpose of doing his work as providing financial stability for his family in a way that meant he was fully in control. The reason Stuart chose to do his work (running his own business) was because he naturally enjoyed being an entrepreneur. Stuart's work purpose therefore linked to his values, and his choice of work had come about because of his knowledge of his best skills.

Making adjustments at work

From the previous activity, you can identify the main areas that need change. Work often needs adjustment as a result of undesirable impact in the following areas:

- ✔ **Beliefs.** Your beliefs about your work may be holding you back. Perhaps you think that you're 'entitled' to be stimulated by what you do and need to re-think that belief so you can be more proactive about finding ways to increase stimulation for yourself.

- ✔ **Motivation.** Your motivation may need re-adjusting by making a change in the way you approach work.

- ✔ **Freedom.** You may feel the need for more freedom and autonomy in your work.

- ✔ **Support.** You may require more support and recognition from those around you.

- ✔ **Pressure.** Your work may overload you and cause you unhelpful stress.

- ✔ **Responsibility.** You may feel disconnected from your work and want to take more responsibility in order for you to become more engaged in what you do.

- ✔ **Environment.** You may be unfulfilled with your current environment – from a simple issue of 'same desk, same four walls' to having really outgrown your current job and company.

Book I

Plotting a Course: Your Job and Career Plans

Using Table 1-2 as your example, write down the commitment in each area that moves you closer to your ideal work. Here's what Stuart had to say about his paid work of running his own business:

Table 1-2	Commitment Statements to Move You Closer to Your Ideal Work
Change my beliefs	'The business will not collapse if I delegate more, in fact it will benefit from fresh energies directed at some areas.'
Focus on my motivation	'I'm looking forward to harnessing the creative energy I get from my art to see how I can solve business problems more effectively.'
Enjoy more freedom	'Setting a goal of getting home on time more often will stop me feeling chained to the business.'
Get more support	'My office manager (Jo) is ready for development and is really committed to the business – she will thrive on being asked to support me more and take on new responsibilities.'
Generate less pressure	'Spending time with my children will help me de-stress.'
Take more responsibility	'I want to be more self-responsible about my time. I'm shocked to see how much time I coast along thinking I'm working hard. Staying late has become a habit.'
Change my environment	'Don't feel the need for a change here, although Jo has some ideas to move the team around to stimulate new work relationships. I'll keep an open mind!'

Improving Your Current Job

If evaluating your job has made you realise that your current work isn't meeting your needs, you may now be formulating a plan to make radical changes. You may decide that although you want to change certain aspects of your current role, it basically meets a lot of your requirements for a satisfactory work situation. On the other hand, you may feel ready to take a deep breath and search elsewhere for a new position (see the section 'Finding Your Dream Work'). But you probably have to serve notice, meet obligations, and hand over projects before you can cross the next threshold. Even if your change is relatively organic – such as acquiring or developing a new skill so that you can progress to the next level in your current organisation – a shortfall remains between your ambitions and where you are now.

Keeping your focus

You need to work out how to focus your attention on the here and now at work while setting your sights on your next goal. And in the process of 'making the best' of your current situation you may also discover some new wisdom to inform your next step. You may realise that you can make changes in your current job that improve your situation.

Senti started life coaching with one clear objective – to escape from her current role before she got fired! Although she admitted that she probably wouldn't really be fired (she was a careful and conscientious manager), she hated the relationship she had with her boss so much that she *felt* as if it were true. She was intensely unhappy because although she knew where she *didn't* want to be, she had no clue about the next best step.

During coaching she worked through the steps she needed to take to resolve her stalemate. She realised that deciding exactly on her next career move was not the most urgent priority. She faced the fact that some of her own beliefs about herself were contributing to the poor relationship she had with her boss. Unless she found more assertive ways of behaving, she would find herself in a similar position in any new role she undertook.

Senti set herself two main goals – to identify and begin to take action to secure the job of her dreams, and to address her relationship with her boss. The second goal was hard work because part of her had already written off her current position and was focused on the future. She worked hard on her self-esteem and confidence, which allowed her to stop taking her boss's style personally. In turn, this helped her boss to see Senti's talents clearly at last. Three months later, he offered Senti a promotion to manage a new project.

After some thought Senti accepted the new role. It would enhance her skills considerably and was in an exciting area of the business that interested her. Her biggest surprise was that she found that her new role took her pretty close to the dream job she'd begun to identify for herself. Using coaching, Senti's new-found self-confidence gave her the courage to identify business needs that she was uniquely fitted to address.

Like Senti, you may discover through coaching that the external factor that you think is the problem with your current work role – the pay; the way you're managed; the pressures of deadlines – may be secondary to the internal factors that you can control by applying and developing your natural skills. Here are some suggestions that can help you to improve your enjoyment of work:

✔ **Practise assertive communication.** If you feel frustrated at work, your needs are not being met. Be clear with yourself about what you need from your role – is variety more important to you than a fixed routine? You may find ways of creating a more varied structure to what you do but you may need the okay from your boss to make changes. State what will work best for you clearly and directly as early as possible rather than fuming quietly over a situation. This helps you avoid any tense confrontations further down the line when the boredom has really got to you.

✔ **Remember what motivates you.** When you're clear on your values, you can link all that you do to these motivating forces. If elements of your job feel stressful at times and you wonder why you stick with it, think about what your job gives you that helps you live your values. Perhaps your salary supports the lifestyle you want, or the recognition you receive for meeting deadlines feeds your sense of accomplishment and self-belief. Keeping a focus on the end result helps you put your job into a whole-life perspective.

✔ **Catch yourself 'being in the moment'.** A sign that you're performing well is when you get absorbed in what you're doing and lose track of time. With a little practice, you can place yourself 'in the moment' even when you're bored or frustrated. Simply focus on what you are doing as if your life depended on it, or as if it were the most fascinating thing you've ever encountered, or try to recall the feeling you had when you completed this task for the very first time. This trick won't always turn a boring task into the highlight of your day, but making the effort to switch your mental state is often enough to jolt you out of negativity and help you deal effectively with the routine so you can move on to more interesting tasks.

✔ **Remember that the only things that are ever fully in your control are your own thoughts, behaviour, and actions.** No matter how little you deserve it, you sometimes fall foul of the bad mood of a colleague or boss. You can allow this to throw you off course or you can put yourself in their shoes and decide on a course of action that accommodates the unfavourable circumstance and still gets you where you need to be. Sometimes that means tackling the behaviour and sometimes it means giving the other person space to work through their bad mood without you taking it personally. Focus on what you can control – your *own* mood and behaviour – and you're more likely to help the other person get back on track too.

✔ **Take a rain check with yourself every couple of hours.** If you know you tend to prefer the company of others rather than working alone, how can you inject some human interaction into your task to help you regain energy to continue? Think about the different ways you can carry out simple or routine tasks that increase your enjoyment. If you have a mailing to pack up for the post can you get some other people involved to make it more fun? Or would you prefer to sit by a window with a nice view and let the routine task act like a calming meditation? These little choices can make a huge difference to how you feel about what you do and help to put you more in control of your work.

Dealing with negative situations

Book I

Plotting a
Course:
Your Job
and Career
Plans

You may love your work but find that the people around you drain your
energy and lower your mood, your confidence, or your conviction in what
you do. You can protect yourself from the most damaging effects of negativity
by understanding that people often exhibit bad behaviour when they feel
trapped, and sense that they lack power and choice.

Boredom and disengagement can lead to apathy, which can put a damper on
the enthusiasm and proactivity of entire teams. When you succumb to apathy
you get hijacked by lethargy, cynicism, and a feeling of pointlessness, and it's
easy to pick this mood up from other people and join in. Coach yourself to
avoid this mood by asking yourself, 'What am I feeling frustrated about? What
is causing me to feel trapped and out of control? What can I do to positively
support the team or proactively challenge this problem?'

A quite different form of negative behaviour results from the temptation to
indulge in gossip and hearsay. Damaging gossip can stem from fear and self-
protection, directing the attention away from the gossiper. And the effects are
often very negative – encouraging back-biting between departments, and
destroying trust. All of this can be quite exciting – for a while – until the negative energy means that the biter ends up getting bitten. Coach yourself to
steer away from indulging in gossip by asking yourself, 'How can I direct my
energies to fuel a more productive fire?' Before you pass on information
about a co-colleague to a third party, ask yourself three questions: 'Is what
I'm about to say true? Is it positive and constructive? Is it useful and relevant
to the person I'm talking to?'

Finding Your Dream Work

This section looks at the options you have when you know that progressing
your career means leaving for pastures new. Finding your dream work starts
with knowing what you really love to do in a work context. The following
activity helps you to identify what you relish doing at work.

Find a quiet spot and sit comfortably, taking a few moments to breathe
deeply and relax. Close your eyes and ask yourself the following question:

> *If a miracle happened and when I open my eyes I have the perfect work for
> me, what would that look like? What would I do for the next 24 hours?*

Think about exactly what would happen, planning out each hour of the day
exactly to your taste and preferences. You can include scenarios that may
seem impossible and beyond your current grasp. The end result of your visualisation is not to create an accurate blueprint, but to give you clues to the
key elements of your perfect work day.

Floating into a career change

For the last 30 years, Richard Nelson Bolles has published an annually updated manual for job hunters and career changers called *What Colour is Your Parachute?* The manual contains some great exercises to identify specific skills and give you ideas on how and where you might apply them (although the manual is more specific to the United States job market). Take a look at the companion Web site `www.jobhuntersbible.com`, which has additional guidance on how to search the Internet for job-hunting resources.

What has your miracle created for you? Is it an extension of your current work, maybe just a few steps away from where you already are? Or is your dream work something so wildly different from your current job that you can't see how you can ever make it happen? You already have all the resources you need to get your dream job, no matter how many challenges stand in your way. Of course, the further away your dream job is from your current skill set and reach, the stronger your passion must be for pursuing it so that you can maintain the momentum when the going gets tough.

Make sure your passion is well rooted in what's really important to you in your life as a whole before committing to the road ahead.

Start bringing your dream job closer to home by collecting adverts for roles that approximate or match it. Some may be a little out of your reach right now but you can also include adverts in your dream job folder that are a few steps closer to where you are currently. By researching and referring to your ideal role, and thinking about how you can prepare yourself for getting there, you'll find that your goal becomes much more realistic.

Knowing your job search goal

What did you discover about your dream job from the activity in the preceding section? To what extent is that role in your reach right now? Your strategy for exploring the job market differs depending on how many steps you need to take to get to your ultimate destination. Your goal may be:

- ✔ **Wanting change for its own sake.** You probably like elements of your current job a lot, as well as being frustrated over others. Essentially though, your main motivation for moving is to re-enthuse yourself in a fresh environment. Positive change for its own sake is really your key driver. You can make this change in your work fairly easily and quickly because you don't need to change many factors to re-enthuse yourself. Start by looking around at other departments within your company to get a fresh perspective. A secondment (temporarily transferring to another position) may be just the trick to satisfy your need for a change or springboard you to a new role.

✔ **Increasing your challenge.** You want to get to the next level, or even the one beyond that. Promotion and a rise in salary may be key motivators for you. You're ready to compete in the job market, demonstrate that you can stretch yourself, and prove you're worth the increased financial investment for a new employer. You need to prepare for the healthy competition you may face – think about your CV, your interview technique, and the research into the market you need to do. When you've done this groundwork, change can happen quickly.

✔ **Expanding your horizons.** You have your sights set on a long-term goal of broadening your skills base. Maybe you see the next few years as a platform for ultimately setting up your own business, so your next move is about gaining lots of broad experience as preparation. You may need to move a little sideways to get the long-term benefit of a different skill set. This career goal may take longer to achieve because you want to change a number of factors and need to demonstrate you can adapt to a whole new work arena.

If your dream job involves acquiring a new skill or re-training, take a look at www.learndirect.co.uk for a wealth of information and resources on practical study and qualifications to help you.

Working the market

When looking for a new job, you can go it alone by sending out speculative CVs to job adverts, posting responses on Internet job boards, or working your networks (the following section is about using your current network of people to your advantage). You can also use recruitment consultancies. You may want the strength of an expert behind you who can give you support, advice, and can market you with skill.

If you decide to use a recruitment consultancy, choose two or three and build up good relationships with your contacts there. Sign up to a consultancy with a national network to benefit from their extensive resources, and one or two smaller local consultancies who can give you the very best service. Agree how you'll keep in touch with your consultant – don't assume they'll call you. Be memorable and ensure you're at the forefront of their mind when a juicy role comes up.

Using your networks

A high proportion of career moves, especially at a senior level, are word of mouth introductions (the 'hidden' job market). But you don't have to be a serial networker to take advantage of this route. When you're searching for your dream job, don't hold back from telling the people around you your wish list for your next move, and ask them to consider people they know who may help you. Your acquaintances may not know a potential employer, but they may know someone in the right industry who can offer you helpful information to help you prepare. Or someone in your network may be able to practice interview techniques with you or review your CV. Ask yourself:

> *What do I need to close the gap between where I am now and where I want to be? Who can help me do that?*

Getting Recognition for Your Work

Even the most high-minded and self-aware person needs the right kind of feedback and recognition in order to feel that their work is worthwhile. But giving and receiving feedback can be tricky. Sometimes you may fear to confront a problem, or feel embarrassment at the idea of offering or receiving gushing praise. Many problems at work are caused by people hoping that the problem disappears, or that they don't need to say 'well done' because you've obviously done a good job. However, studies show that even negative feedback, poorly delivered, is preferable to no feedback at all.

Coaching yourself to give and receive feedback at work not only helps you to develop your work abilities, but also enhances your own self-awareness, empathy, and ability to come up with solutions.

Getting feedback

Do you look forward to getting feedback in appraisals and one-to-ones? Or do you simply find them pointless and irrelevant? Appraisals can sometimes feel too focused on looking at how you measure up to a common standard – and you are, of course, an uncommon, unique individual. While the company perspective is essential, both parties benefit when the review is really meaningful for the person being reviewed. Try to see your formal review as a free, and very powerful, coaching session and help your appraiser to tailor the session to your needs – you get a lot more out of your review and also project a proactive, professional image.

Book I

Plotting a
Course:
Your Job
and Career
Plans

Ask yourself the following questions:

- ✔ What opportunities do I have to get formal feedback at work? How can I encourage more constructive feedback opportunities?

- ✔ What benefits do I currently get from formal feedback at work?

- ✔ On a scale of 1–10, how much do I enjoy this kind of feedback and feel motivated by it?

- ✔ How can I get increased benefits and feel even more motivated by formal reviews?

Here are three suggestions for getting more out of your formal review process:

- ✔ If you are nervous or apprehensive, explain so in good time so that your appraiser can come up with ways of reassuring you. This might be as simple as finding a less formal room to conduct the meeting in – facing your appraiser across a cold, forbidding boardroom table is off putting for many people.

- ✔ Be clear about the focus for the feedback session well in advance and prepare any relevant documentation. If you have facts at your fingertips, you waste less time and present a good impression.

- ✔ Ask for specific examples of behaviour (good and bad) and an explanation of exactly why the behaviour did/didn't match up to expectations. Ask for suggestions for maintaining/improving your performance in the future.

If you're self-employed, you can still benefit from setting up a feedback process through self-coaching, and listening to your customers and suppliers. Here are some annual review questions you can ask yourself:

- ✔ What were my successes over the last year? What has inspired me most?

- ✔ What have been my main challenges and how have I overcome them? What have been my biggest obstacles and what am I learning from these?

- ✔ What do my customers think about me, my business, and my products/services? (Ask them!)

- ✔ How do my suppliers and partners feel about our working relationship? (Ask them!)

- ✔ What skills have I developed and what have I learnt about myself?

- ✔ What new personal goals can I set for the coming year?

- ✔ What support do I need?

- ✔ How can I measure my success?

What is your personal wish list for an effective feedback session? What action can you now take?

Promoting your personal brand

Getting recognition at work is all about helping others to see what your unique contribution is. You may feel that selling yourself and your skills is egotistical, especially if you tend to be naturally modest about your achievements. Perhaps you tend to hide your 'light' and find that over time you begin to feel a little resentful that people don't always notice or appreciate your good work. Or you may take the opposite view and grab the limelight as often as you can, only to find that those around you push you back down into place. Getting the balance right is tricky. You may feel that you have to adopt a different work persona and play office politics in order to be successful, but the truth is that most people hate spin, and the last place they want to have to deal with it is at work.

In what ways do you put up a façade at work? Do you sometimes present a show of blustery confidence when you're really quaking in your boots? At times this is helpful, but at other times it may prevent you from getting the support you need. If you manage staff, do you think you always need to know the answer to every problem? What impact does this have for you and the team, on those occasions when you don't know the best solution? How can you present an authentic you at work and maintain the respect of others?

Think of yourself as a business. What are your unique selling points? Yes, you have skills, but how do you package and present these skills to the world in a way that is unique to you? Getting used to thinking about how you project your personal brand can help you to develop versatility. After all, you are uniquely your brand and you can also change that brand as you wish, according to the 'market' you're in. So you may choose to display your more extrovert image in a meeting or you may let people see your reflective, thoughtful side, depending upon your audience and what's required.

Looking to the Future

What are the trends you see developing in your work choices? You may feel you have to run to keep up with the pace of change, but if you regularly coach yourself through your work choices you can set your own pace, and establish your own standards of excellence.

Book I

Plotting a
Course:
Your Job
and Career
Plans

Progression in your work life need not always equate to promotion up the ranks. Progression may be more about finding ways to remain stimulated in what you do, perhaps taking a sideways move from time to time to re-energise yourself and your skills. Or progression may mean that you move to a different role in a new company every few years. If you've found the work that you feel you were meant to do, making progress may be easy.

Generally, you feel a sense of making progress when you're living your values at work and being your authentic self. And while all jobs have an element of routine in them, you usually feel more inspired if you're able to find new things to learn about yourself and your skills through work.

Here are three things that you can contemplate on a daily basis to measure your progress:

- ✔ **What were my 'wins' today?** This could be successfully negotiating with a supplier, or achieving a deadline.

- ✔ **What have I learnt today?** Maybe you added to your skills, picked up some new knowledge, or discovered a way not to do something!

- ✔ **What can I change as a result of today?** Perhaps you want to revisit your time management strategy as result of experiencing a bit too much stress meeting that deadline, or you decide that you're going to step into future negotiations more readily to take your confidence to another level.

Write down your answers so that you can reflect back on them and witness the cumulative power of these small daily successes, learning points, and significant steps that you've integrated into your working life.

When you think about the work you plan for the future, how prepared are you for it? Do you have a dream to be your own boss, or to create a working life that is independent of your source of wealth – by investing in property for example – so that you have more freedom to choose your work on its own merits? You can think about your future work in the context of a SWOT analysis – considering your strengths, weaknesses, opportunities, and threats – as follows:

- ✔ What are my **strengths** at work?

- ✔ What **weaknesses** am I aware of and how am I working on them?

- ✔ What **opportunities** do I have at work that match my whole-life goals?

- ✔ What **threats** at work may hold me back from meeting my whole life goals?

Coach yourself for your future work by working through the following coaching questions:

- ✔ **Powerful opening question:** What attitudes do I want to develop about work to fulfil my potential throughout my career?

- ✔ **Personal style:** What kind of work am I naturally drawn to? What do I thrive on? What demotivates me? What kind of environments suit me best? Where do I feel most at home when I am working?

- ✔ **Beliefs:** What negative beliefs do I have about work that prevent me from preparing for future challenges?

- ✔ **Motivation:** What image of myself at work is most appealing as my future vision? What would I reach for if I knew that I couldn't fail?

- ✔ **What's working:** What am I doing now to prepare myself for my future working life? How can I develop these behaviours and habits? What's getting in the way of fulfilling my potential? What trends do I see developing now that either propel me forward or hold me back?

- ✔ **Exploring options:** What options do I have to expand my working range? What is the easiest route? What is the most challenging route? What more information do I need before I decided on my options?

- ✔ **Taking action:** What's my first step? How much time can I allocate to planning my approach? How do I know when I am making progress? What can I do to celebrate?

Chapter 2

Getting Motivated

In This Chapter

▶ Understanding what motivation means and what motivates you

▶ Applying motivation theories to your work and social life

▶ Using your understanding to engineer new opportunities for achievement

▶ Getting focused and avoiding procrastination

*Y*our personal motivation is the force that gets you out of bed in the morning and provides you with energy for the work of the day. Have you ever wondered why you seem to be bursting with it some days, and other times it seems to desert you entirely?

Understanding how motivation works so that you can access your natural motivation to help manage the life you want with more confidence and ease is what this chapter is about. It gives you the insight you need to keep moving forward despite the challenges you face.

The most important thing you can take from this chapter is that you don't have to put up with feeling weak and unmotivated. If you deal intelligently with blocks in your natural energy source, you can restore your energy, achieve more with less effort, and feel more at ease with life, more satisfied with yourself, and more confident and powerful in the world.

Driving Forward in Your Life

The more motivated you feel the more inclined you are to push yourself through the things that are holding you back. If you can increase your motivation, you automatically increase your confidence. In the next sections, we look at Abraham Maslow's influential hierarchy of needs to help you gain insight into what motivates you and everyone you come into contact with.

Rising through Maslow's hierarchy of needs

One of the founders of the human potential movement, Abraham Maslow is best known for his work on human motivation. He was fascinated by what makes some people face huge challenges in life, and what makes them refuse to give up despite incredible odds. He developed the model for which he is best known – his hierarchy of needs, shown in Figure 2-1 – to explain the forces that motivate people.

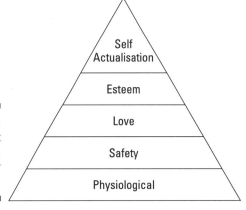

Figure 2-1:
Looking at Maslow's hierarchy of needs.

Maslow saw men and women being constantly drawn on through life by the irresistible pull of unsatisfied needs. He grouped human needs into a hierarchy, which everyone shares and needs to satisfy from the bottom up. This model is widely taught in management development courses, but his work goes far beyond the workplace to the very heart of our humanity.

Maslow believed that you must first satisfy your basic physiological needs for air, water, food, sleep, and so on before any other desires can surface. As a member of modern society, these basic needs are largely taken care of for you, but if you have ever been short of breath under water you know and understand how this first-tier, physiological need dominates everything else until it is satisfied.

But once your physiological needs are met, you automatically shift up to the next level in the hierarchy to your need for safety, – and that now drives you. Again, modern society tends to provide safe environments, but whenever you do feel threatened, you experience an automatic physical response and cannot think of much else until the situation is resolved and you feel safe again.

At the next level, you have to make more personal interventions to ensure your needs are satisfied within the framework that society provides for you. Your needs for love and connection show up here; things you don't automatically get all the time. If your needs at this level are unsatisfied, and you feel isolated or lonely, you find it almost impossible to meet your higher-level needs in any meaningful way.

The next level is where your needs for self-esteem and recognition kick in. These may never have been an issue for you as you struggled to join your group, but now they can become dominant. It is no longer enough simply to belong; now you must have some power and status in the group too – drive a bigger car, become captain of the golf club perhaps, or chair of the school parent–teacher association. This is where most established adults reside most of the time today.

But thankfully, the endless striving does end, and with all your needs taken care of, you eventually arrive at the top of Maslow's hierarchy as a fully developed human being. At the exotically named *self-actualisation* stage, you decide what is truly most important to you in life and your major motivation becomes living and expressing this. Often, this is where you get to give something back to the world that has supported you so royally in your journey up the hierarchy.

Maslow's hierarchy of needs helps to explain so much of the variability in human behaviour. Different human beings can be operating at different levels, and be driven by different needs at any given time. Your motivation may be different on Monday from on Friday with the weekend looming. And of course, you may feel different at work from the way you feel at home. The more you understand what drives you, the better able you will be to use it to achieve the things you want in life.

Greeting the world with grace

Maslow is often associated with motivation at work, but his insights apply equally in social situations where you can use them to help put yourself at ease.

When you find yourself in a new social group – meeting new people at a party or function, for example – you can expect to feel anxious because *at this moment* you are at Maslow's second level, needing to be accepted into this new group. When you're in this situation, the first thing to do is to accept your mild anxiety about it. There's nothing wrong with feeling or admitting that you're nervous (in case the voice inside your head starts accusing you of being a wimp).

Remember, everyone in the room fits into Maslow's hierarchy and is therefore feeling needy at some level. The people you're meeting who are not new to the group are operating at the second and third levels: some are anxious for acceptance, just as you are (and these people will be just as keen to be accepted by you as you are by them); some are motivated by their need for social esteem and need your respect.

Depending on the kind of party this is, you can expect to witness needy behaviours at all levels from hunger and thirst, through sex, connection, companionship, to a close approximation of self-actualisation on the dance floor. Don't judge your fellow partygoers too harshly. In fact, give everyone at the party a break, including yourself. Enjoy the spectacle!

Take on board these new factors in an otherwise ordinary and potentially dull social dynamic by paying attention to the curious and interesting display of need-motivated behaviours going on around you.

If you're curious about the people in the group and really take an interest in what's happening, you come across to others as attentive and a great conversationalist. This is more fun for you, and more fun for the people you meet. Pretty soon everyone will want you at their parties.

Bringing this more curious and attentive version of yourself into social situations lessens your anxiety, because you focus on the impression others are making on you rather than the one you're making on them. You always appear charming to those you meet if you give them the gift of your rapt attention. People are not used to this and they will love you for it.

Taking Charge at Work

Your personal motivation is critical to your performance and confidence in the world, but in work, your motivation is pretty important to your employer too. This has led to motivation becoming the focus of a lot of social science research over the last 50 years, and in this section, we show you how to use some of this for your personal benefit at work.

Looking at usable theory

Maslow's theory about human needs is universal, applying to everyone in all situations. Other important theorists, most notably Frederick Herzberg and William McGregor, have focused on your motivation at work, which is important to you and to your employer. In this section, you can find out how to take more control over your motivation at work and increase this if that is what you need. You will also find a self-test to help you to measure your progress.

Searching for satisfaction with Herzberg

Frederick Herzberg is another motivation guru frequently studied on management development courses (which means that your senior colleagues should have heard about him). His elegant theory reveals the factors that energise you at work and also those that take your natural energy away. He separates out those forces that motivate people, called *motivators*, from those that sap motivation, the *dissatisfiers*. He discovered that these forces operate in a surprising, seemingly illogical way.

Take pay as a universal example. You may think that the money you are paid provides you with motivation, and most employers act as though this is the case, but it simply isn't true in the long term according to Herzberg. Pay is a dissatisfier and not a motivator. If you aren't being paid the rate for the job, your poor pay rate can certainly make you feel dissatisfied, but surprisingly, of itself being paid over the odds doesn't motivate you any further than being paid a fair rate does (although it may bring other factors into play, such as recognition and team status).

Recognition, on the other hand, is a motivator. This is why a good job title, a word of thanks from the boss, or a mention in the in house journal for a job well done can be so motivating.

Table 2-1 contains a list of some of the main motivators and dissatisfiers that Herzberg identified. The dissatisfiers on the left have to be carefully managed or they can create serious dissatisfaction for you, but of themselves they cannot motivate you. The factors on the right are the motivators and give you the drive you need to do your best work, but they don't come into play until the dissatisfiers have first been neutralised.

Table 2-1	Factors Affecting Job Attitudes
Dissatisfiers	*Motivators*
Company policies	Achievement
Style of supervision	Recognition
Relationship with boss	Work itself
Working conditions	Responsibility
Salary	Advancement
Relationship with peers	Personal growth

Notice that the factors in the left column are external to the work itself and are largely imposed on you from outside. The motivators in the satisfaction column are much more personal, in that they tend to be more closely tied to the job you do. They are also more psychological, in that you have personal discretion over how much of them you feel.

If this insight starts to resonate powerfully for you, you may want to read up a bit more on Herzberg's motivation-hygiene theory before having a discussion about it with your boss. The dissatisfiers present in your work may be easy for your boss to neutralise, leaving you unencumbered psychologically to bring your motivation into play.

Unless you feel the presence of the motivators to a degree that has significance for you, you won't be motivated or satisfied at work no matter what else the company does for you.

Mapping McGregor's Theory X and Theory Y

Douglas McGregor's work is less well known to general managers and this is a shame as it focuses closely on management style (one of Herzberg's key dissatisfiers). McGregor brought out the effects of reactionary and over-zealous management practices and policies in his two models: Theory X and Theory Y.

Theory X assumes that, as a worker, you have an inbuilt dislike of working and will shirk as much as you can get away with. Therefore, you need to be controlled to ensure that you put in the effort needed, and you need to be told exactly what to do and how to do it. This can be very damaging to your natural motivation, your job satisfaction, and eventually your self-belief and confidence. Studies suggest that if your boss treats you this way, you may begin to behave as if it were true. (If this is happening to you the feedback model in Book I, Chapter 3 to make this point to your supervisor or departmental representative.)

Theory Y takes the opposite view. It assumes that working is important to you, and as natural to you as the other parts of your life. If your work is satisfying, it becomes a source of drive and fulfilment. You become committed to it and you require little in the way of supervision.

You perform better and are more productive if you are allowed to manage your own workload, output, and so on, because you know so much better than anyone else how to get the best out of yourself. In these circumstances, your supervisor becomes a colleague you can consult when you need a second opinion and who can liaise with senior management to enable you to do the best job possible.

How do these two models compare with your own job situation? The chances are that your own supervision has elements of both Theory X and Theory Y. As ever, the onus is on you to take more control of an element of your life. Once you have knowledge you need to put it to use.

Taking action may require all the confidence you can muster, and in this case it will repay you directly by helping to build your confidence for the future.

The challenge you face is not so much individuals and their personal attitudes but organisation structures and the way jobs are organised. If you supervise a team, or even just work in a team, following Theory Y gives you a far better chance of getting the results you need. Educate your colleagues where you can and help to bring your teams into the 21st century.

Putting theory to the test

In this section, you see how to use the theoretical insights from the preceding sections to build your confidence as you engage with the world. And because most motivation theory is based on the workplace, you start there.

Whether you work for yourself or for someone else, you have to meet your motivational needs. Table 2-2 provides a self-test you can take in two minutes that measures your motivation response at work. If you work alone, modify the questions as necessary to suit your circumstances. Give yourself up to five points for each question – all five if you strongly agree, down to one if you strongly disagree.

Book I

Plotting a Course: Your Job and Career Plans

Table 2-2	Job Motivation Response Self-Test				
Value Statement	*Strongly Agree (5 points)*	*Agree (4 points)*	*Neutral (3 points)*	*Disagree (2 point)*	*Strongly Disagree (1 point)*
I am entirely in control of my work environment. Provided I meet my objectives, I am free to decide how much I do and what work I do next.					
I have established a good working relationship with my boss. She gives me the room to do my job the way I want and I usually deliver what she needs.					
My benefits package and general working environment are okay. When something needs to be looked at, it's usually sorted out in a reasonable time.					
My work colleagues are generally supportive and don't get in my way. We are a good team and each of us serves the group objective pretty effectively. When issues arise, we are usually able to deal with them.					
I get a real buzz from the work I do. I feel closely identified with my output and put the best of myself into it. I wouldn't want it to be any other way.					
I feel that my employer values my work and is in touch with what is going on. They care about my career and look after things so that I don't have to worry about them.					

Book I

Plotting a
Course:
Your Job
and Career
Plans

Value Statement	Strongly Agree (5 points)	Agree (4 points)	Neutral (3 points)	Disagree (2 point)	Strongly Disagree (1 point)
My work is very visible. People know that it is mine, and I take great pride in it. It is not unusual for people to acknowledge the good job I am doing.					
I am allowed to take full responsibility for the quality of my work and for meeting my other objectives and deadlines. My boss knows that I know how to get the best out of myself and lets me get on with it.					
I feel that my work stretches me and allows me to grow. I have the level of challenge and variety that keeps me fully engaged without being overwhelmed.					
My work is an expression of who I truly am at some deeper level. Even if I were not being paid, I would still need to express myself through the kind of work I do. If I were unable to work it would be like losing a limb.					

Use these guidelines to evaluate your score:

- **41–50:** Congratulations, you may have found your life's work. You're working in a job that gives you most of what you need not only for motivation but for your growth and fulfilment too.

- **31–40:** This is still a very good score. You should be able to see the areas that are pulling you down and you can develop some goals for changing them.

✔ **10–30:** You already know this score is not so good. You may need to take more personal responsibility for your motivation at work, which can include changing your job or organization. Take a look at the techniques in Book I, Chapter 3 to help you take more control of your work.

Recognising the importance of achievement

Achieving results in work is not just a matter of pleasing your boss and earning a bonus. It forms an important contribution to your personal sense of significance and wellbeing as you move up the hierarchy of needs (refer to Figure 2-1) and a sense of achievement is top of the list of Herzberg's motivators (refer to Table 2-1).

As you progress in work, you need to think more about what constitutes achievement for *you*. Consider what it is you really want out of your life and your work, and then, without working any harder, you should be able to secure more of it both for yourself and your employer. This increases your sense of fulfilment and satisfaction and provides you with more motivational energy for yet more achievement.

Your relationship to your work is a very influential part of your relationship to the world and all it contains. If you want to achieve your most confident and powerful version of yourself, you need to understand and manage your value and contribution through your work in the world.

Going for the next promotion

Like most people, when a promotion opportunity comes up, you may want to seize the chance to get it immediately (not least because if you don't get it someone else will). But think very carefully about what the promotion may mean for you before you go for it.

It is not uncommon for a successful and happy worker to win a promotion only to become a less successful and far less happy supervisor or manager. When this happens, the person can remain stuck in their new role where their poor performance rules out any further advancement and the organisational hierarchy prevents them from returning to where they were once good and happy.

If you know anyone who has been caught in this way, you understand that it's hardly a recipe for organisational achievement – much less for personal confidence and fulfilment. Armed with the knowledge of this chapter, absolutely no reason remains why it should happen to you.

Before you accept any new role, ask yourself:

- How did things play out for the previous person who held this job? Perhaps they went on to even higher things, or perhaps they were stuck in the role for a long time and didn't appear too happy in it.

- What is likely to happen to you if you remain a while longer in your current role? Is there an even better promotion coming up soon? Would your refusal to take on the promotion offered send a bad or a good signal to your management?

- How could you use the current situation to create the job you want? Would it be possible to change the new job into something that suits you better, retaining, say, some of your current responsibility? Or perhaps it would be possible to split up the new role and take only some aspects of it into your current role?

- How can you use the change on offer to let your colleagues and superiors know that you are thinking deeply about the work you do and are not just in it for the pay cheque? In the longer-term this may be the most valuable aspect of the entire situation.

Now, when the opportunity for promotion comes up, you have a far richer way of evaluating why you are interested in the new role, what it will bring to you other than money and what it will take away. And if you decide to go for it, you bring so much more to the table; making a good impression on your colleagues and leaving you with a big win whether or not you get the role.

Overcoming Procrastination

Question: What's your procrastination all about?

Answer: I don't know. Can I tell you later?

If confidence is about focusing your energy and acting decisively, then procrastination is the direct opposite. Procrastination scatters your energy and puts off acting at all – sometimes you avoid even deciding. You postpone and postpone. You dither about. Perhaps you have a proposal or essay to write and you keep putting it off and putting it off. Maybe it's the tax form to fill out, the cupboard to tidy, the difficult phone call to make, the button to sew on, the cobwebs to dust off the ceiling, or the medical check-up. It – whatever the current it happens to be – never happens.

Unless you're hyper-organised, you probably have something sitting on a 'to do' list that hasn't become urgent enough yet to do something about it. If so, you're qualified to join the procrastination club – if only club members could get a date and venue organised to meet up. Maybe next week.

Procrastination is the ultimate waiting game: waiting for someone else to take the lead; waiting for career change to happen first; and above all waiting for everything to be perfect before you do anything. Procrastination comes when you lack focus and energy. When you're high on focus and energy, the positive result you get is purposeful action – a livelier place to be.

The quick secret to bust through procrastination is to do something, anything, but just get moving. As writers we face the blank page each day. So we start writing anything, even if it's pure rubbish.

In the next sections, we look at practical ideas to allow you to move on with confidence.

Breaking the gridlock

Clients often come to coaching because they are stuck in what we call the *X then Y gridlock* scenario. They have a goal, a dream, something they want to realise, and yet it's not happening. Instead the conversation is around: 'I can't do X until Y.' These are the kind of messages we hear that signify people are putting their lives on hold. Some may be familiar to you:

> 'I can't do the training course until the children are older.'

> 'I can't turn professional until I have sponsorship.'

> 'I can't travel to Australia until my health is better.'

> 'I can't leave/change my job until my partner's business has taken off.'

> 'I can't buy my cottage house by the sea until I'm rich.'

> 'I can't get to the gym until I change jobs, and I can't change jobs until my wife is working too . . .'

> 'I can't lose weight until my wife stops cooking delicious dinners every night.'

. . . and on it goes. The treacle gets stickier by the day. This stuck situation becomes debilitating and reduces energy and focus to an all-time low.

In order to achieve a big dream, most people quite rightly argue that they are limited by not having enough time, money, or energy. However, these are not the sole reasons people get stuck. Essentially, they are struggling because they haven't broken the job into steps.

Try this step-by-step approach to breaking this pattern of gridlock for yourself and for others.

1. **Put aside the idea that you do not have enough time, money, or energy – assume the lack of any or all these elements is not the real problem.**

   Imagine that you are rich enough in time, money, or energy.

2. **State your goal or dream in a positive way and write it down.**

   For example: 'I want to move to a cottage by the sea.'

3. **Ask yourself Question 1: 'Can I do it today?'**

   If your answer is yes, everything is in place, hey presto your dream is complete. However, if it's not – and this is the most likely scenario – then proceed to Step 4.

4. **Ask yourself Question 2: 'What needs to happen first?'**

   Break out all the separate tasks you need to do to accomplish your goal.

   In the example of the house by the sea, the tasks divide into three main activities: Researching the location, finding a more flexible job, and getting the family's agreement.

5. **Loop around the questions in Steps 3 and 4 for each task.**

   Ask yourself Question 1, 'Can I do it today?' and if not, then Question 2, 'What needs to happen first?', until you arrive at a list of activities that you can either do today or you have negotiated with yourself to do on a set date that you write in your diary.

Get the idea? In this way you have broken through the gridlock, and are moving towards your dream.

Biting off smaller chunks

Patience and persistence are valuable qualities to help build the confidence for career change. And when you calmly stick at things, breaking large tasks into smaller ones, you're more likely to get closer to perfection than if you rush at a job looking for a quick fix.

Bob calmly tackles stressful challenges in his job in a global IT team as well as in his hobbies by keeping his cool and seeing large projects as simply a collection of smaller chunks. At work, his job is to help transform the efficiency of an international airline – a seemingly impossible task. Yet he breaks this down into a series of smaller and smaller chunks. First he identifies the critical business processes, then maps business processes onto the existing IT infrastructure. From there he looks at process performance measures, identifies issues, and sets up smaller projects to tackle improvements that will make a difference.

At home, Bob takes a similar approach to large challenges, whether it's building a garden, renovating the house, or flying a glider. When he first decided he wanted to learn to fly, he did his research, found a gliding club, booked on a beginners' course, and set himself a series of challenges that he has quietly ticked off one by one: Flying solo, flying a single-seater glider, an endurance flight, a long cross-country flight. None of these has required any great fuss, as his practical approach is just to 'get on and have a go', knowing that he will gain confidence as he finds out more.

In order to break your own projects into smaller chunks, follow these steps:

1. **Set your big goal.**

   For example, perhaps you want to write a novel.

2. **Set a reasonable and realistic timeframe.**

   Writing a novel could take a year.

3. **Break your goal down into a series of small activities to accomplish within the timeframe.**

   For writing a novel, these activities may include finding a publisher, firming up the story line, and developing your creative writing skills.

4. **Set specific timeframes for each activity.**

   Each novel-writing activity could take several months of work to complete.

5. **Break each activity into a series of daily habits or short projects.**

   So developing your creative writing skills may translate to attending a creative writing evening class and writing for an hour each day.

Organising a project into manageable tasks lets you tackle the largest task with confidence.

Chapter 3

Demonstrating Confidence in the Workplace

*T*he most confident, motivated version of you will be immediately recognisable in the workplace. You will be at ease with yourself and others, straightforward and generous in your dealings with your fellow workers, cooperative and pleasant to work with, ready to laugh at the odd joke, and *very* effective in getting your job done.

So, now it's time to consider how you are in your place of work, and to apply your confidence in your job. This chapter helps you explore your relation to your work and the impact this has on your confidence. You find many ways to increase your confidence and be able to use this to your advantage both in your work and in other parts of your life.

Developing Confidence in Your Professional Life

When you're introduced to someone new, and they ask you the age-old question, 'And what do you do?' how do you answer? So much of your sense of who you are is bound up in your work that the description you offer is a powerful indicator of the meaning that work has in your life and the degree of success you can expect.

Your workplace gives you a constant bombardment of influences, both positive and negative, from the physical environment, the people in it, the tempo and nature of the work, and how closely you identify with what is getting done.

Keep in mind that it is your own responsibility to maintain an attitude that helps you to get everything you need from your work: including a confident sense of pride and well being from doing your job well.

Defining your professional identity

If you're a medical doctor, in the absence of any other information about you, people can reasonably accurately assume a whole lot of things about your ethics, values, social standing, and so on. This is because your identity in society is defined by the work you do. For members of the professions, the magic is in the job title; it defines them to themselves and to others.

If you're not a member of a recognised profession, you don't have all the accoutrements of a professional identity. But it's still essential for you to recognise that you do a professional job that people need and value. In order to feel and act with total confidence, you must get clear about the contribution of the work you do and how it fits into the wider value chain in your organisation and beyond into society.

Try drawing a diagram of your job in its broadest context; like Figure 3-1 filling in the details. No job operates independently of everything else, so how does your role at work fit into the greater scheme of things in your business? Does your company make something, or provide a service that enables others to do their work? Perhaps you help to maintain the home or work environment that enables others to do their work. All of these things are essential for the economy to be successful.

Think about everything you could take pride in around your work. Do you work alone or in a team? (Both need special qualities.) Do you supervise others, do you work remotely from the main office, do you work in the home providing care for your family to allow them to engage fully in the world? All of these are essential for a healthy society.

A work-based sense of self

Some people hold onto a role-based sense of self in the face of an enormous weight of contrary evidence. Nicky is an actress who has spent only two or three years out of the last 10 working in this role. In between times, she has spent many years doing temporary office jobs, waiting on tables in restaurants, or having no job and no income at all. And yet she feels and acts the part of 'actress', albeit one who is temporarily doing something else. The 'actress' part of her self-image is her role identity; the temporary work is what she has to do to pay her bills.

When she goes to parties, as she does often, how do you think she answers the question 'what do you do? 'Does she tell people that she does 'pretty much anything to make ends meet'? Of course not: she tells people she is an actress, and if we haven't seen her recently on television, we know that this includes periods of enforced idleness and probably temporary jobs. Neither she nor we are particularly concerned about her other jobs (even though she spends 75 percent of her time doing them) because they express little or nothing about who she is as a person and what her life is about.

Figure 3-1: The broader context of your work.

The global economy

Your national economy

Your organisation

Your job

Uncovering what you want to do

Of course, it is unlikely that you can step straight into the work of your dreams. You need to build up your skills and experience, make the contacts, gain the profile, and earn the opportunity to make the break. This is quite normal; but if you have no sense of these things, if you cannot see your way ever to getting the work you want, then you have a problem that you need to deal with.

At its highest, your *work* in the world is an expression of your being; something powerful and close to your core. But your job doesn't automatically give you the opportunity to do your chosen work. You need to manage this: take steps to acquire the skills you need and balance your life with voluntary work closer to your ideal as you take the time to develop your career.

Answer the following questions to get a clearer vision of your ideal work:

- **What do you absolutely love about working?** This is an unusual question and you may, like many people when asked it, find it easier to come up with an immediate list of what you don't like about working. Persevere, you will find there are many things you love about working, from a reason to go to town, to the great friends you work with, from the interesting people you meet, to the problems you get to solve, and so on.

  Don't stop thinking until you have written down four or five things, even if they're not available in your current job role.

- **What aspects of your work are you really good at, or have other people told you that you're really good at?** Wow! Include all the things that you know you're good at even if nobody else does. Perhaps you are a good timekeeper, or maybe you are sensitive and caring when your co-workers are feeling down. Perhaps you are good at dealing with the boss, or the customers, or maybe you are excellent at getting on with the job without being distracted.

Stretch your thinking and go for four or five things.

- **What is absolutely essential for you to have available in your work?** This is a great question whether or not you believe your current role gives you what you need. You may include things like meeting people, good money, being part of a team, or the opportunity to learn new things, or the chance to make a real difference.

  Think about what *you* need. How much of it would be available in your current role if you came at it a little differently?

✔ **What do you feel you really ought or would like to be doing?** Many people who want to change jobs lack clarity in their ideas about the work they wish they were doing. So, what is it for you? How much more of the things you really need would be available in the job you would prefer to be doing?

✔ **Finally, what is the truth that your answers whisper to you?** Bring all your other answers to mind. Should you be doing something else? Would it make any difference? Other than giving you more money, do you have clear insight into how you will ensure that your next role supports you better?

Book I

Plotting a Course: Your Job and Career Plans

After answering all these questions, you have a clearer idea than ever before of how you see your work in the world and what about it is most important to you. Now you need to look at the kind of jobs you have been doing. Have they given you what you need? Will they ever? When your work aligns with your values, you can be fully confident and fully empowered in your job. What do you need to change to make it so?

This powerful exercise can help you get in touch with your deeper need for work. You are most powerful and confident in your work when you are able to find jobs and roles that match your developing sense of vocation and purpose.

Finding value in what you do

Uncovering the hidden value in your work is important for your self-respect and contributes to your confidence.

Whether what you do is something you simply fell into, or whether it was a planned and conscious choice, your job defines you in the world more than almost anything else. You should always ask yourself what is valuable about the work you do in the larger scheme of things, and be sure you bring to mind all the hidden value.

If you work for a large company or a well-known branded business, you can take pride in that. Maybe you work for the government, or the local authority. Take a pride in that. If you work with children, or with sick people, or people with special needs, you may also have some sense of vocation and you can take pride in that.

Whatever you do, take pride in your professionalism. *Professionalism* is about knowing what needs to be done and going about it competently. When you adopt a professional approach to your work, you demonstrate your confidence to others that you know what you are doing, which in turn inspires others to be confident in you.

 Eleanor Roosevelt said that the future belongs to those who believe in the beauty of their dreams. A key to confidence is having dreams. Connecting your work with your growing sense of your life's purpose and your dreams is a very powerful means to having that work sing to your soul.

Becoming Assertive

The key to effective communication and relationships with most colleagues in your organisation (including your boss) is a set of personal skills that are usually lumped together and called assertiveness. Assertiveness is one of those acquired skills you need training and practice to acquire.

Assertiveness specialist coaches claim that this skills set is more powerful than any other in business. It can protect and boost your self-esteem, build your confidence, and reduce your stress levels.

Assertive people are generally liked and respected, they respond well in tight spots, and they are not afraid to say 'no'. You know where you are with an assertive person; they don't get put upon.

So what is this miracle skills set called assertiveness? At its core, *assertiveness* is the conviction that every person is equal to every other and that each person has the responsibility to take care of his or her personal needs and rights. There is an implicit acceptance that this applies to all of us, so in claiming it for yourself you also claim it on behalf of all your colleagues.

The fundamentals of assertiveness are

- ✔ You value yourself and others as equals.
- ✔ You have the ability to say 'yes' or 'no' to anyone when you choose, and you do not always choose to offer a reason for it.
- ✔ You embrace and protect your human rights. You stand up for yourself and this is something that you are unafraid to be known for doing.
- ✔ You take responsibility for your own needs and ensure you have them met.

✔ You take responsibility for your own contribution and the value you create. You are not afraid to admit to mistakes nor to ask for help when you need it.

✔ You express your thoughts and feelings honestly, whether positive or negative, and with due respect for others.

✔ You are able to handle conflict when it arises. You are prepared to confront difficult people when necessary or appropriate.

✔ You give and receive feedback honestly and in a straightforward manner. You take the trouble to do this effectively and completely.

✔ You respect these rights in others and understand that they have the same rights as you.

Don't worry if you don't feel you match up to all these points yet. It is important first that you know what they are. As you grow in confidence from working with this book, you will naturally become more assertive and powerful.

Showing Confidence in Specific Work Situations

Several common work situations may test your confidence. This section offers advice on how to manage your confidence in meetings. For more on presentations, turn to Book IV.

You can develop new skills, or *competencies* as they are often called in business, through training and practice. Nothing in business is impossible to master (certainly nothing is as difficult as learning to walk and talk, and most of us manage that). If your employer is asking you to do something for which you do not yet have the requisite skill, you should insist on the training. And if you find yourself struggling with any task at work your first question should always be: How can I acquire the skill to do this better or faster? This will take you forward into growth and confidence, rather than shrinking backward into fear and avoidance.

Demonstrating power and presence in meetings

Have you ever sat in a meeting just bursting to make a telling point only to find that the discussion has moved on before you are able to get it in? Or have you come up with a brilliant idea after the meeting is over and felt if only you could go back in time and make the point everyone would acknowledge you for solving the problem or pointing up the unnoticed flaw in the argument? If you have, then congratulations, you are a fully functioning, normal human being. We've all done it.

The main cause of such missed opportunities is the lack of balance between the *two* conversations that are going on in the meeting: the one in the room and the one in your head. When you are fully present and engaged in the meeting conversation, the conversation in your head fades into the background where it belongs most of the time. When you are feeling nervous or self-conscious, the dialogue in your head becomes predominant and prevents you from being fully engaged in the meeting.

You may feel self-conscious just because you're in unfamiliar territory. Take a few deep breaths to ease the tension, focus on who is in the room, what they're wearing, and so on just to bring yourself fully present.

Understand that this is normal, and ease up on yourself. Accept that the more natural you can be in the meeting situation the more balance you will achieve between your inner and outer dialogues.

If you can become curious about how the external conversation is developing and how the meeting will turn out, you will find yourself naturally focused on the outer discussion. From this position your own ideas and comments come up more naturally and more appropriately, it will be easier for you to make your points and you will grow in confidence.

Above all, relax. Whether the meeting is highly formal and large, or small and routine, the more engaged you become in the business of the meeting, the more effective your contribution becomes.

Rejecting manipulation and bullying

Bullying is all too common in the workplace. Surveys show that millions of people in the UK feel bullied every day at work, which takes a heavy toll on confidence. If you feel you are a victim of serious bullying at work, seek professional help from your HR or union representative, or perhaps your functional director. Bullying is never acceptable, by anyone, in any circumstances.

Whilst the unacceptability of bullying is perfectly clear in cases of physical intimidation or sexual and racial harassment, the less dramatic, lower-intensity form of bullying by shouting, verbal abuse, and manipulation can sap your self-esteem just as surely as a flagrant assault.

The manipulative bully's techniques include sarcasm, unjustified criticism, trivial faultfinding and humiliation, especially in front of others. It can also include your being overruled, isolated, and otherwise excluded from team activities. All this is calculated to sap your self-confidence to make you more of a target.

You protect yourself best by refusing to play the victim. Recognise that it is the bully who is inadequate and needs fixing, not you. Don't be taken in by criticism, even though it may have a grain of truth in it. No amount of improvement in your performance will satisfy your bully; a bully isn't interested in improving you, only in having control over you.

If you seem to attract such people either into your professional or your private life, it may be because you exhibit certain personality traits that mark you as a target for someone with a bullying personality. *This is not your fault.* Table 3-1 contains practical tips on how to offset tendencies that make you easy prey for bully boys (and girls).

Book I

Plotting a Course: Your Job and Career Plans

Table 3-1	Personality Traits and Being Bullied
Tendency	*Counter Behaviours*
You want to please.	Accept that you will never be able to please everyone, especially a bully.
You take on more and more to gain approval.	Set yourself sensible limits.
You find it hard to say 'no'.	Learn how to be more assertive.
You have a strong desire to think well of others.	Be more objective; ask others' opinions.
You want things to be perfect.	Realize that perfection isn't possible and turn to Chapter 9.
You have a strong need to feel valued.	Learn to value yourself (see Chapter 5).
You tend to discount your own contributions.	Ask yourself whether what you're expected to do is fair and reasonable.

Your first step in dealing successfully with a bully is to take control. Acknowledge your need to be more assertive, and look at that section in this chapter. There is almost certainly something you can do to stop yourself being victimised. Consider the following actions. Don't think for too long though, you need to take decisive action quickly:

- ✔ **Let your union or staff representative know about the problem.** Take any advice they offer you, and if this is inadequate check out any help-lines or consult your local Citizen's Advice Bureau.

- ✔ **Talk about the situation to your colleagues (if they will discuss it).** Find out if anyone else is suffering and if others are aware of what is happening to you. Others may be suffering in silence.

- ✔ **Start a diary and keep a written record of all incidents.** You may need this detailed evidence later if things come to a head but more likely it will act as a strong disincentive on your bully.

- ✔ **Confront your bully in person if you feel you can, otherwise do it by e-mail or memo.** In firm but non-aggressive language, make it clear what you are objecting to in their behaviour. Keep a copy and any reply. This may end their bullying.

- ✔ **If you decide to make a formal complaint take advice first from HR or your union and follow your company's procedures.** Ask your representatives to help you; this will cut down greatly on the stress on you.

    If you have made a formal complaint, be aware that your bully's job could now be in jeopardy. You need to be able to substantiate your allegations through witnesses or written records, and you may have to confront your bully in an investigation.

If you are not satisfied by the outcome of the internal investigation, take advice on your legal rights. If you leave your job and subsequently make a claim to an employment tribunal, they will expect you to have first tried to resolve the situation using the internal procedures. Any records you have will be heard when the tribunal hears your claim.

Managing Your Boss

Complaints about the boss are commonplace in work life and pretty much inevitable. It will help your confidence to remember that however big and scary your boss may appear to you now, she got that way by having to cope with difficult situations on her own and that underneath she is as vulnerable as you are.

The bottom line with bosses is that they need to get the job done and meet their performance targets. They need their team members to perform effectively and they have strategies for getting the required performance out of their subordinates.

When the pressure is on, bosses become anxious and scared just like anyone else, and that is when problems often show up most.

Anyone who is persistently out of sorts or bad tempered is almost certainly stressed and needs help whether they know it or not. There may be nothing you feel you can do to help your boss with her issues, but you can certainly manage your own.

Dealing with feedback

It is important for your self-confidence that you learn how to manage feedback. If you can receive and give feedback effectively, and especially turn even poorly delivered feedback to your advantage, you will grow massively in confidence and effectiveness at work.

Figure 3-2 shows an example of ineffective feedback to a secretary who fails to use the spell checker in her word processor.

Joan, you've left typos in the weekly review again.

Sorry Mrs Farrell.

Why do you think you have a spell checker? All you have to do is use it and it will find most of them for you?

Sorry Mrs Farrell.

The problem is it makes us all look slip-shod. The work you put out damages the image of the whole department; it reflects badly on me.

Sorry Mrs Farrell.

Yes, well you say you're sorry every time we have this conversation and nothing ever changes. It simply isn't good enough and you are going to have to change. If you don't mend your ways my girl this is going to end in tears, yours. Is that clear?

Yes Mrs Farrell.

Well let this be the last time, or else. I mean it.

Sorry Mrs Farrell.

Figure 3-2: How *not* to give feedback.

Figure 3-3 offers a more professional and effective way of giving feedback that might actually result in a change for the better.

> Joan, thank you very much for the weekly review. Once again you have turned it around very quickly and efficiently.
>
> Thank you Mrs Farrell.
>
> I know we have talked about this before but there are still some typos. Are you having problems using the spell-checker?
>
> Err, yes, I keep forgetting.
>
> Why don't you put a sticky label on the side of the computer to remind you about spell-checking your work and then it will stop happening. It is so easy to use.
>
> Okay Mrs Farrell, I'll definitely do that.
>
> Good Joan; if you need any further training on the system, let me know and I can organise it.
>
> Thank you, I will do.
>
> Once again Joan, thank you for this.

Figure 3-3:
Giving
effective
feedback.

The next sections offer tips for giving and getting feedback.

Giving effective feedback

When giving feedback, whether positive or negative, things generally go most smoothly if you follow a few simple rules:

- ✔ **Be very clear about the information you are imparting and own the responsibility of making the point.** You don't want any grey areas at the end, and you want to make sure that your receiver knows this clear information is coming from you.

- ✔ **Focus on the action you want to take place.** Describe the facts of the situation and how you want them to change. Do not judge or offer opinions about why the problem is arising, you might get it wrong.

- ✔ **Be as specific as possible.** Take a keyhole or laser surgery approach to your intervention. Deal as precisely as possible with the situation and avoid generalisations like *always* and *never*. If your feedback deals with some aspect of behaviour, ensure that it is the behaviour you address and not the character of the person.

Book I

Plotting a
Course:
Your Job
and Career
Plans

✔ **Emphasise the positive aspects of the situation.** This helps the person receiving your input to keep her receiving channels open. If you're correcting an error or making another point that she may receive as criticism, it can be helpful to the receiver if you sandwich the negative point between something positive, both before and after. This is not manipulative if you do it honestly; it is helpful to the person who has to take your point on board.

Turning negative feedback around

Input from your boss that you receive as criticism, nit-picking, or nagging is just an inadequate form of feedback. The information it contains may be valuable to you though, and important to your organisation, so it is worth understanding what your boss is trying to communicate.

If you can see that your boss's criticism of you is just her inadequate way of giving you information, you retain more power in the relationship. You can do two things that may surprise her and turn things around:

✔ Take on board any feedback that may be useful to you in improving your performance and let your boss know what this is.

✔ Ask permission to give your boss feedback on how she can communicate with *you* more effectively. If you do this, follow all the rules on being specific, focusing on the action, and so on from the preceding 'Giving effective feedback' section. Remember, you both share the goal of improving performance.

Getting your boss to keep her promises

The frustration of being offered some benefit or reward but not receiving it can corrupt your relationship with your employer and erode your confidence.

Unfulfilled promises generally fall into one of two cases:

✔ **Case 1:** You believe your boss has promised you something that she doesn't. She may be surprised that you feel a promise has been made.

✔ **Case 2:** You both know full well that the promise has been made and yet it is being delayed for reasons that have not been made clear to you.

In both cases, you feel maligned or abused and your self-esteem and self-confidence will suffer unless you do something about it.

At the root of both cases is a problem with communication. In Case 1, you may have unintentionally translated a good intention by your boss into a promise. In Case 2, the ambiguity may be deliberate. Your boss may simply have made the promise to keep you quiet without intending to fulfil it any time soon. Fortunately, the remedy for both is simple and it is the same action.

What you do, as a professional person of integrity, is put down in writing in the form of an email or memo any important exchanges. In clear and straight-forward language, write down what you believe has been agreed. Figure 3-4 gives an example.

Figure 3-4:
Putting an under-standing in writing.

> Dear Boss
>
> Thanks for seeing me yesterday to discuss my pay rise. I'm obviously delighted that you have agreed to my request and I'm looking forward to receiving it. When will this be by the way? (This is the first question my wife will ask me). Do please confirm a date and let me know if there is going to be any delay.
>
> Thanks and regards

Of course, if you have the presence of mind in the discussion to ask when the reward will take effect, you will already know the promised date and you can include it in your note.

How will your boss react to this written input? In the majority of cases, your note simply confirms what your boss agreed to do, and your confirmation acts as a reminder. If you send it as an email, your boss can forward it to her PA, HR, or payroll with a confirmation that she has agreed to your note and a request for action. Then it will be done – easy for everyone.

But what happens when your boss doesn't agree or doesn't take action? In the case of a misunderstanding, your note is likely to evoke an immediate response from your boss pointing up the mismatch. Will she be annoyed? Maybe, a little bit, since the issue has returned so quickly, but it is far better to identify her mistake in communication immediately and give her the chance to rectify it. You can apologise if necessary to maintain rapport, and immediately ask when you can expect the reward. If she can't give you any indication, then you are probably being fobbed off, which is Case 2.

So what will be your boss's reaction to your note if she is using delaying tac-tics? You will catch her out and force her hand. If she continues to be evasive, then you know she is simply stringing you along. You won't have your reward, but you will have your integrity restored. You may be annoyed, but it will not be directed at yourself. You may use your annoyance to give you the motivation to do something about changing your dishonest boss by changing your job.

Telling your boss she's wrong

At the heart of confidence is trust: Trust in yourself, trust in others, and trust that things will turn out okay. Telling your boss that she's wrong requires that you feel all three, so let's take a look at the structure and dynamics of the situation.

First, bear in mind that neither you nor your boss is infallible. Everyone makes mistakes from time to time; everyone makes errors of fact and judge-ment. This is perfectly human. What matters most in business is what you do to remedy the immediate problem and what you can then do to stop the situ-ation occurring again.

If you are sure that you are correct about your boss's error or misjudgement, then you owe it to her to point it out before the damage gets worse. Here is where you need trust in yourself. No matter what gap there may be in age, prestige, salary, experience, or levels in the hierarchy, you are just as valu-able a human being as your boss and you owe it to her, person to person, to point out her error. If you do this with respect and a little care (for example, not in front of your colleagues or in the middle of a meeting), your boss will remember and respect you for your honesty and tact.

If you have some evidence ready to support your judgement that she has made an error, use it discreetly. It can help your boss to come to terms with her error more quickly but spare her blushes with others. If you point out your boss's errors in public, she won't thank you for it.

If you have an honest and straightforward remedy, offer it to help fix her mis-take quickly. Don't become wedded to your solution, though, as she may choose another.

Fundamentally, being assertive and acting to inform your boss of the error is what counts. You will grow in confidence from your taking the action and so, if she is any good as a leader at all, will your boss.

Casting Off Your Cloak of Invisibility

More often than not, the reason nobody is acknowledging the great job you are doing is because your superiors and colleagues are too busy worrying about their own performances. Don't be afraid to seize the opportunity to take powerful action to bring your excellent work to the attention of your boss and colleagues.

The following formula creates a winning situation for everyone. If you use it, you set yourself apart as the one in a thousand employees who cares enough about performance to take it on.

Follow these steps:

1. **Ask your boss to define exactly what she wants from you in order for you to get a five-star annual appraisal.**

   The more detailed this is the better. Get her to spell out, from her point of view, what *good* looks like, then play it back: 'So if I do this, this, and this, and avoid that and that, you will think I'm doing an excellent job, right?' Once you have agreement, write it down (but don't send it anywhere just yet).

2. **Ask the same question of others who depend on you or are affected by your performance.**

   These may be customers or a group of colleagues who use your output in some significant way. Find out, from their perspective, what good looks like, play it back, get their agreement, and write it down for your own use later.

3. **Pull it all together into job objectives that you can realistically achieve.**

   You have a lot of detailed input on how other people depend on you and what they need you to do well in order to be happy with your performance.

4. **Spell out what you feel you can reliably deliver to your boss, colleagues, and customers.**

   Present them with a document that outlines the objectives you're committed to achieving (perhaps with training or some other assistance) and get their agreement to it (you may need to negotiate and compromise).

Doing the work to put together an action plan helps you achieve a number of really important objectives:

- ✔ Composing a job specification that is relevant, detailed, achievable, and creates value.

- ✔ Letting your boss and colleagues know what to expect from you and that they can rely on you to deliver.

- ✔ Laying a solid basis for renegotiating expectations and outcomes should anything change.

You have a perfect right, a duty even, to check in with your colleagues periodically to ensure they are happy with your performance. And each time you do so it will remind them of what a good and dependable job you do.

Dealing Confidently with Corporate Change

As change managers know, change tends to trigger a cycle of reactions and feelings. These fall into a sequence of predictable stages, irrespective of whether the change is planned or unplanned. Figure 3-5 shows a simple change curve.

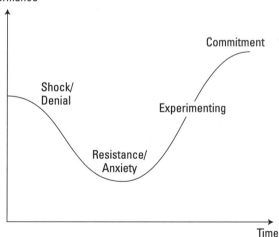

Figure 3-5: Changing with the change curve.

The time you spend at each stage and the intensity of your reaction depends on your personality and the nature of the change. To make a successful transition, however, you have to work through all the stages. The stages are

- **Shock or Denial:** Your natural response to this may be to minimise the impact of the change by trivialising it or denying that it exists.

- **Resistance and Anxiety:** This stage is characterised by your strong emotions and also feelings of flatness, accompanied often by a loss of confidence. You may have difficulties in coping with the new circumstances, which makes it hard to accept the changes.

- **Experimenting:** Activity now increases as you test new ways and approaches towards the change. You may have firm ideas of how things should be in relation to the new situation and feel frustration as the inevitable mistakes are made.

- **Commitment:** By this stage, you will have adopted new behaviour and accepted the change. You're working well and confidently with the new situation. You may reflect on how and why things are different, and attempt to understand all the emotion and activity of the previous stages.

Getting through rejection

One of the messages coaches give out loud and clear is that it's a normal part of growth *not* to be chosen for any given role or assignment. If you set out your stall to be successful then you need to be prepared to learn from the experience of being rejected. Often a valid reason exists and you can benefit from the disappointment.

One of the most valuable approaches to rejection is to embrace change and disappointments from the mindset that it's simply feedback rather than failure. For every company that wins work, several others lost the work. For every successful candidate at an interview, a number got a rejection call.

Rejection is not about you as a person, but about your skills and style not being appropriate at this time for this company or customer.

Winners stay professional and persist for the long term. Confident people welcome feedback and continue to learn.

Taming the threat of redundancy

As jobs and roles get made redundant, and not people, you can only be made redundant if you see yourself as your job. You may find yourself out of work for a while, and it certainly won't be of your choosing, but you will avoid the quite ridiculous and yet soul-destroying label of being redundant yourself.

Fully embrace the notion of work being something you choose to do for yourself and sometimes – often – you pursue this through a job role. Now you have a clear distinction between the work you have taken on in the world and the medium through which you are currently engaged in your work. This is a far healthier relationship to your job and one that allows you to have much more personal power.

The way forward is to hold on to who you are and your true purpose and find the work or lifestyle that fits for you right now. Hold on to the idea that this is merely a transition in your life. Confidence is about accepting and embracing the energy of the change and finding the positive lesson for you. Ask someone who has been made redundant six months after the event, and many will tell you that it was the best thing that happened to them – it gave them freedom to move on and was a catalyst for change.

Chapter 4

Asking Yourself the Right Questions

· ·

· ·

*W*hen you know the 'right' questions to ask, you'll get the results you want much faster. Let's be more precise. When we talk about 'right' questions we are looking specifically for incisive ones – those that put your finger right on the nub of an issue, that have a positive effect in the shortest possible time. The 'wrong' questions are those that send you off-course, meandering down dead-ends, gathering interesting but irrelevant information.

Throughout this book, we explain and demonstrate that your language is powerful; it triggers an emotional response in *you* as well as others. This is one reason why you can make a difference as you begin to choose language with increasing awareness. In this chapter, we bring together some of the most useful questions you can ask in different situations to make things happen for yourself and for others. Knowing the right questions to ask might make a difference for you when you want to:

✔ Set your personal compass in the right direction

✔ Make the best decisions

✔ Help others to take more responsibility

✔ Select and motivate people

Before You Begin: Question-asking Tips and Strategies

Before rushing on to the critical question you'd probably like to get answered – 'What are the magic questions that do make a real difference?' – take a quick breather to consider *how* to ask questions when you are working with other people, which is just as important as the *what* to ask.

In this section we encourage you to challenge your personal style and assumptions and adapt your own behaviour to function at your best.

Cleaning up your language

Have you ever wondered how many questions you ask that make assumptions based on what *you* want, and *your* map of reality, rather than what the other person wants? As human beings it's very hard not to project our ideas, our needs, our wants, and enthusiasms on to others – especially those closest to us. You influence other people all the time. You just can't help it. For that reason, most questions are not clean – they *assume* something, as in the famous 'When did you stop beating your wife?' question.

Even the one small word *beating* will have different meanings for each of us. Did you think of *beating* in the context of physical violence or did you think of it in the competitive sense of winning at a *sport* or game?

Therapists go into many years of training to work with their clients like a 'clean mirror' that can simply reflect the client's issues back to them to deliberate on. Some get to shine brighter than others! After all, you already know how much you can communicate just through one raised eyebrow or suppressed giggle. (This was why Freud had his clients lying on a couch while he, as the therapist, sat behind the client's head!)

If you want to be respectful of other people's views, then notice how well you can avoid prejudicing the result of a discussion. Are you telling somebody else what to do based on what you would do yourself?

Beware making generalisations or limiting possibilities. Listen to what you say and if you hear yourself issuing instructions that begin with words like: you must, you should, you ought to, you can't – then it's time to stop directing the action and imposing your stance on others.

Let's suppose you are coaching someone. Maybe it's a colleague, a friend, or a member of your family. In a coaching session, it's essential to begin with a clear aim in mind. So you might ask:

> 'What do we want to work on today?'

The question is simple, direct, and focuses attention on the fact that you're *working* on something.

Coaching is about exploring and challenging clients, leading them on to take responsibility and commit to action. Clean questions help you do that. It's important that suggestions are phrased in such a way that people think for themselves.

So a clean question that directs a client to think carefully for himself or herself might be:

> 'I wonder what that's about?'

Curiosity may have killed the cat, as the saying goes. We've never heard of it killing human beings. A different perspective is: Curiosity is the pathway to understanding. You choose which saying suits you best.

Press the pause button

Silence is golden. It's really helpful to pause for a moment when one person has finished speaking, and in turn let yourself think before you speak.

Pauses give other people critical space to process what you have said and consider their reply.

Simply giving people unhurried time to think within a structured framework of questioning is a huge benefit in business and in family situations, too. Listening to others is a generous act and an undeveloped, undervalued skill in most organisations. In her book, *Time to Think*, Nancy Kline sets out a framework which she describes as a *thinking environment* in which listening creates more productive meetings, solves business strategies, and builds stronger relationships.

To take time to think is to gain time to live (Nancy Kline).

Book I

Plotting a Course: Your Job and Career Plans

Test your questions

If ever you have any doubts about whether your question is appropriate to help a person or situation move on to a better place, stop and ask yourself:

- ✔ 'Is my next question going to add value in this conversation? Is it taking us closer to where we want to go? Is it going to move us further apart?'

- ✔ 'What is the outcome or result I'm looking for here?'

Make positive statements the norm

When we say to you, don't think of a pink elephant, what happens? Yes, of course, you immediately think of a pink elephant, you just can't help it! Similarly, if we say to a child: 'Don't eat those sweets before tea, now!' What happens? The child is compelled to *eat the sweets* – you have inadvertently issued a command.

The brain doesn't distinguish the negatives – it ignores the 'don't' and thinks 'do'. Better to say to your child: 'Tea's coming, so save your appetite for just two minutes.'

Figuring Out What You Want

Knowing what you want can be the greatest challenge. It's a constantly moving feast. There may be times when you get what you *think* you wanted, yet you're disappointed because it turns out that it wasn't what you *really* wanted at all! So to figure out what you *really* want, you have to ask yourself two questions: 'What do I want?' and 'What will that do for me?'

What do I want?

If there's one great question that the powerful set of personal development tools known as Neuro-linguistic Programming forces you to ask, it's: 'What do I want?'

Book I

Plotting a
Course:
Your Job
and Career
Plans

Help in discovering what you want to do

Does your career make you feel as if you're treading water just to keep your head above the surface? Then here are a few free Web sites that can help you start moving again. They offer many tips on career decision-making and management:

✔ **The Career Key** (www.careerkey.org) by Dr Lawrence K Jones and other academics specialising in career development. Much of the work is based on legendary John Holland's six basic personality types. You're given a list of jobs that may be appropriate for each of the personality types.

✔ **Online Personality Tests** (www.2h.com) aren't scored but focus on you as a person who works. (When you get to the site, click on *Personality Tests*.)

✔ **Queendom's Best Tests for Career Hunters** (www.queendom.com) doesn't pretend to be scientific, but it does offer a collection of career-focused quizzes, ranging from personality to owning a business. (When you reach the site, click on *Tests & Profiles*.)

✔ **Keirsey.com** (www.keirsey.com) contains links to understanding and taking the Keirsey Character/Temperament Sorter tests, a kissing cousin to the Myers Briggs test.

✔ **Team Technology** (www.teamtechnology.co.uk) – with the slogan 'you can't change who you are but you can change the role you play', this site is based around the Myers Briggs test and the role of the individual within teams.

✔ **All the Tests** (www.allthetests.com) – just in case you're getting a taste for this kind of thing, there's no shortage of online test covering personality types and careers and this site presents a sample of what's out there.

Sometimes you know very clearly what you don't want. This is a good starting point. When you know what you don't want, flip it over and ask yourself: 'What is the opposite?' And then check with yourself again: 'So, what is it that I do want?'

As you begin to articulate your answers, explore some details and allow yourself to dream a little. Imagine yourself in the future; fast forward your personal movie to a time when you have got what you want and maybe more besides. Employ all your senses and ask yourself what does that feel like, sound like, look like? Are there any smells or tastes associated with getting what you want? Check inside with yourself as to whether it seems right. Does it energise and excite you? And if you feel anxious or exhausted, that's a clue that something's wrong.

What will that do for me?

Once you've thought about what you want, and some words and ideas have come to you, then the next check question is: 'What will that do for me?' You may have a goal in place – it might be to bid for a new business project, or to take up a new sport, or to quit your work and go trekking in Nepal.

Ask yourself this question: 'What will that do for me?' And ask the same question three times – really drill down until you hit some core values that make sense for you. Otherwise you'll be choosing to do things that really take you meandering down the side lanes rather than staying on track for where you want to get to.

Keith was a successful, high-flying salesman who was evaluating his performance in his job. When he first worked with an NLP coach, his priority was to focus on developing specific skills he needed in place. His primary focus was to pave his succession route to become the next sales director in his company.

After a few sessions in which his coach asked him what he wanted and what that would do for him, he delved further into what he really wanted, taking into account all aspects of his life and work. He realised that if he achieved this career goal, he would have to give up much of the freedom and flexibility that his current role gave him. He realised that much of the new desirable role meant he'd be commuting into town in the rush hour, stuck most of the day at a desk in the corporate headquarters agreeing targets, budgets, and sorting out the legalities of the company pension schemes. ('I'd be like a puppy chained to a desk.')

In fact he thrived on being out with customers and winning deals. The promotion would not give him what he really wanted. With this realisation, he chose to reset his career direction and take his skills into another part of the corporation. From there he was able to use his initiative to open up new international sales territories.

Making Decisions

You make decisions all the time: whether to go to work or stay at home, what to have for lunch and supper, whether to accept an invitation to see a film, how much you should spend on a new computer or holiday, to lay on a Christmas party with your folks or not?

So let's imagine that one sunny day you're happily working at your job and there's a call from a head-hunter: there's a new job on offer, you're the person they'd like, and by the way, it means shifting your home base to a town by the sea 200 miles away. You weren't even considering a change, but you're flattered, so you go and talk to them. The deal looks pretty attractive and, wow, wouldn't it feel good to be working near the sea in hot weather like this? But, there's a niggling little voice inside you saying: 'Is this the right thing to do? Are you sure?'

Should you go for it or should you stay doing what you know best? How can you decide this one?

Here are four key questions that you can ask yourself, or someone else, to guide you in making a decision – a life-changing one or something smaller.

- ✔ What will happen if you do?
- ✔ What will happen if you don't?
- ✔ What won't happen if you do?
- ✔ What won't happen if you don't?

The four questions you have here are based on Cartesian logic and you may find them referred to as *Cartesian Co-ordinates*. All you need to remember is that they offer some powerful linguistic patterns that enable you to examine a subject from different angles.

The decisions can be major – shall I leave my wife, shall I move house, change career direction, have a baby? The questions focus your attention and challenge your thinking. When you reach the last question, you may stop and think, 'That's confusing.' Good. This means you're arriving at a breakthrough in your thinking.

If you make a change in one area of your life at the expense of another area, the chances are that that change is not going to last. So, for example, if you moved jobs but had to give up important interests or friendships where you currently live, then that change isn't going to make you happy in the long term, so you probably would not stick with it.

Don't take our word for it; try the questions out now on something you're deliberating. You'll see the questions encourage you to check out your decision based on the impact on the whole of your environment, in a healthy way – what we call an *ecology* check.

Challenging Limiting Beliefs

People's thinking may be stopping them from achieving a much sought after goal, but there are three simple questions you can ask that challenge such thinking. To help others (or yourself) overcome a limiting belief, you ask a series of three questions, explained in the following sections.

The way to ask the questions is to give people plenty of time to talk about an issue, then, as you sense they've 'got it off their chest', at that point begin asking the questions.

✔ **Question 1: 'What do you assume or believe about this that limits you in achieving your goal?'**

Ask this question three times until you're sure you've reached the heart of the matter – what NLP describes as a limiting belief. As you delve deeper, you may say: 'That's right, and what else is there about this that limits you?'

For example, the person may be thinking: 'I'm not good enough.' 'Nobody will let me.' 'I just don't know how.' When you hold a negative position like this, then you stop yourself from doing what you need to do to achieve what you want.

✔ **Question 2: 'What would be a more empowering belief, one that is the positive opposite of that?'**

This question flips the limitation over to the positive side. For example, the positive opposite of the assumptions and beliefs above would be stated positively as: 'I am good enough.' 'Somebody will let me.' 'I do know how.'

With this second question, your colleague or client may get confused or even cross because it is a challenging one to answer. Yet, it's a critical one to hold onto if you're going to get a switch in perspective and come up with a more empowering belief that helps someone shift forward. So stick with it.

✔ **Question 3: 'If you knew that (new freeing belief) . . . what ideas do you now have to help you move towards your goal?'**

This question completes the process. At this point, your client comes up with his or her own ideas as to how to move forward: 'Oh well, if I knew that I was good enough, then I would do XYZ.'

The way this questioning works is to put somebody into an 'as if' way of thinking. If you act with the belief that something can happen, then you will find the behaviours to get there.

A managing director who wanted to be successful in her business was struggling to make a decision on having a child. Her limiting belief was: 'It is not possible to be a good mother and a successful businesswoman at the same time.' By working through the three questions, she evaluated the new opposite assumption that: 'It is possible to be a good mother and a successful businesswoman at the same time.'

By working in this 'as if' framework, that is, operating as if it was possible to do both well, she opened up many ideas on how she could run the company differently in order to pursue motherhood at the same time as being successful in business. Not only did she go on to have two healthy well-adjusted children, she also put in place more flexible policies that benefited the men as well as the women in the company.

Finding the Right Lever for Change

Carl Jung, one of the twentieth century's leading thinkers in psychology, once famously said, 'We cannot change anything until we accept it. Condemnation does not liberate, it oppresses.' And he was right because the first step to coping with change is to accept that it is happening. Then you are in a position to proactively work with it and give yourself choices rather than wait to be on the receiving end of whatever happens to you.

Three requirements need to be in place for change to happen. You must:

- ✔ Want to change
- ✔ Know how to change
- ✔ Get or create the opportunity to change

In the following sections, you delve further into the logical levels. As you explore, keep in mind one important question: 'How can you make change easy for yourself?'

In all of the questions we raise in the following sections, we have applied them to you as an individual. You can ask the same questions about your organisation, too.

Environment

The environment is about time, place, and people. It's the physical context where you hang out. It's about finding the right time and the right place. If you want to become fluent in a new language, then the easiest way to learn would be to go and live in the country for a while, fully immerse yourself in the culture, ideally by living with the natives. You would be in the best place to learn. Similarly, if you wanted to learn a new software package, then it would make sense to move onto a project to work with a person or team that applied it in their business. Again, the environment would be conducive to learning, which is itself a type of change. The timing would also be critical – you cannot learn if the time is not right for you – maybe if you're tied up with other needs.

Some *environmental* questions to ask yourself when you sense that you are not in the right place or this is not the right time for you to get what you want:

- ✔ Where do you work best?
- ✔ Where in the world do you want to explore?
- ✔ What kind of people do you like to have around you? Who makes you feel good, energised, and comfortable? Who makes you feel drained? Or do you prefer to work alone?
- ✔ What time of day do you feel good – are you up with the lark in the mornings or a night owl?

Questions such as these will give you the right kind of data so you can decide what environmental issues you can work on.

Behaviour

Your behaviour is all about what you actually say and do, what you consciously get up to. In NLP terms, behaviour refers to what you think about as well as your actions. It also points out that all your behaviour is aimed at a purpose, it has a positive intention for you.

Change at the behavioural level is easy to make when you have a real sense of purpose, it fits with your sense of identity, and your beliefs and values.

Some *behavioural* questions to ask yourself when you think that you may need to change your behaviours in order to get the results you want:

Book I

Plotting a
Course:
Your Job
and Career
Plans

- ✔ Do your behaviours support your goals?

- ✔ Do they fit with your sense of who you are?

- ✔ What do you do that makes life interesting and fun?

- ✔ What do you find yourself saying habitually? Can you detect any patterns?

- ✔ What do you notice about other people's words and sayings?

- ✔ How aware are you of people's behaviour – how they walk, the tone of their voice, and their smile?

- ✔ What colour changes do you observe in people as they talk?

- ✔ How does your breathing change and when?

- ✔ What body language do you adopt in different circumstances?

- ✔ What do you sound like?

Maximising effective behaviours

In order to create positive change, then it's worth developing the behaviours and habits that serve you well. Often small changes have an incremental effect. If you are slimming to fit into a new outfit, then eating a healthy salad each day in place of your sandwiches would be a valuable habit to cultivate. In the same way, if you are trying to improve your meetings at work, then a good behaviour for a team would be to set clear beginning and end times.

When writing this book, and with deadlines pressing, we listened to the advice of successful writers. The one key message that we took away was the value of writing something every day – whether 200 words or 2,000 words. (We heard of one famous author who wrote precisely 600 words each day even if that meant stopping in mid-sentence.) An easy behavioural change for us to make was to get up early each morning and begin each day writing for a couple of hours. By focusing our energy at the start of the day, we felt a real sense of purpose and a clear identity as *Dummies* authors.

Practising the right behaviours until they become habitual will increase your capability. How many great sports people or musicians are born wielding a tennis racket or violin? Yes, they may have natural talent, but the key lies in their hours of dedicated practice and willingness to go that extra mile. One of our tennis coaches reminisced about teaching UK tennis star Tim Henman as a young lad. Tim was the one who was prepared to get out there and hit balls long after the others had had enough. The golfer Tiger Woods is renowned for being out on the golf course before anyone else. To stay at the top of the game requires constant hard practice.

Modifying unwanted behaviours

What about the unwanted behaviours, the things you do and wish you didn't do, silly habits such as smoking or poor eating habits? The reason they become hard to change is because they are linked to other higher, logical levels involving beliefs or identity.

'I'm a smoker' = a statement about identity.

'I need to have a cigarette when I get stressed' = a statement about belief.

'He's a big, strong lad' = a statement about identity.

'He can't live on salad and fruit' = a statement about belief.

To make change easier you can create a new identity for yourself such as 'I'm a healthy person' with beliefs such as 'I can develop the right habits to look to after myself'.

Capabilities

Capabilities are your talents and skills. They lie within people and organisations as highly valuable assets. These are the behaviours that you do so well that you can do them consistently without any seemingly conscious effort. Things like walking and talking are skills you learned without ever understanding how you did that. You are a naturally great learning machine.

Other things you've learned more consciously. Perhaps you can fly a kite, ride a bicycle, work a computer, or play a sport or musical instrument. These are skills you will have deliberately learned. Perhaps you're great at seeing the funny side of life, listening to friends, or getting the kids to school on time. All valuable skills that you take for granted and others could learn. You're likely to remember the time before you could do these things, while you probably can't recall a time before you could walk or talk. Organisations build core competencies into their business processes, defining essential skills that are needed to make the company function at its best.

NLP focuses plenty of attention at the capability level, working with the premise that all skills are learnable. It assumes that anything is possible if taken in bite-size pieces or chunks. The HR director of one of the UK's most

Book I

Plotting a
Course:
Your Job
and Career
Plans

prestigious retailers told us recently: 'We recruit primarily on attitude: once this is right, we can teach people the skills they need to do the job.'

Yet even attitudes can be learned and changed so long as you find the desire, know-how and opportunity to learn. The question to hold on to is: 'How can I do that?' Bear this in mind for yourself as you go through every day. The NLP approach is that by modelling others and yourself, you become open to making changes and developing your own capabilities. If you want to do something well, first find someone else who can do it and pay close attention to all of their logical levels.

Here are some *capability and skills* questions to ask yourself when you want to make an assessment of your capabilities and see where you can learn and improve:

- ✔ What skills have you learned that you're proud of – how did you do it?

- ✔ Have you become expert at something that serves you less well – how did that happen?

- ✔ Do you know someone who has got a really positive attitude that you could learn from – how could you learn from them?

- ✔ Ask other people to say what they think you are good at.

- ✔ What next? What would you like to learn?

As you build capability, the world opens up for you. You are in a position to take on greater challenges or to cope better with the ones you struggle to face.

Beliefs and values

Beliefs and values are the fundamental principles that shape your actions. They direct your life and yet often you may not be aware of them. What *you* believe to be true is often going to be different from what other people believe to be true. Here, we're not talking about beliefs in the sense of religion – rather your perception at a deep, often unconscious, level.

Lee is an amateur club golfer with a passionate desire to launch his career on the international circuit. He believes he has the same potential as top golfer Tiger Woods and that he too can create a living as a professional golfer. Such beliefs drive his capability – he is highly competent in his game. His beliefs also drive his behaviours – he can be found determinedly practising on the golf course every day of the year and he works at developing relationships with the media and sponsors. And his beliefs also determine the environment where he spends much of his time – when not on the golf course, he'll be working out in the gym.

Likewise values are the things that are important to you, what motivates you to get out of bed in the morning, or not – criteria such as health, wealth, or happiness. Beliefs and values and the way we rank them in order of importance are different for each person. This is why it's so difficult to motivate a whole team of people with the same approach. One size does not fit all when it comes to beliefs and values.

Values are also rules that keep us on the socially acceptable road. We may seek money, but our values of honesty keep us from stealing it from other people. Sometimes there will be a conflict between two important values – such as family life and work. In terms of making change, understanding beliefs and values offers huge leverage. When people value something or believe it enough, it's an energising force for change. They are concentrating on what's truly important to them, doing what they really want to be doing, and becoming closer to who they want to be. They are in a place that feels right and natural for them. Beliefs and values drive us and influence the lower levels of capability, behaviour, and environment. Thus all the levels begin to come into alignment.

Often we work with people who move from one job to another with increasing dissatisfaction. IT director, John, is a case in point. Every two years or so he'd get fed up, decide it was time for a change, and apply for another similar job with more money, a better benefits package, in a new location, hoping that things were going to be better somewhere else. He simply made changes at the environmental level – new company, new country, new people. 'It will be better if I work in New York.' As he began to evaluate his own values and beliefs he realised that some essential ingredients were missing. He'd invested time and energy into taking an MBA and valued professional learning and development as important. Yet he always ended up in 'hire and fire' organisations which were too busy to invest in their people or to work strategically: places that drained his energy. His beliefs and values did not match those of the organisations that he worked in. Once he understood this, he took his skills to a prestigious international business school that valued his learning and gave him the opportunity to develop further.

Here are some *beliefs and values* questions to ask yourself when you sense that there's a conflict at this logical level that is hindering you getting what you want:

- ✔ Why did you do that? Why did they do that?
- ✔ What factors are important to you in this situation?

Book I

Plotting a
Course:
Your Job
and Career
Plans

✔ What is important to other people?

✔ What do you believe to be right and wrong?

✔ What has to be true for you to get what you want?

✔ When do you say 'must' and 'should' and 'must not' and 'should not'?

✔ What are your beliefs about this person or situation? Are they helpful? What beliefs might help me get better results?

✔ What would somebody else believe if they were in your shoes?

Armed with the answers to these questions, you may want to work on your beliefs and values to ensure that they support you through difficult times. As you question your beliefs about yourself you may choose to discard some of them that no longer serve you well.

In business change management programmes, you often hear talk of 'winning the hearts and minds' of people. This means you need to address people's beliefs and values. Once the right beliefs are firmly in place, NLP suggests that the lower levels – such as capability and behaviour – will fall into place automatically.

Identity

Identity describes your sense of who you are. You may express yourself through your beliefs, values, capabilities, behaviours, and environment, yet you are more than this. NLP assumes that a person's *identity* is separate from their *behaviour* and recommends that you remain aware of the difference. You are more than what you do. It separates the intention that lies behind your action from your action itself. This is why NLP avoids labelling people. 'Men behaving badly', for example, does not mean the men are intrinsically bad, it's just bad behaviour.

There's a saying that one of our corporate clients quotes: 'Easy on the person. Tough on the issue.' This is a positive management style consistent with the NLP premise that people make the best choices open to them, given their own situation at any time.

If you want to give feedback to encourage learning and better performance, always give very specific feedback about what someone has said or done in terms of the *behaviour* rather than commenting at the *identity* level. So, instead of saying: 'John. Sorry mate, but you were just awful.' Try instead: 'John, it was difficult to hear you at the meeting because you looked at the computer all the time and had your back to the audience.'

Here are some *identity* questions to ask yourself when you have a sense of conflict around your identity:

✔ How is what you are experiencing an expression of who you are?

✔ What kind of person are you?

✔ How do you describe yourself?

✔ What labels do you put on other people?

✔ How would others describe you?

✔ Would other people think of you as you wish?

✔ What pictures, sounds, or feelings are you aware of as you think about yourself?

A greater awareness of self is a valuable insight in any journey of personal change. Too often people try to change others when changing themselves would be a more effective starting point.

Purpose

This 'beyond identity' level connects you to the larger picture when you begin to question your own purpose, ethics, mission, or meaning in life. It takes individuals into the realms of spirituality and their connection with a bigger order of things in the universe. It leads organisations to define their *raison d'être*, vision, and mission.

Man's survival amidst incredible suffering depends on true self-sponsorship that goes beyond identity. Witness the resilience of the Dalai Lama driven from Tibet or the story of Viktor Frankl's endurance of the Holocaust in his book *Man's Search for Meaning*.

As we become older and approaching different life stages, it's natural to question what we're doing with our lives. Sometimes there will be a trigger to inspire action and light up our passion. A friend and logistics manager in industry, Alan, travelled to Kenya on holiday and saw at first hand the educational needs of the country. Thus began a powerful one-man campaign that took over his life and led him to create an international charity taking educational materials into Africa thanks to his personal passion to make a difference. On speaking to him about it, he would often say. 'I don't know why me. It's mad, but I just know I have to do this.' His purpose was stronger than his identity.

Here are some *purpose* questions to ask yourself when you want to check whether you are steering your life in the right direction for yourself:

- For what reason are you here?
- What would you like your contribution to be to others?
- What are your personal strengths that you can add to the bigger world out there?
- How would you like to be remembered when you die?

In *The Elephant and the Flea,* management guru Charles Handy conveys the passion that comes from a sense of mission and underlying purpose. He talks of the entrepreneurs featured in *The New Alchemists*, another book by Handy and his wife, the portrait photographer Elizabeth Handy, as people who leap beyond the logical and stick with their dream:

> 'Passion is what drove them, a passionate belief in what they are doing, a passion that sustained them through the tough times, that seemed to justify their life. Passion is a much stronger word than mission or purpose, and I realise that as I speak that I am also talking to myself.'

Checking in with Yourself

In order to keep on track to where you want to get, either on a daily basis or longer term, it can be helpful to question yourself. So allow us to leave you with a final checklist of questions to ask yourself each day.

Daily checkpoint

What do I want?

What will that do for me?

What's stopping me?

What's important to me here?

What's working well?

What can be better?

What resources will support me?

If you accept the NLP presupposition that there's no such thing as failure, just feedback, then you won't be afraid of asking questions in case you get answers you'd prefer not to hear. Tune into the feedback you get for yourself as well as others as you ask the right questions.

Book II
Showcasing Yourself with a StandOut CV

'Come now, Mr Scrimfold, aren't you a little too old to ask your parents to help you with your contract of employment?'

In this book . . .

A high quality CV is essential for anyone who wants to get ahead in their career. The chapters in this book help you to get to grips with writing a CV that suits your own situation. Inside you'll find dozens of useful examples and great advice on the structure and language to use when creating your CV.

Here are the contents of Book II at a glance:

Chapter 1

CVs and the Changing World of Recruitment

In This Chapter

▶ The welcome return of good-looking CVs

▶ The dangers of online screening for your CV

▶ Your rights in background checks

▶ The rise of specialist sites and company portals

▶ The regimentation of the Information Age

▶ How humans interact with paper CVs

*L*ook out everyone! Here comes the third big technological wave that's sweeping across the employment landscape. A word to the wise right from the start – getting to grips with the recruitment revolution is more critical to your job-hunting hopes than you may imagine.

Historically speaking, we raced through the first two waves in record time. In the ten years of the 1990s, job hunters learned to write (1) scannable CVs and (2) ASCII plain text CVs. The third wave is with us now, and this book describes this new technology – technology that's the basis for rethinking how you prepare your CV.

Formatted e-CVs and *online screening* are the two most dramatic developments turning up in large- and medium-sized companies in developed nations across the globe. We tell you about these two big changes in some detail and how they impact your CV. Then, in the remainder of this chapter, we give an overview of other big changes coming your way. You can find out about the rest of these changes in the rest of this book.

Below, you can read about the current state of the recruiting industry, which can help you to better understand what's happening now and what will happen next to your CV as it makes its way through the workplace steeplechase.

Unintended Consequences from a Seismic Shift in CVs

In our networked employment world of online CVs, e-mail, and applicant management systems, some of the vaunted technologies of the 1990s that were created to save recruiters' time and effort have measured up. But other technologies have produced unintended consequences brought about by staggering numbers of online CVs. The glut of CVs overloads recruiters, who are struggling to separate qualified from unqualified applicants for the jobs they're trying to fill.

These CVs are plucked from cyberspace by many elements of online recruiting that include the following: search engines, Web-savvy recruiters, job Web sites, corporate Web sites with career portals, CV distribution services, and newsgroups. But where are all these CVs coming from?

As one recruiter complained to colleagues in a recent online discussion:

> *Most job searchers no longer read job descriptions. Job ads have become a lot like horoscopes: every applicant thinks a job description describes him or her perfectly. Or if there isn't a fit at all, many job seekers reason that if they're not right for this position, maybe there's something else within the company that they're good for. Armed with an Internet connection, a list of job boards, and a CV, a job searcher can crank out about 100 applications in less than four hours.*

Job searchers aren't solely responsible for the high CV volume in cyberspace. Corporate human resources (HR) departments contribute to the nearly unmanageable workload when they fail to develop clear job requirements or use puzzling company jargon. These deficiencies force job searchers to work blindfolded, attempting to decipher inadequate postings of who or what a company is seeking.

Sometimes, the company is vague or purposely paints a rosier cast on a job than reality supports. A number of my newspaper column readers have written to me complaining that the positions they accepted are very different from their job descriptions; a single example is an undisclosed requirement to travel frequently and wear a beeper 24 hours a day.

Meet the recruiting tribe

The term *recruiter* in this book is used to indicate any professional who plays a role in bringing candidates to a hiring manager's attention. The recruiter *screens* candidates, and the hiring manager *selects* candidates. The presumption is that candidates brought to a hiring manager have been checked out and possess the qualifications to do the job being filled. All recruiters read CVs.

✔ **Internal recruiters** employed by a company are also called *in-house recruiters, or corporate recruiters*. They are salaried and eligible for bonuses based on meeting targets.

✔ **External recruiters,** commonly called *headhunters* or *executive search consultants,* may also be called *third-party recruiters,* (recruiting) *agency recruiters,* or *independent recruiters*. They recruit for a variety of companies and are further divided by the way they are paid for their services:

✔ *Retained recruiters* are paid fees whether or not a search produces the candidate hired for the job. Retained recruiters may work on yearly retainer contracts and, like outside solicitors, are called upon when their help is needed.

✔ *Contingency recruiters* are paid on the transactional model – they get their money only when they deliver a candidate who is hired by their client.

Contingency recruiters vastly outnumber retained recruiters. Until the mid-management level, contingency recruiters may produce better results for your career advancement, but retained recruiters may offer the best opportunities at upper-management levels.

Book II

Showcasing Yourself with a StandOut CV

The end result is that because of job seekers who apply for virtually every published job they come across – regardless of qualifications – and employers who write fuzzy job descriptions, the recruiting system is awash in CVs. Recruiters say most of them are unusable. Consider these examples:

✔ A recruiter working a career fair complains that, of 8,000 CVs left at his company's stand, about 60 made it back to the company's HR office. The others failed to meet the requirements of the open positions.

✔ Another recruiter reports a recent experience in which her agency posted a position for a project manager on major job boards and other free job-related sites. Some 654 applicants responded, of which 6 percent met 80 percent or more of the job's requirements and 11 percent met 51–79 percent of the job's requirements. But 82 percent failed to meet more than half of the job's requirements, and it took the recruiter two days to review the CVs to determine which ones were useful.

From the recruiter's viewpoint, taking the time to filter out about eight of ten applicants who weren't at all qualified for the job means that much less time can be spent doing in-depth assessments and negotiating and closing offers to the right candidates.

Hooray! The Return of the Handsome CV

The vast number of e-CVs are spun in plain text. They may read cleanly and easily for a computer, but for a human, they are eye-wateringly dull and likely to lead to sagging chins and glazing eyes amongst recruiters. Fortunately, help is here through better technology.

Do you remember – or perhaps you're too young to remember – those handsome CVs with the compelling embellishments: attractive formatting, appealing typefaces and fonts, boldfaced headings, italics, bullets, and underlining? Embellishments that were refreshing to read until technology all but killed them off a decade ago in favour of the electronically correct but tearfully tiresome online ASCII plain text CV?

Well, the wonders of the Web will never cease, and smart technology is bringing back those good-looking specimens we grudgingly gave up in the 1990s to make sure our CVs arrived intact over the Internet. The handsome CV is making a welcome return for those CV readers who grow bleary-eyed looking at pure text day in, day out.

The new technology gang

The thrust for updated technology permitting handsome CVs to flourish comes from vendors selling technology known as *applicant tracking systems* (ATS) and *applicant management systems* (AMS). An ATS is any system, whether in software form or paper, that manages both a company's job posting and its data collection (of CVs and applications) to efficiently match prospective candidates to appropriate job openings. An AMS includes features of ATSs plus other functions, such as automated online screening.

Goodbye plain text, farewell scanning

As CV management technology evolves at breakneck speed, the end approaches not only for ASCII plain text CVs but also for scanning CVs into a system. This allows you to attach your fully formatted, word-processed, handsome CV directly into the applicant system from a Web portal. Submitting your CV through a Web portal eliminates the labour-intensive, error-plagued scanning process and allows line (department) managers who make hiring decisions to view an aesthetically pleasing formatted CV in its full glory complete with bold text, underlining, and pleasing fonts.

A portal is an entryway. A Web portal for CV submission is either a company Web site's career portal; a job site, such as Fish4Jobs or Monster; or another Web site, such as one operated by a college career centre or professional society.

Book II

Showcasing Yourself with a StandOut CV

How the systems work

In older applicant tracking systems, CVs are routed to managers by e-mail. A paper CV can be scanned and converted to a text file in order to do this, but the result is often an eyesore, full of errors introduced through the optical scanning process (optical scanners don't always recognise letters correctly).

Many reviewing managers see an error-studded CV and either assume that the applicant is not a detail-oriented person or that HR did a slovenly job in screening. Another feature of older systems is managerial overload. A manager could easily receive more than 20 e-mailed CVs daily in addition to all her other e-mail.

Newer systems send the manager only one e-mail: 'Check your portal. You have new CVs to review.' When the manager opens the portal, all the CVs are listed with a hot link to either the MS Word document or an HTML (*HyperText Markup Language*) version of the Word document. If the system includes an online screening component, the manager may choose not to look at all the CVs, but reduce their number by looking for certain specific requirements.

When the manager finishes reviewing the CVs, the appropriate recruiter in HR is automatically advised of the manager's interview choices. This streamlined process improves the staffing workflow and shortens the time it takes to bring a new employee onboard.

The rush to get onboard

New software releases by the major vendors of applicant management systems allow you to take advantage of the handsome CV option. Smaller vendors are expected to follow suit quickly or be placed at a competitive disadvantage. All major software programs accommodate these functions:

✔ Take in fully formatted, word-processed (MS Word, for instance) CVs as an attachment

✔ Inventory the CVs in the original format (most often MS Word)

✔ Send CVs downstream to hiring managers in their original formats

The fact remains that plenty of older systems that cannot handle the formatted handsome CV are still in use. These older systems continue to put new CVs into plain text database storage.

If your CV is already in a database at a company that has recently upgraded its applicant management system technology, your CV will remain in plain text. If you hope to work for a particular employer that already has your plain text CV in its database, should you bother to send in a handsome CV? We would.

Online Screening Comes of Age

Traditionally, employers checked out candidates' qualifications for a position during or after a job interview. Today's emerging technology allows automated selections to take place before the interviews are held. Online screening technology is a direct response to the congested CV marketplace. Online screening has an enormous effect on your CV's acceptance and, if you don't make it through online screening, the technology can banish your CV to the database basement.

Online screening is known by various terms – *pre-screening* and *pre-employment screening,* to mention two. By any name, the purpose of online screening is to verify that you are, in fact, a good fit for the position and that you haven't lied about your background. Employers use online screening tools (tests, assessment instruments, questionnaires, and so forth) to reduce and sort applicants against criteria and competencies that are important to their organisations. Sounds a touch futuristic for these shores? Don't you believe it; a survey of 500 UK companies revealed online screening of job applicants rose from 12 percent in 2000 to 54 percent by 2001, and has continued to rise ever since.

Alastair Cartwright, the Commercial Director of recruitment consultancy Enhance Media, explains why:

> *What we've seen in online recruitment is a surge going back five years now that created a lot of response and generated a lot of CVs. The problem was that companies didn't have the technology to sift through them so that*

instead of saving money they ended up having to take on extra staff to deal with the response. That defeated the object, so they have since developed a number of ways to deal with that. The likes of Royal Bank of Scotland and Abbey National have now completely done away with the CV for their graduate programmes – instead using online personality tests. Another approach is that of United Biscuits where they start off with ten 'killer' questions which have to be answered before a candidate can be considered.

The kind of questions you're likely to encounter in online screening include:

- Do you have a valid work permit?

- Are you willing to relocate?

- Can you demonstrate a proven track record of managing a corporate communications department? (The specific area of management will change from job to job, of course.)

- Is your salary requirement between £25,000 and £40,000/year? (Of course, the salary figures inserted here will change from job to job.)

Answering 'no' to any of these questions disqualifies you for the listed position, an automated decision that helps the recruiters thin the herd of CVs more quickly, but that could be a distinct disadvantage to you, the job searcher. Why? Well, without human interaction, you may not show enough of the stated qualifications, but you may actually have compensatory qualifications that a machine won't allow you to communicate.

On the other hand, professionals in shortage categories benefit by a quick response, such as nursing. For example: *Are you a Registered Nurse?* If the answer is 'yes,' the immediate response, according to a recruiter's joke, is 'When can you start?'

Book II

Showcasing Yourself with a StandOut CV

Online info

Use of online screening in its traditional form has been on the rise for some time, but a growing trend of employers using the internet to search for information about candidates also exists. A recent survey by Joslin Rowe reveals that 20% of recruiters have used social networking sites, such as Facebook and MySpace, and 68% have used search engines such as Google. A similar survey of 600 employers, commissioned by business networking site Viadeo, found that 23% of employers said that the information they found online about potential candidates influenced their decision to progress the job application or not.

Online screening can be described as an automated process of creating a blueprint of known requirements for a given job and then collecting information from each applicant in a standardised manner to see whether the applicant matches the blueprint. The outcomes are sent to recruiters and hiring managers.

Sample components of online screening

The following examples of online screening are not exhaustive, but they are illustrations of the most commonly encountered upfront filtering techniques:

- **Basic evaluation:** The system automatically evaluates the match between a CV's content and a job's requirement and ranks the most qualified CVs at the top.

- **Skills and knowledge testing:** The system uses tests that require applicants to prove their knowledge and skills in a specific area of expertise. Online skills and knowledge testing is especially prevalent in information technology jobs where dealing with given computer programs is basic to job performance. Like the old-time typing tests in an HR office, there's nothing subjective about this type of quiz: You know the answers, or you don't.

- **Personality assessment:** The attempt to measure work-related personality traits to predict job success is one of the more controversial types of online testing. Dr Wendell Williams, a leading testing expert, says that personality tests expressly designed for hiring are in a totally different league than tests designed to measure things like communication style or personality type: 'Job-related personality testing is highly job specific and tends to change with both task and job,' he says. 'If you are taking a generic personality test, a good rule is to either pick answers that fall in the middle of the scale or ones you think best fit the job description. This is not deception. Employers rarely conduct studies of personality test scores versus job performance and so, it really does not make much difference.'

- **Behavioural assessment:** The system asks questions aimed at uncovering your past experience applying core competencies that the organisation requires (such as fostering teamwork, managing change) and position specific competencies (such as persuasion for sales, attention to detail for accountants).

- **Managerial assessments:** The system presents applicants with typical managerial scenarios and asks them to react. Proponents say that managerial assessments are effective for predicting performance on competencies, such as interpersonal skills, business acumen, and decision making. Dr Williams identifies the many forms these assessments can take:

- **In-tray exercises** where the applicant is given an in-tray full of problems and told to solve them

- **Analysis case studies** where the applicant is asked to read a problem and recommend a solution

- **Planning case studies** where the applicant is asked to read about a problem and recommend a step-by-step solution

- **Interaction simulations** where the applicant is asked to work out a problem with a skilled role player

- **Presentation exercises** where the applicant is asked to prepare, deliver, and defend a presentation

- **Team assessments** where the applicant is asked to work with other candidates to solve a problem or make a presentation

- **Integrity tests:** The system attempts to measure your honesty with a series of questions. You can probably spot the best answers without too much trouble.

Pros and cons

From your viewpoint, here's a snapshot of the advantages and disadvantages of online screening:

- ✔ **Advantages:** (A) In theory, a perfect online screening is totally job-based and fair to all people with equal skills. Your CV would survive the first cut based only on your ability to do well in the job. (B) You are screened out of consideration for any job you may not be able to do, saving yourself stress and keeping your track record free of false starts. (C) If you're judged a close match, you're halfway through the hiring door.

- ✔ **Disadvantages:** (A) The creation of an online process is vulnerable to human misjudgement; I'm still looking for an example of the perfect online screening system. (B) You have no chance to 'make up' missing competencies or skills. (An analogy: You can read music but you don't know how to play a specific song. You can learn it quickly, but there's no space to write 'quick learner'.) (C) Tests may lead to test faking – not you, but job searchers who do find ways to cheat put you at a disadvantage. (D) You may be screened out of contention by impersonal software because you aren't Web savvy, but with a little computer coaching, you could do very well in the job.

Level playing field for salaries

When employers demand your salary requirements before they'll schedule an interview, you are at a disadvantage in negotiating strength. But with hundreds of Web sites giving out salary information (try Workthing – www.workthing.com), the tables are turning.

You can, with a few clicks, get a ballpark estimate of your market worth. For an additional sum, you can get a detailed report on your market value. With this information, you become a more informed and more equal partner in the negotiation. If your market rate is £45,000/year and you answer the question earlier in this section, 'Is your salary requirement between £25,000 and £30,000 per year?' you can answer 'no' and keep looking.

Background checks

Background checks are another component of online screening. They're booming in this era of ongoing security concerns. With your permission, employers can dig into your personal and employment history. Since employers are liable if they hire someone who doesn't have the right to work in the UK, they can claim, quite fairly, that they have to do a certain amount of checking. Bear in mind, however, that equal opportunities legislation means that they must run exactly the same checks on everyone. Any company that asks for background information about one applicant, without doing the same for another, risks falling foul of discrimination laws.

So that you will be very careful about the accuracy of the information you convey during an online screening, here is a list of the information that an employer can legitimately look into:

- ✔ **Work status:** Since the onus is now on the employer to check that you've got correct immigration status, they can ask for a National Insurance number, birth certificate, or passport as proof that you are entitled to work in the UK.

- ✔ **References:** References are a tricky issue in the UK, as employment lawyer Colina Greenway of Klegal explains: 'You can't ask for a copy of your reference from the person who gave it, but you can ask for it from the person who receives it. Even then it is subject to questions of breach of confidence. No one is obliged to give a reference, but if you give one, it must be accurate and complete. If it is misleading, then the referee could be liable. As a result a lot of employers give a very standard reference mentioning no more than dates of employment, the job title and perhaps the salary.' As companies seek to protect themselves from liability, these bland references are increasingly common. That means you shouldn't necessarily worry if that's what your company gives you, nor does it necessarily ring alarm bells with prospective employers.

✔ **Positive vetting:** Detailed background checks are rare in the UK, and while there are exceptions, such as the security services, employers are normally careful to ensure that they have specific consent from any job applicant.

✔ **Medical records:** A company has to demonstrate that a) it requests the same information from all applicants and b) that this information is necessary to fulfilling the job.

✔ **Credit history:** There are financially sensitive jobs that may require credit history, but remember that, under the UK's strict Data Protection laws, companies can't get access to any information that you can't. You have the right to request a copy of your own credit history. Credit histories are collected and stored by two companies, Equifax (`www.equifax.co.uk`) and Experian (`www.experian.co.uk`).

✔ **Criminal record:** Companies don't generally request your criminal record – instead you should apply for and supply a copy in a process known as *disclosure*. The body responsible for this is the Criminal Record Bureau Disclosure service (the CRB). Some employers may request your criminal record from the CRB themselves, but can only do so with your permission. More information is available at `www.disclosure.gov.uk`. There are different degrees of disclosure, ranging from the basic (which does not include 'spent' or outdated offences) to the fully detailed.

Bear in mind that certain employers – for example schools and care organisations – have a particular duty to protect the vulnerable. These employers don't accept the simple disclosure and expect a fully detailed record.

When online screening questions ask for specific details such as your National Insurance number, think twice before supplying it. You can't be sure who is reading the information you're sending. A National Insurance number and a CV are all the data a crook needs to steal your identity. Substitute a series of '9's in the space where the NI number is a required field. Give your NI number only when you're confident that the data is going to the right place.

Book II

Showcasing Yourself with a StandOut CV

Your rights in background checks

Finding derogatory information about you is not necessarily sufficient to officially disqualify you from employment. Deficiencies must be shown to be job-related, and any screening must be done equally for all.

To ensure that you are being treated fairly in a background check, remember the following:

- You must give signed permission for background screening to take place.

- You must apply for your own criminal record to be disclosed.

- You have the right to request a copy of any and all data about you that is held on a computer.

- You can insist that inaccurate information be corrected or deleted and that outdated information be stripped from your record.

To find out more about your rights, including Data Protection and employment legislation, take a look at the Department of Trade and Industry's site at www.dti.gov.uk, or try the Advisory, Conciliation and Arbitration Service's site at www.acas.org.uk.

Watch your back in screening rejection

The first thing to do to get your CV on the favoured short list of candidates: Be sure that you don't get knocked out by online screening simply because you don't know enough about the topic. Spend enough time cruising job sites and company Web site career portals to get a feel for the kinds of online screening that are apt to come your way. Take a few tests on company career portals where you really don't want to work to gain experience and increase your comfort level.

What about the online free psychology tests that aren't job specific? Don't bother with these baseless pop psychology instruments for this purpose – unless you feel you just need to get some practice interacting with online tests.

As for background checks, what can you do to protect your career against harm? Before you sign releases permitting the screening to take place, make sure your records in credit bureaus are correct. You can order a credit report from one of the national credit bureaus – Equifax or Experian – to correct errors. You can also order a credit report from each of the bureaus (they may have differing information about you) from their Web sites (www.equifax.co.uk and www.experian.co.uk).

Book II

Showcasing
Yourself with
a StandOut CV

Jumping through hoops

Job seekers complain that recruiters expect you to do far too much work before giving you an inkling that you're a contender for a position. When you post your CV, you may be instructed to also fill out a lengthy job application, breaking down your CV item by item, and filling out a long skills summary. You may be asked to do all this task online or through autoresponder e-mail. When these demands are made, turn to your completed worksheets for a quick tool.

Can your CV be turned away?

What if you get low grades on answering the screening questions – can the employer's system tell you to take your CV and get lost? In fact, companies don't 'bin' a CV for the simple reason that they have to keep them to defend themselves in the event of accusations of discrimination. It's only natural, however, that if a company sets criteria and you don't measure up, you're not doing yourself any favours. As Rob Brouwer, MD of Monster UK, recently said:

> *Using [screening assessments] to better understand candidates' skills ensures that employers need only ask the most suitable job seekers to interview. This reduces recruitment costs and increases the likelihood of finding a candidate that is a good fit for an organisation.*

The bottom line is, if you don't score well in screening questions, your CV will be exiled to an electronic no-hire zone even if it isn't physically turned away.

More Big Changes on the Workplace Horizon

In addition to the handsome CV and online screening trends, other developments also influence how effectively your CV travels. Employers and job seekers alike are making great use of the Internet, and over two-thirds of UK employers now accept online applications, so having both a paper and an electronic CV has become more important than ever.

Job sites

Surveys report that the big general employment sites (such as Monster, WorkThing, and TotalJobs) aren't always the ones responsible for high numbers of job offers. In part, the reason is due to the growth of specialist sites and company Web career portals.

Company Web career portals

Almost all big corporations now operate company Web sites with career portals. This makes it easy to directly apply to the companies that you'd most like to work for.

Employee referral programmes

The practice of employers asking their own workforce, 'Do you know anyone who might be good for this job?' has blossomed into widely used formal employee referral programmes in which bonuses are paid for each candidate hired. A strongly referred candidate is usually seen as preferable to someone off the street. In tempo with advertising, employee referral programmes rise when too few unemployed look for work and slow down when too many unemployed look for work.

Profile-based systems

Profile-based systems are designed to bypass keyword searches entirely by standardising data fields on which the recruiter can search.

Basically, you dissect small pieces of your overall self-marketing information into specific data fields (boxes), which are filed in a company or job site database. You may use the site's automated CV-builder, answer lengthy questionnaires, cut-and-paste data from your plain text CV – or, in some systems, you may be asked to build a profile of yourself online.

Profiles often require that you express your preferences by naming your desired salary range, work location, job function, travel, work schedule, and so forth (a version of online screening).

Some companies, such as Predict Success.com and HR Technologies specialise in helping employers develop online competency questions used to develop the applicant's profile. The profile is measured against a position model to predict whether a person has the skill set to succeed in a position.

Creating a standardised format that compares apples to apples is done for the convenience of recruiters. If you have superb qualifications, profiles can lift you above the competition. But, because the vast majority of job seekers don't fall in that category, profiling can work against you. In profiling, you are negotiating 100 percent on the employer's terms without the opportunity to express unique skills, an uncommon experience mix, or compensatory characteristics if certain requirements of data fields are missing in your background. The image of 'robo-CV' comes to mind when we think of profiles!

XML technology

A decade ago everyone thought that *HyperText Markup Language* (HTML) CVs would be the next big thing, but the technology never really took off. Most employers tell me that they receive less than 1 percent of their CVs in HTML.

XML *(eXtensible Markup Language)* is the new technology that allows staffing systems and payroll systems to talk to each other. An independent, non-profit worldwide consortium of companies, HR-XML, is attempting to develop standards for exchanging workforce staffing and management information between HR specialists.

HTML is a series of tags that are hidden (embedded) in a Web document and that point out how to mark up the text and pictures. HTML tags include layout descriptions to say, for example, that this text is in bold, or double size, or should be in a box in the top left-hand corner. XML is an extension of HTML that adds new tags so that the document not only 'knows' that this line of text is in bold, but that it is also the name of the job applicant. Similarly XML tags can say that not only is this text in a box, but also that it is a list of previous jobs or an address field. The idea is that, if properly tagged, any CV laid out with XML would be readable by recruiter databases without any further modification.

Volatile job market

Economists say the *human capital marketplace* (latest buzzword for job market) should expect endless cycles of hiring/layoff at the same company. This prediction seems reasonable if the past decade is a clue, suggesting you keep your CV current, register with online job agents, maintain a network of employment contacts, remain visible in professional organisations, and follow tips for handling temporary jobs on your CV.

Human networking

If you are a job seeker with doubts about your job qualifications, age, or employability and fear you may run into a brick wall on the Web, stick with human-based job search. Networking in person still has a value, and you can find tips on finding employment the old-fashioned way throughout this book, but be aware that things are changing. A 2006 survey by Personnel Today revealed that over 70 per cent of organisations use online recruitment methods, whether by advertising on a commercial job board or using their own corporate Web sites, or both, and this trend is likely to continue.

But don't throw out your paper CV

Despite the growing use of technology, your paper CV still has its place. Professionals in the e-recruiting industry have been trying to exterminate paper CVs for a half-dozen years, proclaiming them all but dead. But paper CVs are alive and well and will survive for use in local or regional job markets during the next decade – perhaps even longer. Among reasons why paper survives:

- **Paper to have and to hold:** Hiring managers, as well as recruiters, may like a tangible paper to feel, view, and save.

- **Job fairs:** Using e-CVs at some brick-and-mortar job fairs is possible, but paper CVs are the norm because they're easy to distribute.

- **Advertising mail address:** Job ads that include postal addresses keep the paper alternative in place.

- **Employee referral programmes:** Companies that haven't converted employee referrals to Web processes often retain a form that instructs referring workers to clip a paper CV to the form before submitting a name to the HR department.

Really, Must You Have a CV?

Periodically, job guide writers, with bullet-proof self-assurance, assert that CVs are unnecessary baggage. These critics insist that the best way to find a job is to network and talk your way inside. Just ignore them; they're kidding nobody but themselves. The only people for whom the no-CV advice is okay are those who can leave talk-show hosts struggling to get a word in edgewise. Very few people are extroverted and glib enough to carry the entire weight of their employment marketing presentations without supporting materials.

More importantly, you need a CV because most employers say that you need a CV. Employers don't have time to take oral histories when you call to 'ask for a few minutes of time to discuss opportunities'. Those days are gone. A StandOut CV that's easily read and absorbed saves employers' time and shows that you're aware of this new reality.

Book II

Showcasing Yourself with a StandOut CV

Even if – as a corporate executive's child, pal, or hairdresser – you get yourself handed a job on a plate, somewhere along the way you'll need a CV. At some point, people who make hiring decisions insist on seeing a piece of paper or a computer screen that spells out your qualifications. CVs are an important first step on the road to the perfect job.

CVs open doors to job interviews; interviews open doors to jobs.

Chapter 2

Getting Your CV Out There

. . . .

In This Chapter

▶ Succeeding with a ten-step placement plan

▶ Using personal job agents

▶ Unravelling the real deal about job sites

▶ Safeguarding your privacy and credentials online

▶ Networking inside and outside companies

▶ Following up in professional style

. . . .

*T*his chapter puts the cart before the horse. The water skier before the boat. The train before the engine. You get the point?

Suggestions on how to distribute your StandOut CVs before you've written a word come up front in this book because so much has changed during the past couple of years that knowing how you'll *use* your CV could help you do a better job of *writing* your CV.

Ready? Try on these ideas for size.

Marketing Your CV in Ten Steps

No matter how good your CV, it needs to get read to be appreciated. Follow these steps to get your CV to the right place:

1. **Target your job market.**

2. **Make a master list of job leads.**

3. **Take care of housekeeping chores.**

4. **Draft your CV(s).**

   5. **Draft back-up self-marketing CV content.**

   6. **Draft your cover letters and cover notes.**

   7. **Review today's submission technology.**

   8. **Save your CVs and cover letters in useful formats.**

   9. **Determine your online CV strategy.**

   10. **Keep track of your progress.**

The following sections explain these steps in detail.

Step 1: Target your job market

You may not know precisely what you want, but having one to three choices can shorten your search. Choose an occupation, industry, company size, and location you think you'd like. For example, you may want a job, using your education in electrical engineering, in a medium-sized company in Sheffield or the Thames Valley. Or you may want to work in a non-profit organisation as an event planner in Westminster. In both cases, you'd want to check out specialist sites for your occupation.

You can be flexible and change directions if opportunity strikes.

Step 2: Make a master list of job leads

Identify and research potential employers that may be a good fit. At each company, try to uncover the name of the individual who is responsible for hiring people for the position you want. Here are resources for your list:

- ✔ **Job sites:** Big super sites like Jobsite, TotalJobs, and Monster, and specialist sites that relate to your occupation and job title, industry, and geographical location.

- ✔ **Newspapers:** Classified and larger display job ads, plus business page articles.

- ✔ **Business directories, trade publications, and other sources of company information:** The Financial Times (www.ft.com), Hoover's Online (www.hoovers.com/uk), and PR Newswire (wwww.prnewswire.co.uk), are three examples.

- ✔ **Networking groups:** Both local and functional; both online and offline.

- ✔ **Recruiting firms:** Independent, third-party.

✔ **Professional organisations:** In your career field.

✔ **College or university:** Glean contact details of your friends and peers from school or college from Friends Reunited (`www.friendsreunited.com`) or social networking Web sites such as Facebook (`www.facebook.com`) and MySpace (`www.myspace.com`); school ties can sometimes help you out (unless you were the school bully!).

✔ **People:** Family, friends, neighbours, former co-workers, bankers, social organisation members, job club members, former professors.

✔ **Referrals:** Acquaintances and friends who work at companies you admire, and referrals from people you contact who don't know of a job opening but can give you more names to contact.

Step 3: Take care of housekeeping chores

There are many 'little extras' that can help get your foot in the door. Some of the better ideas include:

✔ **Get a free e-mail address:** You can get a free e-mail address from Hotmail (`hotmail.com`) or Yahoo! (`yahoomail.com`). Be sure to check each and every one of your e-mailboxes every day. And while you're at it, why not rent a post office (PO) box and install a phone with an answering machine if you intend to add that layer of privacy to your search.

If you're a student, definitely get another e-mail address. Most college students get a free e-mail address on campus that ends with the extension.ac.uk – a dead give-away for student status. Many employers, who really want from one to three years' experience, won't consider CVs with .ac.uk in the e-mail address. Get another address for job hunting so that you can at least make the first cut.

✔ **Consider using split personalities:** Suppose you want to present yourself as a candidate in two occupations or career fields in the same database. You're looking for a job as a convention planner or a market representative. Or as a controller or internal auditor. Most databases are programmed to replace CV number one with CV number two, under the assumption that CV number two is an update.

If you want to be considered for two types of jobs, consideration may come automatically as a job computer searches the CV database for keywords. But if you want to double up to be sure, use your full name on CV number one. On CV number two, cut back your first and middle names to initials and change telephone numbers and e-mail addresses.

✔ **Self-send first:** Before sending out your CV, send it to yourself and a friend to compare and correct. It's surprising what you can miss the first time around.

✔ **Double-check your Web page:** Before making your Web CV address public by putting it on other types of CVs, review your site for links that you may have forgotten you added in a more carefree period. Stories of links to employment-killing naked lady pictures and bawdy jokes continue to circulate. And don't provide links to your school class or professional society; employers may slip out and find better candidates than you. Finally, if confidentiality is important, don't forget to password-protect your Web page. When employers call, give them the password. If you don't know how to password-protect your site, ask your Web site host or Internet service provider for instructions.

✔ **Practise online testing:** Some employers, weary of having their databases crammed with candidates who don't meet their skill standards, are requiring that jobs seekers take a screening test before their CVs are allowed inside (see Book II, Chapter 1 for more about screening).

✔ **Be mindful of legal issues:** Remember that CV banks must obey equal opportunities laws: Don't reveal any potentially discriminatory information (age, race, gender, religion, sexual orientation) by e-mail to a representative of a CV bank or job site that you would not reveal in a telephone call or during an in-person job interview. Assume the information will be passed on to employers.

✔ **Bookmark favourite job sites and search tools:** Add your favourite sites to your Internet Bookmarks and, on a regular basis, make a focused search by job title, industry, or geographical location. You could, for example, ask a site to show a list of all open jobs for emergency medical technicians in Glasgow.

Step 4: Draft your CV(s)

Create more than one CV if possible. Shape several different CVs: one general version plus several others that address the finer points of functions you want to do – for example, accountant, internal auditor, tax specialist.

Make sure your CV contains the relevant keywords because, in a word-matching keyword search, your CV will be stuck to the bottom of a database if it lacks the required words.

Step 5: Draft back-up self-marketing CV content

Create mix-and-match text blocks for a fast tune-up of your CVs and cover letters. Write a variety of paragraphs and store them on your computer. Need ideas of what to say in the paragraphs? Read over CVs of others in your field and be inspired. Then, when you must quickly put together a CV targeted to a specific job – and none of your full-blown CV versions are perfect – your inventory of text blocks gives you a running start.

Step 6: Draft your cover letters and cover notes

Draft several cover letters and the shorter version, cover notes. *Cover Letters For Dummies* (Wiley) offers state-of-the-art tips on writing dynamic statements.

Book II

Showcasing Yourself with a StandOut CV

Step 7: Review today's submission technology

The handsome CV is making a comeback (we're really glad about this – see Book II, Chapter 1). But until the new technology completely drives out the old, telephone an employer about any job that's very important to you and enquire about that specific company's technology. When in doubt, paste your ASCII text cover letter and CV in the body of the e-mail message and attach a formatted MS Word CV. The ASCII CV is backup in case the employer is using an old system and can't or doesn't download your formatted CV.

Step 8: Save your CVs and cover letters in useful formats

Ready your CV packages for battle by saving them on your hard drive and a floppy disk if you transmit CVs from more than one location. If you move around a lot, you may want to have a password-protected copy stored on your ISP's server. That way you (and only you) can access it, edit it, and send it wherever you have web access. Most ISPs allow plenty of storage space for this. Wherever you choose to save your CV, one version should be in MS Word and the other in ASCII plain text.

Making sure that the right people get it

If you send your CV to a hiring manager (good idea), send a duplicate to the human resource department. Note this effort in your cover letter to the hiring manager, which means that not only is the human resource professional not treated disrespectfully, but the hiring manager gets to keep your CV as a constant reminder of you instead of having to send it down to HR.

Making 100 per cent sure that you have the right names for both of these individuals shows that you have a flair for accuracy and that you care enough about the company to do your homework properly. A quick phone call to a company's reception desk usually equips you with the right people's names.

Step 9: Determine your online CV strategy

If privacy issues are of concern to you, you may choose any of several strategies:

- ✔ **Conservatively confidential:** No online posting of your CV, except as a response to specific job listings or to a targeted mailing list of potential employers. You take care to protect your identity. You plan to work with one or more recruiters (you understand that third-party recruiters are paid for finding the best candidates and will likely ignore you if you are spread all over the Net and can be hired for free).

- ✔ **Moderate exposure:** In addition to the conservative exposure just mentioned, you are highly selective about the CV databases and personal job agents you submit your CV to. You may or may not cloak your identity. You understand the privacy policy of the job sites you select.

- ✔ **Full visibility:** You are unemployed and need a job quickly. You post to every logical job site you can find. You want immediate action and are pulling out all the stops. You have read this chapter and know the pros and cons of such a move.

Step 10: Keep track of your progress

Don't let important aspects of your online activity get away from you. Keep records of where you submitted your CV, which personal job search agents are alerting you to the best job posts, and which source of job listings are proving to hold the most potential for you. Make mid-course corrections when needed.

When should your CV arrive? Mondays are busy days, and Fridays are practically the weekend. Try for arrival on Tuesday, Wednesday, or Thursday.

Sending Your CV the Right Way to the Right Places

Deciding whether to post your CV at a big job site or stick with the traditional paper CV is a decision deserving some thought. The following sections explore the options.

Book II

Showcasing Yourself with a StandOut CV

The good and bad of big online job sites

Even Net-savvy job searchers write to us saying they're becoming disenchanted with big online job sites:

Warning: Watch out for the black hole at major job boards

Recruiter Mary Nurrenbrock doesn't sugar-coat it when describing her view of the practice of responding to jobs advertised on the major job boards:

'When you respond to openings directly through job boards, your CV usually ends up in a black hole, a passive database. If you are responding right from the board, it's going to HR. Bad move. These guys are up to their eyeballs and usually don't even really know what the hiring manager is looking for. That is, if the HR person even sees the CV in the passive database.

'You need to get to the hiring manager, not HR. How? When you visit a job board and see a job that looks like it's a fit (you notice I didn't say that it looks interesting), go to that company's Web site and get a name. Most of the corporate sites have profiles. Get the name of the VP Marketing, CEO, CMO – whoever the open position is likely to report to.

'Figuring out the address isn't hard. Look under the press releases where you'll usually find a company contact e-mail address. Use the same format – joe_bloggs@, joe.bloggs@, jbloggs@ – to send your CV. If it bounces back, try a different format. If that doesn't work, try to get the address from the company receptionist. If all else fails, snail mail it.

'What usually happens next is that the hiring manager sends your CV to HR. But we are trying to avoid that, right? No, we are trying to avoid the black hole. Now the HR person is looking at a CV that came to her from an internal source. Big difference!'

I keep sending CVs for jobs to big job boards (generalised super sites), however I never hear anything back from them. As yet, I have never been contacted. I fill out the CV and make it specific to the job advertised. What am I doing wrong?

I have sent out my CV to a number of positions posted on sites like (big job board), and I have noticed that a number of these positions stay posted for weeks on end. What is the average response to jobs posted on the Web? Are people actually hired from these sites?

Back in 1995, a time when dinosaurs ruled the earth in terms of the Internet, advisers, including us, urged job seekers to get aboard the Web wagon or be left behind. The message was received around the world. Over a decade later, the online novelty has vanished as millions of job seekers found out how easy it is to pop a CV online and have done so.

The giant job boards do offer several advantages when you're floating your CV:

- ✔ Excellent for entry-level jobs with big corporations like Microsoft and Proctor & Gamble.
- ✔ Excellent for job searchers with broadly applicable skills, such as sales and marketing.
- ✔ Excellent for a number of fancy tools, such as job title converters that help job seekers figure out what their job title would be in other companies or career fields.
- ✔ More focused sections or channels (like healthcare and legal jobs) are being added to emulate the appeal of the niche job sites.

You shouldn't decide that, because of the low rate of hires, you're never going to speak to the Web again and that's that. As unsatisfying as the Web can be for the actual hook-up of people and jobs at the moment, the clock won't be turned back. Consider online searching as merely one more option in your tool kit.

Our recommendation? Use one or two major job boards, and devote the rest of your online time to the specialist sites and the corporate sites.

Specialist Web sites: Why smaller may be better

The super-generalised job sites – TotalJobs, Monster, and Jobsite – have been compared to broadcast TV, appealing to a very wide, diverse audience. Specialist sites, by contrast, operate a narrowcast model more like cable networks where channels like UK Gold and MTV are targeted to very specific groups of viewers.

The future of online job searching: Specialist and specificity

Generic broad-based Web recruiting is giving way to narrowly focused recruiting. And as go the recruiting sites, so go your CVs. We don't even want to guess how many specialist sites sit on the Net waiting to welcome computer-loveable CVs, but there are more than you could shake your CV at. Every profession, locality, industry, and lifestyle is joined by networking hubs and entre-preneurial watering holes catering to the select Web communities they target.

Specialist sites, by their nature, are more liable to appear and then melt away than their big generalist brothers. To get an idea of what's out there, try looking at directories that list the specialist sites, rather than trying to find each and every one individually. Some sample directories of specialist recruiters include the listings at Support4Learning (`www.support4learning.org.uk/jobsearch/jobs_special.htm`) or the UK Jobs Guide (`www.ukjobsguide.co.uk`), which has a handy listing of specialist recruitment sites.

Book II

Showcasing Yourself with a StandOut CV

When specialist sites shine

The reasons to customise your job hunt by posting your CV on small sites are the following:

- More focused job listings for your purposes.

- Fewer cumbersome procedures to post a CV.

- More control over what your CV looks like. Big general job boards tend to insist on a chronological job history format when using a project-oriented or functional approach may be more to your advantage.

- May limit listings by headhunters, which make up a heavy percentage of ads on super sites. Headhunters often don't name the potential employer, which could be a problem if it's your own company.

- Appear to have a higher percentage of mid- and upper-management jobs than the general super sites.

- Many job seekers say they like the smaller specialist sites' manageable size, better quality listings, and community feel.

Hail the corporate Web site

In the days before computers and the Internet, when you went directly to companies to apply for a job – without knowing whether any openings were available – the job search method was called 'direct application'. Today, you can still use the direct application method, but you do it online at corporate Web sites that recruit through their *career portals* (gateways).

Guide to online resources

The comings and goings of dot.coms/dot gones means that finding reliable advice online is a bit of a moving target. That said, a few organisations can help make sense of the range of sites on offer in the UK. Support4Learning (www. support4learning.org.uk) is a general site aimed at students and those in the education sector but if you go to its Jobsearch section (www.support4learning.org.uk/job search), you'll find a guide to using UK online recruitment agencies and an updated list of who's who and what's what in the job market. Although this site is intended for students and teachers, it's a pretty good guide to the scene for anyone looking for work online.

For registered members, the Chartered Management Institute (www.inst-mgt.org.uk) also has links to listings pages lurking under the slightly misleading title of 'Managing Yourself' (www.inst-mgt.org.uk/external/man skill/self.html). Here you can find a list not only of job hunting sites but also of careers portals, advice centres, career development advice, and such things as stress management and emotional support sites.

UK Recruiter (www.ukrecruiter.co.uk), intended for use by the recruitment industry itself, also provides a lot of helpful advice and links. You don't have to hanker after a career in headhunting to benefit from UK Recruiter's inside information and horse's mouth advice on job hunting and current online recruitment sites.

The following sections offer some things to bear in mind when submitting your CV to a corporate Web site.

Target your search

Although major commercial job sites, such as Monster.com, are centralised, the universe of corporate Web sites is decentralised. Exploring that universe is time consuming. You can easily spend two hours taking the measure of just one or two corporate career portals, picking up details of what you should know to maximise opportunity.

Begin by compiling a list of prospective employers. To prioritise the list, you can use company briefings on Hoovers (www.hoovers.com/uk) and other online company directories, as well as information from newspapers and business magazines.

Another way to compile your list is to search large job sites – job boards, such as Jobsite or TotalJobs – to sort opportunities by location, by job function, or by industry. Verify appealing job ads on the corporate Web site.

Notice company interests

As you scan a corporate career portal, back up to the company home page and click to press releases, annual report, and general areas for any edge you can use to enhance your application when you move to the careers area.

Understand procedure

About the only standard advice for sending your CV to corporate Web sites is to submit information in a digital version only. Skip postal mail and fax (see the sidebar 'Why two-for-one doesn't add up' for why).

Pay attention to specific instructions on each corporation's site. Some corporate Web sites ask you to attach your CV. Others require that you cut and paste it into a standard form, or use the site's CV builder.

 If you attach your formatted CV (my preference if it's an option) and can't decide whether to kick off with an objective and or skills summary, try both, like this.

Objective: Position at (name or type of company) in (general location) requiring a stand-out performer with the following skills and characteristics: (insert your keyword profile, as discussed in Book II, Chapters 3 and 4).

Additionally, don't be surprised if you're asked to take online employment tests. Be ready to provide good information on your skills and interests.

 Some corporate sites won't accept anonymous candidates who cloak their identity.

Book II

Showcasing Yourself with a StandOut CV

Job seeker connects through specialist site

An acquaintance of ours, David, a consultant, spent more than 30 minutes building his CV on a super job site, filling out multiple screens of information and tick boxes. David wasn't a happy bunny because he already had a CV he liked, but he went along with the drill. Nothing happened.

David finally tried a local job board, a community site. Happily, this site let David cut and paste his own CV. Within a day, David got two calls for interviews that fit his requirements while his mandated super job site CV slept the sleep of the dead.

Why two-for-one doesn't add up

To make doubly sure that your CV is in a database for a job you really want, should you postal mail a duplicate hard copy as a backup in case a clerk messes up the electronic file?

No. When the company's career page directs you to e-mail your CV or to submit it via the company's online CV builder, do not send in a hard copy to the HR department because the hard copy would more than likely be scanned, found to be a duplicate, and deleted. This unnecessary extra work causes a scowl on the poor scanning operator's face and doesn't get you anywhere. The only time to send in a hard copy is to a hiring manager.

If company managers wanted duplicates to clog their files with paper, they wouldn't have installed the more efficient electronic recruiting systems.

As technical reviewer Jim Lemke says, 'With any system, once you submit your CV, you are in the pond. There is no need to send another CV through the system at the same time.'

Use paper CVs to rescue your career

Remember that the Web is just one more pebble on the employment beach. A big pebble to be sure, but, let's face it, some job hunters are never going to get past the E-Gatekeeping Godzilla (Internet recruiting systems) because they are too old, too young, have the wrong skills, or whatever.

Evaluate why your online search isn't working

Is your online job search in trouble? Review this checklist and see which reason(s) could be at fault. Some job hunters:

- Strike out in e-job search because they refuse to invest the effort to learn the ropes.

- Come up with zero online because they just don't get this Internet thing, never did, never will and no longer care.

- Never lift off with their searches because their CVs lack the right keywords and accomplishment content.

- Bump into a wall of silence because their skills are not in demand and possibly are obsolete.

- Are ignored in today's youth culture because they're older ('overqualified') than the people employers want to hire.

> ✔ Don't make it past the online screening programs because they lack the knowledge, competencies, skills, or ability to respond correctly to programmed questions.
>
> ✔ Never hear back because employers just aren't on a hiring spree.

Could this be you? Before cursing the darkness of a failed job search, decide whether you want to (A) improve your online search techniques or (B) decide the computer is rotting your mind and ditch the whole digital thing.

Go back to finding jobs the classic way

If you have reason to think you belong in the Internet expatriate class and your chances of finding a job by e-efforts (even if the 'e' stands for excellence) are nil, my best suggestion is head back to job hunting the way it was before the Web arrived and wasted your time.

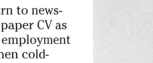

Use your paper CV as your marketing tool of choice when you turn to newspapers and trade publications to find out who's hiring. Use your paper CV as your calling card while networking person to person and finding employment thanks to human intervention. Use your paper CV as your ace when coldcalling hiring managers, many of whom dislike reading computer screens and like the feel of a piece of paper in their hands.

As we often say, when the machines seem to be beating you, use people to beat the machines. Some good opportunities will always be captured the old-fashioned way.

Taking Online Issues into Account

As you submit your CVs electronically here, there, and everywhere, you need to be aware that there are tricks and tips specific to using the Web. These sections address those related to sharing your CV.

E-mail, post, or fax

A reader's letter to us: 'A very simple, but important question: If you are asked to e-mail, fax, or post a CV to a prospective employer, what is the best way to send it?'

When a delivery mode preference isn't specified, we'd suggest e-mail because it's easier to inventory in a database and send downstream to hiring managers. Next choice, we'd send it by post (making sure it is scannable) and, as a last resort, fax.

Respecting the difference between CV posting and CV blasting

Which do you do? Not sure? Well, CV posters understand the difference between quality and quantity and choose to place their CVs only on a few select sites. By contrast, CV blasters indiscriminately chuck out CVs like confetti all over the Internet.

CV posting

CV posting should be an exercise in thoughtful placement. If you do it yourself, you exercise 95 percent control. The other 5 percent is a wild card – despite privacy statements, job sites and corporate Web sites have been known to 'migrate' CVs to databases you don't know about. (Read about privacy protection issues later in this chapter.)

If you decide to post to a limited number of sites, heed these tips:

- Choose sites where you need not register first to search for jobs.

- Determine the control you have over your CV. On a case-by-case basis, what you want is the ability to choose when to release your CV to an employer listing a job you may want. The ability to say 'yes' or 'no' really shouldn't be negotiable if you want to control your own information.

- Determine the access you have to your CV. You want to be able to edit it (adding new facts or targeting it each time you apply for a different job), delete it entirely, and if your CV is expunged after a certain time period, you want to be able to easily renew it.

If you do want to post with caution but also want to save hours and hours, consider a CV-posting service that allows you to choose which sites receive your CV, give login information for each site, and allow you to apply directly to each site. Posting services allow you to select industry categories to apply to and so leave the job of finding industry specific recruiters to someone else. The service is usually free – take a look, for example, at CV Poster (www.cvposter.com).

CV blasting

You may already have received an e-mail pitch urging you to reach thousands of search, recruitment, and placement firms. At least a half-dozen CV distribution services ask you to let their companies carpet-bomb the Web with your CV.

At first glance, that kind of CV blasting may seem like a smashing idea, an easy way to get your CV out there and in front of every face that matters. But after you think it through, you'll probably change your mind – there's a big difference between getting your face noticed where it counts and putting yourself right in the face of those that count.

Ed's attachment etiquette

'If you are attaching something, consider the following guidelines when doing so', says Ed Struzik, president of BEKS Data Services, Inc. (beks@beksdata.com). Struzik speaks from a dozen-years' vantage point in providing outsourced CV processing services and applicant tracking system consulting to numerous Fortune 100 companies.

Do Not attach **EXE files.** An EXEcutable file could contain a virus, and no one will chance having the hard drive or network infected.

Do Not attach **ZIP files.** Who's to say the ZIP file doesn't contain an infected EXEcutable. And besides, can your CV be so large that you have to ZIP it?

Do Not attach **password-protected documents.** How would you expect someone or something to open it without the password?

Do Not attach **documents with contact info in headers or footers.** This one seems innocent enough. But the fact is, doing a 'Select All' to copy/paste your CV may not capture your name, address, etc. if they are in header or footer data.

Do Not attach **documents with text boxes.** Another seemingly innocent situation. But again, doing a 'Select All' to copy/paste your CV may not get the text box.

Do Not attach **forwarded messages.** In most mail systems, you have the option to 'attach' a forwarded message or 'include' the text of a forwarded message. For a number of reasons, choose 'include' the text.

Remember that many company firewalls (the software that protects their system from unwanted intruders) may be set to simply strip-out any pictures or attachments. Even HTML may be switched off in the email reader at the other end, meaning that your beautifully embellished CV or cover letter is trimmed down to lowest-common denominator text without your knowing. If in doubt about what file formats will work, go for the simplest you can, and if you want to send attachments and other stuff, then take the trouble to ask whether they can get through.

Indiscriminate posting of your personal information can trigger a wave of career failures and personal problems, which are intertwined with privacy issues. See the 'CV confidential: Protect your privacy' section later in this chapter to find out how these disasters can happen.

One irate hiring manager tells of a CV blaster for IT (information technology) who began bombarding her with forwarded and unsolicited CVs even though she didn't have open jobs at that time. When the CV load proved to be too burdensome to comply with the company policy on replying to each job seeker, the hiring manager told the CV distribution service to stop. The hiring manager was frustrated not only because a large number of the forwarded CVs lacked contact or name information but also because she felt sorry for the job searchers who'd paid money for the CV blasting services and were actively on the market looking for work.

The hiring manager's parting comment: 'These job seekers should know that (A) they are paying to reach recruiters without jobs or (B) to have their CVs forwarded in a way that cannot be responded to. They should use their money for something else.'

As About.com's Allison Doyle points out, however, 'Some CV blasting services will let you target only recruiters who asked to be put on a list to receive CVs in specific industries and geographic regions and will send you a list of the recruiters your CV was sent to.'

There are other reasons to avoid services that send out a tornado of CVs, which are covered in the following sections.

We do not recommend CV blasting for a number of reasons, including the following:

- ✔ Negative perceptions of CV 'spamming' (junk mail)
- ✔ Recruiter distaste for shop-worn CVs
- ✔ Loss of control over your own CV

Gerry Crispin and Mark Mehler (CareerXroads consultants and experts on the recruiting industry) agree that CV blasting is ill-advised:

We are absolutely not in favour of sites that promise to distribute job seekers' CVs to 'hundreds of subscribing recruiters and employers'. Most charge a fee, and it's a waste of money. Privacy and disclosure is too important, and while you may not care today, you certainly will tomorrow.

Realising that CVs live forever

After your CV leaves earth to live in the stratospheric reaches of the Web, you can't control it. It may turn up anywhere, anytime – including on your boss's desk.

But what if you've been cagey – wink, nudge, say no more – and only listed events prior to your current job? Can't you just tell your boss that the CV is old, posted before you took your present position, and you have no idea how or why it's still alive? Sure you can, but the missing information describing your present employment is probably your best selling strength if you're on the market.

Moreover, employers are realising that as soon as your CV is up in Web lights, you'll continually be contacted if you seem to have what's wanted somewhere. And if you're having a bad day, you might just be tempted to say, 'I'm gone.'

What to do when you're all alone by the telephone

No matter how picky you were about the job sites where you posted your CV – including big national job boards and small specialist sites alike – if you're getting no action after a month to six weeks, whisk back your CVs from their current locations and post them elsewhere.

What about corporate Web sites you haven't heard from? Leave your CV in these databases.

Consider them lifers unless you decide they need refreshing or the company's policy requires deletion of unused CVs after a specified time period – usually six months to a year.

By the way, repeated postings of the same CV won't make a positive difference, and may, in fact, make you look like a loser.

Book II

Showcasing Yourself with a StandOut CV

Most online job boards, such as Monster, enable job seekers to block their name, contact details, and current employer's name on their CV's so that their current (and/or previous) employer can't find them on the CV database.

Marked for life

Individuals who put their CVs on the big national job boards two years ago are still hearing from recruiters and companies even though they have accepted other employment. Not only do the CVs live on eternally, but they may also find their way to unintended databases.

Even job seekers who report that they deactivated their CVs on the boards where they originally posted them hear from places they never knew received their CVs. 'Marked for life' is the way one job seeker put it.

The chances that your CV will escape from its designated space are multiplying.

CV scraping

Job ads have long been openly 'scraped' – a term for what happens when robots/spiders scour the Web looking for job listings and collect them on a second and unrelated site.

Now, CVs are being scraped, too. Ethical scrapers send you an e-mail and ask if you'd like to be included in the second database and are guided by your response. But most scrapers treat CVs like a commodity, don't get your permission, and take your CV to places unknown. When you don't know where your CV is, how can you call it back to make changes? Or withdraw it entirely?

Remember, online CVs may never die. They just blow like tumbleweed through the wastelands of the Web.

Recruiters keep their distance

One more reason not to spread your CV all over the map: When you're targeting the fast track to the best jobs, nothing beats being brought to an employer's notice by an important third person – and an independent recruiter qualifies as an important third person.

We've already seen how employers are becoming resistant to paying independent recruiters big fees to search the Web when they theoretically can save money by hiring in-house corporate recruiters to do it. That's why recruiting agencies need fresh inventory that employers can't find elsewhere. If you want a third-party recruiter to present you, think carefully before pinning cyber wings on your CV.

CV confidential: Protect your privacy

Identity theft may be the worst-case scenario, but it isn't the only life-altering problem that can arise when you put your business on e-street.

You can lose your current job, if you have one. 'Many employers do search for their employees' CVs in job site CV databases and search engines,' explains Susan Joyce, CEO of Job-Hunt.org, who tracks the privacy issue. 'When employees' CVs are found grazing in someone else's pasture before noon', says CareerXroads' Mark Mehler, who consults with countless company managers, 'they may be on the street by the end of that same day.'

A recent survey by the Cranfield School of Management and a BT working group showed that of UK SME's (Small and Medium-sized Enterprises), just under three quarters had the facility to monitor employees' e-mail. By UK law, a company can't just listen in to your mail for the fun of it, but it is allowed to monitor your mail to establish a number of things, including whether or not those communications are relevant to the business. Any system that uses keywords will have little trouble spotting employees who are sending CVs. Companies are encouraged to have clear policies that explain to their staff just what kind of e-mail monitoring they indulge in. But many don't. Because all companies have the right to dip into mail to ensure that the business you're minding is theirs, a little discretion goes a long way.

Who can you trust?

People in the UK benefit from one of the most protective approaches to data. Both UK and European legislation are very strict about what information you can store about someone and just who you can pass it to. Despite this, there can't be many of us who have never received junk mail or spam from someone who has clearly begged, borrowed, or stolen our details.

Be stingy with your CV

In addition to losing control of your CV, its wide availability can cause squabbles among contingency recruiters over who should be paid for finding you. An employer caught in the conflict of receiving a CV from multiple sources, including internal CV databases, will often pass over a potential employee rather than become involved in deciding which source, if any, should be paid.

A CV and an NI number are perfect building blocks for identity theft or harassment. Be wary of who you give them out to. Any reputable job site will guarantee confidentiality, but mistakes happen, and software 'scraping' programs (explained in the section 'CV scraping') snap up details without permission. If confidentiality is key, then it may pay to keep mum.

You can decide whether you want to be a victim of your CV's lack of privacy protection. Just remember: Problems could happen tomorrow or years from now because online CVs live eternally on the Internet.

Safeguarding your identity

In some recruitment circles, job seekers who protect their identity are more desirable than those who don't, notes Susan Joyce (CEO of Job-Hunt.org). Employers assume you're employed and have an existing job you are protecting. The downside in cloaking your identity is that some recruiters and potential employers won't accept anonymous CVs.

What should you do? We suggest you take that chance. After all, privacy protection doesn't mean relying on assurances from job sites that they're protecting your privacy for you. Here's how to look out for yourself: *Transform all identifying information into generic information.* But won't going generic hurt your chances of being hired? Maybe. Maybe not. There's a trade-off.

Combining suggestions by job hunt authority Susan Joyce, career expert and author Martin Yate, recruiter Steven Gatz, and ourselves, here's a roundup of techniques to help you avoid colliding with your boss, identity thieves, criminals, and other problems on the information highway:

- ✔ **Your name:** Replace your true name with an e-mail alias. Use a serious e-mail name, such as MEngineer. Or make up a name followed parenthetically by the words 'screen name' – Able Smith (Screen Name). Or refer to yourself as someone like 'Confidential Candidate' or 'Confidential Systems Analyst'. Or, using a special e-mail address that you maintain for just this purpose, just enter seven nine's – 9999999 – for each field requiring name, address, and phone number. Even if the original site sends your CV on to other sites, your personal information is never revealed.

✔ **Your contact information:** After obtaining a free e-mail account with Yahoo!, Hotmail, or the like, train yourself to check it daily. Use this address as your chief point of contact. If you feel you need to flesh out your contact information, for a street address, rent a post office box and use an unlisted telephone connected to a message recorder. Again, check regularly.

Recruiters often search by area and postal codes, so you may want to use the real ones in those spots, followed by fake numbers – most postal codes come in two parts, often of three letters or numbers. The first part is good enough to narrow down your location for a recruiter – offering the last two or three digits will usually narrow it down to a couple of houses which may be more information than you want to give. Here's another good tip: Under pain of torture, never use your business e-mail address as your CV contact point. You risk being flayed alive when your boss finds out.

✔ **Your current employer:** Omit the name and replace it with a generic, but accurate, description. Nuts n' Bolts Distributors, Inc becomes 'small construction supplies distribution company'. Microsoft becomes 'multinational information technology company'. For company location, Cadbury Schweppes in Birmingham becomes 'FTSE food and drink company in the Midlands'. The flip side of that coin is that your current company may be your biggest selling point for your next. As Joe Slavin, MD of Fish4Jobs points out, 'Employers are searching on keywords so that if a candidate uploads a CV that says they are currently working for Pepsi, then Coke will see that and give them a call immediately.'

✔ **Your job title:** If your job title is uncommon (like 'head geek' – yes, these sorts of titles do exist!) or, in combination with other facts, would identify you, use a generic title. However, if the title you choose could be misleading in any way, indicate that you've switched it – Network Engineer (position-equivalent title). South-East regional gadget marketing director becomes 'Home Counties marketing manager of gadget-class products'. If your job title is generic, such as 'Editor' or 'Sales Representative', just go ahead and use it.

✔ **Prior employers:** You probably won't need to sanitise information about earlier employers unless you're in a small industry where everyone knows everyone else and can figure out who you are by your work history. In that case, continue to camouflage yourself with the use of generic terms for the past ten years. Instead of 'Five years with Jackson Plastics as a research design engineer', substitute 'respected plastics company' for Jackson Plastics.

Listing previous employers by name, title, and dates of employment (research design engineer, 1992 – 1997, Jackson Plastics) can strip you of stealth options. A suspicious boss can check personnel files for your old CV.

✔ **Education:** Use either your degree and institution (MA, Durham University) or your degree and date (MA, 1987). Using all three makes you identifiable through Old Boy's associations or Friends Reunited. A really determined, suspicious manager may even be able track you down if you use both your undergraduate and advanced degrees by cross-checking academic lists. Of course if you're living with that kind of suspicion, you may well be in a hurry to get out anyway.

If one or both of your degrees are from a prestigious institution, ride on those coat tails, leaving off dates. Or just list your advanced degree and decide whether the college or a recent graduation date is most important in qualifying you.

✔ **Accomplishments:** Veil defining accomplishments with generic language. No to 'Lead design engineer on development of DayNight onboard navigation component – headed a team of eight design engineers with a project budget of £7 million'. Yes to 'Led a large task force in a multi-million pound automotive technology launch.'

✔ **Certifications and licenses:** Showing national or local certification isn't high risk, but professional associations may publish their member lists, and licenses are often easy to track down. That's why you generally should not list the date or precise location certifying your professional designation or granting your license.

✔ **Memberships:** Be careful which organisations you include. Exclusive or unusual bodies may identify you more precisely than you think.

If taking all these precautions seems a little paranoid, choose only the stealth strategies you think you need to protect your privacy. Admittedly, too much of a masquerade-ball environment can be off-putting to recruiters and employers.

Targeting the best lists for your e-mail CV campaign

A targeted e-mail CV campaign is a sophisticated and often highly effective strategy for a job search campaign, and it's best used for senior-level jobs. The formula is simple: You use a commercial list of selected independent recruiters and companies that logically could hire you, and you contact them with e-mail – or a combination of e-mail and post.

Let us play mind-readers for a minute and answer the questions that we think you might have.

Q: But isn't a targeted mailing campaign just an updated version of the old broadcast letter that most experts say doesn't work and that they'd rather drink bleach than recommend?

A: They are both about reaching-out, but these methods have substantial differences between them. The broadcast letter typically is sent indiscriminately to all addresses on direct-mail lists. The targeted e-mail campaign depends on careful matching of potential employers to the requirements of the job seeker. The quality of the list is a make-or-break factor.

Q: Are these e-lists new?

A: They're not new, but the e-databases that create the lists became a stand-alone tool only within the past several years. E-databases have the power to customise a list of recruiters by specialisation – both by industry (energy companies) and functional field (quality control). The way they're being used is very different than the old lists of the last century.

Yesteryear's recruitment e-databases were like the original television show, *Charlie's Angels*, featuring soft plots and good manners. Today's powerful e-databases are like the new hyper-action feature film of the same title that blows its heroines through skyscraper glass windows. The old e-databases were offered on disk or CD-ROM and updated periodically; new versions are on the Web, and the premier products are updated daily. Earlier versions were produced by information vendors and resold by outplacement, executive marketing, and CV writing firms as an optional service; today's renditions are directly accessible to individual consumers.

The best lists are not free, but they include a mail-merge feature allowing you to send your cover letter and CV yourself. You can hire it done if you're not comfortable with computers.

Q: Is a targeted e-mail campaign a good bet if you don't have a degree?

A: Yes, if you use a CV letter instead of a CV; a letter doesn't flag your missing degree and gives you a chance to explain if a recruiter or employer calls you.

Q: What else is needed to find a good job by a targeted mail campaign?

A: You need good credentials and employers that are hiring your bundle of skills. Additionally, the following factors make the difference:

- ✔ You must address your mail campaign to a hiring decision-maker by name, not 'Marketing Manager' or 'President'.

- ✔ Excellent marketing materials help attract employer interest. If you lack writing skills, hire a specialist to prepare them. The mailing package can consist of your CV and cover letter or note – or a combination CV letter.

- ✔ In the best targeted mail campaigns, you or your agent follow up with telephone calls to recipients within a week of the transmission. Anyone can be your agent for this purpose, paid or unpaid.

Q: Which is best – e-mail CVs or post CVs?

A: The Internet recruiter Reed (www.reed.co.uk) recently ran a survey of over 400 UK recruiters to find out who they would choose if they were faced with two equal candidates, one with a paper CV and one with a digital CV. Seventy-eight percent of recruiters said they'd take the candidate with the e-CV. Furthermore, 63 percent said they would favour people with e-CVs when selecting for

interviews. Reasons given included the fact that e-CVs are 'faster and more efficient to deal with . . . whether they arrive by e-mail, through a company's own
web site, or from an external Internet job site'. On a more subjective note, a
third of recruiters noted that they saw candidates with paper CVs as being likely
to be computer-illiterate or simply 'behind the times'. Diana Sabey, Director of
Product and Content for Monster UK & Ireland, said that 'People who apply
online are more "with it". It shows that they know how the internet works'.

It's a pattern that varies around the country. According to Reed, the areas
least likely to handle their CVs digitally are Yorkshire and the North-East. At
the other end of the scale, London-based employers are the most likely to use
electronic CVs with over 44 percent of employers in the capital receiving 90
percent or more of their CVs electronically. Generally speaking, two out of
five recruiters say that they now receive over 90 per cent of CVs electronically. Only 15 per cent of recruiters do not accept CVs via the Internet at all.

E-mail is easy to inventory in databases and to forward CVs to clients. Send
two e-mail versions – your formatted attachment and also an ASCII text
within the body of your e-mail.

**Q: Can you give an example of a real-life successful targeted e-mail
campaign?**

A: There is an e-mail campaign story we especially like. This one involves a
father in top management and his son in sales. The father's search cost
£1,000; his son's £250.

The father, Craig (not his real name, we're just too nice to embarrass him!), is
a 50-something senior telecommunications executive earning a six figure
salary. In his previous position, Craig had turned a 'fallen dot.com' into a positive cash-flow business. After the flood of red ink was cauterised, the owners
of the business decided to step back in, and Craig was out.

On Craig's behalf, an e-mail campaigner focused on retained executive
recruiters and on venture capital firms specialising in the telecommunications
industry. More than 1,600 e-mails were sent with Craig's cover letter and CV.

After five days, Craig had four major hits for executive jobs through recruiting firms in various parts of the country. Delighted, Craig began to proactively work those four leads. Craig's job search continued for 12 weeks,
during which he reached final-interview status for all four positions. Two
didn't pan out. The third company put him through 12 interviews before
selecting the other short-listed candidate. As this book went to press, the
fourth and favourite opportunity remains viable.

At the same time, Craig's son David (also not his real name) was looking for
a better sales job. David's e-mail campaign went to 400 selected potential
employers. Results were quick, and David began his new and much superior
job within six weeks of the campaign.

Book II

**Showcasing
Yourself with
a StandOut CV**

Q: If targeted e-mail campaigns are so powerful, why doesn't everyone use them?

A: Targeted e-mail campaigns can be pricey, and they don't always work. You should be earning in the £50,000 and up range if you want to pay for a full-on turnkey campaign. And they aren't for everyone. You can do them yourself at a substantial time cost until you learn the ropes. Or you can hire a specialist if you have the money to pay for services. E-mail CV campaigns work best when you are contacting executive recruiters and when companies are hiring in your field.

Branching Out to Make Use of All Your Job-Finding Options

Networking (read *human interaction that includes employee referrals*) is rated number one in hiring results. That said, putting the following tools to use will be a great help to you.

Seeking endorsement through employee referral programmes

If you want fast action and special interest in your candidacy for a job, book your CV for the *employee referral programme* (ERP) tour. That is, identify companies where you'd like to work. Start with ten and then move on to a second batch of ten. And so on.

At each target company, network your way to an employee. You may already know some of the people inside a few companies. When you don't know a soul, keep asking someone who knows someone who knows someone. After you identify a contact, enlist that employee's aid in forwarding your name for employment.

Building a corporate insiders network sounds like hard graft, and it is. But this is a gift to yourself that keeps on giving – your efforts could pay off big, not only for your next job but also for a number of ever more responsible positions in coming years.

Formal Employee Referral Programmes are still in their infancy in the UK, where only an estimated 18 per cent of companies use this approach. In the US they are now the number one source for new employees. ERPs are used by

74 percent of *Fortune* magazine's '100 Fastest Growing Companies'. Nonetheless the ERP approach is likely to grow since experience suggests that candidates hired through employee referrals stay longer and settle in faster than those hired through other methods, including the Internet and headhunters.

Sometimes, employees cruise available openings and forward them to friends with the click of a mouse. But you can't sit back and wait for the call to come. To remain on the ERP tour, stay in touch with your employee contacts regularly. Formal ERP or not, networking pays dividends and 'jobs for the boys (and girls!)' doesn't have to be a term of exclusion.

Shape of things to come? Taking a dip in talent pool programmes

Swimming in a company talent pool isn't the same as trying to capitalise on an employee referral programme, which is described in the previous section. Building a network of employees ready to refer you to their companies could result in a fast job hunt, at least theoretically, while managing to get yourself in company talent pools could stretch out your search or produce future jobs.

The talent pool concept is a new idea – except perhaps to professional sports teams where emerging talent pools are often called 'schools of excellence'. But just as a newcomer from the school of excellence isn't guaranteed a place on the bench, let alone the pitch, so a company talent pool member isn't guaranteed a job with that company.

What exactly is a company talent pool? Some recruiting industry consultants describe the talent pool function as a kind of customer service to woo potential future employees. Corporate use of online screening and communication tools (see Book II, Chapter 1) is used to identify well-qualified applicants who could fill a variety of positions in a given company. Once tapped for the talent team-in-waiting, recruiters and candidates are supposed to maintain two-way communication (chiefly e-mail and e-newsletters), staying in touch as needed. Others see the talent pool differently, instead using the term to mean a database of passive job hunters who aren't actively seeking a job at the company but whose faces might fit. Executives Direct (www.executives-direct.com) is one such example of the passive job hunter pool.

Talent pools are an idea from the US. As the pool idea takes off on the other side of the pond, it will surely wing its way over to this side, so keep an ear open. Just because you find yourself in the pool doesn't mean you can relax. Splash around, get noticed – or in this case make quite sure you continue to send interesting or pertinent (job change) messages to the recruiter who got you included in the pool in the first place.

Asking job agents to stand guard

Millions of people change jobs each year, voluntarily or involuntarily. Because of diminishing job security, increased ambition, and new technologies, many people are locked into a perpetual job search. Sounds like a grind, and it can be. A job agent could be what you need to lighten the load and let you know you when a job you want comes along.

The basics are, well, basic

The nitty-gritty of engaging a *personal job agent* is simple but varies slightly among job sites. Most personal job agents are free to job seekers, but some come with membership in fee-based sites. On the job sites of your choice, you fill out a template to produce a profile of the job you want: your desired occupation, job title, industry, location, and salary range. You may have to provide a profile or use the site's CV builder to provide a profile of your qualifications. You supply your e-mail address and go on with your life.

Now, for the part about the cyberservant who comes to tell you that 'Employment is served': When a fresh job ad comes to a chosen career site that's a pretty good match for your profile, the site's personal job agent sends you a circumspect e-mailed message. The employer is identified in the message. If you're interested, you say 'Yes, release my CV to this employer', and if not, 'No, don't release my CV to this employer'.

If you're mobile and have high-demand skills, personal job agents are the best thing since headhunters to add zest to your career management fortunes. Best of all, they do all the hard work so you don't have to.

Let the job come to you

You may have a way out of interminable job hunt pressure. If you're not in a hurry, you can post your career-move preferences on each of your chosen job sites and then sit back and wait for employers to find you – perhaps even being offered opportunities you would never have found on your own initiative.

We are witnessing the rise of what recruiters call 'the passive job seeker' and the job search tools that serve them. A *passive job seeker* is employed and is not actively on the market, but is always interested in exploring the 'right offer'. It is good to be king, and it is good to be a passive job seeker. A passive job seeker isn't too easy to get, so he or she is valued above all others. After all, if a passive job seeker is employed doing a particular job, someone must think that person is good at it, right?

Are you a passive job seeker? Congratulations! You can use any of hundreds of personal job agents that will keep their ears tuned to the job market, and when a promising position you might like comes to their attention, they'll tip you off with an e-mail alert.

Just as the devil is usually found in details, the downside is in the ratios: Each personal job agent has tonnes more registered job seekers than job vacancies. Like 250,000 job hunters and 4,000 job openings. So don't count on personal job agents to come through if you need to get a job fast.

Following-Up – an Act of Job Finding

The vast majority of employers – as many as eight of ten according to some surveys – that use digital recruiting systems (applicant management systems) send out an automatic receipt of your application, commenting that if they want to talk to you, they'll make contact. The response rate of third-party recruiters is unclear, but if you are a potential candidate for a job opening they're trying to fill, you'll hear back fairly quickly; if not, you may get an auto response or none.

Even when an auto response is sent, job searchers say they're underwhelmed, with the boilerplate e-mails seeming next to meaningless. Whether or not you get an underwhelming Web response, you run the risk of sounding particularly needy if you then call to ask a transparent question, 'Did you receive my CV?' Instead, try something a little more professional sounding – some version of:

I've had another job offer, which prompts me to ask if you had planned to contact me within the week.

We suggest other ways to make contact later in this section.

Bear in mind, however, that in these transitional times, the majority of smaller employers still don't use a digital recruiting system. If you send a CV to a workplace without a digital system (you know because you called first to check), calling later to ask, 'Did you get my CV?' *is* a good question.

Reaching out when you don't 'have mail'

The reasons that employers ignore applicants who send their CVs are many. They range from too few staffers to handle the clerical response task to uncertainty about whether the position actually will be filled. No matter. For your purposes, you must take the offensive and follow up.

If you've had previous contact with the recipient of your CV, the nature of that experience (stranger, referral, friend, telephone call, personal meeting) will suggest whether your follow-up is a thank-you letter or some other kind of communication, such as carrying out the employer's direction: 'At your suggestion, I forwarded my CV . . .'

If you've had no earlier contact with your CV's recipient, e-mail or telephone your follow-up. Which is best – e-mail or telephone? We recommend you use the medium that makes you feel most confident and comfortable.

Book II

Showcasing Yourself with a StandOut CV

If you've had an auto response and know your CV is in the database, you can ask what happened to it:

Was my CV a match for an open position? Was my CV passed onto a hiring manager? Can you tell me which manager?

After you know your CV has been routed to a hiring manager – or you have personally sent your CV to that hiring manager – don't call the human resource department because HR will automatically consider you for all open job requisitions. Try to contact the hiring manager, who is the one who makes the decision to hire you or not hire you. If your CV was passed onto a departmental hiring manager and you can uncover the manager's name, try calling that manager early in the morning or late in the day. Lunch is not a good time.

Beating that frustrating voicemail

What should you do when you try to reach the manager but can't break through voicemail? Leave a short message showing upbeat interest, not desperation:

My name is Steve Shipside, and I'm calling you because I've successfully outgrown my job, and you have a reputation for running a progressive department. I think you have my CV. If you like what you see, we should talk – 01234 567 890. The best time to reach me today is between 2 and 6 pm. I look forward to hearing from you.

Pronounce your name clearly and say your telephone number at a moderate pace. Give the hiring manager a chance to write it down without replaying the message. Otherwise, the manager hears a 'garbledrushofwords' and decides 'Idon'thavetimeforthis' and moves on.

How often should you call? Some very smart experts suggest calling every ten days until you're threatened with arrest if you call again. But busy employers insist that – unless you're in sales or another field requiring a demonstration of persistence – after you're certain your CV was received, call two weeks later, and then no more than once every six weeks. An excessive number of telephone calls brands you as a pest. Instead, send notes or e-mail with additional facts about your qualifications, ideas to solve a problem you know the company is facing, or just an expression of your continuing interest in working for the company and the manager.

Everyone agrees that, in this increasingly impersonal world, effectively following-up on the CVs you send out is becoming harder and harder. But the challenge of getting your CVs into the right hands means going beyond transmission to connection with as many recruiters and employers as you reasonably can manage.

Chapter 3

Choosing the Right Format

In This Chapter

▶ Selecting your best format

▶ Using handy templates

▶ Comparing format features

*C*V *format* refers not to the design or look of your CV but to how you organise and emphasise your information. *Different format styles flatter different histories.* This chapter helps you choose a format that highlights your strengths and hides your shortcomings.

An extensive line-up of CV formats follows. A template that you can use for developing your own CV illustrates each of the formats in this chapter. Survey the lot of them before deciding which one best tells your story.

CV Formats

At root, formats come in three family trees:

✔ **Reverse chronological:** The reverse chronological lists all employment and education, beginning with the most recent and working backward.

✔ **Functional:** The skills-based functional shouts what you can do instead of relaying what you've done and where you did it.

✔ **Hybrid:** The hybrid or combination is a marriage of both formats.

These three family types have spawned several other formats:

✔ **Accomplishment:** highlighting specific achievements rather than general experience

✔ **Targeted:** point for point directed at a specific job

✔ **Linear:** relating what you have to offer as a series of short lines

✔ **Professional:** slightly more long-winded with emphasis on detail of professional qualifications

✔ **Keyword:** in which words are specially selected to make the CV attractive to keyword-based computer searches

✔ **Academic curriculum vitae:** very long (up to ten pages) biographical statement usually for academia

✔ **International curriculum vitae:** a professional format with some modifications to suit target countries with different layout expectations

Table 3-1 gives you a breakdown of which format to use when.

Table 3-1	Your Best CV Formats at a Glance
Your Situation	**Suggested Formats**
Perfect career pattern	Reverse Chronological, Targeted
Rookie or ex-military	Functional, Hybrid, Accomplishment, Targeted, Linear
Seasoned ace	Functional, Hybrid, Accomplishment, Keyword
Tech-savvy	Keyword
Business	Reverse Chronological, Accomplishment, Targeted
Technical	Keyword, Targeted, Accomplishment, Reverse Chronological
Professional	Professional, Academic Curriculum Vitae, Portfolio
Government	Reverse Chronological, Professional
Arts/teaching	Professional, Portfolio, Academic Curriculum Vitae
Job history gaps	Functional, Hybrid, Linear, Targeted
Multitrack job history	Functional, Hybrid, Targeted, Keyword
Career change	Functional, Keyword, Targeted
International job seeker	International Curriculum Vitae
Special issues	Functional, Hybrid, Targeted

The following sections explore each type of CV format so that you can choose the style best for you and your skills.

The narrative format is an outdated chronological format that starts with the oldest facts and works forward to the newest facts. A pretentious variation of the narrative format uses the third person as though you were writing a biography. We don't bother to even discuss them, and we strongly suggest that you don't use either one.

Reverse Chronological Format

The *reverse chronological* (RC) format, shown in Figure 3-1, is straightforward: It cites your employment from the most recent back, showing dates as well as employers and educational institutions (college, vocational-technical schools, and career-oriented programs and courses). You accent a steady work history with a clear pattern of upward or lateral mobility.

Book II

Showcasing Yourself with a StandOut CV

Strengths and weaknesses

Check to see whether the RC's strengths are yours:

- ✔ This up-front format is by far the most popular with employers and recruiters because it is so, well, up-front.

- ✔ RC links employment dates, underscoring continuity. The weight of your experience confirms that you're a specialist in a specific career field (social service or technology, for example).

- ✔ RC positions you for the next upward career step.

- ✔ As the most traditional of formats, RC fits traditional industries (such as banking, education, and accounting).

Take the weaknesses of the reverse chronological format into account:

- ✔ When previous job titles are at variance with the target position, this format does not support the objective. Without careful management, it reveals everything, including inconsequential jobs and negative factors.

- ✔ RC can spotlight periods of unemployment or brief job tenure.

- ✔ Without careful management, RC reveals your age.

- ✔ Without careful management, RC may suggest that you were stagnant in a job too long.

REVERSE CHRONOLOGICAL FORMAT

YOUR NAME

Home Address

City, County , Post Code

(###) ###-#### (Phone) (###) ###-#### (Fax) ###@###.# (E-mail)

Objective:

A position that uses your skills.

SUMMARY

- Number of years of work experience, paid and unpaid, relevant to target position
- Achievement that proves you can handle the target
- Another achievement that proves you can handle the target
- Skills, traits, characteristics – facts that further your ability to handle the target
- Education and training relating to the target (if unrelated, bury in resume body)

PROFESSIONAL EXPERIENCE AND ACCOMPLISHMENTS

20## - Present   Job Title   Employer, Employer's Location
A brief synopsis of your purpose in the company, detailing essential functions and the products and customer base you managed.
- An achievement in this position relevant to objective (do not repeat summary)
- A second achievement in this position relevant to current objective
- More accomplishments (awards, recognition, promotion, raise, praise, training)

20## - 20##   Job Title   Employer, Employer's Location

Detailed as above.

20## - 20##   Job Title   Employer, Employer's Location

Detailed as above but more brief

19## - 20##   Job Title   Employer, Employer's Location

Detailed as above but more brief

EDUCATION AND PROFESSIONAL TRAINING

Degree(s), classes, seminars, educational awards and honours.
Credentials, clearances, licenses.

Figure 3-1:
The tried-
and-true,
basic
reverse
chronologi-
cal format.

Who should use this format and who should think twice

Use the RC if you fall into any of these categories:

- ✔ You have a steady school and work record reflecting constant growth or lateral movement.

- ✔ Your most recent employer is a respected name in the industry, and the name may ease your entry into a new position.

- ✔ Your most recent job titles are impressive stepping-stones.

- ✔ You're a savvy writer who knows how to manage potential negative factors, such as inconsequential jobs, too few jobs, too many temporary jobs, too many years at the same job, or too many years of age.

Think twice about using the RC under these circumstances:

- ✔ You have a lean employment history. Listing a stray student job or two is not persuasive, even when you open with superb educational credentials enhanced with work experience.

With careful attention, you can do a credible job on an RC by extracting from your extracurricular activities every shred of skills, which you present as abilities to do work with extraordinary commitment and a head for quick learning.

- ✔ You have work-history or employability problems – gaps, demotions, stagnation in a single position, job hopping (four jobs in three years, for example), re-entering the workforce after a break to raise a family.

Exercise very careful management to truthfully modify stark realities. However, you may find that other formats can serve you better.

Instructions

The StandOut way to create an RC is as follows:

- ✔ Focus on areas of specific relevance to your target position or career field.

- ✔ List all pertinent places worked, including for each the name of the employer and the city in which you worked, the years you were there, your title, your responsibilities, and your measurable achievements.

Book II

Showcasing Yourself with a StandOut CV

The RC template included in this chapter is generic and doesn't show how to handle problems such as unrelated experience. You can group unrelated jobs in a second work history section under the heading 'Other Experience', 'Previous Experience', or 'Related Experience'.

Functional Format

The *functional format,* shown in Figure 3-2, is a CV of ability-focused topics – portable skills or functional areas. It ignores chronological order. In its purest form, the functional style omits dates, employers, and job titles. But employers don't like it when you leave out the particulars, so contemporary functional CVs list employers, job titles, and sometimes even dates – but still downplay this information by briefly listing it at the bottom of the CV. The functional format is oriented toward what the job seeker *can* do for the employer instead of narrating history.

Strengths and weaknesses

The strengths of the functional format are

- ✔ A functional CV directs a reader's eyes to what you want him or her to notice. It helps a reader visualise what you can do instead of when and where you learned to do it. Functional CVs salute the future rather than embalm the past.

- ✔ The functional format – written after researching the target company – serves up the precise functions or skills that the employer wants. It's like saying, 'You want budget control and turnaround skills – I have budget control and turnaround skills.' The skills sell is a magnet to reader eyes!

- ✔ It uses unpaid and non-work experience to your best advantage.

- ✔ It allows you to eliminate or subordinate work history that doesn't support your current objective.

The weaknesses are

- ✔ Because recruiters and employers are more accustomed to reverse chronological formats, departing from the norm may raise suspicion that you're not the cream of the crop of applicants. Readers may assume that you're trying to hide inadequate experience, educational deficits, or who knows what.

FUNCTIONAL FORMAT

YOUR NAME

Address, City, Postcode (###) ###-#### (Phone), (###) ###-#### (Fax), ###@###.## (E-mail)

Job Title You Desire

More than (# years paid and unpaid) work experience in target area, contributing to an (achievement/result/high ranking in industry/top 5% of performance reviews). Add accomplishments, strengths, proficiencies, characteristics, education, brief testimonial – anything that supports your target job title.

PROFESSIONAL EXPERIENCE AND ACCOMPLISHMENTS

A Top Skill (pertinent to objective)

- An achievement illustrating this skill and the location/employer where you earned it*

- A second achievement illustrating this skill and the location/employer where you earned it*

*Omit locations/employers if your work history doesn't present a clear sense of progression and purpose.

A Second Top Skill (pertinent to objective)

Detailed as above

A Third Top Skill (pertinent to objective)

Detailed as above

A Fourth Skill (optional – must relate to objective)

Detailed as above

A Unique Area of Proficiency (pertinent to objective)

- An achievement testifying to this proficiency, including the location/employer*

- A list of equipment, processes, software, or terms you are familiar with, reflecting your familiarity with this area of proficiency*

- A list of training experiences that document your proficiency*

*Omit locations/employers if your work history doesn't present a clear sense of progression and purpose.

EMPLOYMENT HISTORY

20## – Present	**Job Title**	Employer, Location
20## – 20##	**Job Title**	Employer, Location
19## – 20##	**Job Title**	Employer, Location
19## – 19##	**Job Title**	Employer, Location

PROFESSIONAL TRAINING AND EDUCATION

Degrees, credentials, clearances, licences, seminars, training

Book II

Showcasing Yourself with a StandOut CV

Figure 3-2:
No experience? Use the functional CV format.

✔ Functional styles may leave unclear which skills grew from which jobs or experiences.

✔ A clear career path isn't obvious.

✔ This format doesn't maximise recent coups in the job market.

Who should use this format and who should think twice

This CV is heaven-sent for career changers, new graduates, ex-military personnel, seasoned aces, and individuals with multitrack job histories, work-history gaps, or special-issue problems.

Job seekers with blue-chip backgrounds and managers and professionals who are often tapped by executive recruiters should avoid this format.

Instructions

Choose areas of expertise acquired during the course of your career, including education and unpaid activities. These areas become skill and functional headings, which vary by the target position or career field. Note any achievements below each heading. A few examples of headings are: 'Management', 'Sales', 'Budget Control', 'Cost Cutting', 'Project Implementation', and 'Turnaround Successes'.

List the headings in the order of importance and follow each heading with a series of short statements of your skills (refer to Figure 3-2). Turn your statements into power hitters with measurable achievements.

Hybrid Format

The hybrid, a combination of reverse chronological and functional formats, satisfies demands for timelines as well as showcases your marketable skills and impressive accomplishments. Many people find the hybrid – or one of its offspring – to be the most attractive of all formats.

Essentially, in a hybrid, a functional summary tops a reverse chronological presentation of dates, employers, and capsules of each position's duties. Figure 3-3 gives you a template for this format.

HYBRID FORMAT

YOUR NAME

Address, City, Post Code

(###) ###-#### (Phone)

(###) ###-#### (Fax), ###@###.## (E-mail)

Objective: Position as (job title) using (#) years' experience in skills key to target.

SUMMARY OF QUALIFICATIONS

Number of years in area of target position

Related education, training and accreditation

An achievement pertinent to objective

Traits that reinforce your candidacy for this position

Other accomplishments, characteristics, proficiencies

SUMMARY OF SKILLS

Technical skills • Processes • Computer software

ACCOMPLISHMENTS AND EXPERIENCE

Job Title, Top Proficiencies Used   Employer, Location

A Top Skill (pertinent to objective)

- Accomplishments made while in this position

- Several related achievements from position, pertinent to this skill and the objective

Another Skill (pertinent to objective)

- Several achievements pertinent to this skill and the objective

                                                             20## - Present

Job Title, Top Proficiencies Used   **Employer, Location**

Detailed as above

                                                             20## - 20##

Job Title, Top Proficiencies Used   **Employer, Location**

Detailed as above

                                                             19## - 20##

PROFESSIONAL TRAINING AND EDUCATION

Degrees, accreditations, licences, clearances, courses

Figure 3-3:
The hybrid format – the best of both worlds.

Book II

Showcasing Yourself with a StandOut CV

The hybrid style is similar to the contemporary functional format – so much so that making a case for distinction is sometimes difficult.

Strengths and weaknesses

A hybrid format combines the strengths of both the reverse chronological and functional formats, so check out those earlier sections. Its weakness is that it contains more 'frills' in the form of highlighted accomplishments and achieved goals than a very conservative employer may prefer.

Who should use this format and who should think twice

The hybrid is a wise choice for newcomers, ex-military personnel, seasoned aces, those with job history gaps or a multitrack job history, and individuals with special-issue problems.

Career changers or job seekers needing more appropriate formats, such as functional or portfolio, should skip the hybrid.

Instructions

Build a functional format of ability-focused topics and add employment documentation – employers, locations, dates, and duties.

Accomplishment Format

Definitely not a boring read, an accomplishment format immediately moves your strongest marketing points to centre stage, grabs the reader's interest, and doesn't let go. If you want a rhyme to remember: Use flash and dash to go for cash.

A variation of the hybrid CV, the accomplishment format (shown in Figure 3-4) banners both qualifications *and* accomplishments. This is the format of choice for many executives – particularly in traditionally mobile industries, such as advertising, communications, and publishing.

ACCOMPLISHMENT FORMAT

YOUR NAME

Address   Phone number: (###) ###-####   E-mail: #####@##.##
City, Post Code   Message and/or fax number(s): (###) ###-####

OBJECTIVE: Position as (job title) using skills and experience accumulated over (#) years. (Or use a Summary, as in the hybrid format.)

QUALIFICATIONS:

- Number of years' experience that is pertinent to objective

- Your record of improvement or reputation in the industry

- Specific skills and training related to objective

- Areas of specialised proficiency

- Work ethic traits demonstrating candidacy and a constructive attitude

- Procedural familiarities

- Technological familiarities

ACCOMPLISHMENTS:

In any order, list accomplishments (quantifying with numbers and percentages when appropriate) that elaborate such achievements as

- Competitive skills, technological proficiency, professional aptness

- Improvements, innovations

- Revenue-saving strategies

- Promotions, raises

- Increasing responsibilities, management and troubleshooting functions

- Praise from employers and/or co-workers

- Training rendered, training received

PROFESSIONAL EXPERIENCE:

Job Title	Employer, Location	20## - 20##
Job Title	Employer, Location	20## - 20##
Job Title	Employer, Location	20## - 20##
Job Title	Employer, Location	19## - 19##

EDUCATION:

- Academic and professional accreditation(s), emphasis

- Universities, schools, courses (attended or in progress)

Book II

Showcasing Yourself with a StandOut CV

Figure 3-4:
The accomplishment format really lets you strut your stuff!

Formats to use when the executive recruiter calls

Executive recruiting is usually a response to an employer's known problem in a given business area. Accomplishment formats, along with reverse chronological and targeted styles, are well equipped to tell employers how you can solve their problems.

When an executive recruiter calls, ask for enough details about the position's problem areas to give you ammunition for whipping out a made-to-order CV. If you're a candidate, the recruiter may be happy to have as many as four readable pages about your background, as long as you grab his or her attention on the first page. Remember that most executive decision makers favour reverse chronological presentations, so use conservative language in drawing attention to your accomplishments on this format. See Book II, Chapter 5 for more information about the language of CVs.

Strengths and weaknesses

This format offers benefits similar to those of functional and hybrid styles noted earlier in this chapter. Readers who prefer a reverse chronological style may view the accomplishment format as too jazzed up.

Who should use this format and who should think twice

Use the accomplishment format when

- ✔ **You're considering using a functional or hybrid CV style.** You're a career changer, new graduate, ex-military personnel, seasoned ace, or have a multitrack job history, work history gaps, or special-issue problems. The accomplishment presentation is especially effective for individuals whose work history may not have been smooth but was, at times, bright with great successes.

- ✔ **You're returning to payroll status after a period of self-employment.**

If you've climbed career steps without a stumble, use a reverse chronological format instead of the accomplishment format.

Instructions

List accomplishments in order of importance, making chronology a secondary factor. Close with a summarised reverse chronological work history.

Targeted Format

A targeted format, tailored to a given job, is VIP (very important person) treatment. Targeting is persuasive because everyone likes to be given the VIP treatment.

The targeted style is written to match point-for-point a specific job offered by a specific employer.

The template in Figure 3-5 is but one way to build a targeted CV. You can equally benefit with other format options springing from the functional or hybrid branches of the CV family. You choose.

Strengths and weaknesses

The strength of the targeted format is that it shows the employer that you're a good match for the position. Its weakness is that you may not be readily considered for other jobs.

Who should use this format and who should think twice

Pretty much everyone stands out with a targeted CV. Ex-military personnel can translate milspeak to civilianese, newcomers can equate their non-paid experience to employer requirements, and seasoned aces can reach deep into their backgrounds to show, item for item, how they qualify. This format is a good choice for people with strong work histories but a few spots here and there.

The targeted format isn't a great idea for anyone lazy about doing research – the success of the targeted CV depends on lining up data ducks in advance.

Book II

Showcasing Yourself with a StandOut CV

TARGETED FORMAT

YOUR NAME

Address, City, Postcode

(###) ###-#### (Phone), (###) ###-#### (Fax), ###@###.### (E-mail)

Objective: Position as (title of job that employer offers) using your (#) of years' experience in skills that are essential and specialised to the position.

SUMMARY OF QUALIFICATIONS

- Number of years in area of target, explaining similarities to objective position/duties

- Related education, training, accreditation – specifically those the employer will appreciate

- An achievement directly related to target

- Traits reinforcing your candidacy for this position, specifically those the employer requires

- Other accomplishments, characteristics, knowledge either rare or prized in the field

SUMMARY OF SKILLS

Technical skills the employer wants • Processes the employer uses • Computer and software skills the employer needs

ACCOMPLISHMENTS AND EXPERIENCE

Job Title   Employer, Location   20## – Present

   A Top Skill (pertinent to objective)

- Accomplishments made in this position targeting the employer's priorities or customer base

- Several other related achievements from position, pertinent to skill and objective

   Another Top Skill (pertinent to objective)

- Several achievements pertinent to this skill and the objective

Job Title   Employer, Location   20## – 20##

Detailed as above

Job Title   Employer, Location   19## – 20##

Detailed as above

PROFESSIONAL TRAINING AND EDUCATION

Degrees, accreditations, licences, courses

Figure 3-5:
Use the targeted format to hit the bull's-eye with a specific employer.

When CVs and research are beyond reach

You say you're not sure you want to do enough research on a position to write a targeted CV? Definitely not a StandOut mind-set, but you're still ahead of an applicant who wrote the following query to the human resources department of a big company (We did not make this up):

Dear Sirs, I would very much like to send a CV to you, but I haven't the slightest idea how to fill out a CV, and I can't remember the dates or addresses for any of it anyway. So if that is going to keep me from being employed by your company, then to hell with it! Otherwise, call me in for an interview and a job.

Book II

Showcasing Yourself with a StandOut CV

Instructions

Find out what the position demands and write – fact for fact – how you offer exactly those goods.

If you can meet better than 80 percent of the position's requirements, you've got a shot at an interview; if less than 80 percent, don't hold your breath waiting for your telephone to ring.

Linear Format

A linear format (line by line – hence, *linear*) relates the benefits you offer in short spurts of achievements, winning moves, and the like. An offspring of the reverse chronological format, the linear doesn't get into great detail; it sparks curiosity to meet you and find out more. Check out the template in Figure 3-6.

This spaced-out variation of the reverse chronological format lacks a job objective section and opens with a skills summary instead. Plenty of white space is the hallmark of this achievement-highlighted document.

Career advisers pin a blue ribbon on this format.

LINEAR FORMAT

YOUR NAME

Address, City, Postcode

(###) ###-#### (Phone), (###) ###-#### (Fax), ###@###.### (E-mail)

QUALIFICATIONS SUMMARY

- Number of years' work experience, paid and unpaid, pertinent to objective position

- Accomplishments that prove your unique candidacy for this position

- Skills geared toward the objective position or company

- Other things the employer will like to know – proficiencies, characteristics, achievements, training, credentials, education

PROFESSIONAL EXPERIENCE AND ACCOMPLISHMENTS

20## – Present   **Job Title**   Employer, Employer's Location

- An achievement made during this position that is pertinent to current objective, detailing job skills and responsibilities

- A second achievement made during this position also pertinent to current objective

- More accomplishments (awards, recognition, promotion, raise, praise, training)

*Divide description according to titles held with employer, listing titles as subheadings.

20## – 20##   **Job Title**   Employer, Employer's Location

Detailed as above.

EDUCATION AND PROFESSIONAL TRAINING

Degree(s), university, year

Top achievement

Other seminars, awards, honours, credentials, clearances, licences

COMMUNITY LEADERSHIP

Memberships and other offices in community organisations

Figure 3-6:
The logical linear format appeals to many employers' eyes.

Strengths and weaknesses

The pluses of linear CVs are

✔ Linear CVs are very easy to read quickly, particularly in a stack of CVs a foot high. Instant readability is increasingly important as harried recruiters struggle with the clock, and baby boomers become middle-aged readers whose eyes don't enjoy poring over pages sagging with text.

✔ Because the format presents your starring events in a line-by-line visual presentation, your achievements aren't likely to be overlooked as they would be if buried deep in a text paragraph.

The minus is that you can't pack as much information into a linear format (remember the white space), but, with careful planning and good writing, you can pack plenty of sell.

Who should use this format and who should think twice

This format works to showcase career progression – steady as you go. If that's you, use the linear.

Job seekers with gaps in employment, too many jobs, few advancements, or scant experience as well as those who've seen enough sunrises to be on the shady side of 50 should avoid the linear.

Instructions

Write down your achievements and other necessary data, look at the big lumps of text, and then divide and conquer. Think white space.

Professional Format

A professional format, also called a *professional vitae,* is slightly long-winded (say, three to five pages) but factual. It emphasises professional qualifications and activities. This format, shown in Figure 3-7, is essentially a shortened academic curriculum vitae.

PROFESSIONAL FORMAT

YOUR NAME

Address, City, Postcode

(###) ###-#### (Phone), (###) ###-#### (Fax), ###@###.### (E-mail)

EDUCATION AND PROFESSIONAL TRAINING

Degrees, credentials, awards, achievements, honours, seminars, clearances, licences

OBJECTIVE: A position that uses your talents, with an emphasis on your special skills.

SUMMARY

- Number of years' work experience, paid and unpaid, relevant to target

- Accomplishment(s) that prove your unique talents as a candidate for this position

- Strengths geared toward the objective position or company

- Other things the employer will like to know – proficiencies, characteristics, achievements, training, credentials, education

PROFESSIONAL EXPERIENCE AND ACCOMPLISHMENTS

20## – Present   **Job Title**   Employer, Employer's Location

A brief synopsis of your purpose in the company, detailing essential functions and products you managed and your customer base.

- An achievement pertinent to target

- A second achievement also pertinent to target

- More achievements — awards, recognition, promotion, raise, praise, training

19## – 20##   **Job Title**   Employer, Employer's Location

Detailed as above but more brief

*List three previous jobs with the same detail as above; divide jobs according to job title, not employer.

Figure 3-7:
The long but effective professional format is perfect for certain careers.

Strengths and weaknesses

The professional CV is mandatory for certain kinds of positions; your choice is whether to send this type or go all the way and send an academic curriculum vitae.

But be aware that professional CVs are reviewed under a microscope; every deficiency stands out. Adding a portfolio that shows your experience-based work skills may compensate for missing chunks of formal requirements. Just make sure that any unsolicited samples you send are high quality and need no explanation.

Book II

Showcasing Yourself with a StandOut CV

Who should use this format and who should think twice

Professionals in medicine, science, and law should use this format. Also use it when common sense or convention makes it the logical choice.

For most non-professionals, especially managers, the professional format is tedious.

Instructions

Begin with education, professional training, and an objective. Follow with a summary of the main points you want the reader to absorb. Follow that information with details of your professional experience and accomplishments.

Follow the template in Figure 3-7, paying attention to accomplishments. Just because you present yourself in a low-key, authoritative manner doesn't mean that you can forget to say how good you are.

Keyword Format

Any CV can be a keyword CV. It becomes a keyword CV when you add a profile of *keywords* (nouns identifying your qualifications) anywhere on any type of format. We like front-loading a keyword preface at the top of the CV.

The template shown in Figure 3-8 is a format that works well for computer scanning. Support your keywords with facts but don't repeat the exact phrasing in a keyword profile and in other parts of your CV – vary your language. Repetition must be handled with thought.

Strengths and weaknesses

Virtually everyone benefits from using a keyword profile – it functions like a skills summary. Job seekers sending CVs by e-mail or postings on the Internet should always include keywords.

A minority of recruiters dislike a keyword preface. Their objection: 'It appears to be a check-box-oriented approach to doing a CV.' This weakness isn't likely to get you rejected out-of-hand, however. If the body of the CV supports your keywords (which it should if it's StandOut quality), and you can do only one CV, it's worth the risk.

Who should use this format and who should think twice

Most job seekers should consider the keyword option. Technical people can't leave home without it.

However, top management executives (the £300,000-a-year-and-up kind) are unlikely to be recruited from CV databases. Executive recruiters do, however, construct their own in-house databases. In building these in-house databases, they may import from public-domain databases that input information from traditional CVs and other sources.

Instructions

As Figure 3-8 shows, you begin with your contact information, followed by a keyword profile, an objective, several strengths, and reverse chronological employment history.

You may choose not to use a front-loaded keyword profile but rather a one-paragraph qualifications summary or a skills section composed of brief (one- or two-line) statements. The more keywords (or skills) in your CV, the better your chances of being summoned for an interview.

Keep in mind these keyword CV tip-top tips:

✔ Use as many valid keywords as possible in your CV, but if you place a keyword summary at the top of your online CV, 20 to 30 keywords are enough in one dose.

✔ Computers read keywords in any part of your CV, so if you use a summary, avoid redundancy.

If you use an acronym, such as LSE , in your summary or opening profile, spell out London School of Economics later. If you mention that you have 'four years of experience with three PC-based software programs', name the programs elsewhere: Excel, RoboHELP, QuickBooks.

Book II

Showcasing Yourself with a StandOut CV

Academic Curriculum Vitae

The academic *curriculum vitae* (ACV) is a comprehensive biographical statement, typically three to ten pages, emphasising professional qualifications and activities. A CV of six to eight pages, ten at the most, is recommended for a veteran professional; two to four pages is appropriate for a young professional just starting out (see the 'Professional Format' section earlier in this chapter).

If your CV is more than four pages long, show mercy and save eyesight by attaching an *executive summary* page to the top. An executive summary gives a brief overview of your qualifications and experience.

Among various possible organisations, the template in Figure 3-9 (a variation of the hybrid format but with exhaustive coverage) illustrates a line-up of your contact information, objective, qualifications summary, skills summary, and professional background.

Strengths and weaknesses

An ACV presents all the best of you, which is good, but for people with ageing eyes, an ACV is reading-intensive. More important, weaknesses in any area of your professional credentials are relatively easy to spot.

KEYWORD FORMAT

YOUR NAME, Address, City, Postcode

(###) ###-#### (Phone), (###) ###-#### (Fax), ###@###.### (E-mail)

Key Words: General nouns, phrases, and terminology known to be valued in the position and industry; specific Key Words descriptive of duties and proficiencies necessary to position; specific terms known to be priority to employer/company applying to, including credentials, years of experience, areas of familiarity, and equipment involved

Objective: Title of opening, using the following highlights of your background:

- Number of years' work experience, paid and unpaid, relevant to target

- Accomplishments that prove your unique suitability for this position

- Strengths geared toward the objective position or company, education, credentials, and training

PROFESSIONAL EXPERIENCE AND ACCOMPLISHMENTS

20## – Present   **Employer, Employer's Location**

Present Job Title

A brief synopsis of your purpose in the company, detailing essential functions and products you rendered and customer base.

- An achievement related to current objective

- A second achievement also related to objective

- More achievements, awards, recognition, promotion, pay rise, bonuses, praise

- Equipment used, processes, procedures (in noun form)

20## – 20##   **Employer, Employer's Location**

Job Title

Detailed as above but more brief

19## – 20##   **Employer, Employer's Location**

Job Title

Detailed as above but more brief

19## – 19##   **Employer, Employer's Location**

Job Title

Detailed as above but more brief

EDUCATION AND PROFESSIONAL TRAINING

Degrees, classes, seminars, awards, achievements, honours, credentials, clearances, licences

Figure 3-8:
The keyword CV is a great format to submit to CV databases.

ACADEMIC CURRICULUM VITAE

YOUR NAME

Curriculum Vitae

Address, City, Postcode

(###) ###-#### (Phone), (###) ###-#### (Fax), ###@###.### (E-mail)

Objective (optional): Position as (title of position employer offers) using your (#) of years' experience in (skills essential for and specialised to the position).

SUMMARY OF QUALIFICATIONS

- A summary of your education, proficiencies, and career pertinent to target
- Number of years in objective area, explaining similarities to job and its responsibilities
- Related education, training, and accreditation, reflecting employer's goals/ priorities
- An achievement directly related to target
- Traits reinforcing your candidacy for this position, specifically those asked for by the employer and those generally in demand in the field
- Other accomplishments, characteristics, knowledge either rare or prized in the field

SUMMARY OF SKILLS

Topics of speciality or innovation within field • Areas of particular familiarity • Software equipment • Processes • Terminology relevant to target • Languages

PROFESSIONAL BACKGROUND

EDUCATION

Degrees:

> Ph.D., institution, date of degree (or anticipated date), specialisation
>
> M.A./M.Sc., institution, date of degree, emphasis, concentration
>
> B.A./B.Sc., institution, date of degree, class of degree

Courses: Those taken, honours, seminars, number of units, G.P.A. (if a recent graduate)

Other Accreditations: Licences, clearances

Academic Achievements: Appointments, nominations, leaderships, scholarships, grants, awards, praise, recognition, accomplishments

Affiliations: Societies, associations, clubs, leagues, memberships

PH.D. DISSERTATION

> Title, advisor, director
>
> Abstract summary (4-5 sentences) discussing content and methodology

HONOURS, AWARDS, AND ACADEMIC ACHIEVEMENTS

Appointments, nominations, leaderships, awards, praise, scores, recognitions, accomplishments, fellowships, scholarships, grants (including B.A./B.Sc)

Book II

Showcasing Yourself with a StandOut CV

Figure 3-9: Brevity definitely isn't a feature of the academic CV (continues on the next page).

TEACHING EXPERIENCE

Job Title, Top Proficiencies Used   Employer, Location 20## - Present

    A Top Responsibility (relevant to objective)

- Accomplishments made in this position, targeting the employer's priorities/ mission

- Several other achievements from this position, pertinent to objective

    Another Skill (appropriate to objective)

- Several achievements from this position, pertinent to objective

Repeat pattern for each position.

RESEARCH EXPERIENCE

Positions, locations, dates, descriptions of research pertinent to target position

TEACHING INTERESTS

RESEARCH INTERESTS

PUBLICATIONS

List all those you are willing to show the search committee. Include works in progress or pending. Cite works as follows:

- "Title of work," Name of publication/publisher *(Newsletter, Newspaper, Magazine, Journal, Book),* location of publisher , date of publication, volume number (v.##), issue number (#.#), series number (#.#.#), page numbers (# - #).

PRESENTATIONS AND PUBLIC APPEARANCES

Include conference papers and research reports. List as follows:

- "Title of presentation," location of presentation , date (20## - 20##); optional synopsis of content and/or purpose of presentation, audience, results, and so on.

PROFESSIONAL AFFILIATIONS

- A society, association, league, or club with which you associate, position held, 19## - 20##

- And so on.

RECOMMENDATIONS

Names and contact information of three to four references willing to write recommendation letters

CREDENTIALS

Address where the recipient can access your career/placement file

Figure 3-9:
Continued.

Who should use this format and who should think twice

Anyone working in a PhD-driven environment, such as higher education, think tanks, science, and elite research and development groups, needs to use this format. Anyone who can avoid using it should do so.

Instructions

Create a comprehensive summary of your professional employment and accomplishments: education, positions, affiliations, honours, memberships, credentials, dissertation title, fields in which comprehensive examinations were passed, full citations of publications and presentations, awards, discoveries, inventions, patents, seminar leadership, foreign languages, courses taught – whatever is valued in your field.

Book II

Showcasing Yourself with a StandOut CV

International Curriculum Vitae Format

The international CV is *not* the same document as an academic CV. Think of an international CV as a six-to-eight-page excruciatingly detailed CV (Figure 3-10 gives you a template). Although it solicits private information that's outlawed in the UK, such as your health status, the international CV is favoured in some nations as a kind of global ticket to employment.

The international CV is usually a reverse chronological format that includes your contact information, qualifications summary, professional background, education, and personal information. Some European countries prefer the chronological format, which lists education and work experience from the farthest back to the present.

Strengths and weaknesses

International employment experts say that if you don't use this format, foreign recruiters may think you're hiding something. But keep in mind that the international CV format intrudes into private areas of your life.

INTERNATIONAL CV FORMAT

YOUR NAME

Curriculum Vitae

Home Address, City, State/County, Country, Province, Postcode

Include international codes:

(###) ###-#### (Phone), (###) ###-#### (Fax), ###@###.## (E-mail)

Objective (optional): Position as (title of position employer offers) using your (#) years'
experience in (skills essential and specialised to the position).

SUMMARY OF QUALIFICATIONS

- A summary of your education, proficiencies, and career pertinent to target

- Number of years in area of objective, explaining similarities to it/its responsibilities

- Related education, training, and accreditation, reflecting employer's goals/ priorities

- An achievement directly related to target, something that the employer needs

- Traits reinforcing your candidacy for this position, specifically those asked for by the
  employer and those generally in demand in the field

- Other accomplishments, characteristics, knowledge either rare or prized in the field

- Travelling in field, countries visited, improvements made, distinctions, and so on

SUMMARY OF SKILLS

Topics of speciality or innovation within field • Areas of particular familiarity • Software
equipment processes • Terminology relevant to target • Languages

PROFESSIONAL BACKGROUND

EMPLOYMENT

Job Title   Employer, Location   **20## - Present**

A Top Responsibility (relevant to objective)

- Accomplishments made in this position targeting the employer's priorities/mission
- Several other achievements from this position, pertinent to objective

A Skill (appropriate to objective)

- Several achievements from this position, pertinent to objective

Repeat pattern for all jobs.

PROFESSIONAL HONOURS

All honorary positions, awards, recognitions, or titles, with locations, 19## - 20##

Figure 3-10:
The
international
CV is an
option when
applying for
jobs outside
your home
country
(continues
on the next
page).

PUBLICATIONS

- "Title of work," name of publication/publisher *(Newsletter, Newspaper, Magazine, Journal),* location of publisher (country, languages, city and state or major city), date of publication, volume number (v.##), issue number (#.#), series number (#.#.#), page numbers (# - #)

Repeat pattern for all publications.

PRESENTATIONS AND PUBLIC APPEARANCES

- "Title of presentation," location of presentation (country, city, state, province, language), date (20## - 20##); optional synopsis of content and/or purpose of presentation, audience, results, and so on

Repeat pattern for all presentations.

PROFESSIONAL AFFILIATIONS

All societies, associations, leagues, or clubs, positions held, locations, 19## - 20##

EDUCATION

Degrees:

Ph.D., institution, date of degree (or anticipated date), specialisation

M.A./M.Sc., institution, class of degree, date of degree,

B.A./B.Sc., institution, class of degree, date of degree,

Give equivalents of these degrees for other countries

Courses: Those taken, honours, seminars

Other Accreditations: Licences

Academic Achievements: Appointments, nominations, leaderships, scholarships, grants, awards, praise, scores, recognitions, accomplishments

Affiliations: Societies, associations, clubs, leagues, memberships

DOCTORAL DISSERTATION

Title, advisor, director

Abstract summary (four to five sentences) discussing content and methodology

HONOURS, AWARDS, AND ACADEMIC ACHIEVEMENTS

Appointments, nominations, leaderships, awards, praise, scores, recognitions, accomplishments, fellowships, scholarships, grants, (including B.A./B.Sc./equivalents).

PERSONAL INFORMATION

- A sentence or so that describes personal attributes pertinent to employer's interests. Think positively, omit negatives, and highlight goal-oriented, functional characteristics that hold the promise of a good worker-employer relationship and reliably good work product. Present specific work-related examples of these personality highlights and explain how they are significant to the employer. Without exaggerating, accentuate the positive and include all favourable quotes from employers and co-workers, political officials and other public servants, and members of the clergy, volunteer organisations, and non-profit organisations.
- Age, marital status (single, engaged, married)
- Hobbies and leisure activities (travel, clubs, sports, athletics, collections, subscriptions)
- Volunteer service, public service

Figure 3-10: Continued.

Who should use this format and who should think twice

Use this format if you're seeking an overseas job and don't object to revealing information that may subject you to discriminatory hiring practices.

Individuals who feel strongly about invasions of privacy or who aren't willing to be rejected out of hand because of gender, religion, race, age, or marital status should avoid this format and negotiate for a bare minimum of personal information.

Instructions

Formality prevails with the international CV. In Japan, for example, job hunters still fill out standard forms, available at Japanese bookshops.

- ✔ If you're applying in a non-English-speaking country, have your CV trans-lated into the appropriate foreign language. Send both the English and the native-language version.

- ✔ Unless it's untrue, mention in the personal section that you have excel-lent health.

- ✔ Suggest by appropriate hobbies and personal interests that you'll easily adapt to an overseas environment.

- ✔ Hand write the cover letter that goes with your CV – some European countries are keen on handwriting analysis as a screening device. If your handwriting is iffy, enclose a word-processed version as well.

In addition, make sure that your cover letter shows a sincere desire to be in the country of choice.

The Rise of the e-CV

The Net (Internet) is the world's biggest computer network. The Web (World Wide Web) is a graphical overlay on the Internet that makes possible sound, film, video, and various special effects, as well as text.

With the Net and the Web as background, boundless change is inevitable in the way we do business, and the CV industry is no exception. The transformation within the CV industry is irreversible. The newest trends are described in Book II, Chapter 1, but these two developments underpin all CV change:

- ✔ An amazing acceleration of computer software over the past 15 years drives the reinvention of the way you *prepare and submit CVs* and in the way others *read and manage them.*

- ✔ The Internet, in connecting the globe's computers, continues to restructure forever the way CVs are sent from one place to another.

These two developments sparked the explosion of the e-CV. Millions and millions of e-CVs float like inexhaustible soap bubbles throughout cyberspace each day. Their collective volume threatens to overwhelm the recruiting industry.

Book II

Showcasing Yourself with a StandOut CV

Stop and ask directions

When you're not sure what technology is being used where you send your CV (which, today, is most of the time), telephone or e-mail the employer's human resource department or company receptionist and ask the following question:

In submitting my CV, I want to be sure I'm using the correct technology at your organisation. Can I submit my CV to your company electronically?

If the answer is yes, then ask:

Can I send my CV as an attachment?

If the answer is yes, then ask:

If I send my CV as an attachment (MS Word), will managers see my CV in the original format, or do you convert the attachment to text?

If the company converts the original CV to a pure text CV, avoid a bad wrap. Send your CV as a plain text (ASCII) file. Why? Some systems that convert an attachment to text do so at the expense of readability. They mess up the line-wrapping formatting so badly that the result looks as though your typing is tacky. Figure 3-11 shows an example of a plain text CV that began life as an attachment.

TARGET COMPANY
Category: Consulting Services
Description of my ideal company:
To obtain a position in the Information Technology field which
provides a challenging atmosphere conducive to professional
achievement and the ability to advance while contributing to
organisational goals. To work for a company that lives a credo
and holds commitment to personal integrity and pursuit of
excellence as core values.
TARGET LOCATIONS
Relocate: Yes
UK South West/East   France   Germany
Spain
WORK STATUS
I am an EU resident authorised to work in the UK or any other
EU member state.
EXPERIENCE
7/2000 - Present   Broadbase Software, Inc.
Thames Valley Business Park,
Reading Application Consultant
?   Install and configure Broadbase Foundation and Brio
Enterprise Server to create a decision support environment.
?   Customise out-of-the-box Broadbase Applications and Brio
Reports to customers decision support needs.
?   Reverse engineer transactional databases with Erwin to
build a logical dimensional model for physical deployment onto
Broadbase db.
?   Create custom applications in Broadbase Foundation
Application Workbench to perform ETL into physical dimensional
model within Broadbase db.
?   Administer Broadbase db.
?   Provide support after engagement is over for problems
that may arise.
?   Work mainly on transactional systems in SQL Server,
Sybase, and Oracle. To develop dimensional models for
analytical reporting from Brio or MS OLAP server.
9/1999 - 7/2000 Genesis ElderCare   Kensington, London
Senior Application Analyst (Applications DBA)
Designed an assessment database to track patient medical
outcomes and company defined scoring system

Figure 3-11:
What can
happen
when you
don't use
ASCII.

CV production, 1-2-3!

Are you puzzled about where to begin, what to write first, and what to do next? Follow these steps that we recommend to fire up your CVs after you've created the core document, from which all targeted CVs flow.

1. **Create your CV in a word-processing program, such as MS Word.**

   Stylise the CV to reflect your persona by choosing a typeface you like. Visually emphasise focal points with boldface, bullets, and underlined characters, as well as words. Save as 'yourname.doc' (like 'SteveShipside.doc'). This document is your fully formatted CV for general usage. Print paper copies as needed.

   Limit yourself to using characters found on a standard keyboard so that they translate correctly. For example, use asterisks to mark bulleted items, and forget about using the fancy arrows you can choose in the MS Word program.

2. **Convert your formatted CV (MS Word) into plain text by following these steps:**

   1. Choose Edit ⇨ Select all.

   2. Click the Start button; then click Programs ⇨ Accessories ⇨ Notepad. When a Notepad window opens, and paste your CV from the fully formatted original in Step 1.

   3. Still in Notepad, choose Format ⇨ Word Wrap.

      Some minor tweaking may be necessary to line up dates and job titles if they were indented or you used bullets in your formatted CV.

   4. Save the resulting document in Notepad (by choosing File ⇨ Save) as **yourname.txt** (for example, SteveShipside.txt).

   This is your plain text (ASCII) e-CV, which is compatible with all systems for use in e-mailing and posting to job sites.

3. **Use either your .doc file (created in Step 1) or .txt file (created in Step 2) to import your e-CV to other applications, such as an Adobe Acrobat PDF file.**

   You also can save your MS Word document as HTML from MS Word's Save As dialog box.

That's it. You're ready to roll.

Book II

Showcasing Yourself with a StandOut CV

A Roundup of Other Formats and Styles

A few adventuresome job seekers are experimenting (or soon will be) with newer CV formats, developing distribution technology and imaginative styles of communication. Take a quick look at possibilities that can't be classified as mainstream methods, but may be just the vehicle you need to find the job you want.

Portfolios

Samples of your work, gathered in a portfolio, have long been valuable to fields such as design, graphics, photography, architecture, advertising, public relations, marketing, and education.

Often, you deliver your portfolio as part of the job interview. Some highly motivated job seekers include a brief version of a career portfolio when sending their CVs, although recruiters say that they want less, not more, paper. Still others create online portfolios and try to entice recruiters and employers to review them.

A career portfolio is rarely used today but is a job-searching tool that may rise in future popularity charts as the work force moves more briskly among jobs, often working on short-term projects as contractors. The portfolio is a showcase for documenting a far more complete picture of what you offer employers than is possible with a CV of one or two pages.

Getting recruiters to read it is the problem.

If you believe that a portfolio is your best bet, put it in a three-ring binder with a table of contents and tabs separating its various parts. Mix and match the following categories:

- **Career goals** (if you're a new graduate or career changer): A brief statement of less than one page is plenty.

- **Your CV:** Use a fully formatted version in MS Word.

- **Samples of your work:** Include easily understandable examples of problem solving and competencies.

- **Proof of performance:** Insert awards, honours, testimonials and letters of commendation, and flattering performance reviews. Don't forget to add praise from employers, people who reported to you, and customers.

- **Proof of recognition:** Here's where you attach certifications, transcripts, degrees, licenses, and printed material listing you as the leader of seminars and workshops. Omit those that you merely attended unless the attendance proves something.

✔ **Military connections:** The military provides exceptionally good training, and many employers know it. List military records, awards, and badges.

Make at least two copies of your portfolio in case potential employers decide to hold on to your samples or fail to return them.

Your portfolio should document only the skills that you want to apply on a job. Begin by identifying those skills; then, determine what materials would prove your claims of competency.

Educator Martin Kimeldorf is responsible for the recent popularisation of career portfolios. Browse a library of Kimeldorf's portfolio samples at `amby.com/kimeldorf/portfolio`.

Book II

Showcasing Yourself with a StandOut CV

Direct letters: A CV alternative

The broadcast direct letter – postal mailing or e-mailing to megalists of companies asking for a job – is an old strategy widely panned by career advisers. But in the hands of experts and sent to a targeted list, the strategy can work surprisingly well.

E-Mail networking newsletters: A CV supplement

Job seekers, usually over 50, who have special knowledge of a topic (such as classic cars or music) as well as computer savvy, are publishing free newsletters and writing blogs as a vehicle for reminding their network core that they're still between gigs.

Choose What Works for You

The big closing question to ask yourself when you've settled on a format is this: Does this format maximise my qualifications for the job I want?

If the format you've chosen doesn't promote your top qualifications, take another look at the choices in this chapter and select a format that helps you shine.

Chapter 4

Contents that Make a Difference

∙∙

In This Chapter

▶ Using the StandOut CV to get a better job

▶ Doing your research to create StandOut CVs

▶ Understanding the parts of your CV

▶ Making each part impress the reader

∙∙

*Y*ou say you're ready to step out and find a terrific job? You say you're tired of selling off a piece of your life in return for forgettable pay in go-nowhere jobs? Or you're fed up with starving as a student? You say you want a job that speaks fluent money with an interesting accent? Sounds good. But that's not *all* you want, you say? You also want *meaningful* work.

We understand. What you want is a job that you love to get up in the morning to do and that pays major money, has first-class benefits, provides a real sense of self-worth and achievement, doesn't disappear overnight, and maybe sends you off on pleasant travels periodically. Something where the present makes you feel alive, the future makes you feel optimistic, and the whole thing brings a fuzzy warmth to both you and your bank manager.

Those StandOut jobs are going to people who, with StandOut CVs and self-discipline, have found out how to outrun the pack. This chapter tells why you need a StandOut CV to make the new workplace work for you.

A global knowledge revolution, as far-reaching as the Industrial Revolution, is changing business. And business is changing the job market. No one is immune to being made redundant as the Job For Life goes the way of the dodo. The good news is that more resources to help us find new work connections have appeared during the past decade than in all of previous history.

Deciding what information to put into your CV isn't difficult if you remember the basic purpose of those few sheets of paper – you're showing that you can and will provide benefits to an employer.

Every company wants to be able to read your CV, knowing that you'll be able to 'do exactly what it says on the tin'. Regardless of how many sophisticated bells and whistles you add, the words of your CV must tell employers just how well you can do the job they want done.

Your CV as a Sales Tool

A CV used to be a simple, low-key sheet or two of paper outlining your experience and education, with a list of references at the end. That kind of CV is now a museum piece.

By contrast, your StandOut CV is a specially prepared sales presentation. Created as a sales tool to persuade a potential employer that you're the best one to do the job you seek, your CV is a self-advertisement that showcases your skills. With a series of well-written statements that highlight your previous work experience, education, and other background information, your CV helps prove what you say about your achievements, accomplishments, and abilities. It tells an employer you have a positive work attitude and strong interpersonal skills.

As a sales tool, your CV outlines your strengths as a product:

✔ The skills you bring to the organisation

✔ The reason you're worth the money you hope to earn

✔ Your capacity for doing the work better than other candidates

✔ Your ability to solve company or industry problems

In every statement, your CV strategically convinces employers that you can do the job, have positive work attitudes, and can get along with others. Your CV – whether stored in the rapidly expanding electronic universe or on paper – helps employers see how they could benefit by interviewing you.

Tailor Your CV to the Company and the Position

When do you need more than one version of your CV? Most of the time. Following the usual approach, you develop a core CV and then amend it to fit specific positions, career fields, or industries.

Nothing beats a perfect or near-perfect match. Suppose a company sports a job opening requiring A, B, and C experience or education. By designing your CV for the target position, you show that you're well endowed with A, B, and C experience or education – a very close match between the company's requirements and your qualifications.

What should you do when you want to change careers, and you don't know exactly to what? Sorry, but you're not ready to write a StandOut CV. First, you need to clarify your direction through either introspection or professional careers advice.

The benefits of research

Research is the key to tailoring your CV to the company your want to work for or the job you know you'd excel at.

By researching a company and industry to customise your CV and determine new job prospects, not only do you gain the firepower to create a StandOut CV, but you build an arsenal of data points to use in interviews.

You won't use every scrap of research, of course. Some data will be useful only for impressing your future co-workers at the next office party. The problem is knowing which data is surplus and which is necessary; glean as much information as time and your study habits permit. In general, the higher the level of job you seek, the more research you need to do in order to be seen as the best candidate for the job. Certainly, if you're writing a CV for a dream job, then pull out all the stops.

Finding out about the company

What does your CV reveal about you? Right off the bat, your CV reveals whether you're willing to take the time to discover what a prospective employer wants done that you're well qualified to do. It shows the health of your judgement and the depth of your commitment to work. Your impulse may be to assume that you can write a CV out of your own head and history – that dogged, time-eating research makes a nice add-on but is not essential. Don't kid yourself. At the core of a StandOut CV is research, research, and more research.

For a comprehensive approach, educate yourself about the company's history, growth and acquisition record, products and services, corporate philosophy on outsourcing, sales volume, annual budget, number of employees, division structure and types of people it hires, market share, profitability, location of physical facilities, and how recently and deeply it has downsized personnel.

Research into your prospective company – in this usage, *company* means non-profit organisations and government agencies as well as private companies – lets you glimpse how you may fit into the company and what you can offer it. Research gives you a sound basis for selecting those areas to include in your CV that demonstrate good judgement and commitment to the goals of your prospective company.

When you know what an employer is willing to employ someone to do, you can tell the employer why you should be the one to do it. *In a tight job race, the candidate who knows most about the employer has the edge.*

Resources for company research

Pulling together the information to write StandOut CVs used to be such a chore that CV writers could spend weeks running down all the facts they needed, visiting libraries for books and newspapers, and traipsing down to Companies' House for annual reports. Mercifully, research is far easier today with a multitude of tools at your beck and mouse-call. To be comprehensive, line up the usual suspects in printed form – directories, annual reports, newspapers, magazines, and trade journals. Then scout the Internet. Following are some sites you may find helpful:

- ✔ **Prospects** (www.prospects.ac.uk): The official UK graduate careers Web site, Prospects includes advice on what jobs would suit you and a database of UK company profiles.

- ✔ **CAROL** (www.carol.co.uk): This site offers company reports online. You name it – balance sheets, profit and loss, financial highlights, and so on – and you can find it here. A valuable source of information that's free to use (registration required though).

- ✔ **CEO Express** (ceoexpress.com): This site covers fewer industries than you might expect, but the wealth of research and information about each industry is impressive. The site offers a large number of links to business magazines and business news Web sites.

- ✔ **Corporate Information** (corporateinformation.com): Type in the name of a company and get a list of sites that report on that company. Or select an industry and get a list of companies in that industry, plus news, overviews, and a short write-up about the industry.

- ✔ **Heriot-Watt University Careers Service** (www.hw.ac.uk/careers). The information at this site isn't exhaustive, but you can find a useful round up of company sites.

- ✔ **Hoover's Online** (www.hoovers.com/uk/): This site offers a business information database with a ton of information about companies, contact information, key officers, competitors, business locations, and industry news.

- ✔ **Europages** (www.europages.com). A business directory priding itself on 500,000 companies listed from 33 European countries.

- ✔ **Kellysearch** (www.kellysearch.co.uk). Kellysearch is a search engine for UK companies. It breaks the companies down into over 100,000 product headings. Free to use.

- ✔ **Financial Times** (www.ft.com). The full glory of the FT online is only available to subscribers, but with the free trial period, you can still make good use of the pink pages without digging deep.

Book II

Showcasing Yourself with a StandOut CV

Some companies even have employee message boards – forums where employees swap notes on life in their company. These message boards are usually for employees of large companies and can be a useful way of getting a more human take on what seems like a faceless giant corporation. Be aware of their limitations, though. If *you* know that a company has a dedicated message board, then that company knows as well. If the forum is monitored, either formally or informally by the company, criticism will most likely be muted. By the same token, be careful of the extreme opposite: grievance sites run to criticise large companies. These sites often feature a name that spoofs the company itself, and people post messages to the site anonymously. These sites can also feature a torrent of abuse. Some of the criticism you read at grievance sites may be valid, but anonymity gives some people a feeling of freedom to let rip without reflection, and anyone with a grudge gets to present a one-sided version of events. The proverbial pinch of salt comes in handy.

Finding out about the position

The ultimate StandOut CV, like a custom-made suit, is tailored to the job you want. After researching the target company and position, you can make your CV fit the job description as closely as your work and education history allow.

At minimum, find out the scope of the position and the skills the company is looking for. The next sections give you more information about how to research your next job and what you can do with this information.

Creating a position analysis

Many companies develop what is called a *candidate specification,* which describes the competencies, skills, experience, knowledge, education, and other characteristics believed to be necessary for the job.

Grab this idea and turn it around. Prepare a counterpart – your own *position analysis.*

The content you're looking for to put in your position analysis includes the major responsibilities, technical problems to be solved, and objectives for the position, as well as competencies and skills, education required, and so forth.

Resources for position research

Find the data for your position analysis in a number of places:

- ✔ **Commercial job descriptions:** Buying job descriptions is pricey, so try libraries or friends who work in HR offices. A limited number of free job descriptions are available on the Web; find them with search engines by typing in **job descriptions**.

- ✔ **Recruitment advertising** (print and online): Look online for job ads for the career field and occupation you want. Although some descriptions are notoriously vague, many companies have learnt their lesson and now specify precise requirements for positions to be filled. On the print side, newspaper recruitment ads are happy hunting grounds for the data you need to write your position analysis.

- ✔ **Occupational career guides:** The US Department of Labor's *Occupational Outlook Handbook* (www.bls.gov/oco) contains career briefs that describe the nature of the work for popular occupations. Remember that, while it is still widely referred to over here in the UK, its job descriptions can show its US origins. Double check this information against UK descriptions wherever possible.

After writing your position analysis, you're ready to roll in composing a StandOut CV.

The Parts of Your CV

To make your contents easy to access, organise the facts into various categories. Here are the essential parts that make up a CV:

- ✔ Contact information
- ✔ Objective or summary statement (if appropriate – see below)
- ✔ Education and training
- ✔ Experience
- ✔ Skills
- ✔ Competencies

> ✔ Activities
>
> ✔ Organisations
>
> ✔ Honours and awards

You can also include these other sections:

> ✔ Licenses, work samples
>
> ✔ Testimonials

To increase the likelihood that your CV positions you for an interview, take the time to understand the purpose of the different CV parts, which we explain in the following sections.

Book II

Showcasing Yourself with a StandOut CV

Contact Information

No matter which format you choose, place your name first on your CV, followed by contact information:

> ✔ **Name:** If your name isn't first, a computer may mistake Excellent Sales Representative for your name and file you away as 'Ms Representative'. You may want to display your name in slightly larger type than the rest of the contact information and in boldface, to make it clear who's CV the reader is holding.
>
> ✔ **Postal address:** Give a street name with the house/flat number, city, county, and post code. If you're a student or member of the armed forces who will be returning home, give both addresses, labelled Current Address and Permanent Address. You can add operational dates for each address. But don't forget to delete a date after it's passed. Otherwise, you will look like a product whose shelf life has expired.
>
> ✔ **Valid telephone number:** Use a personal number, where you can be reached or where the recruiter can leave a message.
>
> Don't allow children to answer this line. Don't record a clever message – play it straight, as potential employees might not want to leave a message on an answer phone with an amusing message from Eric Morecambe on it. If you must share a telephone with kids, emphasise the need for them to answer the phone professionally and to keep their calls short. Consider getting a cheap, pay-as-you-go mobile as a unique number/answering machine just for job hunting.
>
> ✔ **Other contact media:** Use any or all of the following, if available to you: e-mail address, mobile phone number, telephone answering service number, and Web page address.

What about using company resources? Should you ever use your employer's e-mail address or letterhead? Many employers see an employee's use of company resources to find another job as small-time theft. In certain situations, however, you can use your company's help. For example, a company that's downsizing is expected to provide resource support for outplacement. When you're ending a contract project for which you were hired, your employer may allow you to use company resources. Indicate permission to use them in your CV's cover letter: 'The project for which I was hired is finishing ahead of schedule; my grateful employer is co-operating in my new search.'

Is it okay to list your work telephone number on your CV? In a decade when employers have been tossing workers out without remorse, it's a tough world, and you need speedy communications. The practical answer is to list your work number – if you have a direct line and voice mail or a mobile phone. To show that you're an ethical person, limit calls to a couple of minutes – just long enough to arrange a meeting or an evening call back. Avoid the issue by using your personal mobile phone to call back during your lunch break.

Hooks: Objective or Summary?

Your StandOut CV needs a hook to grab the reader's attention. The hook follows your name and contact information and is expressed as a *job objective* or as an *asset statement* (also called a skills summary) – or some combination of the two.

A job objective can look like this:

> **Objective:** Assistant to Executive

A skills summary can look like this:

> **Summary:** Over 14 years of progressively more responsible office support experience, including superior computer skills, with a well-earned reputation for priority-setting and teamwork.

Or a job objective can be linked to a skills summary:

> **Objective:** Assistant to Executive, to keep operations under firmer control, using computer skills, contemporary office procedures, and pleasant manner with people.

However it is fashioned, the hook tells the recruiter what you want to do and/or what you're qualified to do.

Debate rages among career pros over the topic of objective versus summary.

- ✔ Objective backers say that readers don't want to slog through a document, trying to guess the type of position you want and how you'd fit into the organisation.

- ✔ Summary advocates argue that a thumbnail sketch of your skills and other competencies allows you to be evaluated for jobs you haven't identified in your job objective – a serious consideration in this age of CV database searches.

A quick guideline taken from a sampling of six recruiters, as reported in *Job Choices* magazine, is this: 'Objective statements are essential for recent graduates, summary statements for seasoned professionals.'

On balance, we agree with the recruiters. An objective may be a self-defeating force for seasoned aces with well-established career paths, whose insistence on a particular job objective may be seen as rigid and for those whose CVs will be stored in electronic databases. But an objective is rearly essential for job seekers who are short on experience or don't have a clear idea of what they'd like to do, but know the general direction.

What you really need in your CV is *focus,* whether you style it as a job objective or as a summary.

Book II

Showcasing Yourself with a StandOut CV

The job objective statement

Weigh these considerations when deciding how to help readers visualise what you could do in the future for them.

When to use an objective

Use a job objective when:

- ✔ You're a new graduate or a career changer exiting the military, the clergy, education, or full-time homemaking. A job objective says what you're looking for.
- ✔ You have a greatly diversified background that may perplex some employers.
- ✔ You know the job being offered; make that job title your job objective.

Advantages of an objective

Most studies show that employers prefer objectives for quick identification purposes. They like to see the name of their job openings and/or companies at the top of a CV. Because you cite those achievements that support your objective and forget random experiences, the finished product (when done well) shows that you and the desired job are a well-matched pair.

Disadvantages of an objective

Do you have the time to write a CV for each position (or career field) to which you apply? A narrow job objective may keep you from being considered by the same employer for other positions. And if the objective is too broadly focused, it becomes a meaningless statement.

The skills summary (asset statements)

A summary statement announces who you are and identifies your strengths. A summary can be stated in paragraph form or in four to six bulleted quick-hits, such as:

- ✔ Recruited and trained more than 300 people

- ✔ Installed robotics, standardising product, reducing retraining cost by 16 percent

- ✔ Slashed initial training costs from £800,000 to £650,000 within one year

- ✔ Created dynamic training culture to support the introduction of a new product

Take a look at the sections that follow for tips on when a summary statement is best.

When to use a summary

Use a summary statement when:

- ✔ You're a person with widely applicable skills. Recruiters especially like a skills summary atop a reverse chronological CV because it lets them creatively consider you for jobs that you may not know exist.

- ✔ You're in a career field with pathways to multiple occupations or industries (an administrative assistant, for example).

- ✔ You know that your CV is headed for an electronic database and you want to be considered for multiple jobs.

Advantages of a summary

A summary can be more appropriate to status – senior executives, in particular, can let their records speak for them. Recruiters believe that what you're prepared to do next should be pretty evident from what you've already done. Another argument is premised on psychology: Employers aren't known for being overly concerned with what you want *from* them until they're sure of what you can do *for* them.

Disadvantages of a summary

A summary doesn't explicitly say what you want and why the employer would want you. The technique of specifying a job objective in a cover letter attached to a skills-summary CV is common; the problems arise when the cover letter is inadvertently separated from the CV or the CV is passed out alone, as at a job fair. Furthermore, the fact that a skills summary CV leaves many doors open is a double-edged sword: Your accomplishments don't thrust you toward a specific target, so you may be abandoning a success strategy that's been proven again and again.

Education and Training

While both education and training are all about learning, the first is normally taken to mean more general academic subjects (such as arts or sciences) while the second is seen as vocational or directly job related. In the real world such distinctions are rarely so clear since a literature qualification may be truly job related for a would be publisher, and a certificate in motorbike mechanics may have little bearing on the desired job in stock-broking. Think through all and any of the educational/training qualifications you have to your name and decide which are going to make a potential employer see you as a hot property.

- ✔ List your highest degree first – type of degree, subject you read, college name, and date awarded.

- ✔ New graduates should give far more detail on course work than seasoned aces who've held at least one job for one year or more.

- ✔ Omit secondary school if you have a university degree.

- ✔ If you have a vocational or technical certificate or diploma that required less than a year to obtain, list your secondary school as well.

- ✔ Note continuing education, including seminars related to your work.

- ✔ If you fall short of the mark on the job's educational requirements, try to compensate by expanding the continuing the education section. Give the list a name, such as 'Professional Development Highlights', and list every impressive course, seminar, workshop, and conference that you've attended.

What's first – education or experience?

The general rule in CV writing is to lead with your most qualifying factor.

With certain exceptions (such as law, where your choice of university may be considered throughout life), lead off with experience when you've been in the workforce for at least three years. When you're loaded with experience but low on credentials, list your school days at the end – and perhaps even omit them entirely if you didn't graduate.

Young people just out of school usually start with education, but if you've worked throughout school or have relevant prior work history, start with experience.

Young readers, if your research shows that a prospective employer wants education and experience, provide a summary linking them together as interdependent. For example, explain how your education was part of your professional experience, or how your experience was an education itself. Following this consolidation, create a heading under which you can merge both sections – such as 'Professional Preparation' or 'Education, Training, and Employment'.

Experience

Describe – with quantified achievements – your present and previous positions in reverse chronological order. Include dates of employment, company names and locations, and specific job titles. Show progression and promotions within an organisation, especially if you've been with one employer for aeons.

Consider using more than one Experience heading. Try headings, such as 'Accounting and Finance-Related Experience', 'General Business Experience', and 'Healthcare and Administration Experience'. This is yet another way of reinforcing your suitability for the job you seek.

Some CV formats use a more rigid approach than others, allowing little leeway as you fill in the blanks. Most formats, however, leave all kinds of room for stacking your blocks in a way that does you the most good.

Skills

Skills are the heart and soul of job finding and, as such, encompass a variety of experiences. These are examples of skills:

Collaborating, editing, fundraising, interviewing, managing, navigating (Internet), researching, teaching

Top accomplishments

Top 12 accomplishments that most interest employers:

- ✔ Increased revenues
- ✔ Saved money
- ✔ Increased efficiency
- ✔ Cut overheads
- ✔ Increased sales
- ✔ Improved workplace safety
- ✔ Purchasing accomplishments
- ✔ New products/new lines
- ✔ Improved record-keeping process
- ✔ Increased productivity
- ✔ Successful advertising campaign
- ✔ Effective budgeting

Book II

Showcasing Yourself with a StandOut CV

And here are some more skills:

> Administering social programmes, analysing insurance facts, advising homeless people, allocating forestry resources, desktop publishing, co-ordinating association events, designing home furnishing ads, marine expedition problem-solving, writing police reports.

And some more:

> Dependable, sense of humour, commitment, leadership, persistence, crisis-resilient, adaptable, quick, results-driven.

And these are still more skills:

> Brochures, UNIX, five years, 100 percent quota, telemarketing, senior management, spreadsheet, MBA, major accounting firms.

As you can see, a very broad definition encompasses what can constitute a skill, and using skills as a basic element of your CV may surprise you. We include them here because they've taken on new importance, and the concept of 'skill' has changed in the past two decades. Skills used to be thought of in the classic meaning of general and industry-specific abilities. Recruiting industry professionals expand the term to include personal characteristics, as well as past employers, special knowledge, achievements, and products.

 Because the term is widely used in job searching today, a *skill* is any identifiable ability or fact that employers value and will pay for. That means that 'five years' is a skill, just as 'word processing' is a skill; employers pay for experience and competence.

Where do skills belong on your CV? Everywhere. They are the basic ingredients of every CV – so season every statement with skills. Skills are indispensable.

Whether you use an e-CV or a traditional paper CV, you must name your skills or be left behind.

Skills are one part of the emerging concept of *competencies,* a discussion of which immediately follows.

Competencies

Competencies is a broader concept than *skills*. Competencies and skills differ in that skills are applications of knowledge to solve a problem or perform an act. The competencies concept includes skills as well as behaviours required in a career field position, such as persuasiveness or persistence in sales and marketing. Richard H Beatty, co-founder and board member of HR Technologies (www.hrscope.com), a leading competencies software firm, expands the concept's meaning: 'Competencies are the knowledge, skills, characteristics, and behaviours essential to successful performance of a job.'

But human resource professionals don't share universal agreement about the precise composition of *competency-based programs.* Some employers establish enterprise-wide *core competencies* that apply to all employees no matter what their position. The employer's signature core competencies (such as teamwork, goal setting, and trustworthiness) are meant to aid in selecting new employees who are aligned with the company's mission and objectives. Essentially, the employer tries to figure out what makes its best performers tick (identify their competencies) and hire more people like them.

Some employers add to core competencies a number of *role competencies* that relate to the position held – an engineer's role competencies differ from an accountant's, for example.

The following overview launches you on the road to understanding the nuts and bolts of the emerging *competency-based recruiting model.*

Competencies in the corporate arena

Most users of competency-based models are large corporations. The idea hasn't yet trickled down to the mass of employers. Each employer chooses the enterprise-wide core and role competencies that it prefers. Some employers articulate only a few enterprise-wide core competencies, and others have a dozen or more. An employer may have hundreds or even thousands of role competencies, assigning 20 or 30 to each position.

The competencies theory is an intellectual child of the 1990s, but its popularity has surged only recently. Although the competencies concept is more commonly used in job interviewing, job seekers are beginning to integrate competencies into their CVs as growing numbers of employers adopt the approach to improving the quality of hiring.

Competencies basically fall into two distinct classifications: *behavioural competencies* and *technical competencies.* Behavioural competencies – where most of the recent employer emphasis has been – are further divided into two distinct types. The two types are behaviours that are *job relevant* (important to job success) and behaviours that are *culture relevant* (important to fitting in well with the organisation's culture of work environment).

Here's an illustration of the differences between the two:

- ✔ **Technical competencies:** These are the specialised knowledge and skills needed to solve the key problems faced in a given position and get the results expected of the job.

  Technical competencies for a sales position include product knowledge, market knowledge, customer knowledge, market trends, pricing, competitor products/ pricing/strategies, closing skills, knowledge of sales tactics, and techniques, for instance.

- ✔ **Behavioural competencies – job relevant:** These are the personal characteristics of excellent performers in the job.

  Descriptions of job-relevant behaviour in a sales position include self-confident, investigative, strategic, open and friendly, relationship builder, networker, good listener, strong communicator, attentive, responsive, and service-oriented.

- ✔ **Behavioural competencies – culture relevant:** Many of the corporate *core competencies* come into play here. The core competencies reflect the behaviour and attributes that the company's senior management believes are important to the organisation's long-term survival and success.

  Descriptions of culture-relevant behaviour in a sales position include team-oriented, client-focused, change agent, strategic visionary, and consistently improvement-oriented.

Competency-based CVs

Most good CVs focus on knowledge, skills, and accomplishments. They only hint at competencies required to do the work. To capture behavioural competencies on a CV, you must show how your accomplishments confirm your competencies. Or to turn it around, you must show how your competencies made it possible for you to hit the back of the net.

Competencies focus on how an employee contributes value (benefits) to the employer and on what's actually accomplished.

As an example, to connect your behaviours with your accomplishments, you can say something like this:

> Product development: Created new mid-market segment supporting an annual growth rate of 20 percent in a flat industry, demonstrating high energy and business acumen.

In the above example, the verb 'demonstrating' connects the accomplishment (Created new mid-market segment supporting an annual growth rate of 20 percent in a flat industry) with the behaviours, or competencies (high energy and business acumen). Other verbs you can use to bridge the two types of information include the following:

- ✔ Confirming
- ✔ Displaying
- ✔ Exhibiting
- ✔ Illustrating
- ✔ Manifesting
- ✔ Proving
- ✔ Revealing

Very little outcome data has yet been collected on the construction of competency-based CVs. But here's a formula if you want to try your hand at incorporating competencies into your StandOut CV: After noting your measurable accomplishments, add your personal behavioural competencies that made them possible.

Try to find out whether the target company has adopted the competencies model. Try these strategies:

- ✔ If you belong to professional organisations, look at the organisation's membership directory, try to find someone you know who works at the place where you're applying, and inquire about the company's competencies and any change in culture the company is trying to engineer.
- ✔ Look for the competencies tip-off on the company's Web site. You may find the company's core competencies embedded in its mission statement.

> ✔ Call the company's human resource department and ask, 'Do you use a competencies model in recruiting?' If yes, ask whether you can obtain a lexicon of the company's core competencies and the role competencies for the target position. Sometimes, the HR specialist will reveal the competencies and sometimes not. But you're missing a bet if you don't ask.

If the company uses the competencies model, apply the StandOut advice we mentioned just above. After noting your measurable accomplishments, add your personal behavioural competencies that made them possible.

Competencies statements don't make good keywords, and the company won't uncover your CV based on your behavioural competencies. So why do it? Accomplishment and skill keywords initially snag the interviewer's attention, but when he or she sees that you've also included competencies statements, the interviewer will note that no moss is hanging from your hair and that you understand the emerging competency model. This sophistication is a plus for interviewing purposes.

Be on guard against taking one particular wrong turn that spills the beans on any misunderstanding you may harbour about competencies. Some CV writers recognise competencies as a buzzword, but they don't know much about its workings. To compensate, they try to update keyword profiles or functional listings by pouring old wine into new bottles, which they then label 'Core Competencies'. That's a mistake. If you do this, HR professionals who 'get it' will know that you don't.

Find more competency information through your professional organisation, search engines (such as Google), personnel publications, and books with the word 'competencies' in the title.

Activities

Activities can be anything from hobbies and sports to campus extracurricular participation (but not ones that take place after you've been to the pub!). The trick is to analyse how each activity is relevant to the target job; discuss skills, knowledge, or other competencies developed; and list all achievements. Make sure that this section doesn't become meaningless filler.

In addition, avoid potentially controversial activities. Stating that you're a keen member of a fox hunt won't endear you to animal-loving recruiters. If you've been able to research the reader and have found that you two have a common interest, however, that interest is worth listing on the CV, so that it can become an icebreaker topic during an interview.

Book II

Showcasing Yourself with a StandOut CV

Organisations

Give yourself even more credentials with professional and civic affiliations. Mention all-important offices held. Relate these affiliations to your reader in terms of marketable skills, knowledge, and achievements. A high profile in the community is particularly important for sales jobs.

Just as you should be careful about which activities you identify, so too should you be sensitive to booby traps in organisation memberships.

✔ Listing too many organisations may make the reader wonder when you'd have time to do the job.

✔ Noting that you belong to one activist or protest organisation may work in your favour, but reporting your membership in five such organisations may raise red flags. The recruiter may worry that you're a troublemaking activist who's willing to exhibit poor work performance and unacceptable behaviour in order to create a public issue if you're due to get fired.

✔ And, of course, you know better than to list your membership in religious or political organisations (unless you're applying for a job that requires such membership). They don't apply to your ability to do the job, and some readers may use them to keep you out of the running.

Honours and Awards

List most of the achievements for which you were recognised. If the achievement had zero to do with work or doesn't show you in a professional light, don't take up white space with it; for example, you probably wouldn't list a Yard of Ale drinking award (unless you're applying for a job as a beer taster, of course).

Licences and Samples of Your Work

If you're in the legal, certified accounting, engineering, or medical profession, you need to add to your CV the appropriate licence, certifications, and other identifications required for the position. For a professional CV, you may also need to list descriptions or titles of specific work that you've done or include samples of your work along with your CV. If asked to include samples of your work, be selective about what you send. No brainer: Make sure that your samples have no obvious flaws or errors.

What To Do about the Salary Question?

Some people like haggling, but when the thing being bought or sold is yourself most of us get a little nervous. Stating your salary expectation up front is something that's often expected by potential employers, but there is always the fear that you can undersell or overprice yourself. Maybe you want this interesting new job and are prepared to accept less than you were previously paid but are afraid of selling yourself short in the process.

Book II

Showcasing Yourself with a StandOut CV

Salary history and requirements

One approach is to never mention salary on your CV. If a job ad asks for your salary history or salary requirements, revealing those figures in a cover letter puts you at a disadvantage if you've been working for low pay – or if you've been paid above the market rate. This is not to say that you refuse to disclose salary – that doesn't reflect well – only that you prefer not to advertise it until asked. That doesn't always work, however, not least since profile forms on job sites and online personal agents almost always ask for your salary information. If you decide to participate, state your expectations in a range (£xxx to £xxx), and include the value of all perks (benefits, bonuses), not just salary, in your salary history.

But first, do two things:

- ✔ Research the market rate for someone with your skills and experience. Start with the Web sites like Monster (www.monster.co.uk) that also provide salary comparison engines.
- ✔ Find out why the smart money advises against being too quick to pipe up with hard figures on the money you've made and the money you want.

What can you expect in return for revealing salary information, job unseen? You get a chance to name your price and hope you find takers, many of whom will want to talk your price down. Ask around and read widely on the Net. Absorb all you can – salary negotiation is as complex as buying a house.

References

In an earlier time, when supply and demand were roughly in balance, employers didn't always bother to check references. Small employers still may not, but midsize and large companies, afraid of making a hiring mistake, are more likely to pay heed to references. Depending on the nature of the job, employers can legally investigate your credit history, as well as any record of criminal convictions, particularly for jobs in sensitive areas such as caring jobs or education.

Nevertheless, references *don't* belong on your CV. Instead, create a second document filled with the names, correct telephone numbers, and addresses of references. Supply this sheet only when requested by an interested potential employer – don't burn out your references by allowing too many casual callers access to their names and contact information.

If a personal reference is given, they may get in touch, but that is increasingly rare since liability issues mean most references are now deliberately non-committal and bad references have all but ceased to exist. That is not a license to invent references, however, because Sod's law dictates that if just once in your life you choose to embellish a reference, that will be the one time when it is checked, or the referee turns out to be a personal friend of the employer.

Following are some key suggestions for managing your references:

- ✓ **Choose your references carefully.** List referees who have direct knowledge of your job performance. If necessary, go beyond your immediate supervisor and include past or present co-workers, subordinates, customers, suppliers, members of trade associations, or anyone else who can praise your work. With the exception of your immediate boss, never – *never* – list a reference until you have gained that person's permission to do so. Make a dry run: have a brave friend call your references to make certain that no sly naysayers are hiding behind friendly faces.

    Employers are not legally bound to provide references, and as a result of the Employment Equality Regulations, employers can face legal action if they wrongly indicate that a former employee is unsuitable.

- ✓ **Coach your references.** If you are applying for a job that specifically requests referees to be listed, choose and prepare your referees accordingly. Providing them with your CV is standard operating procedure. Go further: Write a short script of likely questions with a summary of persuasion points under each question. In addition to general good words about your industriousness, creativity, and leadership, focus on the industry. If you're applying to a financial institution, suggest that your references dwell on trustworthiness, conservatism, and good judgement. If you're applying to a high-tech company that has proprietary software and inventions, ask your referees to stress your ethics and loyalty.

✔ **Write your own reference letters.** A letter of reference isn't particularly effective, but it's better than nothing in cases where a company nosedives out, your boss dies, or the referee is difficult to reach. When you want a reference letter, go after it StandOut style: Offer to draft or even to prepare for signature a letter of praise for your referee to sign. Routinely arrange for a reference letter when you leave a job. Remember that some companies have a policy of not supplying references; if that's the case, ask for a letter to that effect to show that that not having a reference letter isn't a reflection on you.

Book II

Showcasing Yourself with a StandOut CV

Application forms: Take them seriously

Although many job hunters tend to underestimate the importance of formal application forms, these tiresome profiles are legal documents. Lies can come back to bite you. Stick to the facts as you follow these rules and push some paper:

✔ If allowed, take the application home; photocopy it in case you spill coffee on your first effort.

✔ Verify all dates of employment and salaries to the letter.

✔ Enter the full name and last known address of former employers. If former employers are no longer available, don't substitute co-workers.

✔ If asked for salary history, give your base salary (or add commission and bonuses), omitting benefits.

✔ Give a complete employment history in months and years, including trivial three-week jobs that you wisely left off the CV.

If you stint on telling the whole story, you leave a loophole of withholding information that later can be used against you if the employer decides that you're surplus to requirements.

✔ Unless you have a condition directly affecting your ability to do the job for which you are applying, you need not elaborate on any disability.

✔ Divulge any criminal record required of you. Check out the Criminal Records Bureau disclosure site (www.disclosure.gov.uk) or call the CRB on 0870 9090 811 to find out what offences have 'expired' and can be wiped off before job hunting.

✔ Be honest about having collected unemployment benefits (but remember that repeaters are frowned on); if you're caught lying about it later, practise your farewell speech.

✔ Autograph the application; you've been honest – why worry?

✔ **Stamp out bad references.** If you were axed or pressed to resign – or you told your boss what you thought and quit – move immediately from spin control to damage control. Even if you were cool enough to obtain a letter of reference before you left, you absolutely must gulp down the bile and try to neutralise the reference.

Appeal to a sense of fair play or guilt. Sometimes, just saying that you're sorry and you hope that the employer won't keep you from earning a living will be enough. Sometimes, though, it won't. When you've done all you can to try to overcome a bad reference you can't avoid supplying, such as your previous bosses, you still have options:

- Drown the poor reference in large numbers of favourable references.

- If you know that your potential employer will want to speak to your previous employer, make it clear that you do not expect them to prejudice your chances of future employment. For legal reasons the worst you can normally now expect from a previous employer is a refusal to give a reference. If you think that your previous employer may prejudice your chances of a new job take legal advice from your nearest Citizen's Advice Bureau.

- Continue your job hunt, concentrating on small firms that may not check references or that may be more inclined to take a chance on someone.

No matter how super-powerful you've made your CV, weak or poor references can wipe out your job chances. That's why you write the sample question-and-answer scripts and the reference letters, and that's why you take the first step to patch things up with former adversaries. Your employment is a much higher priority by far to you than it is to reference-givers.

Chapter 5

Winning with Words

. . . .

. . . .

Words are powerful. They can be surprisingly emotive, and if carefully chosen, they are astonishingly powerful tools. When chosen wisely, a few words can change the world: Bishop Desmond Tutu reinvented an entire country with just two when he dubbed South Africa the *Rainbow Nation*. It took just one word, *glasnost,* to herald the end of the Cold War and a new spirit of co-operation. John Lennon managed to squeeze the hopes of a generation into the word *imagine.* Winston Churchill needed only two words to bind Russia to the *Iron Curtain.* A brief four words memorialised Martin Luther King's vision: *I have a dream.* And in a single sentence, John F Kennedy set the challenge for a generation: *Ask not what your country can do for you, but what you can do for your country.*

The right words can change your life. Samuel Taylor Coleridge once said that the definition of *prose* was 'words in their best order' and the definition of *poetry* was the 'best words in the best order'. You may not be setting out to write *Kubla Khan,* but if you want your CV to soar off the page and sing to the recruiter, you'd best make sure you, too, are using the best words in the best order.

This chapter helps you in your hunt for the right words to build a StandOut CV. It shows you how to use *StandOut words* (action verbs, such as *improve, upgrade,* and *schedule,* the described your strengths) and *keywords* (nouns, like *technology transfers, PhD organic chemistry,* and *multinational marketing,* that demonstrate essential skills). It also explains CV grammar.

StandOut Words Can Bring Good News

Use power-play verbs to communicate your abilities and accomplishments. A punchy delivery keeps these achievement verbs campaigning for you. The important thing is to choose words of substance and power that zero in on your abilities and achievements. Take a look at the StandOut words that follow and check off those words that work for you.

Here are some things to remember when you choose your StandOut words:

- Try not to use the same word twice on your CV – the thesaurus in a word-processing program can give you more possibilities.
- Never use two words where one better one will do.
- Little words never devalued a big idea.

StandOut words for administration and management

advised	initiated	prioritised
approved	inspired	processed
authorised	installed	promoted
chaired	instituted	recommended
consolidated	instructed	redirected
counselled	integrated	referred
delegated	launched	reorganised
determined	lectured	represented
developed	listened	responded
diagnosed	managed	reviewed
directed	mediated	routed
disseminated	mentored	sponsored
enforced	moderated	streamlined
ensured	monitored	strengthened

examined	motivated	supervised
explained	negotiated	taught
governed	originated	trained
guided	oversaw	validated
headed	pioneered	
influenced	presided	

StandOut words for communications and creativity

Book II

Showcasing Yourself with a StandOut CV

acted	edited	proof-read
addressed	enabled	publicised
arranged	facilitated	published
assessed	fashioned	realised
authored	formulated	reconciled
briefed	influenced	recruited
built	initiated	rectified
clarified	interpreted	remodelled
composed	interviewed	reported
conducted	introduced	revitalised
constructed	invented	scheduled
corresponded	launched	screened
costumed	lectured	shaped
created	modernised	stimulated
critiqued	performed	summarised
demonstrated	planned	taught
designed	presented	trained
developed	produced	translated
directed	projected	wrote

StandOut words for sales and persuasion

arbitrated	judged	purchased
catalogued	launched	realised
centralised	lectured	recruited
consulted	led	reduced
dissuaded	liaised	reported
documented	maintained	researched
educated	manipulated	resolved
established	marketed	restored
expedited	mediated	reviewed
familiarised	moderated	routed
identified	negotiated	saved
implemented	obtained	served
improved	ordered	set goals
increased	performed	sold
influenced	planned	solved
inspired	processed	stimulated
installed	produced	summarised
integrated	promoted	surveyed
interpreted	proposed	translated
investigated	publicised	

StandOut words for technical ability

analysed	expedited	operated
broadened	fabricated	packaged
charted	facilitated	pioneered
classified	forecasted	prepared
communicated	formed	processed
compiled	generated	programmed

computed	improved	published
conceived	increased	reconstructed
conducted	inspected	reduced
co-ordinated	installed	researched
designed	instituted	restored
detected	integrated	revamped
developed	interfaced	streamlined
devised	launched	supplemented
drafted	lectured	surveyed
edited	maintained	systematised
educated	marketed	trained
eliminated	mastered	upgraded
excelled	modified	wrote
expanded	moulded	

Book II

Showcasing Yourself with a StandOut CV

StandOut words for office support

adhered	distributed	managed
administered	documented	operated
allocated	drafted	ordered
applied	enacted	organised
appropriated	enlarged	packaged
assisted	evaluated	planned
assured	examined	prepared
attained	executed	prescribed
awarded	followed up	processed
balanced	formalised	provided
budgeted	formulated	recorded
built	hired	repaired
charted	identified	reshaped
completed	implemented	resolved

contributed

co-ordinated

cut

defined

determined

dispensed

improved

installed

instituted

justified

liaised

maintained

scheduled

screened

secured

solved

started

StandOut words for teaching

acquainted

adapted

advised

answered

apprised

augmented

briefed

built

certified

chaired

charted

clarified

coached

collaborated

communicated

conducted

co-ordinated

delegated

delivered

demonstrated

designed

developed

directed

dispensed

distributed

educated

effected

empowered

enabled

enacted

enlarged

expanded

facilitated

fomented

formulated

generated

grouped

guided

harmonised

implemented

influenced

informed

initiated

innovated

installed

instituted

instructed

integrated

lectured

listened

originated

persuaded

presented

responded

revolutionised

set goals

stimulated

summarised

trained

translated

StandOut words for research and analysis

administered	detected	interviewed
amplified	determined	invented
analysed	discovered	investigated
applied	documented	located
articulated	drafted	measured
assessed	edited	obtained
audited	evaluated	organised
augmented	examined	pinpointed
balanced	exhibited	planned
calculated	experimented	prepared
charted	explored	processed
collected	extracted	proof-read
compared	focused	researched
compiled	forecasted	reviewed
composed	found	riveted
concentrated	generated	screened
conducted	grouped	summarised
constructed	identified	surveyed
consulted	integrated	systematised
critiqued	interpreted	unearthed

Book II

Showcasing Yourself with a StandOut CV

StandOut words for helping and caring professions

advanced	encouraged	reassured
advised	expedited	reclaimed
aided	facilitated	rectified

arbitrated	familiarised	redeemed
assisted	fostered	re-educated
attended	furthered	referred
augmented	guided	reformed
backed	helped	rehabilitated
balanced	instilled	repaired
boosted	liaised	represented
braced	mentored	served
clarified	ministered	settled
collaborated	negotiated	supplied
comforted	nourished	supported
consoled	nursed	stabilised
consulted	nurtured	streamlined
contributed	obliged	translated
counselled	optimised	treated
demonstrated	promoted	tutored
diagnosed	provided	unified

StandOut words for financial management

adjusted	economised	reported
administered	eliminated	researched
allocated	exceeded	reshaped
analysed	financed	retailed
appraised	forecasted	saved
audited	funded	shopped
balanced	gained	secured
bought	generated	sold
budgeted	increased	solicited
calculated	invested	sourced
computed	maintained	specified
conciliated	managed	supplemented

cut

decreased

developed

disbursed

dispensed

distributed

doubled

downsized

marketed

planned

projected

purchased

quadrupled

reconciled

reduced

systemised

tested

tripled

underwrote

upgraded

upsized

StandOut words for many skills

accomplished

achieved

adapted

adhered

allocated

appraised

arbitrated

arranged

articulated

assured

augmented

collected

communicated

composed

conceptualised

conserved

contributed

co-ordinated

demonstrated

dispensed

evaluated

executed

facilitated

forecasted

founded

governed

guided

illustrated

improved

increased

initiated

integrated

interpreted

invented

launched

led

navigated

optimised

organised

originated

overhauled

performed

prioritised

promoted

proposed

reconciled

rectified

remodelled

repaired

reshaped

retrieved

solved

stimulated

streamlined

strengthened

trained

upgraded

validated

won

Keywords Are Key to Finding You

Recruiters and employers use keywords to search and retrieve e-CVs in databases for available positions. Keywords are chiefly nouns and short phrases. That's your take-home message. But once in a while, keywords can be adjectives and action verbs. Employers choose their own list of keywords – that's why no list is universal.

In computerised job searches, keywords describe not only your knowledge base and skills but also such things as well-known companies, big name colleges and universities, degrees, qualifications, and professional affiliations.

Keywords identify your experience and education in these categories:

- Skills
- Technical and professional areas of expertise
- Achievements
- Professional qualifications
- Other distinguishing features of your work history
- Prestigious education and training background or former employers

Employers identify keywords, often including industry jargon, that they think represent essential qualifications necessary for high performance in a given position. They specify those keywords when they search a CV database.

'Keywords are what employers search for when trying to fill a position: the essential hard skills and knowledge needed to do the job', is how systems and staffing consultant James M Lemke classifies the words that describe your bundle of qualifications.

Rather than stopping with action verbs, connect your achievements. You managed *what?* You organised *what?* You developed *what?* Job computers look for the *whats,* and the whats are usually nouns.

Having said that, never say never. Employers scanning for management and administrative positions may search for verbs and adjectives that define soft skills – 'assisted general manager', 'outgoing personality', 'self-motivated'. But job computers normally prefer a hard skills diet. If your CV has the sought-after keywords, the employer zooms you into focus; if not, you're overlooked for that particular job.

Obviously, keywords are arbitrary and specific to the employer and to each search-and-retrieve action that the employer wants done. The following lists provide a few examples of keywords for selected career fields and industries.

Keywords for administration and management

administrative processes	facilities management
Bachelor's degree	front office operations
back office operations	office manager
benchmarking	operations manager
budget administration	policy and procedure
change management	production schedule
crisis communications	project planning
data analysis	records management
document management	regulatory reporting

Keywords for banking

branch manager	loan management
branch operations	loan recovery
commercial banking	portfolio management
construction loans	retail lending
credit guidelines	return on investment (ROI)
debt financing	trust services
first in, last out (FILO)	turnaround management
financial management	Uniform Commercial Code Filing
investment management	Workout
investor relations	

Keywords for customer service

account representative

call centre

customer communications

customer focus groups

customer loyalty

customer needs assessment

customer retention

customer retention innovations

customer service manager

customer surveys

field service operation

key account manager

order fulfilment

order processing

product response clerk

records management

sales administration

sales support administrator

service quality

telemarketing operations

telemarketing representative

Keywords for information technology

automated voice response (AVR)

chief information officer

client/server architecture

cross-functional team

data centre manager

director of end user computing

disaster recovery

end user support

global systems support

help desk

multimedia technology

network development analyst

project lifecycle

systems configuration

technology rightsizing

vendor partnerships

Keywords for manufacturing

asset management

assistant operations manager

automated manufacturing

capacity planning

logistics manager

manufacturing engineer

materials co-ordinator

on-time delivery

cell manufacturing

cost reductions

distribution management

environmental health and safety

inventory control

just-in-time (JIT)

shipping and receiving operation

spares and repairs management

union negotiations

warehousing operations

workflow optimisation

Keywords for human resources

Bachelor or Master degree

college recruitment

compensation and benefit

cross-cultural communications

diversity training

disciplinary and grievance

job task analysis

labour contract negotiations

leadership development

IPD and certificates

organisational development (OD)

recruitment specialist

regulatory affairs

sourcing

staffing

succession planning

team leadership

training specialist

wage and salary administration

Book II

Showcasing Yourself with a StandOut CV

Keywords are the magnets that draw non-human eyes to your talents.

Where to Find Keywords

How can you find keywords for your occupation or career field? Use a high-lighter to pluck keywords from these resources.

✔ **Printed and online help-wanted ads:** Highlight the job skills, competencies, experience, education, and other nouns that employers ask for.

✔ **Job descriptions:** Ask employers for them, check at libraries for books or software with job descriptions, or search online. To find job descriptions online, just enter the term *job descriptions* on a search engine, such as Google (www.google.co.uk).

✔ **Your core CV:** Look through to highlight nouns that identify job skills, competencies, experience, and education.

✔ **Trade magazine news stories:** Text about your career field or occupation should be ripe with keywords. Media that have strictly sober style guides, such as *The Economist* and *The Financial Times* are often good sources of hype-free description.

✔ **Annual reports of companies in your field:** The company descriptions of key personnel and departmental achievements should offer strong keyword clues.

✔ **Programmes for industry conferences and events:** Speaker topics address current industry issues, a rich source of keywords.

✔ **Internet search engine:** Plug in a targeted company's name and search the site that comes up. Look closely at the careers portal and read current press releases. You can also use Internet search engines to scout out industry-specific directories, glossaries, and dictionaries.

Just as you should keep your CV up to date, ready to move in a flash if you must, you should also keep a running log of keywords that can help you reconnect to a new job on a moment's notice.

Chapter 6

Overcoming Deadly Dilemmas

. . . .

. . . .

*I*f you're tempted to skip over this chapter, which deals with reshaping perceptions, go ahead and fly by – just as long as you're no older than 35 and have five years of experience that precisely matches the requirements for a job that you want. Otherwise, sit down, read up, and get ready to fight your corner.

This chapter spotlights major CV components that need spin control to ward off an early burial for your CV. These components are the quintessential and potential chance-killing perceptions that stem from your age; the abundance of your experience; and the experience that seemingly isn't there when you return to the job market. Other dilemmas include unexplained spaces in your job history, stumbles in the workplace, or physical characteristics.

All the common rejection issues covered in this chapter call for a spot of CV *spin control,* or putting the best face on a perception.

Too Much Experience

Leading off the line-up of CV headaches is the four-letter word that's 10 letters long: *Experience.*

The E word's pejorative status is justified. Not only is inappropriate experience – too much or too little – often the real reason that you're turned down, but it's also too frequently a cover story for villainous rejections that are really based on anything from bias to bad breath.

Too many qualifications or ageism?

A reader who's rounding the 50s curve, writes that his qualifications for a training position are superior but too ample. He explains:

Preoccupation with age seems to be the pattern. I'm rarely called for an interview; when I call after sending a CV in response to an ad or a networking contact, I'm told I'm too experienced for the position – 'You seem to be overqualified.' How can I keep my CV from looking like lavender and old lace?

Ageism is often the subtext behind the *overqualified* objection. Deal with it by limiting your work history to the most recent positions you've held that target the job opening. To avoid seeming too old or too highly paid, limit your related experience to about 15 years for a managerial job and to about 10 years for a technical job. Concerns about how you moved up so fast will arise if you only go back 10 years for a managerial job, but 10 years is believable for a technical job, many of which won't even have been in existence for that long.

What about all your other experience? Leave it in your memory bank. Or if you believe that the older work history adds to your value as a candidate, you can describe it under a heading of *Other Experience* and briefly present it without dates. Figure 6-1 gives an example of a CV that shows recent experience only.

The recent-experience-only spin doesn't work every time, but give it a try – it shows that you're not stuck in a time warp, and it's a better tactic than advertising your age as one that qualifies you for carbon dating.

If the employer is notorious for hiring only young guns, rethink your direction. Try to submit your CV to employers who can take advantage of your expertise, such as a new or expanding company operating in unfamiliar territory. Past experience suggests that even with legislation on your side, you'll still have to work hard to overcome deeply entrenched prejudice.

Fortunately, a new tool has come along in the past several years admirably suited to this purpose: Savvy job hunters now turn to the Internet's discussion groups to check out job leads, to name names of saint and sinner companies, and to ask about company cultures and anti-discriminatory practices. Based on your occupation, you can choose among the many millions of discussion groups available through forums and newsgroups. You may, for example, want to connect with other architects, financial planners, or technical writers. Use the keywords of your target employment field to find specific discussion forums by searching for **discussion forums** on a UK-focused search engine like www.yahoo.co.uk. Make sure you click on UK Only option unless you want to look at US discussion groups, too. If you are interested in US groups, try taking a peek at forumdirectory.net and forumscentral.com.

A bit harder to navigate, but with a complete 20-year archive, Google Groups (http://groups.google.co.uk) allows you to wade through most newsgroups.

What if the overqualified objection is just that and not a veil for age discrimination? The employer legitimately may be concerned that when something better comes along, you'll be out the door like greased lightning.

If you really prefer to take life easier or to have more time to yourself, you can be forthcoming with that fact in your CV's objective. Writing this kind of statement is tricky. You risk coming across as worn-out goods, ready to kick back and listen to babbling brooks while you bank the salary. When you explain your desire to back off an overly stressful workload, balance your words with a counter statement reflecting your energy and commitment, as in the example in Figure 6-2.

Book II

Showcasing Yourself with a StandOut CV

Too much experience in one job

A reader writes:

I've stayed in my current and only job too long. When my company cut thousands of workers, we received outplacement classes. I was told that job overstayers are perceived as lacking ambition, uninterested in learning new things, and too narrowly focused. What can I do about this?

Spin strategy A: Divide your job into modules

Show that you successfully moved up and up, meeting new challenges and accepting ever more responsibility. Divide your job into realistic segments, which you label as Level 1, Level 2, Level 3, and so on. Describe each level as a separate position, just as you would if the levels had been different positions within the same company or with different employers. If your job titles changed as you moved up, your writing task is a lot easier.

RECENT EXPERIENCE ONLY

Work Experience

FEIN AND SONS – Operating from Limehouse, East London.
Sole Proprietor, Broker.

Estate agent, development, asset management, and consulting. Specialising in eight-and nine-figure acquisitions, shopping centres, and commercial space, obtaining entitlements and economic analysis. Personal volume: over £30 million.

SONNHAARD LTD. – Canary Wharf, London. 2000-20XX.
Marketing Manager.

Real estate development corporation. Primary project: Playa del Sol, a residential development on Spain's Costa Daurada. Sourced architect, designers, and contractors. Limited liability company built 60 custom luxury homes by architect Jacques Donnaeu of Toulouse. Supervised 10 sales representatives. Sales gross exceeded £10 million, selling 58 homes ahead of project schedule by six months.

EUROPEAN CONFEDERATION OF ESTATE AGENTS – London. 1992-2000. **Executive Vice President.**

International trade association with 190 member companies, 15 affiliated organisations, and 300 service members who provide goods and services to members. Annual convention attended by over 2,000 executives. Responsible for creating formal information-sharing programme and database on local and pan-European real estate legislation. Increased membership by 200%, administering seven-figure budget, with staff of five professionals.

Other Experience

• BBH & Co., **Executive Vice President.** Administered six-figure budget and supervised 27 managers. Directed recruitment and marketing activities.

• CSU Manchester, **Development Director.** Managed £10 million project to expand university campus grounds by 30%. Maintained campus construction budget within promised budgetary and time constraints, including contracting and materials.

• TRADE ALTERNATIVE, **Commercial Properties Manager.** Marketed, leased, and acquired £300,000 in commercial property. Catered to such upmarket clientele as high-end law firms.

Figure 6-1:
Focusing on recent experiences is an effort to avoid the problem of being seen as too old.

Figure 6-2:
This positive CV statement shows that, although you no longer want a leadership role, you still want to be a productive employee.

> Energetic and work-focused, but no longer enjoy frenzied managerial responsibility; seek a challenging non-managerial position.

Spin strategy B: Deal honestly with job titles

If your job title never changed, should you just make up job titles? *No.* The only truthful way to inaugurate fictional job titles is to parenthetically introduce them as 'equivalent to . . .' Suppose that you're an accountant and have been in the same job for 25 years. Your segments might be titled like this:

- Level 3 (equivalent to supervising accountant)
- Level 2 (equivalent to senior accountant)
- Level 1 (equivalent to accountant)

To mitigate the lack of being knighted with increasingly senior job titles, fill your CV with references to your continuous salary increases and bonuses and the range of job skills you mastered. In a world in which people are often rewarded with grandiose titles instead of pay rises or responsibility, the fact that you have been rewarded with more solid benefits may speak well of you.

Spin strategy C: Tackle deadly perceptions head-on

Diminish any perception that you became fat and lazy while staying in the same job too long by specifically describing open-ended workdays: 'Worked past 8 pm at least once a week throughout employment.'

Derail the perception you don't want to learn new things by being specific in describing learning adventures: 'Attended six terms of word-processing technologies; currently enrolled in adult education program to master latest software.'

Discount the perception that you're narrowly focused by explaining that, although your employment address didn't change, professionally speaking, you're widely travelled in terms of outside seminars, professional associations, and reading.

Spin strategy D: When nothing works, try something new

When you have followed these recommendations note for note but are still sitting out the dance, take a chance on something new.

Highlight the issue

In a departure from the normal practice of omitting from your CVs reasons for leaving a job, consider indicating why you're making a change after all this time.

Neutralise the issue burning in every employer's mind: 'Why now? Why after all these years are you on the market? Excessed out? Burned out?' If the question isn't asked, that doesn't mean it isn't hanging out in the recruiter's mind. Even though you may be seen as a mouldering antique, reveal yourself as interested in current developments by adding this kind of phrase in your objective:

Focusing on companies and organisations with contemporary viewpoints

In an even more pioneering move to solve the same problem, create a whole new section at the tail of your CV, headed *Bright Future,* with a statement such as the one in Figure 6-3.

Figure 6-3:
This add-on may make the difference between being perceived as stodgy and unambitious and being seen as dynamic and experienced.

BRIGHT FUTURE
Layoffs springing from a new management structure give me the welcomed opportunity to accept new responsibilities and bring a fresh challenge to my work life.

Consider contract work

An employer's perception of highly experienced people may be that they're too rigid and hold expectations that the new environment will replicate the old – a perception that assassinates their job prospects.

Sometimes, going the extra mile to prove you're dynamic and experienced, as well as generous and forward-looking, still doesn't generate job offers. This is particularly true for professionals over 40 in technical fields.

An example from a reader:

'I have a PhD in physics and more than 20 years of computer programming experience, including Fortran, C/C++, ADA, HTML, and Java. At my own substantial expense, I'm currently completing a year's course work in Cobol, Visual Basic, Web-page administration, and advanced LAN theory.'

The reader laments that he hasn't had a nibble on a job interview. Yes, he's tried the work experience remedy.

'I enrolled for work experience, but after I donated 40 hours to the company, building five computers for free for them, the company pulled out of the programme, negating a verbal agreement to give me hands-on experience. Because I have a doctorate, almost routinely I'm asked, 'Why would you want to be a programmer?' The implication is that I'm overqualified. The reality is that ageism is alive and well, and employers are unwilling to pay for senior talent.'

In such cases, we advise seasoned personnel to consider contract work. For contract work, start your CV with a keyword profile and include as many skills as you legitimately can.

You can find other ideas of how technical personnel can surmount 'over-qualified' objections and age discrimination on Web sites such as Math and Engineering Links (www.phds.org). More UK-specific sources of help, include the Campaign Against Age Discrimination in Employment (CAADE) which you can contact at www.caade.net. There's also a guide to the relevant legislation at The Employers Forum on Age – a body campaigning for 'an age diverse workforce' in the UK (www.efa.org.uk). For the government line on encouraging age diversity, there's also Age Positive, which has advice on job seeking as well as useful links (www.agepositive.gov.uk).

> **Book II**
>
> **Showcasing Yourself with a StandOut CV**

Too Long Gone: For Women Only

A woman re-entering the world of work still has it tough. Usually, Mum's the one who puts her career on hold to meet family responsibilities. When she tries to re-enter the job market, by choice or economic necessity, she feels as though she's been living on another planet, as this letter shows:

Employers don't want to hire women if they've been mothers and out of the market for more than a year or two. You know what, for the last 10 years, I've worked my rear-end off! Don't they understand that? Doesn't intelligence, willingness to work hard, creativity, attention to detail, drive, efficiency, grace under pressure, initiative, leadership, persistence, resourcefulness, responsibility, teamwork, and a sense of humour mean anything these days?

Every characteristic that this reader mentions is still a hot ticket in the job market, but the burden is on mothers to interpret these virtues as marketable skills.

- ✔ Grace under pressure, for example, translates to *crisis manager,* a valuable person when the electricity fails in a computer-driven office.

- ✔ Resourcefulness translates to *office manager,* who is able to ward off threatening calls from credit collection agencies.

- ✔ A sense of humour translates to *data communications manager,* who can cajole a sleepy technical whiz into reporting for work at two in the morning for emergency repair of a satellite hovering over Europe.

You can't, of course, claim those job titles on your CV, but you can make equivalency statements: 'Like a crisis manager, I've had front-line experience handling such problems as electrical failures, including computer crashes.'

If you're a returning woman, develop a StandOut CV, like the one shown in Figure 6-4, that connects what you can do with what an employer wants done using the tips in the following sections.

Look back in discovery

Review your worksheets (see Book II, Chapter 7) to spot transferable skills that you gained in volunteer, civic, hobby, and domestic work. Scout for adult and continuing education, both on campus and in non-traditional settings.

Re-examine the informative television programs that you've watched, the news magazines that you've monitored. Go to the library and read business magazines and trade journals to make a lexicon of up-to-date words, such as 'Please compare my skills' and not 'I'm sure you will agree'.

REENTRY

JOY R. NGUYEN
12 Watt Road, Northampton, Northants, NN40TJ   01933 456 123

SUMMARY OF EXPERIENCE
More than five years' experience in event-planning, fundraising, administration, and publicity. More than nine years' experience in administration for retail and manufacturing firms. B.A. in Business IT with Human Resource Management.

NONPROFIT/VOLUNTEER SERVICE

2002-Present   **Wellingborough Women's Association, Wellingborough**
                    Membership Committee Chair
Planning, organising programs, exhibits and events to recruit association members. Coordinated annual new member events.

1994-2002   **Northants Telephone Samaritans**
                 Member, Board of Directors and Executive Committee
Spearheaded expansion of Telephone Samaritans organsiation. Designed programs, procedures, and policies, monitoring trustees in the conversion of a £1 million switchboard and greeting rooms facility. Led £75 million fundraising campaign.

- **Fundraising Chair**, 1994-1996, Raised funds for entire construction project, establishing hundreds of donors and supervising project. Sourced contractors and directed fundraising activities, using strong interpersonal and networking skills.

HOME MANAGEMENT EXPERIENCE

- **Scheduling**: Assisted business executive and two children in the scheduling of travel and 16,000 miles of transportation. Arranged ticketing, negotiated finances of £5,000 in travel expenses.
- **Conflict Resolution**: Arbitrated personal, business issues. Effective interpersonal skills.
- **Relocation**: Took care of the relocation of entire family, coordinating moving services, trucks, and packing schedules.
- **Budget & Purchasing**: Managed family finances, including budgeting, medical, dental insurance packages, two home purchases, three car purchases, expenses and taxes. Developed financial skills.

ADDITIONAL PROFESSIONAL EXPERIENCE

1994-1996   **Sunrise Books, Northampton**
                 Assistant Manager, Sales Representative
Managed daily operations of coffee house and bookshop, managing a staff of 11. Supervised entire floor of merchandise and stock. Purchased all support goods.

- Spearheaded store's first sales campaign, resulting in tripled sales.
- Designed system for inventory analysis, streamlining purchasing and display control.
- Redirected staff duties for more effective work hours.
- Promoted from sales to supervisor in 38 days; three months later to asst. mgr.

EDUCATION
Bachelor of Arts (Hons), Business Information Technology with Human Resource Management, 1994, Coventry University

Figure 6-4:
A sample CV showcasing the skills of a domestic specialist re-entering the work world.

Book II

Showcasing Yourself with a StandOut CV

Avoid tired words like *go-getter* and *upwardly mobile.* Yesteryear's buzzwords, such as *management by objective* and *girl Friday* won't do a thing to perk up your image, and will, in fact, make you look as old as Rosalind Russell – the original girl Friday.

In recounting civic and volunteer work, avoid the weak verbs: *worked with* or *did this or that.* Instead say, *collaborated with.* What other strong verbs can you think of to sound more businesslike? Try taking a look at Book II, Chapter 5 for inspiration.

Incorporate professional terms

The use of professional words can help de-emphasise informal training or work experience. But you must be careful when doing this to show good judgement about the work world.

Professionalising your domestic experience is a tightrope walk: Ignoring it leaves you looking like a missing person, yet you can't be pretentious or naive. Don't say *housewife;* say *family manager.* Be very wary of using the word *domestic* when describing what you do because the term has been pretty much hijacked and tends to conjure up images of Nigella Lawson. Refer to *home management* to minimise gaps in time spent as a homemaker, and be sure to fill the home management period with transferable skills relevant to the targeted position.

Delve into what you did during your home management period. You did not hold a paid job, but you did do important unpaid work. Dissect your achievements to find your deeds – they can be impressive. Examples range from time management (developing the ability to do more with less time) to budgeting experience (developing a sophisticated understanding of priority allocation of financial resources). Other examples include using the telephone in drumming up support for a favourite charity (developing confidence and a businesslike telephone technique) and leadership positions in school committees (developing a sense of authority and the ability to guide others).

Despite more than three decades of media attention to skills developed by homemakers, employers continue to be dismissive of parenting and other abilities acquired inside the home. Many employers believe that identifying yourself as a domestic specialist is no more workplace-useful than claiming to be a 'seasoned husband' or 'experienced friend'.

Make your homemaker skills difficult to disrespect by showing their relevance to a given career field. Be careful to avoid sounding as though you attended a workshop where you memorised big words, however.

Selected home-based skills

Don't overlook these skills that you may have acquired inside the home. We've included a few examples of occupations in which they can be used. This illustration assumes that you lack formal credentials for professional-level work. If you do have the credentials, upgrade the examples to the appropriate job level.

- ✔ **Juggling schedules:** Paraprofessional assistant to business executives, physicians. Small service business operator, dispatching staff of technicians.

- ✔ **Peer counselling:** Human resources department employee benefits assistant. Substance abuse programme manager.

- ✔ **Arranging social events:** Party shop manager. Non-profit organisation fund-raiser. Art gallery employee.

- ✔ **Conflict resolution:** Administrative assistant. Customer service representative. School secretary.

- ✔ **Problem-solving:** Any job.

- ✔ **Decorating:** Interior decorator. Interior fabric shop salesperson.

- ✔ **Nursing:** Medical or dental office assistant.

- ✔ **Solid purchasing judgement:** Purchasing agent. Materials buyer.

- ✔ **Planning trips, relocations:** Travel agent. Corporate employee relocation co-ordinator.

- ✔ **Communicating:** Any job.

- ✔ **Shaping budgets:** Office manager. Department head. Accounting clerk.

- ✔ **Maximising interior spaces:** Commercial-office real estate agent. Business furniture store operator.

Book II

Showcasing Yourself with a StandOut CV

Whatever you do, you can't ignore the issue – like where have you been for the past few years? When you lack skills developed outside the home in community work, you have to do the best you can to pull out home-based skills.

The WorkingMums Web site (www.workingmums.co.uk) specialises in advertising job vacancies for mothers returning to the workforce, both part- and full-time.

Use years or use dates – not both

Some advisers suggest that, in referring to your home management years, you use a *years-only approach* and list years, not dates, as in Figure 6-5, to avoid the gap in paid work experience.

Figure 6-5:
Examples
of the
years-only
approach
to list
household
manage-
ment skills.

•   *Family Care 10 years*
Child care, home operations, budgeting, and support for a family of four. Participation in
parent/school relations, human services, and religious organisation

---

•   *Leadership Positions*
Vice President, St. Aidan's County High School PTA; Chair, Fund-Raising, Carlisle Oxfam
shops; Subcommittee Chair, Budget Committee, First Baptist Church

---

This approach is unlikely to make a favourable impression on a person who
hires often. Employment professionals prefer concrete facts and dates. But
the years-only CV can work at small businesses where the hiring manager
also wears several other hats and doesn't pay much attention to hiring
guidelines.

Don't make the mistake of using both forms on the same CV, assigning dates
to your paid jobs but only years to your homemaker work.

Know the score

Gender bias lives, and, of course, you should omit all information that the
employer isn't entitled to, including your age, marital status, physical condition, number and ages of children, and husband's name. Even though the law
is on your side, in today's interview-rationed job market, your CV must qualify you more than the next applicant. If you've been out of the job market for
some years, you have to work harder and smarter to show that you're a hot
hire. To help in your quest, seek out seminars and services offered to women
re-entering the job market.

Job Seekers with Disabilities

As it stands, British law states that any employer with over 15 employees is
legally bound to give disabled workers the same rights as their able-bodied
colleagues. That covers any part of the employment process, including job
interviews, career development, and promotion. As part of this, the employer
must try to accommodate the disabled by changing work hours where

necessary, arranging relevant training, and physically changing the work-space for accessibility where required. Of course every case is different, and some disabilities will rule out suitability for certain types of jobs, but grey areas like these can be tackled case by case with a bit of help. The Disability Rights Commission (DRC) is there to help you, and your local job centre should have a Disability Employment Adviser (DEA) to talk to about potential problems. You can also find a helpful overview of the Disability Discrimination Act at `www.disability.gov.uk` and further help from the Advisory, Conciliation, and Arbitration Service (ACAS) at `www.acas.org.uk`.

To find out whether you're covered by existing disability discrimination legislation, take a look at the definition of disabled at the Disability Rights Commission (DRC) Web site (`www.drc-gb.org`) or phone them. A confidential advice service, the Benefit Enquiry Line for People with Disabilities, is also available on 0800 882200.

Book II

Showcasing Yourself with a StandOut CV

The DRC watches your back to prevent discrimination based on your disability, but recruiters may still weasel around the law to avoid what they perceive as a liability. Use street smarts: When you can't win and you can't break even, change the game. In your game, spin control begins with choosing whether to disclose your disability on your CV. Use these tips:

- ✔ **If your disability is visible, the best time to disclose it is after the interview has been set and you telephone to confirm the arrangements.** Pass the message in passing: 'Because I use a wheelchair for mobility, I was wondering if you can suggest which entrance to your building would be the most convenient?'

- ✔ **Alternatively, you may want to reserve disclosure for the interview – it's a personal judgement call and while it is illegal for a potential employer to discriminate against you on the basis of a disability this is a less than perfect world.** Some people prefer not to give employers any extra time in which to dwell on the disability before having the chance to meet the abled part of the package.

- ✔ **If your disability is not visible, such as mental illness or epilepsy, you need not disclose it unless you'll need special accommodations.** Even then, you can hold the disclosure until the negotiating stage once you've received a potential job offer.

No matter what you decide to do, be confident, unapologetic, unimpaired, and attitude-positive.

Gaps in Your Record

Periods of unemployment leave black holes in your work history. Should you (A) fill them with positive expressions such as *family obligations,* (B) fill them with less positive but true words such as *unemployed,* or (C) show the gap without comment?

Choosing B, *unemployed,* is dreary. Forget that! Choosing C, *leave-it-blank-and-say-nothing,* often works – you just hope that it isn't noticed. My choice, however, is A: Tell the truth about what you were doing but spin it in a dignified, positive way. A few examples: 'independent study', 'foreign travel', and 'career renewal through study and assessment'.

An infoblizzard of tips has been published on how to repair CV holes. Unless you were building an underground tunnel to smuggle drugs, the principles are simple:

- ✔ Present the time gap as a positive event.

- ✔ Detail why it made you a better worker – not a better *person,* but a better worker with more favourable characteristics, polished skills, and mature understanding, all of which you're dying to contribute to your new employer.

How can these principles be applied? Take the case of a student who dropped out of college to play in a band and do odd jobs for four years before coming back to finish his biology degree and look for a job. The student knows that employers may perceive him as uncommitted. In the CV, he should treat the band years like any other job: Describe the skills that were polished as a band leader. Identify instances of problem solving, teamwork, leadership, and budgeting.

You do the real problem solving in the cover letter that accompanies such a CV, as for example in Figure 6-6.

Figure 6-6: Excerpt explaining a job gap in a cover letter.

After completing two years of undergraduate study, it was necessary for me to work to continue my education. Using my talents as a musician, I organised a band and after four years was able to continue my education. I matured and learned much about the real world and confirmed that an education is extremely important in fulfilling my career goals.

Fudging the dates

Recent employment surveys in the UK have revealed that 50 per cent of all CVs submitted by job applicants contained at least one falsehood, and a staggering one in five CVs contained 'significant' inaccuracies. The report found that discrepancies about employees' accurate employment dates were the most common lies.

The chief mistake people make is assuming that a positive explanation won't sell. Instead, they fudge dates from legitimate jobs to cover the black holes. You may get away with it in the beginning. But ultimately, you'll be asked to sign a formal application, a legal document. If you haven't been entirely frank or up front, then those fudges may come back to haunt you. In the event of a company wanting to dump staff without paying severance benefits, the first thing they'll do is check for those they can claim got their positions under false pretences. Lies on applications, even if they surface years into a subsequent career, can be used by a cynical company to save money on severance. Lying isn't worth the risk – it's a mistake.

Another method of papering-over glaring gaps is to include all your work under 'Work History' and cite unpaid and volunteer work as well as paid jobs.

Suppose that you've been unemployed for the past year. That's a new black hole. Some advisers suggest the old dodge of allowing the recruiter to misperceive the open-ended date of employment for your last job: '2000–' as though you meant '2000–Present'. The open-ender solution often works – until you run into a reader who thinks that it's way too calculating.

Black holes are less obvious in a functional format, as discussed in Book II, Chapter 3. *If you can't find a positive explanation for a black hole, say nothing.*

If you possess a not-so-pristine past, stick with small employers who probably won't check every date on your CV.

Resources to Solve Many Dilemmas

The array of CV dilemmas known to humankind is too long, too challenging, and too complex to comprehensively chronicle in this dollop of space.

Book II

Showcasing Yourself with a StandOut CV

The consultant/entrepreneur gap

Professional and managerial job seekers are routinely advised to explain black holes by saying that they were consultants or that they owned small businesses. Not everyone can be a consultant, and there's substantial risk in the small-business explanation.

If it should happen to be true that you were a consultant, name your clients and give a glimmer of the contributions you made to each. If you really had a small business, remember: Employers worry that you'll be too independent to do things their way or that you'll stay just long enough to learn their business and go into competition against them. Strategic antidotes: Search for a business owner who is within eyeshot of retirement and wouldn't mind your continuing the business and paying him or her a monthly pension. CV antidotes: Describe yourself as 'manager', not 'CEO' or 'president', and if you have time, rename your business something other than your own name: 'River's End Associates' not 'Theresa Bronz, Ltd'.

The topic of strategies for ex-offenders, for instance, needs its own book to adequately address this issue. Fortunately, there are a few people out there to help. For advice on job hunting with a less than desirable record, try getting in touch with the Apex Trust, which aims to promote employment opportunities for ex-offenders. You can find the Apex Trust at www.apextrust.com or call on 0870 608 4567.

Spin Control Is in the Details

A white ruffled blouse stained only slightly with one dab of spaghetti sauce is 99 percent clean. But every person who sees you wearing it at a public event remembers the red spot, not the white part of the blouse. Similarly, you can have a 99 percent StandOut CV, but any one of the deadly perceptions identified in this chapter can ice it without your knowing why. Practice spin control – present possible negative perceptions in a flattering light.

A positive explanation goes a long way in overcoming a CV land mine. It doesn't work all the time, but it works some of the time, and all you need – for now – is one good offer to hit the job jackpot.

Omit inappropriate data

The best way to handle some land mines on your CV is to ignore them. Generally, revealing negative information on a CV is a mistake. Save troublemaking information for the all-important job interview, where you have a fighting chance to explain your side of things.

Stay away from these topics when constructing a CV:

- Firings, demotions, forced resignations, and early termination of contracts
- Personal differences with co-workers or supervisors
- Bankruptcy, tax evasion, or credit problems
- Criminal convictions or lawsuits
- Homelessness
- Illnesses from which you have now recovered
- Disabilities that don't prevent you from performing the essential functions of the job, with or without some form of accommodation

Should you ever give reasons for leaving a job? In most instances, CV silence in the face of interview-killing facts is still the strategy of choice. But the time has come to rethink at least one special issue: losing a job.

Now that jobs are shed like so many autumn leaves, losing a job is no longer viewed as a case of personal failure. It may be to your advantage to state on your CV why you left your last position, assuming that it was not due to poor work performance on your part. If you were downsized out, the recruiter may appreciate your straightforward statement, 'Job eliminated in downsizing.'

But remember, if you elect to say why you lost one job, for consistency, you have to say why you left all your jobs – such as for greater opportunity, advancement, and the like.

Book II

Showcasing Yourself with a StandOut CV

Chapter 7

Moving from Worksheets to Your Finished CV

. . . .

In This Chapter

▶ Focusing on what you want and do not want

▶ Sizing up your education and training

▶ Examining your skills and competencies

▶ Writing worksheets, summaries, and asset statements

▶ Producing great-looking CVs

. . . .

*1*f there were a Grand Prix pit crew to fine-tune your CV in this modern age, it would consist of you, you, and you.

That is, everything in your StandOut CV starts with what you want and can do, and how effectively you write it down. This chapter helps you do exactly that by guiding you through the compilation of three self-discovery documents. You work through this task in the following three steps:

1. **Detailed worksheets on which you write all employment-related aspects of your life to date.**

2. **Summary worksheets on which you write key information drawn from your detailed worksheets.**

3. **Asset statements (power-packed self-marketing statements drawn from your summary worksheets), which you can use to open your CV or cover letter with a flourish.**

Step 1: The Detailed Worksheets

The worksheets in this chapter are your first line of defence against repeating sour experiences in your previous jobs, and they also help you to reincarnate cherished experiences in your future jobs. If you haven't held a job before, this chapter can help guide you to the kind of position that you'll most appreciate.

Think of the worksheets in this chapter as a kind of Swiss Army Knife, giving you the tools to get in touch with your innermost thoughts and desires about the following:

- ✔ The real reasons you left previous jobs
- ✔ Beneficial transferable lessons you learned in previous jobs
- ✔ The components that you really must have in a job to be happy
- ✔ The skills and responsibilities that you most enjoy using
- ✔ The skills and responsibilities that you never want to use again

Knowing what you have to offer

You can't present the best of yourself until you have a handle on the goods and that means a lot more than simply listing your better points and looking for inspiration in your successes.

William Bolitho, a writer and journalist for what was then *The Manchester Guardian,* pretty much summed it up when he exclaimed: 'The most important thing in life is not to capitalise on your gains. Any fool can do that. The really important thing is to profit from your losses.'

On these pages you get a chance not only to capitalise on your gains but also to profit from your losses in your chosen career. Make copies of the New Job Worksheet, which begins on the next page, for each job you want to review.

If, at the end, you think that maybe your chosen career was the problem then back up and pursue the issue of career choice in *Changing Careers For Dummies,* by Carol L McClelland, PhD (Wiley).

New Job Worksheet

(Photocopy and complete one worksheet for each relevant job.)

Reasons for Leaving Job

Employer: _____ From:_____(Year) To:_____(Year)

What did you most like about your job here, and why did you apply for it in
the first place? _____

_____

_____

_____

_____

_____

_____

What did you most dislike about your job here? _____

_____

_____

_____

_____

_____

Why did you choose to leave (pay, title, no promotion, unfulfilling)? _____

_____

_____

_____

_____

_____

Book II

**Showcasing
Yourself with
a StandOut CV**

Areas of Highest Performance

Of the skills you used here, which gave you the most satisfaction (give example)? Why? _____

_____

_____

_____

_____

_____

Of the duties, which made you feel your best? Why? _____

_____

_____

_____

_____

_____

Which skills and responsibilities would you like to use in your next job? __

_____

_____

_____

_____

_____

What You Never Want to Do Again

Of the skills you used here, which were the least fulfilling? _____

_____

_____

_____

_____

Which tasks did you dread most? Why? _____

_____

_____

_____

_____

Your Most Attractive Attributes

In your leisure activities, which competencies and skills have you used that

can transfer to your next job? _____

_____

_____

_____

_____

Book II

**Showcasing
Yourself with
a StandOut CV**

Note: Don't bother writing a summary of this exercise; its message will be indelible in your mind.

Working the worksheets

Each worksheet that follows looks at your life in a wide-angle, rear-view mirror and then narrows the focus by suggesting that you target the most useful and vital accomplishments and competencies.

Many people lose the CV derby because they merely report where they have worked and enumerate the duties they were assigned. That information alone won't roll over the competition. You need to provide effective answers to the following questions:

- ✔ What did you accomplish?
- ✔ What value and competencies did you bring to a specific position?
- ✔ What did it matter that you showed up at the office most days?
- ✔ How have you put your education to work?
- ✔ What good has your education done anyone?

Harried career? Use worksheets to rethink your direction

Do you find yourself working too many hours a week and neglecting other parts of your life – friends, family, hobbies, community, and spiritual activities?

Women are especially prone to burnout from the work-go-round grind of rising early, struggling through the day, falling asleep wondering how they'll get it all done, and then getting up again the next morning and starting all over.

Do you really want a career change?

If you're overwhelmed and overworked, the worksheets in this chapter can help you with more than CV preparation. You may be ripe for a career change – or a flexible work schedule, telecommuting, or starting your own business.

Use the worksheets as a diary for discovery.

Use these worksheets to fuel an introspective look at who you are and where you've been. Think of them as a kind of work/life diary to identify the experiences you most enjoyed and did well at, as well as those you never want to repeat.

The personal inventory you create in these worksheets can take you a long way toward identifying solutions to a work/life dilemma that's eating away at your happiness. You may realise that you really don't want a career that's all-consuming – you want one with more balance. The personal inventory you create for CVs also serves as a straightforward tool to guide you toward a more fulfilling future.

The *identification* and *measurement* of *results, outcomes,* and *achievements* are what make recruiters book you for interviews.

Begin your personal inventory now. Fill out these worksheets, which appear on the following pages:

- ✔ **Education and Training Worksheet:** This worksheet outlines your education and training experiences.

- ✔ **Paid Work Worksheet** and **Unpaid Work Worksheet:** These worksheets help you identify your competencies, knowledge, and abilities.

- ✔ **Hobbies/Activities-to-Skills Worksheet:** This worksheet helps you translate your hobbies and activities to skills that employers look for.

- ✔ **Employability Skills Worksheet:** This worksheet helps you identify your personal characteristics.

Education and Training Worksheet

Name of institution/program _____

Address/Telephone _____

Year(s) attended or graduated _____

Degree/diploma/certificate_____

Class rank (if known) _____

Work-relevant study

(Photocopy and complete one worksheet for each relevant course.)

Course_____

Knowledge acquired_____

_____

_____

Skills acquired _____

_____

Accomplishments (with concrete examples) _____

_____

Relevant projects/papers; honours _____

_____

Keywords/StandOut words_____

Quotable remarks by others (names, contact data) _____

_____

_____

Book II

Showcasing Yourself with a StandOut CV

Paid Work Worksheet

(Photocopy and complete one worksheet for each job.)

Name of employer _____

Postal address, e-mail address, telephone _____

_____

_____

_____

Type of business/career field _____

Job title_____ Dates _____

Direct supervisor's name, contact information (if good reference; otherwise,

note co-workers or sources of good references) _____

_____

_____

_____

Major accomplishments (Promotion? Awards? Business achievements –

'increased sales by 30 percent' or 'saved company 12 percent on office pur-

chases'? What credit can you claim for creating, implementing, revamping,

designing, saving? Jog your memory by recalling problems faced and action

taken.) _____

_____

_____

_____

Problems faced _____

_____

_____

Action taken _____

_____

_____

_____

Skills acquired _____

_____

_____

_____

Knowledge/abilities acquired _____

_____

_____

_____

Job responsibilities _____

_____

_____

_____

Keywords/StandOut words _____

_____

_____

_____

_____

Quotable remarks by others (names, contact data) _____

_____

_____

_____

_____

Unpaid Work Worksheet

(Photocopy and complete one worksheet for each relevant unpaid job.)

Name of employer   _____

Type of organisation   _____

Volunteer job title   _____Dates _____

Direct supervisor's name, contact information _____

_____

Major accomplishments (What credit can you claim for creating, implementing, revamping, designing, saving? Jog your memory by recalling problems
faced and action taken.) _____

_____

_____

_____

Problems faced _____

Action taken _____

Skills acquired _____

Knowledge/abilities acquired_____

Keywords/StandOut words_____

Quotable remarks by others (names, contact data) _____

_____

_____

_____

Hobbies/Activities-to-Skills Worksheet

(Photocopy and complete one worksheet for each relevant work-related activity.)

Name of hobby, organisation, club (location)_____

Dates _____

Title/position (officer/member) _____

Elected (yes/no) _____

Accomplishments _____

_____

_____

_____

Work-related skills acquired _____

_____

_____

Knowledge/abilities acquired_____

_____

_____

Keywords/StandOut words_____

_____

_____

Quotable remarks by others (names, contact data) _____

_____

_____

_____

Book II

Showcasing Yourself with a StandOut CV

Employability Skills Worksheet

(Photocopy and complete one worksheet for each relevant position.)

Name of company/supervisor _____

Aspects of your work ethic that the employer appreciated _____

_____

_____

Example _____

Facets of your personality that the employer valued _____

_____

_____

Example _____

Name of co-worker/client/industry contact _____

Aspects of your work ethic that the person appreciated_____

_____

_____

Example _____

Facets of your personality that the person valued _____

_____

_____

Example _____

Keywords/StandOut words_____

_____

_____

Step 2: The Summary Worksheets

The worksheets you filled out in the preceding section are rich in raw material for the worksheet summaries in your next step toward a glorious StandOut CV. On your worksheet summaries, highlight the data that most clearly show how well you qualify for the job (or jobs) you desire.

Photocopy the blank Summary Worksheet and fill out one copy for each job that catches your eye. In the left column, jot down what the employer wants. You obtain this information from job ads, job descriptions, and occupational literature. If you're working with a recruiter, the data should be easy to get.

In the right column, drawing from your worksheets, make note of how well you fill the bill. How good is the fit between each requirement and your qualification?

When the job calls for specific skills, an employer doesn't necessarily care how or where you obtained the requisite skills in the summary worksheet, so the headings in the left column merely say Skills Required.

By contrast, the headings in the right column of the summary worksheet correspond to other worksheets in this chapter. They are noted specifically as yet another reminder to include your skills obtained from any source, paid or unpaid.

The more successful you are at tailoring your CV to fit a specific job, the more likely you are to be in the final running.

Summary Worksheet

The Employer Wants ➡ You Have

Education and Training Required	Education and Training Skills Including Achievements
1)	
2)	
3)	
4)	
5)	
6)	
7)	
8)	
9)	
10)	
Skills/Knowledge/Abilities Required (Competencies)	**Paid** Skills/Knowledge/Abilities
1)	
2)	
3)	
4)	
5)	
6)	
7)	
8)	
9)	
10)	

Summary Worksheet

The Employer Wants ➡ You Have

Skills/Knowledge/Abilities Required (Competencies)	**Unpaid** Skills/Knowledge/Abilities
1)	
2)	
3)	
4)	
5)	
Skills/Knowledge/Abilities Required (Competencies)	Hobby/Activity Skills Including Achievements
1)	
2)	
3)	
4)	
5)	
Employability Skills Required (Personal Characteristics)	Employability Skills Including Achievements
1)	
2)	
3)	
4)	
5)	

(2 of 2)

Book II

Showcasing Yourself with a StandOut CV

Step 3: Drafting Asset Statements

To open a CV or cover letter, you may want to use an *asset statement*. An asset statement is essentially a skills summary – although other ingredients of competencies can be inserted, specifically your knowledge, abilities, and personal characteristics. An asset statement is known by many names in the recruiting industry. Some of these other names are:

- ✔ Highlights statement
- ✔ Keyword summary (or profile)
- ✔ Marketing summary
- ✔ Objective summary
- ✔ Power summary
- ✔ Professional history capsule
- ✔ Profile section
- ✔ Qualifications summary
- ✔ Synopsis

The asset statement typically contains the three to five best skills (sales points) that support your job aspiration. The exception to this definition is the keyword profile, which uses a listing (rather than sentences) of virtually all the relevant skills you possess.

The data in your asset statement need not be proven with examples in this brief section – for now, it stands alone as assertions. In effect, you are saying, 'Here's who I am. Here's what I can do for you.' This is a tease, encouraging the reader to hang in there for proof of what the opening claims.

The information you've written in the previous worksheets paves the way for your powerful asset statements. Figure 7-1 gives you examples of power-packed asset statements.

Human Resources manager

Well-rounded experience in all human resource functions. Focus: Benefits and Staff Relations. Managed an HR staff of 200,000-population city. Reputation for progressive programmes attractive to both city and employees.

Marketing account executive

Award-winning marketer with impressive performance record in Internet merchandising. Proficient in international conventions and customs. Attentive to details while focusing on the big picture. Excellent at organising, tracking, and managing projects. Relate well to both customers and co-workers.

Book II

Showcasing Yourself with a StandOut CV

Construction manager

General construction-manager experience covers all areas: start-up and financing, site selection, building design, and construction. Hire and train. Work ahead of schedules. Rehired several times by same developers.

Communications graduate

Figure 7-1: Asset statements that turbo-charge a CV.

Entry opportunity in print or broadcast news. Completing rigorous communications degree. Work experience as editorial associate in newspaper columnist's office, achieved top performance review; editor of college newspaper; instructor of adult students at writing lab.

Why you need asset statements

An asset statement opens your CV with a bang but provides several other benefits as well:

- ✔ **Summary page:** Asset statements can be expanded to an entire summary page, which you place atop a reverse chronological CV (in effect turning your reverse chronological CV into a hybrid CV format, as discussed in Book II, Chapter 3).

- ✔ **Old successes:** An asset statement can revive a fading job achievement. Suppose you have an achievement that took place four or five years ago and is now needed to qualify you for a job. By amplifying the old achievement in a summary statement (and perhaps choosing a functional format for your CV), you don't bury it in a bazaar of your past jobs. When crystallised in a focused power summary, the golden oldie achievement still works for you.

- ✔ **Basis for achievement statements:** Asset statements provide the raw material for achievement sections (paragraphs) and brief (one- or two-line) high-voltage statements that you use later in your CV.

Data in achievement statements must be proven by *examples,* the best of which are *quantified.* Measure, measure, measure!

What's the difference between an asset statement and the achievement statements that are used later in your CV? The difference is that in an *achievement statement*, you should incorporate documentation, or 'storytelling', to authenticate what you're saying. By contrast, *asset statements* are credible without examples or results.

E-Z asset statements

Remember, you don't have to prove what you say right there in the opening statement or summary – but you do have to prove it later in your CV in achievement statements. Here's a collection of fill-in forms to start you off. Just fill in the blanks.

- ✔ After __ (number of years, provided the number is not too high) years in _____ (your occupation), seek opportunity to use extensive experience and _____ (your favourite skills) as a (your target position).

- ✔ Knowledge of (your expertise) and familiarity with _____ (type of product, industry, or clientele). Seek position as _____ (job title) using intensive experience as a _____ (occupation).

✔ Developed new _____ which resulted in increased _____; maintained an aggressive _____ program that increased employer's revenues by __%. Seeking a position as a _____ (your objective) in an organisation needing expertise in _____ (your top skills).

✔ A position as a _____ (a job slightly higher in rank than your top employment), specialising in _____ (a skill unique to you).

✔ A _____ (type of) position that needs _____ (list skills and accomplishments). Demonstrated by _____ (list of paid and volunteer responsibilities and successes). Will _____ (an improvement that your prospective employer appreciates).

✔ Offering _____ (your field) skills in _____ (related industry), with ability to solve _____ (one or more problems common in the field), including _____ (your top skills).

✔ Encyclopaedic knowledge of _____ (your top skills in technical aspects of position), familiarity with _____ (qualifying duties of position), and effective management of _____ (your lesser job-related skills).

Book II

Showcasing Yourself with a StandOut CV

Aim for powerful but true statements

Wait until the next day to review your finished asset statement. Did you get carried away with fantasy writing? Ask yourself, 'Can I live up to this advance billing?' If not, tone it down to reality – that is, your *best reality*. Unfortunately – you smooth writer, you – when you land a job based on hype that you can't back up, you'll be renewing your job search.

After working your way through Step 1 (worksheets), Step 2 (summary worksheets), and Step 3 (asset statements), you're ready to put your keyboard in action, either electronically or on paper. The following tips apply chiefly to paper, but some suggestions apply to formatted online CVs as well.

Write Until It's Right

Can you write a decent CV in nanoseconds? Several CV books on the market sport titles insisting that you can do just about that. Don't be taken in. A well-developed CV requires adequate ripening time to form, mellow, and develop – you must think, write, think some more, rewrite, proof-read, get feedback, and rewrite.

All too many job hunters scatter hundreds of thrown-together CVs. Then they wait. Nothing happens. Why do you think nobody bothers to call with an interview offer? Perhaps thrown-together too often gets thrown out?

If you don't want to be left behind because of a thrown-together CV, write a StandOut CV. It works.

Paper CVs That Resonate

Although the market is moving away from paper CVs toward digital CVs, tree-and-ink products are here for the foreseeable future. Here's how to look outstanding on paper and make the first cut in the employment screening process.

Take the time to make sure your CV is as strong as it can be to attract the employer who has the right job for you. The CV samples in Book II, Chapter 8 can give you a good idea of the variety of clean-cut, appealing CV designs you can adopt.

Word processing

You need a computer equipped with word-processing software to produce your CV. Typewritten copies are still acceptable, but most people don't type well enough to produce crisp, clean, sparkling copies. If word processing is not yet one of your skills, scout out a word-processing class – you'll need this ability in nearly any job you take. In the meantime, find a friend who can key in your CV. If you have the skill but not the tools, can you use a friend's computer? How about a computer at a school's computer lab or career centre, or a Web café, or your local public library? If none of these is possible, take your hand-written CV to a professional office support firm and hire someone to do the production work.

Unemployed people can use computers for free at job centres and libraries across the country.

Printing

Producing your CV on a laser or inkjet printer is today's standard. The old-fashioned dot matrix printers lack the firepower to print CVs that compete in today's job market. If you photocopy a core CV – rather than custom-tailor each CV to the job at hand – make sure that the copies look first-rate. No blurring, stray marks, streaks, or faint letters.

Paper

How good must your paper be? For professional, technical, managerial, and executive jobs, the stock for a paper CV should be quality paper with rag content, perhaps 25 percent, and a watermark (a faint image ingrained in the paper). Office supply stores, small printing firms, and speciality-paper mail-order catalogues offer a wide range of choices. Restrict the colour of your paper to white or off-white, eggshell, or the palest of grey. Print on one side of the sheet only.

The ink on a StandOut CV is evenly distributed across each page, which is best achieved with a smooth paper stock. The image evoked by a high-quality paper is diminished when it looks as though the ink just didn't flow consistently – the print looks alternately dark or faded, may be streaky or smeared. Linen (*textured*) paper is impressive, but the ink from a laser printer or photocopier may not move smoothly across a sheet, making your CV hard to read. Try before you buy. If there's the slightest doubt about readability, switch to laid (*smooth*) paper.

The quality of paper is immaterial when your CV is to be scanned into job computers or spun across the Internet. Hiring managers never see the quality of paper or printing you have selected.

Open spaces

Which style of reading do you prefer: a paper so packed with text that your eyes need a spa treatment before tackling it or a paper so generous with white space that you *want* to read it? Too many people, hearing that they must not exceed one page, try to cram too much information in too little space.

A ratio of about one-quarter white space to text is about right. Line spacing between items is vital. Do not justify the right side of the page – that is, do not try to have the type align down the right side of the page – leave it ragged. Right justification creates awkward white spaces. An overcrowded page almost guarantees that it will not be read by younger recruiters and hiring managers who grew up in an age of television and web pages. And older readers? Their eyes won't take the wear and tear of too many words crashing in too small a space. White space is the master graphic attention-getter.

Typefaces and fonts

A *typeface* is a family of characters – letters, numbers, and symbols. A *font* is a specific size of typeface. Helvetica is a typeface; Helvetica 10-point bold, Helvetica 12-point bold, and Helvetica 14-point bold are three different fonts.

No more than two typefaces should appear on one CV; if you don't have an eye for what looks good, stick to one typeface. Either Times New Roman or Helvetica used alone is a fine choice for your CV. But if you want to mix the two typefaces, we recommend that you choose Helvetica for the headings and Times New Roman for the text and lesser headings.

Paying attention to the spacing of your CV contributes much to its readability. Printing your name in small capital letters can be pleasing. Using larger type for headings (12 or 14 pt.) or boldface can give necessary prominence. Use italics sparingly – you don't want to overdo emphasis, and italicised words lose readability in blocks of text.

Design structure

Your name and contact information can be left aligned, centred, or right aligned. Look at examples in Book II, Chapter 8. Here are some other tips:

- Some recruiters suggest that you type your name right aligned because they thumb through the right-hand corner of CV stacks.

- Aim for a tasteful amount of capitalisation and bold lettering for emphasis.

- Important information jumps in the recruiter's face when set off by bullets, asterisks, and dashes.

- Typos and spelling errors are unacceptable. They are seen as carelessness or a lack of professionalism. It is far better that we have spelling mistakes in this book than you have one in your CV. In the tens of thousands of CVs mistakenly sent to us for review, spelling has, at times, been creative. One man claimed to be *precedent* of his company. Do you think he was a good one? Use your computer's spell-check feature, read your finished CV carefully, and ask a friend to read it also.

- Do not staple together a two- or three-page CV or put it in a folder or plastic insert. The CV may be photocopied and distributed, or it may be scanned into a database. To minimise the risk of a page becoming an orphan, put a simple header atop each page after the first: your name and page number. In a multiple-page CV, you may want to indicate how many pages there are ('page 1 of 2', for example) in case the pages get separated. You can also put the page number at the bottom.

Chapter 8

A Sampling of StandOut CVs

. . . .

In This Chapter

▶ Model CVs for various skill and experience levels

▶ Model CVs for seven different career fields

. . . .

*P*repare to meet the graduates of StandOut boot camp, from entry- to management-level job seekers. Real people wrote the originals of these CVs, but we tore them up and rewrote them to meet StandOut standards. All names and contact information are fictional, but the raw selling power behind every one is real.

Although StandOut formats (illustrated by the templates in Book II, Chapter 3) are loaded with selling-power, they're by no means rigid – not every section heading works for every CV. Choose your section headings carefully to flaunt your strengths.

In the interest of not chopping trees, we chopped material – that is, some CVs in this chapter would have been two pages had we not eliminated text. Occasionally, as another conservation measure, we used ampersands (&) to replace the word *and*. Should you use ampersands on your own CV? Yes, but very gingerly. Ampersands are okay for

- ✔ Company names
- ✔ Copyrights
- ✔ Logos
- ✔ Phrases common in the targeted industry, such as 'P & L Statements' (Profit & Loss)

Otherwise, spell out the word *and*.

This chapter gives you a selection of StandOut model CVs.

ASSISTANT RETAIL MANAGER
ACCOMPLISHMENT/COMPUTER FRIENDLY

> Contact data too
> close together to scan

John Straw

2424 Heavensent Lane, Purley, Surrey CR8 23Z   0208 987 654   E-mail: jstraw@aol.com

OBJECTIVE

Position as **assistant retail manager** using my eight years of experience in retail, technical sales, and software experience.

SUMMARY

- Hard-won and successful experience in many aspects of retailing: sales, marketing, operations, training, and service.

- Can open and manage retail software and other technical products. Qualified as assistant manager of retail store; qualified as department manager of superstore. Managed new retail location ranking in top ten of 64 stores within first year.

- Internet/World Wide Web merchandising start-up study.

> Web merchandising is buzzword:
> "start-up study" means Straw studied
> topic, is ready to implement new selling
> technology for new employer.

HIGHLIGHTS OF SKILLS:

- Opening, operating **new locations**
- **Growing sales**: make **customer-first**
- **Budgeting, extending credit**
- **Recruiting** and interviewing
- **Training** and retraining staff
- **Telemarketing**
- Product display
- Promotion, advertising strategies
- **Software licensing, electronics, purchasing**

- All major **point-of-sale equipment**
- **Computer skills:** PCs and Macs; Excel, Lotus 1-2-3, QuickBooks, Aldus Pagemaker, CAD, CorelDraw, Desktop Publisher, Windows Office including Word
- **Internet skills:** World Wide Web, e-mail, FTP

> Can be made
> computer friendly by
> eliminating vertical
> design lines

PROFESSIONAL EXPERIENCE:

Video Box, Sanderstead, Surrey -- Customer Rep   2003-Present
Customer service, product display, inventory maintenance, video rentals, and returns. "Best help I've had in five years," (Owner Sanderstead Showers).

Custom Names, Warlingham, Surrey -- Consumer Service Representative   2002
Extensive retail sales and technical support for software, computer equipment, satellite TV, electronics, and home theatre equipment. Maintained average monthly sales of £20,000, ranking fourth in sales. Heavy telemarketing component.

The Cutting Edge, Whyteleafe, Surrey -- Assistant Manager   2000-2002
Serviced upscale clientele in high-end software, electronics, and video game shop. Handled sales, purchasing, staff training, work schedules, product inventory and display, technical support for electronics and software, bank deposits, and staff management.

John Straw

Software Bug, South Croydon -- Night Manager   1997-2000
Evening management of software retailer. Innovative sales strategies brought shop from 47th in
sales ranking to 8th in a 64-store chain. Other work: employee recruiting and dismissal,
training, retraining, scheduling, staff management, technical support. Awarded Employee of
Month four separate months.

Temp-a-Medic, West Croydon -- Healthcare Staffer   1996-1997
Matched healthcare temps with hospitals in Croydon and surrounding areas. Developed
organisational skills, calm resilience when chaos threatened, and acceptance of high-pressure,
detail-reliant environment. Sold new accounts at seven hospitals.

EDUCATION
Two-thirds of the way through an Open University Bachelor of Arts degree; expect degree
June 2004.

VOLUNTEER AND PERSONAL EXPERIENCE

– Coach, Warlingham Warlocks Water Polo team. Team drawn from across Surrey of more
than 30 youths, ages 7-12. Grateful for opportunity to develop strong interpersonal, cross-
generational, cross-cultural, and community networks. Proven talent with teamwork,
organisation, people of various economic classes.

– Interests include computers, electronics, water polo, swimming, computer drafting, and
freehand illustration.

> Straw's goal is completion of college degree.
> To indicate intent to enroll for more than 3-6 hours
> per semester while working in retail, noted for long
> hours, would be risky.

Book II

**Showcasing
Yourself with
a StandOut CV**

CHEMIST
PROFESSIONAL/COMPUTER FRIENDLY

DIXON MARBEND
123 Moon Road, Huntingdon, Cambs, PE9 3DF   01223 584-0150

Chemist ←

> Objective replaced with job title, summary follows – personalises the format.

Six years' research experience with increasing responsibility and successful record of instrumentation and scientific achievement. Speciality: Silicon. Designed computer systems (mainframe to micro) for laboratory instrument automation, including patented design. Published presenter.

EDUCATION

- Ph.D., Chemical Design & Engineering, Cambridge University.
  Dissertation: Manipulation of Luminescent Porous Silicon Structures
- Master of Science, Chemistry, Trinity College, Cambridge
- Bachelor of Science (2:1), Physics, Trinity College, Cambridge University

EXPERIENCE AND ACCOMPLISHMENTS

> Quantifies achievements and responsibilities.

2000-present   **Research Assistant, Cambridge University**
- Patented procedure for "Engineering of Luminescent Images on Silicon" and co-authored seven publications (see addendum).
- Conducted research investigations of luminescent silicon and spearheaded procedure for illuminating structures with photoelectricity; managed staff of 5 assistants.
- Delivered 14 presentations of results and research in progress to professors in department.
- Tutored 37 undergraduates in research and chemistry theory, increasing teaching skills.
- Purchased £59,000 in chemicals and equipment for starting research lab.

1999-2000   **Research Assistant, Cambridge University**
- Built non-vibrating 1.5 ton aluminium platform for NMR management.
- Assisted professor with construction of super-conducting NMR spectrometer.
- Designed and manufactured integrated circuits in lab.

> Shows results of achievements.

1999   **Research Assistant, Cambridge University** ←
- Investigated methods for feature distortion in scanning tunnelling microscopy.

> Minimises less relevant jobs.

1998-1999   **Laboratory Assistant, Cambridge University**
- Prepared and maintained delicate equipment and chemicals for chemistry labs, ensuring maximum performance and efficiency.
- Worked with 57 teacher assistants and students, developing training skills.

TECHNICAL SKILLS ←

> Skills section added to format, enhancing abilities and using more KeyWords.

Steady state photoluminescence
Raman, FTIR, and UV-Vis spectroscopy
Inert atmosphere (Schlenk and dry box)
Standard electrochemistry/photochemistry
AFM, STM, and SEM

Machining aluminium and Plexiglas
Macintosh: Word, KaleidaGraph,
Canvas, Aldus PageMaker, MacDraw,
Hypercard, Chem 3D, Excel, Internet

(1 of 2)

DIXON MARBEND
01223 584-0150

PUBLICATIONS

"Engineering of Luminescent Images on Silicon." Marbend, Patent No. 1,234,567; Jan 1, 2003

"Silicon Technology." Saynor and Marbend in *2003 Cambridge University Press Yearbook of Science Technology*; C.U.P. 2003, 123-4

"Optical Cavities in Silicon Film." Saynor, Curbin, and Marbend in *Electrochemic Journal*, 2003, 21

"Emission from Etched Silicon." Marbend and Piner in *Material Research Symposium*, 2002, 12, 3456-7

"Colour Image Generation on Silicon." Marbend and Saynor in *Chemical Science*, 2002, 123, 4567-8

"Porous Silicon Micro-Dension." Marbend and Saynor in *Physics Applied*, 2002, 45, 678-9

"Stoichiometric Cadmium Electrodeposition." Krass and Marbend, *MaterialChem*, 2001, 1, 23

HONOURS, MEMBERSHIPS & PRESENTATIONS

Chemical Symposium Research Fellow, Undergraduate Honours Fellows, Winter Research Fellow

Chemical Symposium, Chemical Alliance, Electrochemistry Association

Marbend, Saynor and Curbin. *Emission from Etched Silicon.* Presented at 123rd Chemical Symposium, Oxford, January 2003

Marbend. *Porous Silicon Micro-Dension.* Presented at 234th Chemical Alliance, London, January 2003

> New scanning software reads italics; old ones do not. Marbend telephones RezReader to determine scanning software. When old programs are used, Marbend substitutes a second version of his CV, replacing italics with quotes around same typeface used in rest of CV.

HEALTH CLUB MANAGER
REVERSE CHRONOLOGICAL/COMPUTER FRIENDLY

> Larson's boss doesn't know she's job hunting: note "Confidential" and work telephone number with mention to keep calls to arrangement-making only.

Hilda Larson *** CONFIDENTIAL ***

347 Appleview Drive, Luton, Bedfordshire LU4 321   Work (brief messages only) 01582 555 9876
E-mail: hlar@aol.com

> Larson leads with graduate degree because health clubs are subject to legal liability for client injuries, aggravated by employees without credentials.

Objective and Qualifications:

Health and Fitness Industry Management: Master's and undergraduate degree in Health and Fitness. Eight years' individual and group health education and exercise leadership. Extensive background in equestrian skills, dance, gymnastics, martial arts, swimming, and strength work. Use wellness and preventative-medicine techniques.

Professional Experience:

5/01-Present   University of Luton Centre for Disease Research & Health, Luton, Beds.
• **Health Promotion Specialist, Researcher, Exercise Physiologist**
Provide monthly nutrition testing and counselling to 120 individuals, 300 in group. Conduct health and fitness classes – 350 per month. Organisation and promotion skills recognised with selection for Health Promotion Co-ordinator to Building a Better Bedfordshire Programme.

10/99-5/01   Wheaton College Health and Fitness, Wheaton, Beds
• **Instructor and Program Consultant**
Produced bimonthly newsletter, wellness counselling, and campus-wide publicity, leading to 25% membership increase in health and fitness club in 3 months.

11/99-5/01   Fitness Plus Enterprises, Luton, Beds
• **Personal Fitness Trainer, Group Exercise Instructor**
Taught group exercise classes and designed personal fitness programs for 550 individual clients. Popular trainer among special groups (disabled and elderly).

5/99-7/99   Aerobics Activity Centre, Luton, Beds
• **Assistant to the Associate Director**
Designed activity program, teaching, lecturing, and performing market research.

9/98-5/99   University of Luton, Beds
• **Graduate Teaching Fellow**
Designed and taught. Advised 24 independent study projects for undergraduate students. Wrote two proposals to Health/Fitness Department Chair, initiating development of new graduate instruction program, resulting in a £3,000 grant.

(1 of 2)

Hilda Larson 01582 555 9876

Education:

It's okay to list the education section on the 2nd page because Larson refers to it in the Qualifications section.

Master of Health Science, University of Luton, 2000
Bachelor of Science, Honours, Kinesiology, University of Luton, 1996
Guest Scholar, Physical Education Professional Division, University of Luton, Winter and Spring 1999

Certifications:

2003   RSA Exercise to Music Certification
2001   British Amateur Body Building Association certificate
2000   Central YMCA Personal Trainer qualification

Presentations:

- Building a Better Bedfordshire Programme, Summer 2003
- Sport Cardiologists and Nutritionist National Conference, Spring 2000
- Buen Salud Annual Gathering, Madrid, Spain, Spring 2000
- University of Luton Individual Fitness Design, Autumn 1999

Conferences:

- World Fitness IDEA International Conference, Olympia, London, 2003
- IDEA Personal Trainer's Conference, Luton, Beds, 2003
- Better Bedford Wellness Conference, Bedford, Beds, 1999

Awards and Honours:

- Academic Honours, University of Luton, 1993 and 1994
- Cross Cultural Awareness Award – CRE/Better Bedford, 1984
- Prize for Dance and Gymnastics, University of Luton, 1984

NON-PROFIT MANAGER
REVERSE CHRONOLOGICAL/COMPUTER FRIENDLY

MARY WHITELAND

848 Wilmslow Road, Didsbury,
Manchester, M20 2RN

Tel: 0161 456-9876
E-Mail: mwhite@mci.mail.com

NONPROFIT MANAGER-LAWYER: Significant experience with urban issues and non-profit organisations. Successful manager of complex, multi-million pound programs requiring constant attention to bottom line. Skilled lawyer and negotiator effective in stressful environment requiring personal diplomacy mediation among conflicting groups.

PROFESSIONAL EXPERIENCE

WIGGINS, STANLEY, AND FLAYBACK, Manchester.

Senior Counsel, Professional Liability Section, June 2003 to present

Manage professional liability (34) members including section chiefs, lawyers and clerical staff), and legal work involving approximately (175) failed savings and loans. Expertise in closing investigations, bringing lawsuits, and settling litigation.

> Quantifies achievements

Counsel, Professional Liability Section, November 1998 to May 2003 ◄

> Upward mobility shown by dividing jobs by heading

Managed investigation and litigation of civil claims against (25+) failed savings and loans, as well as liaison with attorneys, accountants, brokers, appraisers, and insurance companies; supervised investigators and counsel, assuring cost-effectiveness. Budgeted more than (£8 million) for S&L project. Worked closely with Serious Fraud Squad.

OSWALD, LEICHT, AND SMITH, Holborn, London. ◄
Associate, September 1996 to September 1998

> Minimises less pertinent jobs

Focused on civil litigation on real estate issues and franchise laws.

FRIENDS OF THE EARTH, London
Project Director, October 1992 to September 1996 ◄

> Includes volunteer work in work history

Directed 30+ volunteers in training project with the aim of establishing national structure for verifying and challenging legality of planning permission, construction, and environmental due diligence operations. Organised national FOE conference on EU legislation.

> Shows results with achievements

EDUCATION

MIDDLE TEMPLE – Bar Vocational Course

GLASGOW UNIVERSITY, LLB

SPEECH-LANGUAGE PATHOLOGIST
PROFESSIONAL & TARGETED/COMPUTER FRIENDLY

Brian N. Hawes

123 Northumbridge Avenue, Newcastle-upon-Tyne NE1 7RU
Tel: (0191) 456-7891 • Email bhaw@aol.com

Speech-Language Pathologist ← Replaces objective with job title

EDUCATION

1996 to 1998, and 2000   **Durham University**
Ph.D., 1993; dissertation pending
Minor: Audio/Visual Media

1994 to 1995   **Durham University**
Master of Science in Speech-Language Pathology
Wrote and produced radio and television commercials and promotional videos

1985 to 1989, and 1995   **Sunderland University**
Upper Second (2:1) Bachelor of Arts in Language
Out-placement work experience serving as multimedia laboratory
Assistant, student government representative, and club president ← Shows extracurricular achievements

Skips summary – saved for cover letter

PROFESSIONAL EXPERIENCE AND ACCOMPLISHMENTS

Describes prestigious employer

1997 to Present   **Radius Vox Laboratories, Newcastle**   **Director**

Firm delivers computer and video imaging and audio signal analysis (voice spectrography). Marketing targets hundreds of physicians and healthcare providers treating laryngeal, craniofacial, dental, and neurologic disorders.

1996 to 1997   **Durham University**   **Lecturer, Researcher**

Restructured research laboratory, adding new facilities for voice analysis, videoendoscopy, and biofeedback. Employed sound spectrography, stroboscopy, photography, and electrophysiologic measurement techniques. Lectured to 233 linguists on articulation and voice disorders analysis. Supervised Orofacial Clinic (staff of 37), developed familiarity with fiberoptic endoscopy, videofluoroscopy, and nasometry. Quantifies advancements

1995 to 1997   **The Sound & Sight Centre, South Shields**   **Speech-Language Pathologist**

Provided assessment and therapy to over 3,000 patients (neurologic, orofacial, vocal, and pediatric). Designed medical forms and computer-based therapy, decreasing procedure time by 30%. Co-ordinated patient referral plans with local medical centres. Shows industry knowledge

OTHER SKILLS AND CERTIFICATIONS

Computer: Windows (latest version), numerous applications, Microsoft certified, AI (Prolog), SAS, and SPSS.
Specialised Certifications: American Speech Association, International Association of Forensic Phonetics, Association of Phonetic Sciences, Zertifikat Deutsch, Goethe Institute Summer Abroad Fellowship, and Lake Search and Rescue Team. Licensed Tennessee Speech-Language Pathologist, FCC Radiotelephone Operator's Permit.

Book II

Showcasing
Yourself with
a StandOut CV

FINANCIAL EXECUTIVE
LINEAR/COMPUTER FRIENDLY

Diana Carter

12 Borough High St.
London
SE1 1LM
(0207) 345-6789
dcart@aol.com

Contact information placed on right
so it can be read easily when recruiter
thumbs through a stack of CVs

Objective: FINANCIAL MARKETS MANAGEMENT POSITION

Experience:

Corporate Commerce Bank, Canary Wharf, London   July 2000 -July 2003
Second Vice President – Global Markets Project Manager

- Developed, outlined, and scheduled 98 conferences covering spectrum of financial risk management issues
- Launched 53-page quarterly newsletter on new products and fluctuations
- Researched and edited copy from technical specialists and regulatory agencies
- Expanded circulation of client newsletter more than 500% in three years
- Managed £1.2 million budget and monitored department expenses
- Provided marketing support for Senior Vice President
- Travelled to Hong Kong, Singapore, and New York delivering educational seminars on derivative products and uses.
- Administered 17 bank personnel policies for seven staff members
- Directed office closure due to downsizing

Divides job by title showing upward mobility

Reason for leaving okay – widespread bank mergers

Assistant Treasurer – Global Risk Management Project Co-ordinator

- Assisted establishment of Risk Management Education & Marketing department
- Created presentation materials for over 30 conferences and education programs in 2001
- Promoted to Project Manager/Second Vice President

PC Leasing Inc., Holborn, London   November 1997-June 2000
Assistant Vice President

- Negotiated and prepared loan documentation for 23 financing lease transactions
- Scheduled and finalised funding with 15 financial institutions

Computer Borrowers Corporation, Millbank, London   May 1996-November 1997
Lease Finance Administrator

- Managed company's secured credit lines, market activity, and interest rates
- Arranged financing for transactions up to £2 million and interim financing for all leases
- Served as financial liaison with 5 departments within the company

Trims down less relevant jobs to focus on target

Education:
University of London
- Currently pursuing an MBA (part-time), two-thirds of course completed

Birkbeck College, London
- Bachelor of Arts in Sociology, May 1993

NUCLEAR ENGINEER
REVERSE CHRONOLOGICAL

Technical jargon – or keywords – used throughout so this is also a keyword CV.

Anthony Barbosa

Graceland Avenue
Leiston, Suffolk
01728 456 7890 Home
0777 321 4567 Mobile
atbarbosa@earthlink.net

CONFIDENTIAL CV

Entire CV stresses accomplishment, impressive striving to demonstrate skill

EXPERIENCE

2003-Present · Giant Power & Light Co.
Reactor Operator, Sizewell C

• Chosen by management to attend Reactor Operator Qualification course

• Passed the National NVQ Exam with a score of 93%

2001-2003 Giant Power & Light Co.
Auxiliary Operator Nuclear, Sizewell C

• Member of operations unit which upgraded the Sizewell C Reactor from a forced shutdown condition on the Site Inspectors watch list to both NRC SALP-1 and INPO-1 ratings, company dual unit record breaking performance, and established world records for BWR single and dual unit continuous operations.

• Operated reactor, turbine, and auxiliary support systems to support the safe, reliable, economical, and environmentally sound production of power.

• Selected by operations management as one of three operators for extended assignments as Radwaste Control Operator, to pursue system, operational, and programmatic upgrades. Received awards for results produced in this area.

• Developed several computer programs to assist the operations unit with managing operator exposure and error free performance.

2001-2002 Giant Power & Light Co.
Radiological Engineer, Sizewell C

• Developed a remote valve decontamination device that saved the power company in excess of £450,000 of critical path time during its first use.

• Performed a hydrogen water chemistry impact study to determine the impact of increased injection hydrogen rates on site exposure.

• Designed the containment and developed procedures used for the recovery of a damaged Americium-Beryllium neutron calibration source

Divides tenure at single employer into segments by job and level reflecting advancement

This is a running head on CV.

CONFIDENTIAL CV

1998-2000
Nuclear Associates   Various sites
Health Physics Supervisor/Lead Technician

- Windwhale Nuclear Generating Station, Suffolk (BWR)

- Paired with GE on full system decon (fuel installed) testing for EPRI

- Hinkley Fort, Somerset OH (PWR)

1997-1998
Careful Waste Management, Ltd   Hartlepool
Field Chemist

- Supervised packaging and shipping of hazardous materials

- OSHA 40-HR Hazmat trained

- On-call emergency supervisor/safety officer for field ops

1989-1997
Royal Navy   Faslane, Scotland
Engineering Watch Supervisor/Lead Engineering Lab Tech

- Managed 13-man engineering watch section in port/underway for Trident sub

- Supervised chemistry and radiological control department

- Article 108 rad con monitor

- Navy prototype staff instructor

EDUCATION

2003 Suffolk University
Master of Science in Nuclear Engineering

1999 University of East Anglia
Bachelor of Arts, Political Studies

INTERESTS

- Competitive offshore sailing, computers, bicycling, backpacking, scuba diving.

Personal interests convey image of competitiveness, technology priority, and healthy activities.

GAP IN HISTORY
TARGETED

Paula G. Cramer

27 Redwing Ave.
Shepherd's Bush, London, W12, 0208 123-4567

OBJECTIVE: KELLEY-KENNEDY PRINTING COMPANY PRODUCTION MANAGER
to use 12 plus years of print production management experience and graphic arts knowledge

QUALIFICATIONS SUMMARY
• Handle all print project phases from design through prepress to final
• Budget management – competent, careful
• Education (college degree plus seminars) in management backs up experience-based skills

SKILLS SUMMARY

Desktop Publishing	Staff Management
Colour Separation Technology	Vendor Contract Negotiations
WP Suite, Lotus 123, MS Office XP, QuarkXPress,	Purchasing
PageMaker, Internet, All Word-Processing Software	Blueline Approvals

ACCOMPLISHMENTS AND EXPERIENCE

Good treatment of two gaps – the first one was nearly three years, the other was six months. You have to read carefully to find the gaps because they are buried in the copy.

Lewisburg Marketing, Acton
PRODUCTION MANAGER AND PRINT BUYER (Direct Mail):
Managed direct mail print production from design development through mail date for 40+
concurrent projects, meeting deadlines for 2.5 million per week, 12/96-3/00
   • Directed prepress, design review, proofing, blueline approval, layout, print and
     finishing schedules. Insured compliance with Royal Mail requirements.
   • Purchased for all job components and effectively managed £5 million annual budget;
     set pricing and contracts for copywriters, designers, and printer negotiations.

The Maupin Company, Hammersmith
PRODUCTION COORDINATOR AND PLANNER
Planned and executed print production needs for clients, co-ordinated efforts of Account Executive,
Designers, and Production Staff, 4/95-6/96
   • Managed estimates, purchasing, job production layout, and projects submission to graphic
     design, camera and stripping, providing proof-reading, scheduling, and blueline approvals,
     working closely with press room manager to meet delivery deadlines.

PRIOR EXPERIENCE

Investment Litho Company, Hammersmith
GENERAL ASSISTANT
Worked part-time throughout college. Learned printing business from master printers, 6/88-6/92

EDUCATION   Goldsmiths College, London- B.A. in Business and Marketing, 1991
                 Open University 12 seminars, management

CAREER CHANGER
PROFESSIONAL & KEY WORD/COMPUTER FRIENDLY

REANNA DUMON
123 Tottenham Court Road, London, W1J 2HP
0207 456-7891
E-mail: rdumo@aol.com

Qualifications Highlights:
Seeking **physical therapist position** using eight years' physical therapy and nursing experience in Switzerland, UK, and Canada. Fluent in French, English, and Spanish. Trauma life-support, ECG, paediatrics, obstetrics, emergency and general nursing, internal medicine.

> Includes KeyWords in summary.

Education:
- Laval University, Quebec, Canada, Physical Therapy Certificate, 2003-2005
- Ste-Foy College, Ste-Foy, Quebec, Canada, D.E.C. in Technical Nursing (equivalent to Registered Nurse in UK), 1992-1995
- Garneau College, Ste-Foy, Quebec, Canada, D.E.C. in Physical Therapy, 1988-1990

Experience:

Royal London Hospital, 2000-20XX
Designed 25-page physical therapy clinic manual distributed to injured patients regarding methods of therapy and preventative procedures to eliminate further injury.
- Nurse: Clinical work: physical therapy, paediatric, obstetrical, and long-term follow-ups, child vaccination, laboratory procedures, home visiting, physical exams, medical evacuations, multidisciplinary case discussions.
  Community Health: school vaccination programme.
  Administration: patient transfers, medical visits, arranging meetings.

> Includes KeyWords in job descriptions.

Ungava Hospital, Nunavik, Canada, 1998-2000
- Co-ordinated physical therapy schedule and programme for 16 patients.
- Paediatrics, obstetrics, general medicine nurse. Monitored staff of 30 paediatric nurses; managed 57 patients.
- Co-ordinated schedule for 37 nurses in general medicine unit, maximising hospital efficiency in patient care and personal organisational skills.

> Gives results.

Canttonnal Hospital of Fribourg, Fribourg, Switzerland, 1997-1998
- Nurse, Department of Internal Medicine. Managed 26 patients, 8 with PT needs.
- Trained 11 interns on internal medicine procedures, enhancing leadership, management, and interpersonal skills to implement teamwork ideal of hospital.

Bassee-Nord Health Centre, Quebec, Canada, 1995-1997
- Performed daily physical therapy sessions with 13 paediatric patients.
- Head Nurse - emergency care, general medicine and paediatrics nurse.
- Promoted to Head nurse in emergency-care unit within first eight months.
- Supervised 23 nursing interns and co-ordinated medicine schedules for 35 patients.

> Because physical therapy, not nursing, is goal, Dumon leads with physical therapy experience, although nursing experience is dominant. Dumon moves in and out of the two professions – PT and nursing.

SEASONED ACE
LINEAR

Stephen Ralston
77 Ridge Road, Coventry, West Midlands
Tel: 024 555-9876 E-mail: sralst@aol.com

Alternative heading
for Objective.

Profile: Property Management professional seeks to use high-quality history in supervisory position. More than 15 years' solid experience A to Z in property management.

Ampersand okay –
familiar phrase.

Qualifications :
- Skilled in profit & loss, reductions, distribution, and financial administration
- Restructure marketing plans strategically, advancing returns in excess of 20%
- Record of enthusiastic achievement of corporate objectives
- Managed multi-family properties in Birmingham, Coventry, and Wolverhampton

Quantifies
achievements.

Book II

**Showcasing
Yourself with
a StandOut CV**

Education and Training:
- **Bachelor of Arts in Education,** University of Wolverhampton
- **College of Certified Property Managers,** Apartment Management, Real Estate Finances and Management

Keywords
throughout.

Professional Certifications:
- Certified Apartment Property Supervisor
- Wolverhampton Real Estate License

White space and
bullets improve
readability.

Professional Experience:

2000-Present   **Senior Asset Manager**   Greengrove Point Properties

- Manage marketing and operations programs for over 2,000 units
- Recruit, train, and hire over 100 employees, maximising $2M in capital improvements
- Consult on fair housing issues, minimising legal consultation costs by $2,000

Quantifies and
gives results of
achievements.

1999-2000   **Regional Manager**   Builder Companies of Birmingham

- Facilitated marketing programs for 10-12 properties throughout Birmingham
- Superintended successful lease-up and operation of 23-story luxury hi-rise property in Coventry
- Directed $2 million renovation of 125 year old property on outskirts of Solihull

1997-1999   **District Manager**   Birmingham Property Management

- Created marketing and operations programs for two properties in West Midlands
- Facilitated $2 million renovation with lease-up three months ahead of schedule
- Maintained 98% occupancy in New Construction lease

Ampersand okay –
company name.

1992-1997   **Area Manager**   Benedict, Young, Dalton, & McMillan

Assistant Manager on 1672 unit property in Birmingham area.
- Led company nationally for two years in leasing, averaging over 120 new leases per month
- Portfolio consisted of 2,000 units and over 100 employees
- Directed monthly regional sales meetings, initiated energy savings program that accomplished $150,000 work done to 14 properties, with profit exceeding $12,000

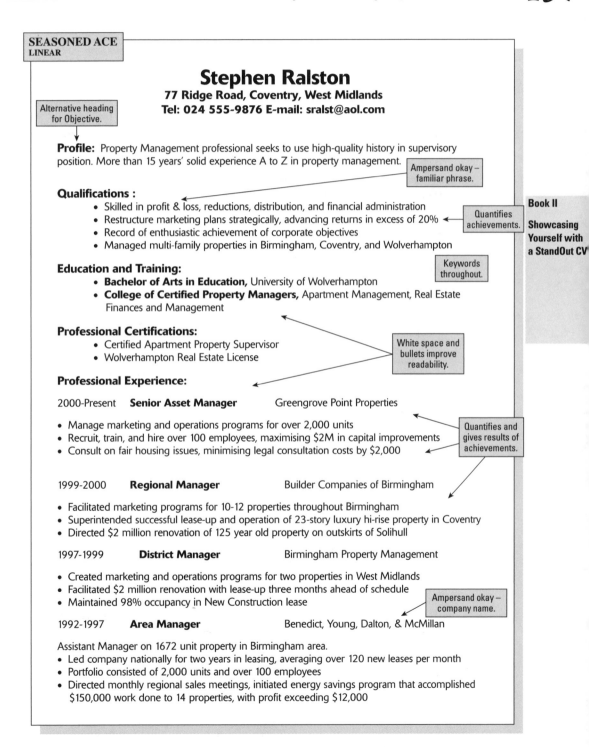

SEASONED ACE
KEYWORD & LINEAR

Ambrose Stenner

13 St Swithins Ave, Exeter, Devon, EX12 1PJ
01290 555 006   Messages taken at 01290 333 800
E-Mail: ambrosesten@aol.com

Objective woven into keyword summary.

Divides jobs by titles, highlighting upward mobility over long period with single employer.

Senior-level sales and distribution management position

12 years' experience in supervisory positions. Sales and distribution experience. Budgeting. Profit & loss responsibility. Customer service. Materials and product management. Employee selection and training. Strategic and tactical planning. Marketing. Facility location. Product training. Labour relations. Manufacturing plant management. Computerised environment and pricing.

Business Experience

1991-Present DUNCAN TRANSIT COMPANY, Exeter
2001-Present   **Director of Aftermarket Business**

Ampersand OK here – familiar phrase.

Profit & loss responsibility for $40 million aftermarket parts division. Supervise 16 sales and 35 distribution staff for sales, marketing, materials management, customer service, distribution, and product management. Serve on Executive Committee for policy making and strategising
- Facilitated strategic plan increasing sales 30%, exceeding 25% assets return
- Chaired integrated software system committee
- Edited sales literature and media campaign for $3 million retail expansion
- Sharpened inventory accuracy to 97.5% with new bar code system, significantly reducing manufacturing downtime

1997-2001   **Corporate Distribution Manager**
Managed warehouse, distribution, and traffic functions for two locations of more than 10,000 stock-keeping units. Assumed plant responsibility for distribution of product to 860 retail stores weekly.
- Designed and relocated new distribution centre on schedule and $200,000 under budget
- Received Star of the Year award from employer for product quality and distribution service levels
- Lowered total distribution cost 24%, saving $1.8M over five years

1991-1997   **Account Manager**
Developed first- and second-level distribution and manufacturing accounts in 30 key market areas, while maintaining in excess of 40 existing accounts in eight states. Conducted sales, product, and technical meetings for distributorship managers and sales staff
- Top company salesperson in 1992, 1993, and 1995
- Increased sales by 220% to $4.4M in two years

Achievement numbers combined for over one year to show high-impact results.

Education

Bachelor of Science, Business Administration, University of Sidmouth
Senior Executive Management Course, Seaton Business School, Dorset

No years given.

Book III
Succeeding at Interviews

'I like a young man who knows where he's going.
If you'll just go through that door while
my directors and I discuss your
promotion application . . .'

In this book . . .

This book gives you easy-to-follow advice about what interviewers want to hear from you, the kind of questions they ask you, and handy hints on how you can prepare yourself. From talking positively about your weaknesses and explaining your unique selling point, to role playing and group exercises, this book can help you to understand the rules of the interviewing game and improve your performance on the day.

Here are the contents of Book III at a glance:

Chapter 1

Understanding What Interviewers Want

In This Chapter

▶ Realising what interviewers want from job candidates

▶ Understanding the skills and qualities sought by employers

Congratulations if you're being invited to attend an interview. Most employers receive dozens or even hundreds of applications for every job – so being invited to an interview means you've already beaten off a large chunk of the competition.

The job market is increasingly competitive, and many interviewers are inundated with too many applications. In this chapter, we share with you the secrets of what interviewers are really looking for, and how to research and prepare the ammunition for your answers.

This book contains plenty of advice and loads of mock answers to tough interview questions. But simply reading through the book won't get you anywhere. What you need to do is figure out how *you* would answer different interview questions by using our answers for inspiration.

Recognising What Interviewers Are Looking For

At first glance, different job adverts seem to be looking for a dazzling array of skills, experience, and qualities. But in actuality, most employers are really looking for three basic factors for finding the right person for the job. These three factors can be summarised as *the three Cs* of interviews:

✔ **Competence:** Interviewers look to recruit people who have the skills and personal qualities to do the job with minimal supervision.

✔ **Commitment:** Interviewers want to give the job to someone who sticks at it. They want a self-motivated person who persists in the face of difficulties rather than gives up at the first sign of trouble.

✔ **Chemistry:** Interviewers want someone that they feel they can get on with. All employers feel they have a unique culture – and want to know that you can fit in with the rest of the team.

Demonstrate your competence and commitment by giving good answers to the many questions thrown at you. You can only create chemistry by using your tone of voice and body language to demonstrate that you are the kind of likeable person who gets on with everyone. Be aware that the interviewers are not only evaluating *what* you say, but also *how* you say it. No matter what section of the book you turn to, be sure to keep the 'three Cs' in mind.

Finding Out about Key Skills and Qualities

When interviewers say they're looking for 'competent' candidates, what exactly do they mean? Well, dozens of surveys have asked employers what they want from potential recruits. This section covers the top ten skills and personal qualities that employers look for.

Interestingly, most of the surveys agree that these skills and characteristics tend to apply to employees at all levels of an organisation and across most industry sectors. So a high-street retailer looking for a shop assistant tends to want more or less the same skills and qualities as an international corporation looking for a senior manager – although obviously to differing degrees.

Communicating with people

Unless you are being hired to work in a sealed room with no contact with colleagues or customers (which we very much doubt!), you need to have good communication skills.

When discussing your communication skills with interviewers, think of examples of occasions when you:

- ✔ Listened to the needs of other people, such as colleagues or customers.

- ✔ Conveyed information to other people – perhaps on a one-to-one basis or to a group of people.

- ✔ Handled difficult situations, such as customer complaints, on the telephone.

- ✔ Used your written communication skills in preparing reports or documents for other people to read.

Influencing others

Although communication skills are important, most employers want people who also have powers of persuasion – being able to win others over or change their minds. In preparing for your interviews, think of times when you have:

- ✔ Had a discussion with someone and helped him or her to see your point of view.

- ✔ Changed someone's mind.

- ✔ Persuaded someone to take a course of action that they were initially not in support of.

Persuasion skills are particularly prized when dealing with customers or clients – for example, in listening to their needs and then selling products or services to them.

Analysing situations

Managers want to hire candidates who can research issues and assess situations. Make sure that you think about times when you:

- ✔ Gathered information about a topic or issue.

- ✔ Broke down a complex problem into a number of smaller issues.

- ✔ Weighed up the pros and cons of different options.

Book III

Succeeding at Interviews

Solving problems

Employers are looking for people who can assess situations and then work out the best course of action to take. Be ready to talk to interviewers about occasions when you:

✔ Made suggestions about how to tackle a problem.

✔ Initiated or participated in brainstorming sessions.

✔ Took a course of action to solve a problem or tackle an issue.

Demonstrating drive and determination

Organisations do not want to hire people who only work when given explicit instructions as to what to do; they want to hire candidates who are self-motivated and can demonstrate a bit of initiative. Think back to times when you:

✔ Suffered a setback or disappointment at work but got back on your feet and got on with a task.

✔ Had an original idea and used it to be more effective or productive at work.

✔ Overcame a difficulty or obstacle that was preventing you from achieving a goal.

Teamworking with colleagues

Employers are constantly talking about the need for employees to work together more effectively as a team. Try to recall instances when you:

✔ Helped someone else in the team with their work or duties.

✔ Resolved conflict or disagreement between other team members.

✔ Provided a team member with a shoulder to cry on.

Effective teamworking is about putting the needs of the team above those of your own.

Developing quickly

Especially for entry-level jobs (including graduate entry roles), employers want people who can develop quickly in the job. Managers don't want to hire people who need a lot of handholding! In preparing for interviews, try to think back to times when you:

- ✔ Became proficient at a task or duty more quickly than others expected.

- ✔ Gained knowledge about a topic or issue because of your hard work and dedication.

- ✔ Picked up a new skill with minimal supervision.

Being flexible and adaptable

Employers want to hire people who are open-minded, accommodating, and willing to help out when the need arises. Try to recall occasions when you:

- ✔ Offered to do overtime to help get a project or piece of work completed on time.

- ✔ Helped someone else even when it was not part of your job description.

- ✔ Changed your mind at work after listening to someone else's point of view.

Book III

Succeeding at Interviews

Planning and organising

Employers are always on the lookout for candidates who can manage their own workload. In order to convince employers that you possess these skills, think about instances when you:

- ✔ Prioritised tasks to meet a tough deadline.

- ✔ Planned out and then completed a project.

- ✔ Organised other people to ensure that a piece of work got done.

Being aware of the bigger picture

Employers complain that a lot of employees have a very narrow-minded view of their work. They don't see the 'bigger picture' of what goes on outside of their team, department, or organisation. Demonstrate that you are aware of the bigger picture by thinking back to occasions when you:

- ✔ Had to liaise with colleagues outside of your department.
- ✔ Found out some interesting information about a customer, supplier, or competitor and then shared it with colleagues.
- ✔ Thought about the impact of your work or duties on people outside of your own team.

Researching the Company

Interviewers want more than a candidate with just the right skills and experience – they want to hire someone who desires working for their particular organisation. And the way to demonstrate that you are keen is to research the company thoroughly so that you can talk confidently about it.

Gathering vital information

Begin your research by reading any information that an organisation sends you – for example, recruitment brochures, prospectuses, job descriptions, and even catalogues of their products or services.

Even if an organisation doesn't send you any information, look at their Web site. If you can't find their site on the Internet, try calling the organisation to ask for the Web address.

Good research can make the difference between success and failure. Make sure that you spend at least a couple of hours reading the organisation's literature and scouring their Web site for information.

Absorb as much information as you can about the company, their aims and objectives, and what they do. At a very minimum, find the answers to questions such as:

- ✔ What are the goals or objectives of the organisation?
- ✔ How many people work for the organisation?
- ✔ Where is the organisation based? Do they operate only within the UK, or in Europe, or globally?
- ✔ Where is their main office or corporate headquarters? How many offices, shops, or branches does the organisation have?
- ✔ What are the organisation's main services or products?

Collecting in-depth information

To find out even more about an organisation, try typing their name into an Internet search engine to see what else you can come up with. Look for information regarding the following list of questions:

✔ When was the company founded? Who were the founders? (This is a particularly important question for smaller organisations.)

✔ What is the name of the organisation's chief executive officer (CEO) or managing director?

✔ Who are the organisation's main competitors? How does this particular organisation differ from its competitors?

✔ What major threats and issues affect the organisation?

✔ Is the company growing and expanding? If so, what are its stated goals and priorities with regards to growth?

✔ How is the organisation performing financially?

Visiting shops and premises

If an organisation has shops, branches, showrooms, or other properties open to the public, visit at least one of them. Even better, try to visit a couple of their premises to get a feel for how the organisation likes to present itself to the public.

Visiting an organisation's premises is particularly important if applying for a job with a retailer. Retail employers often ask candidates what they do and don't like about their shops. If you don't make the effort to visit one of their stores, you may be rejected for not demonstrating enough interest in the company.

Book III

Succeeding at Interviews

Preparing Answers to Common Questions

If you do your research beforehand, you'll have great answers to lots of the questions posed by your interviewers.

The secret to predicting likely topics of discussion during an interview is scrutinising the original advertisement that drew your attention to the job. Always keep a copy of every job advert you apply for so that you can refer to it if invited to attend an interview.

Linking job adverts to key skills

This section shows examples of job adverts and how to identify the key skills, experience, and qualities that you may need to talk about during an interview.

Take a look at the job advert for an office manager that's shown in Figure 1-1. The key words and phrases show questions that interviewers are almost certain to ask candidates applying for this job:

- ✔ **'Experienced office manager':** This phrase tells you that the interviewers will want to know how long you've worked as an office manager.

- ✔ **'Excellent written and oral communication':** Be prepared to give examples of documents that you've written. And, be ready to talk about how you communicate with people both in person and on the telephone.

- ✔ **'Lead a team of four':** Have you led a team in the past? Can you talk about your style of leadership? Be able to give examples of how you built your team, delegated to them, and disciplined them.

- ✔ **'Supporting':** Make sure that you can talk about how you have supported other people in doing their jobs.

Figure 1-1:
Job advert
for an office
manager.

> **Job advert 1: Office Manager**
>
> We are looking for an experienced office manager to help us run our office. You must have excellent written and oral communication skills. You will lead a team of four administrative assistants in supporting a total office of 20 people. In return, we offer a competitive salary for the right individual.

As you can see, you can quite quickly predict many of the questions that the interviewers are likely to ask you. Here's the breakdown of key words and phrases used in the job advert for a sales position, shown in Figure 1-2.

- ✔ **'Self-motivated':** Of course, the interviewers may ask you whether you would describe yourself as self-motivated. But can you give any examples of how you have motivated yourself to achieve goals?

- ✔ **'High-street retailer':** Do you have any retail or customer experience that you can talk about? If not, be ready to talk about why you want to work in retail.

✔ **'Flexible and willing to work shift patterns':** If you have worked shifts in the past, make sure that you mention this. If you haven't worked shifts before, think about some of the difficulties doing so may pose for you – and how you can overcome them.

✔ **'Outgoing personality':** How will you convince the interviewers that you have an outgoing personality? You need to inject plenty of energy into your interview performance, but also think about stories to illustrate how you enjoy spending time with people.

✔ **'Build a career in retail':** This phrase implies that the interviewers are looking for someone who wants to join their company and stay for a number of years rather than someone who sees working in the store as a temporary position. So be ready for questions such as: *What are your longer-term career plans?*

Figure 1-2:
Job advert
for a sales
adviser.

> **Job advert 2: Sales Adviser**
>
> Self-motivated people required! We are looking for sales advisers for a busy high-street retailer. Successful candidates must be flexible and willing to work shift patterns. You should have an outgoing personality and be looking to build a career in retail. Good hourly rates.

Book III

Succeeding at Interviews

Consider these key words and phrases when preparing to go for an executive position, such as the job advertised in Figure 1-3:

✔ **'Working with the sales team':** Prepare to talk about the trials and tribulations of working with sales people. If you haven't worked with sales teams before, then be prepared to explain how you'll go about working with them.

✔ **'Writing marketing materials':** Do you have examples of marketing material that you can talk about?

✔ **'Managing our Web site':** Can you talk about how you have updated another organisation's Web site or at least contributed to one in the past? Are you ready to talk about using software to manage this company's Web site?

✔ **'Dealing with newspapers and trade journals':** Be ready to talk about how you have dealt with journalists in the past. What success stories can you share for how you have promoted a previous employer through working with journalists?

✔ **'Ambitious':** How will you prove to the interviewers that you're ambitious? What major achievements can you cite to demonstrate your ambition?

✔ **'Experience in the IT sector':** Be prepared to talk about other IT companies that you've worked for.

Job advert 3: Marketing Executive

As a fast-growing software company, we are looking to expand our team by recruiting an experienced marketing executive. Responsibilities include: working with the sales team; writing marketing materials including brochures and press releases; managing our Web site; and dealing with newspapers and trade journals. We are looking for an ambitious professional with experience in the IT sector. Contact Laura Hall in confidence for more information on 020 8700 1234.

Figure 1-3:
Job advert
for a
marketing
executive.

Getting Ready to Go

Before you set off, here are a few final thoughts for you in the days before the interview:

✔ **Know the time, date, and location of the interview:** You also need to work out the precise route to get there. If in any doubt as to how long the journey takes, add extra time. Being late is an unforgivable sin.

✔ **Know the format for the interview:** How many interviewers will attend the interview? Is there just one interview, several interviews, or a mixture of interviews and psychometric tests? If you don't know, find out by ringing up the human resources department, the recruitment coordinator, or perhaps an interviewer's personal assistant.

✔ **Have copies of your CV to hand:** Because CVs can go astray, print out a half-dozen copies of your CV and be prepared to give them to interviewers who may not have a copy. Carry the copies of your CV in a briefcase or a plain folder.

✔ **Take a newspaper or business magazine:** If you arrive more than half an hour before the interview, find a local cafe rather than sitting in the interviewers' reception – being too early can signal over-anxiousness.

Nerves can make you sweat and cause your mouth to go dry. Your body odour can become pronounced and your breath may be unpleasant! Deodorise thoroughly on the big day and pop in a couple of breath mints in the minutes before an interview to make sure that the interviewers don't remember you for entirely the wrong reasons.

The telltale signs of a liar

How well do you think you can spot a liar? You may believe you're totally clued up and can see instinctively when someone's fibbing, but numerous scientific studies over the last 30 years show that most of us can only guess when someone tells little white lies. We can even be duped by the most outrageous untruths.

Years of research by Paul Ekman, world-respected for his studies of emotions, reveal that the secret lies hidden in our micro-expressions. Some 42 different muscles move in a person's face to create thousands of different micro-expressions. These change all the time in all sorts of subtle ways. So subtle, in fact, that if you can learn to focus and catch these super-fast movements you have all the information you need to read the liars.

The trouble is that with so many possibilities, any human being finds it hard to register the discrepancies that show a false emotion – a lie. Even the latest generation of machines can't get it right all the time. So who can accurately pick out the naughty tricksters? Ekman's research (*New Scientist* 29 March, 2003) rates the star performers as members of the US Secret Service, prison inmates, and a Tibetan Buddhist monk.

It's probably no surprise that that Secret Service agents would be highly trained to select out dangerous suspects. Prisoners live in an environment of people experienced in crime and deception and need to learn who to trust in order to survive. Meanwhile, Ekman's Buddhist subject had none of these life experiences, but had spent thousands of hours meditating, and appeared to have the sensitivity to read other people's emotions very accurately from their fleeting facial expressions.

Book III

Succeeding at Interviews

Chapter 2

Polishing Your Performance

....

....

*I*magine the scenario: Two candidates both say, *I'm the right person for the job because I have good people skills*. But imagine one candidate mumbling the words in a lifeless fashion, dressed scruffily, avoiding eye contact, and fidgeting nervously, while a well-groomed candidate says the words in a dynamic fashion, smiling and looking eye-to-eye at the interviewers. Who do you think the interviewers are going to give the job to?

Your body language, dress, and tone of voice have important roles to play in convincing the interviewers that you're the best candidate. In this chapter, we talk about ways to make sure that you grab the attention of the interviewers.

Creating the Right Impact

You probably won't be surprised when we tell you that interviewers are looking to recruit motivated and enthusiastic people. But you may be surprised to discover that most of your interpersonal impact comes across not in *what* you say, but *how* you say it.

Research claims that up to 55 per cent of our communication effectiveness is determined by our body language, comprising of our gestures, movements, and facial expressions.

A lot of candidates talk about trying to 'be themselves' during interviews. These candidates say that they tend to warm up only when they get to know people better and that they feel fake in having to 'act up' with interviewers. But remember that interviews are a game of sorts: Interviewers want to hire candidates who are energetic and enthusiastic from the moment they meet, so you need to focus on performing as a dynamic and passionate person – even if that isn't how you normally like to behave until you know people better.

Making eye contact

Eye contact is critical in interviews. Failing to look the interviewers in the eye conveys an impression of nervousness – or that you are embellishing on the truth. Assuming that you don't want to be perceived as anxious or a fraudster, you must develop the skill of making solid eye contact.

However, good eye contact doesn't mean staring at the interviewers throughout your conversation with them. In fact, two rules govern eye contact:

- **Look when the interviewers talk:** Aim to look at an interviewer for at least 90 per cent of the time when he or she is asking questions or otherwise speaking.

- **Look away for part of the time when you talk:** Looking away is okay for a portion of the time when speaking. For example, a lot of candidates tend to look away for a few seconds when they are trying to recall an example. Making more than 90 per cent eye contact when you are speaking will probably freak the interviewers out! Aim to look at them for around a half to two-thirds of the time when you are speaking.

Use *active listening* to demonstrate that you are listening to the interviewers. This means nodding occasionally as they speak and using words and phrases such as *yes*, *uh-huh*, and *I understand* occasionally to signal that you follow what they are saying.

Using your body language

You can tell a huge amount about what goes on inside a person's head by how they use their body language. For example, playing with a ring or repeatedly touching your hair are often interpreted as signs of nervousness. A slouched posture or drumming fingers on a table can be construed as a lack of interest. Follow these tips to project the right kind of image:

✔ **Stand and sit up straight:** Lengthen your body and hold your spine erect. Maintain a straight posture during an interview. Don't let tiredness or nerves allow your shoulders to hunch forwards.

✔ **Stop any fidgeting:** Don't give away any hint of nerves by moving around in a restless fashion. Keep your hands clasped lightly in your lap or rest them gently on the table.

✔ **Use your hands to emphasise key points:** Hand gestures can make people seem more sincere or credible. So use your hands occasionally to underscore key points to make yourself visually more engaging – for example, by turning your palms up and spreading your fingers to indicate sincerity or counting points off on your fingers.

✔ **Avoid crossing your arms:** Some interviewers read crossing your arms as being a sign of defensiveness. So don't do it. However, contrary to popular opinion, you *can* cross your legs – so long as you don't cross your arms across your chest as well.

✔ **Keep your legs still:** Avoid crossing or uncrossing your legs or tapping your feet. Such fidgeting can be unnerving.

Use your hands to emphasise key points only when you are speaking. Keep your hands still when the interviewers are speaking to show that you're listening.

Avoid pointing at the interviewers – this aggressive gesture can seem intimidating.

Creating warmth by smiling

Don't tell anyone, but here's a little secret: Interviewers often hire the candidate that they *like* the most rather than picking the most skilled and experienced person for the job. All interviewers are subconsciously affected by factors such as warmth, rapport, and smiling.

Now, too much smiling makes you come across as a manic Cheshire cat. Following these hints generates an impression of warmth and likeability rather than an unhinged personality:

✔ **Smile as you greet the interviewers:** First impressions really count. So make sure that you are positively beaming when you first meet the interviewers. Project the impression that you are incredibly pleased to be at the interview.

Book III

Succeeding at Interviews

Common vocal mistakes

Job candidates tend to make one of three mistakes when it comes to their voice during an interview. They often:

✔ **Speak in a monotonous voice:** The words seem to fall out of these candidates' mouths without any energy or inflection behind them.

✔ **Mumble words:** The lips of these candidates simply don't move enough to let the interviewers understand what they're trying to say. Unfortunately, interviewers are usually too polite to say that they can't understand you and simply let you mumble on. But you can be certain that they'll give the job to someone that they can understand!

✔ **Speak too quickly or for too long:** Nerves can get the better of some candidates and make them gibber almost uncontrollably or speak for too long. Speak for no more than one or two minutes at a time. If you want to continue a story, check with the interviewers by asking, *Is this useful, shall I go on?*

✔ **Smile when you talk about your strengths or achievements:** Smiling would be incongruous when talking about difficult situations at work. But if talking about positive aspects of yourself and your working life, try to add a smile at some point.

✔ **Smile when you leave the room:** When you say your goodbyes and thank the interviewers for their time, give them another broad smile to show that you enjoyed meeting them.

Using intonation and inflection

Interviewers can spend a couple of days at a time interviewing. And they can feel really bored when all candidates seem to be saying pretty much the same thing. To make the interviewers sit up and take notice of what you're saying, focus on your tone of voice.

Follow these guidelines to come across as an interesting and enthusiastic – but also calm and confident – candidate:

✔ **Introduce inflection into your speech:** Actors sometimes talk of using 'light and shade' in a voice. Occasionally raise the tone of your voice or speed up the pace to convey excitement or passion about a topic. Deepen your voice or slow down a little to transmit seriousness.

✔ **Emphasise key words:** Say key words and phrases a little louder to make them stand out. This tactic is the auditory equivalent of typing important words in a **bold** typeface.

> ✔ **Articulate your words carefully:** If in any doubt as to whether you pronounce your words clearly enough, ask a variety of colleagues for their opinion. Don't ask friends, as they are too used to your way of speaking to give you objective feedback.
>
> ✔ **Think about leaving pauses between sentences:** Remember that full stops appear at the end of sentences. Make sure not to let your sentences all run together.

Intonation and inflection are really difficult to get right. The best way to tell if you sound okay is to tape record yourself saying interview answers out loud and then listen to your responses to see how they come across.

Speaking Out with Confidence

Why is public speaking so nerve-wracking? Why, when confronted unexpectedly by their dream date or their boss, do sitcom characters become incoherent, mumbling idiots (and you laugh because you recognise yourself in the situation)? How can it be that something so natural as speaking, which you've been practising more or less continuously since you first learned to do it, can at times become so difficult?

Children joke about the centipede who loses his ability to walk when someone asks him how he does it; it's the same with speaking. When it becomes self-conscious, for any reason, you get caught up in its mechanics and lose your easy, natural groove.

To find your public voice and gain the confidence to speak out, you need something to say and someone to say it to. And you need something connecting you in that moment to the person or group you're speaking to, which is commonly called *rapport* – a shared view of the world within which there is room for disagreement. To achieve all this, you need to deal with anything standing in the way.

Rehearsing for the big day

To pull off a cracking interview, keep in mind the 'three Ps' of interviewing:

✔ Preparation

✔ Practice

✔ Performance

Saying interview answers out loud can make an enormous difference to your confidence in an actual interview. To observe your body language and expressions, try saying your answers out loud in front of a mirror.

Listening to yourself

Have you ever heard yourself speak on tape? Did you find it a shocking experience to hear your own voice 'from the outside'? It sounds so different from your voice as you experience it from inside your head that you may assume the recording quality is at fault until others confirm that you sound exactly that way in real life. You may have been surprised or dismayed by the poor quality of your diction, or the strength of your accent, and have made an unconscious decision to do something about it or else never speak in public again. However, deciding not to speak in public for any reason is ridiculous and undoable.

Speaking with the local accent and in the regional dialect can be a great help in building rapport. Be proud of your accent, it is part of who you are, but do be prepared to work on your public speaking skills a little in line with the advice in this chapter.

The most common problems with speaking in public are clarity and diction. As your first schoolteacher probably told you, if you sit up and speak clearly you will be heard – heard all over the world.

Breathing to improve your speaking

Shallow breathing is a common problem when you're faced with any kind of public speaking.

Rapid, shallow breathing can reduce the level of carbon dioxide in your blood, which reduces the flow of blood through your body. Then, even though your lungs are taking in all the oxygen your body should need, your brain and body experience a shortage. This can leave you feeling tense, nervous, and unable to think clearly.

The solution, which is well known to singers and those who play wind instruments, is to breathe deeply from the diaphragm or abdomen. If, like most people, you have little idea how to do this, read on.

Feeling how you breathe

First, locate your diaphragm: Place your right hand flat on your stomach just above your navel and below the bottom of your rib cage. Now take a series of short sniffs as though you are trying to detect the smell of something on fire. You should feel the area under your hand moving in and out. This is your diaphragm.

Now, place your left hand on your upper chest just below your collarbone, keeping your right hand over your diaphragm. Take a few normal breaths.

If you're breathing correctly, you feel the rhythmic rising and falling movement of your breathing in your right hand. If you feel movement under your left hand, you're breathing from your chest, and this is not what you want.

Discovering how to breathe through your diaphragm

Breathing through your diaphragm gives you the powerful voice you want. To make use of this technique, follow these steps:

1. **Place your right hand over your diaphragm and your left hand on your chest.**

2. **Purse your lips as though you're about to whistle, and breathe out slowly to a count of five monkeys (count one monkey, two monkeys, and so on to yourself) while tightening your stomach muscles.**

3. **Breathe in slowly through your nose to a count of three monkeys.**

   Feel your right hand rising with the diaphragm.

4. **Pause slightly for two monkeys and then breathe out again to a count of five as in Step 2.**

If you practise this for just a few minutes before every meal and again at odd times throughout the day, you soon become habituated to this more effective way of breathing. Once you get your muscles trained, your diaphragm can do 80 per cent of the incessant work of your breathing for the rest of your life. Proper breathing gives you the platform you need for a powerful voice.

When you're comfortable with diaphragmatic breathing, you can add in another two steps to improve your voice quality further:

✔ In Step 2, instead of pursing your lips, add in a gentle 'Ah' sound for the full exhalation stage. Keep this 'Ah' going until you run out of air.

✔ When you have the rhythm going, drop both your hands to your sides and bounce your shoulders gently but rapidly up and down as you breathe out to 'Ah'. This releases tension from your vocal cords and helps to prepare your voice for speaking.

Now your voice is ready, what are you going to say?

Book III

Succeeding at Interviews

Dressing for Success

Not that long ago, interviewers expected all candidates to turn up in suits. Now, an increasing number of organisations have relaxed their dress codes, and it has become impossible to prescribe how to dress for just about any interview.

Always call ahead and ask about the dress code. Or, if you are at all uncertain, then go on a scouting trip and watch the flow of people as they go in and out of the building where you are to be interviewed. However, even if the majority of the staff seem to dress casually, do be careful as many interviewers may dress smartly specifically for interviews.

Wearing a suit may not always be your best option. For example, people in creative roles in industries such as fashion, advertising, and media often talk scathingly about *suits* – people in (what they see as) boring roles such as finance, operations, and human resources. No matter what, be sure to think about your clothes.

'Getting' the default for men

If in doubt, go smart. Being slightly overdressed is always better than being underdressed (you can always take off your tie and undo a top button). For men, this means the following:

- ✓ **Wear a dark suit:** Navy blue and grey are the most acceptable colours. Black can come across as a bit funereal. And buy a classic cut with a two- or three-button jacket rather than trying to follow the latest fashion.

- ✓ **Wear a plain, long-sleeved shirt:** Pick a pale colour such as light blue or white. If you suffer from sweating, then wear a white t-shirt underneath to prevent wet patches from showing.

- ✓ **Wear a plain silk tie:** Patterns can be distracting. Let your words rather than your tie entertain the interviewers.

- ✓ **Wear black shoes:** Opt for plain lace-ups without fancy buckles. Polish your shoes. One school of thought amongst interviewers says that unpolished shoes are the sign of a disorganised mind.

Understanding the guidelines for women

As for men (see the preceding section), if in doubt, go smart. But women's rules are less rigid, because so many more options are available. However, here are some guidelines if you're unsure about the dress code:

✔ **Wear a neutral or dark-coloured suit:** For interviews with a professional services firm or a big business, wear a suit as opposed to separates. And think carefully before opting for a trouser suit, as a few older, male interviewers are still a bit sexist about women in trousers as opposed to skirts.

✔ **Wear a plain top:** Choose an unpatterned blouse or fitted top in a pale colour. Avoid sleeveless tops and don't go for anything too sexy.

✔ **Keep jewellery to a minimum:** Wear only one pair of earrings and a maximum of one ring on each hand. Avoid thumb rings or too many bangles as they may distract from a professional appearance.

Looking Like You Mean Business

Appearances can be deceptive. They are based on your perceptions more often than reality. By this we mean that you filter information about people based on other people you have met in the past and your own personal prejudices.

When you meet someone for the first time, you are likely to make a judgement in the first 15 to 20 seconds as to whether you like or dislike, approve or disapprove of them. And you may do this based on one aspect of their physical characteristics, dress, and grooming. For example, studies show that people consider men with beards to be less professional than men without.

Your confidence in selecting friends, employees, and partners can be based on your subjective experience rather than objective information. When you get to know the real person beyond the initial façade, your opinion may change.

Confess now. You've probably formed an opinion about people without ever having met them. You see a photo and say 'She's a kind person' or 'She's a smart cookie' or even 'She's a pain in the butt' without having anything more to go on. Consider for a moment what opinions you form of celebrities and members of royalty based on a magazine feature or a brief TV appearance.

Book III

Succeeding at Interviews

The visual impact a person makes provides the strongest data for judging that person. Remember that when dressing for your interview.

Appearing confident

A TV advertisement pictured a woman walking down the street. Her blonde hair was perfectly groomed, she had a spring in her step, a smile on her face, and attracted the admiration of on-lookers, who would whisper: 'Is she wearing Harmony hairspray?' It was a memorable campaign for a low cost way to build self-confidence.

People appear confident if they are dressed in smart or fashionable clothes, if their hair is well cut and managed, if they move with energy, and if they survey the world around them with bright-eyed interest. A person who appears confident may have a voice that's loud and clear or a manner that's warm and engaging. Or they may have expensive accessories or a desirable new car. Perhaps they are the focus of attention or stand out as the leader in a group of people.

Taking a people-watching snapshot is a positive way to help you build your confidence based on your judgements about other people:

1. **Go to a crowded place.**

   Choose a place like a station or airport, a shopping centre, the doctor's waiting room, a gym, or a school playground.

Crowning glory

In 1795, William Pitt put a tax on hair powder, expecting to raise loads of tax because every man and woman with pretensions to style put powder in their hair. He was hoping for around 210,000 guineas in revenue. Unfortunately for the exchequer, the tax raised only 46,000 guineas. Whig leaders opposed to the tax cut off their pigtails in defiance and agreed to abandon the use of hair powder, and the public followed suit.

Today, we still pay tax on hair products – it's a massive international industry with all those shampoos, conditioners, sprays, gels, and mousse, let alone the cost of cuts and colours. Our favourite family hairdresser, Rosy, will vouch for the confidence factor of a new haircut as her customers leave the salon. 'People look and feel ten years younger or older simply according to their haircut. It's not just the ladies, this goes for the men too – shaving off a beard or moustache or going for a new cut with a few coloured highlights can make a guy have much more impact. I know I'm biased, but it's a terrific boost!'

It's easy to get into a habit of repeating the same haircut and style for year after year. For a confidence boost within one hour, find a good hairdresser and go for a new look.

---

2. **Look around until you spot someone who appears confident to you.**

3. **Analyse what it is that makes you think they're confident.**

   Determine what it is about the way they look, carry themselves, and speak that makes you perceive them as confident. Write down three or four things.

4. **Consider how you can imitate or incorporate these qualities in your own behaviour.**

   Now go out and try out your new behaviours and notice the difference.

Making the best first impression

As a struggling young butcher, Tony went off at the crack of dawn to the cattle market in a neighbouring town. To his wife's surprise, he was dressed in his finest suit. His respose to her raised eyebrows was: 'We may be very short of money, but we don't have to look it.'

Like all astute business people, Tony knew that first impressions count. He stood more chance of cutting a better deal if he looked well heeled than if he was hard up. Why else do the most successful companies put smart, enthusiastic, and well-groomed people on the reception desk? They inspire confidence in the organisation. These first impressions are what the marketing folks call 'moments of truth'. If you walk into a shop, an office, or a garage and it looks in disarray or the people are unwelcoming, then all the investment in branding and clever advertising is wasted, because customers avoid doing business with an organisation that gives a bad first impression.

So what impression do you create when you meet someone for the first time? Do you arrive at your interview in a flustered state of disarray with papers flying, or are you neat, organised, and well prepared? Some subtle changes in your image might make you look more confident or inspire others to feel confident about you.

For example, the most basic grooming requires that your face, hair and teeth are neatly brushed and you have no marks of food on yourself or clothing. Check yourself in a full-length mirror before leaving home.

Any tears or threads in your clothes need to be fixed. But you can do better than this. Build time into your schedule to choose clothes appropriate to who you are meeting and where (making sure they are clean and well pressed), to polish your shoes, and for ladies, to apply your make-up.

Book III

Succeeding at Interviews

If you have a very busy week, decide on Sunday night what you're going to wear and save the last-minute morning rush.

Conveying the right attitude with your dress

The style of the well-dressed man about London in the eighteenth century was defined by the Regency dandy Beau Brummell, a chap with 'attitude'. He wore exquisitely cut dark coats over white linen shirts and well-starched neckcloths. Only the waistcoat would display lavish embroidery and design.

Dress codes change with time and place. It pays to notice what those around you are wearing, whether you choose to fit in or stand out with confidence. If you're updating your image, make sure of its appeal to the people you want to mix with. Your smile, sparkly chat, and tidy appearance may do you more favours than designer labels.

You are likely to build stronger rapport with people if you match their dress code than if you look completely different.

A client in the TV world assesses potential newsreaders and presenters by what he calls 'the girl/boy next door' test. He looks for the candidate with a face, dress, and manner that his customers, the viewing public, would invite into their living rooms for a chat. He pays attention to whether candidates convey warmth, friendliness, and an honest sense of humour. These characteristics are much more appealing to the majority of the population than slick, cool, and glamorous.

Dress at work as if you have a more senior role in the organisation. In doing so, you set the unconscious expectation that you are worthy of promotion.

Shopping smart

Actually choosing clothes you can feel confident in isn't very difficult once you know what suits you. Use these tips to ensure smart wardrobe shopping:

- ✔ Buy the size that fits well rather than buying an outfit to slim into.
- ✔ Think about your body type. Some of us are curvy and some are angular. (This is true of both sexes.) If you're curvy, choose shirts with rounded collars and jackets with rounded edges in softer fabrics. Those with a more angular shape look great in sharper cuts, stripes, and firmer fabrics.

✔ Avoid buying clothes in haste. Look when you are not in a hurry to buy and can try on a range of clothes and experiment to refine your choice.

✔ Good-quality coats, bags, and shoes are the best approach to looking great. The rest can be simple.

✔ Invest in smart accessories including belts, watches, and ties/scarves that ring the changes.

✔ Check your wardrobe before you go shopping, so you fill the gaps rather than getting wooed by another impulse outfit.

Buy clothes that can take you anywhere looking good, and you'll feel confident to accept any invitation at a minute's notice.

Getting Off to a Great Start

You may hear people say that most interviewers make up their minds within the first five to ten minutes of an interview. In many cases, it's true – a lot of interviewers judge candidates on what they say and do within those initial few minutes. So make sure that you put in a commanding performance:

✔ Offer a solid handshake.

✔ Demonstrate your enthusiasm.

✔ Make a positive comment.

✔ Be prepared for some chitchat.

✔ Wait until the interviewers indicate for you to sit.

Concentrate on making a great impression in those first few minutes and the interviewers may well warm to you and make the rest of the interview that much more enjoyable. But keep your guard up at all times – listen carefully to every question, never interrupt the interviewers, and think before you speak!

Chapter 3

Preparing Great Questions

· ·

In This Chapter

▶ Demonstrating how much you want the job

▶ Ascertaining your future career prospects

▶ Asking about the organisation's culture

▶ Developing your formal questions into an informal discussion

▶ Gathering positive references

· ·

As the interview draws to a close, the interviewers will almost certainly ask you: *Do you have any questions for us?*

Interviewers often judge candidates on the nature of the questions that you ask. For example, asking about the hours and the number of annual leave days you're entitled to can give them the impression that you are a bit of a slacker, interested only in how little work you can get away with. Or asking about the pay and benefits can make you sound greedy.

In this chapter, we cover how to prepare great questions that not only impress the interviewers but also help you to decide whether this is an organisation that you would actually want to work for.

Never ever say that you have no questions. Saying that you have nothing to ask is a very poor response and signals to the interviewers that you aren't really that interested in the job.

Preparing the Right Questions for the Right Interview

You really do need to do some research to prepare a good dozen or more questions for the interviewers. This way, even if the interviewers tell you a lot about the job and their company, you're still able to ask a few questions at the end of the interview.

Stuck for questions to ask?

If applying for a managerial role, consider asking questions such as:

✔ What are the members of the team like?

✔ Does the team have any issues that need sorting out? Are there any people who are under-utilised?

✔ Who are the key decision makers in the organisation?

✔ What sort of budget would I have for running the team?

✔ What do you see as the main challenges facing the team at the moment?

✔ What style of management is the team used to?

✔ Are there any major milestones or deliverables that you expect the successful candidate to achieve?

✔ What kind of develo   you have for manag

If interviewed for a part-time or job share position, you may want to ask questions such as:

✔ How do you see this position fitting in with the rest of the team?

✔ Do you have any other people in a similar position at the moment? How is the role working out for them?

✔ How would I be expected to hand over work to the other job share person and vice versa?

If the position is a short-term contract, ask a few of the following questions:

✔ Exactly how long is the contract?

✔ What are the deliverables within this time frame?

✔ When do you hope for this project to start?

✔ How likely is it that you may extend the contract or make it a full-time appointment?

✔ Assuming everything goes well, are there any realistic opportunities to join your organisation on a full-time basis?

When aske   ny questions, you may be tempted to say, *No, because we   ered all of my questions in the discussion so far.* The problem is that – even if you are telling the truth – the interviewers may just decide that you simply had not prepared any questions.

The number of questions you want to ask tends to depend on the seniority of the job. For entry level or junior management roles, aim to ask just three or four questions. For senior jobs, you may be expected to have plenty more questions – perhaps as many as ten or a dozen. If you struggle to think of questions when preparing for your interview, take inspiration from the sidebar 'Stuck for questions to ask?'

Always check that a question is relevant to the particular role that you are applying for. For example, *Will I have a development budget?* is not a sensible question for entry-level or junior positions with no responsibilities in this area.

Whatever job you go for, always aim to ask at least three or four questions about the job to demonstrate that you are genuinely interested in being taken on.

When preparing questions to ask an employer, make sure that your questions can only be answered face-to-face by the interviewers. Asking a question easily answered by reading the job advert or their Web site won't help your prospects! Read the company's recruitment brochure (if it has one), job description, and any other documents that they make available to you. The sidebar 'Tailoring your questions' gives you even more advice.

Showing enthusiasm for the job

Here are some questions to ask showing that you are interested in the day-to-day nature of the job itself:

- *In this job, what would I be doing on a day-to-day basis?*
- *Do you have any idea of what proportion of my time would be spent on those tasks?*
- *What kind of training would I get initially?*
- *In practice, how much time would you expect me to spend seeing customers as opposed to being in the office?*
- *Who will be my line manager? What is it like to work for them?*
- *How much contact with customers am I likely to have initially?*
- *How will my performance be measured?*
- *What are the longer-term opportunities for working across the organisation?*
- *Will there be opportunities to work in any of your overseas offices?*

Book III

Succeeding at Interviews

Never forget to prepare questions suitable for each specific interview that you go to. Never take the same questions along to different interviews as the interviewers are bound to see through you. For example, one job advert may be a bit vague about the daily nature of the job, while another may be very detailed – so asking about what you would be doing on a day-to-day basis in the second instance makes you sound poorly prepared.

You can also try to find out why the employer is looking to recruit someone at this time:

- *Why has this vacancy arisen?*
- *How many people are you looking to take on at this point in time?*

Tailoring your questions

Interviewers are most impressed by candidates who can actively demonstrate knowledge of their company. You can really stand out by asking questions that show you've done your research and want to delve even further into understanding the organisation. However, devising questions that are totally pertinent requires more effort on your part. The trick is to mention in passing the source of your knowledge before asking your question. Look at these examples for how to drop your sources into conversation:

✔ *I saw from your Web site that you sell mainly European wines. Do you have any plans to sell New World wines at all?*

✔ *Your brand is well known for its skincare products, and I've read rumours in the papers that you are thinking about launching a fragrance range. Is there any truth in that?*

✔ *One of the press releases on your Web site says that you're planning to double your number of stores in the next five years. Realistically, what promotion prospects will this lead to for people like me?*

✔ *I read in the papers that you plan to close another dozen branches by the end of the year. How is that affecting the morale of the team?*

✔ *That you're seeking to grow the private equity side of the business has been widely publicised. What practical implications would that have for me if I were to join the business?*

✔ *What happened to the previous holder of this position?* and (if that person was promoted) *Of course I'm interested in the next step up, so what did that person do to get that promotion?*

✔ *How quickly are you looking for someone to take on this role?*

✔ *How do you see this role developing?*

Avoid asking questions about pay and benefits until you have been offered a job. In the early stages of the interviewing process, you make a far better impression by appearing interested in the job itself rather than focusing on how much you'll earn.

Checking out future prospects

Employers are usually keen to retain and develop staff rather than let them leave and then have to go through the bother of replacing them. So demonstrating that you're interested in working for the organisation for some years to come is always a good idea.

Here are some questions to ask about your own learning and development within the company:

> ✔ *What is your policy on staff development?*
>
> ✔ *Will I have a development budget?*
>
> ✔ *How do other people at this level tend to spend their development budget?*
>
> ✔ *Are there opportunities to change roles further down the line?*

You can also ask about possibilities for advancement and promotion in the future:

> ✔ *Does a formal appraisal system exist here?*
>
> ✔ *What criteria will be used to judge my suitability for promotion?*
>
> ✔ *How quickly do people in this role tend to be promoted? Is there a minimum length of time that you have to be in the role before you can be considered for promotion?*
>
> ✔ *Does the company encourage people to study for professional qualifications? If it does, what kind of support is the company willing to provide?*
>
> ✔ *What kinds of career paths do people take in the organisation?*

If you want to demonstrate that you take a 'bigger picture' interest in the nature of the organisation, try some of these questions on for size:

> ✔ *How does this department/division interface with others across the organisation?*
>
> ✔ *Are you able to talk about the company's plans for growth?*
>
> ✔ *What sorts of new products/services is the business planning to launch?*
>
> ✔ *Does the company have any plans for mergers or acquisitions?*
>
> ✔ *How stable is the business? Does the company ever have any cash flow problems?*
>
> ✔ *Has the company ever had to make any redundancies? Why? What happened?*
>
> ✔ *Is the organisation planning to restructure or undergo any change programmes in the near future?*

Book III

Succeeding at Interviews

Enquiring about the culture

All organisations have rules and regulations. But *culture* describes the unwritten rules of how to behave at work. You can probably get an idea of the official rules or regulations by reading widely. But you can only get an idea of an organisation's culture by talking to people about it.

Questions about culture are very incisive. At worst, they can appear overly inquisitive so make sure to keep your tone light. And if you sense that the interviewers are prickling at your questions, move off the topic of culture immediately.

Here are some general questions to ask on the topic of organisational culture:

- ✔ *How would you describe the culture of the organisation?*
- ✔ *To what extent do people socialise together outside of work?*
- ✔ *How much autonomy do people really get in this organisation?*
- ✔ *What is it like to work here? What do you most enjoy about the job?*
- ✔ *Obviously you enjoy working here, but what would you say are your minor niggles or frustrations?*
- ✔ *How would you describe morale in the business at the moment?*
- ✔ *What does it take to be successful here?*
- ✔ *What kinds of people don't make it in this organisation?*

We can't stress this point enough – a fine line exists between asking intelligent questions and sounding like a show off! Be sure to think through the impact that each of your questions is likely to have on your interviewers. For example, if applying for a job as an entry-level role in customer service, asking about autonomy in the role would be far less appropriate than when applying for a supervisory role.

Turning Your Questions into a Discussion

When asking your questions, try to sound interested in the answers that the interviewers give. If the interviewers feel that you are genuinely interested in the position and their organisation, they're more likely to start thinking of you as a potential colleague rather than just another candidate.

Never ask a question purely for the sake of asking a question. You want your questions to leave the interviewers thinking that you have a genuine interest in joining their company. Don't rattle through a list of questions simply to demonstrate how clever you are.

As you ask your questions, try to find out more by making comments and asking further open-ended questions, such as:

> ✔ *That's interesting. How did that come about?*
>
> ✔ *May I ask more about that?*
>
> ✔ *So what does that mean for the organisation?*
>
> ✔ *That sounds intriguing – can you tell me more about that?*

Show your appreciation for the interviewers' patience in telling you more by commenting and nodding occasionally. If you fire too many questions at them, the interviewers can quickly feel that they are being interrogated – and that is not the effect you are trying to achieve!

Sending Follow-Up Letters

Interviewers can take days to make up their minds. So you have an opportunity to influence interviewers even after you've left the interview.

If the interviewers are deliberating between you and perhaps one other candidate, then a follow-up letter can just tip the balance. A few well-crafted paragraphs can well be the difference between success and failure.

Consider carefully whether to use e-mail or an old-fashioned letter in an envelope with a stamp on it. E-mail can be useful if speed is of the essence – for example, you know the interviewers have seen all the candidates and plan to make up their minds quickly. On the other hand, e-mail can easily be ignored. If you have the luxury of time, then a letter is much more likely to make a lasting impression.

In your message, try to get across at least two or three of the following points:

> ✔ That you enjoyed the opportunity to meet the interviewer and to hear more about the organisation and the role.
>
> ✔ That you are very interested in the role, the challenge, the team, or the organisation.
>
> ✔ That you have the right attitude, skills, and experience for the job.
>
> ✔ That you would very much like a job offer or to be invited to the next stage of the interview process.

Figure 3-1 shows a sample letter to use as follow-up to your interview; don't copy it word for word, but take a look at what you *can* write.

Book III

Succeeding at Interviews

Dear John,

I thought I would drop you a quick note to thank you for seeing me today. It was interesting to hear about the company's expansion plans. And I could tell that you obviously very much enjoy working there. The more I think about it, the more I would like to be a part of the company's future.

I hope that I managed to convey some of the qualities that would make me the right person for the job. I have nearly ten years' customer service experience in relevant sectors. In addition, I have the temperament and dedication to delivering high standard that would make me an excellent addition to your team.

I look forward to hearing from you soon - hopefully with the good news that you will be inviting me back for a second interview.

Yours sincerely,

Sarah Brown

Figure 3-1: Sending a follow-up after your interview may just tip the balance in your favour.

A lot of people don't like to send follow-up letters to interviewers, saying that doing so is a bit cheesy or feels like begging for the job. But what do you have to lose? Nothing – because if you're unsuccessful you'll never see the interviewers ever again anyway. But think about what you may gain. Just possibly, your letter can land you that job.

Ensuring Your References Are Positive

Many employers make job offers on the condition that your referees say positive things about you – or, at the very least, that they don't say anything hugely negative about you.

Before choosing people as referees, always ask their permission. Ideally, speak to them face-to-face so that you can gauge whether they are likely to make positive comments about you. If these people are reluctant, it may be that they didn't enjoy working with you and would feel uncomfortable commenting encouragingly about you!

If you parted on difficult terms with your last boss, you may not want to ask him or her for a reference. However, any organisation that is thinking of taking you on certainly wants a reference from your last employer. One (slightly sneaky) way round having to get a reference from your last boss is to ask another manager within the company to provide one. Perhaps you worked closely with the marketing manager or a director in another department and can ask one of them to write a complimentary reference for you. However, if a potential employer asks for a reference from your last boss, you may need to come clean.

Book III

Succeeding at Interviews

Chapter 4

Talking about Yourself and Others

. . . .

In This Chapter

▶ Thriving on the questions that interviewers love to ask

▶ Covering essential work skills

▶ Coping with questions about your character

. . . .

*I*n interviewing – as in life – there is both good news and bad. Interviewers tend to be a fairly lazy breed, which means that they often end up recycling the same old questions for interview after interview. For you, that's good news because it means that most interviewers end up asking more or less the same questions as each other.

But the bad news is that you can't simply find out the right answers to give from a book. Sure, we're going to give you lots of examples to illustrate the right sorts of key words and phrases to use. But at the end of the day, make sure that your answers reflect your personality, your skills, and your experience. You need to find ways to stand out from the crowd. So a great answer for an 18-year-old school leaver looking for their first job may be a tad different from what may work for a seasoned 50-year-old executive!

Handling General Questions about Yourself

Let's start with the ten most popular questions asked by interviewers. Giving comfortable responses to commonly asked interview questions is a foot in the door for any candidate. If you go to an interview and the interviewer doesn't ask you at least a few of these gems, well, I'll be amazed!

 Anyone can claim that they are a fantastic leader, a superb problem-solver, a go-getting team player, and an all-round good egg. But just as a lawyer in court needs to cite evidence to substantiate an argument, you need to provide examples to justify your claims. So as you read through the following questions, come up with your own personal example for each answer.

Driving towards great examples

Brrm brrm. The acronym CAR helps you to construct great examples to back up your claims that you are as good as you say you are. Whenever possible, try to explain the following points in your examples:

✔ **Challenge:** What was the problem or opportunity you had to tackle? Set the scene for the story that you are about to tell – but try to do it in only two or three sentences.

✔ **Actions:** What actions did you take to resolve the problem or grasp the opportunity? This is the bulk of your story. Use the first person singular ('I') rather than the first person plural ('we') to describe the actions that you took.

✔ **Result:** What was the outcome of the actions that you took? Generally, try to choose examples that describe successful outcomes.

Coming up with different examples for every skill that you may need to talk about in an interview can be really difficult. So you may end up using a handful of examples to demonstrate multiple skills. For instance, if you were involved in negotiating a deal with a customer, you may have demonstrated skills including researching the customer, writing a presentation, giving the presentation, putting together a business plan, and so on. You can get away with referring back to the same example to illustrate different skills, but each time you do it, don't bore the interviewer by going through all the CAR acronym. Just focus on the actions that you took to demonstrate that particular skill.

Tell me about yourself

This is probably the single most popular question that interviewers use for opening an interview. But don't take the question as an invitation to recount your entire life's history. When you hear this question, answer by pretending that they had actually asked you: *Tell me **briefly** about your professional experience and the relevant qualities that make you a strong candidate for this job.*

Don't make the classic mistake of sharing too much personal information with your interviewer. I've heard too many candidates start by telling the interviewer where they were born and where they went to school and what they studied there. It's not a wrong answer as such, but by telling them about your personal history, your opportunity to sell your experience and relevant skills flies by.

All the interviewer needs is a snapshot – a summary lasting no more than a minute or 90 seconds – of your background and experience. Be sure to prepare one before your interview.

Read the original job advertisement and pick up on the key words and phrases the interviewers are looking for. These may be about certain skills or experience, or perhaps human qualities they want the perfect candidate to have. Squeeze some of these words and phrases into your answer. For instance, if the advert mentions that the employer is looking for 'a supervisor with excellent communication and people management skills', mention any supervisory experience you've gained, as well as the fact that you are articulate and enjoy communicating and liaising with a wide range of people.

Example answers include:

✔ *I am a management consultant with 12 years' experience gained across industries and sectors ranging from financial services and retail to petrochemicals and media. I am responsible for business development activities and last year sold projects totalling £400,000 to clients. On a day-to-day basis, I also manage a team of up to eight consultants and junior consultants. But more than being a good consultant, I like to think of myself as a fair and democratic person as I try hard to listen to my clients as well as my team.*

✔ *I'm currently the floor supervisor at Molly's, which is a busy bar and restaurant in Brighton. I'm responsible for all aspects of management, ranging from stock taking and ordering to end of day cashing up. I run a team of seven staff and am responsible for training, hiring, and firing. The hours can be quite long, but I enjoy it and like the mix of activities from dealing with customers to managing the staff.*

✔ *I've been a childcare assistant for the last three years, working with physically and mentally impaired children between the ages of eight and 14. I've really enjoyed it and have developed some skills such as being creative and being extremely patient. I also spend a lot of time dealing with the children's parents and have to demonstrate really good listening skills with them. I've now decided that I want to expand my horizons and travel, which is why I've decided to change careers into being a holiday rep – but I hope that my creativity, patience, and listening skills will hold me in good stead in this new industry.*

Book III

Succeeding at Interviews

What are your strengths?

From your analysis of the job advert, you can work out the key skills and characteristics that the employer is looking for. Paraphrasing a few of these back to the employer is an effective way to answer this question.

When paraphrasing key skills and characteristics, make sure to change the wording slightly – simply repeating them verbatim will make you sound like a mindless parrot.

A couple of examples:

> ✔ *As an office manager with Global Gadgets, I have excellent organisation skills and really good attention to detail – I'm not the sort of person who does things by halves. I also believe that I have good communication skills in dealing with not only external customers but also all members of the internal team – from the senior managers to the junior researchers.*

> ✔ *I've been told that I'm a very good manager. My team tells me that I give them a lot of freedom in how to do their work, which they really appreciate. They also say that I'm really enthusiastic, so when we're faced with too much work, they tell me that my manner really helps to keep them motivated and calm. My boss also tells me that I'm very innovative in terms of finding new ways of working that cut out inefficiency.*

Have an example up your sleeve to justify each of your alleged strengths. An interviewer can easily ask you, *Why do you believe those are your strengths?*

For example, the Global Gadgets manager mentioned earlier in this section may go on to reply: *As just one example, our company moved offices recently. I had to co-ordinate the entire move and make sure that our server and all of the computers were set up correctly in the new office. At the same time, I dealt with all of our staff and customers to ensure that day-to-day business was not at all disrupted.*

Try to sound confident without sounding over-confident or arrogant. If you're worried about sounding over-confident, use phrases such as *I've been told that I am . . .* and *I believe that I am . . .* rather than just saying *I am. . . .*

What are your weaknesses?

If the interviewer asks about your strengths, they will almost certainly ask about your weaknesses too. Being unable to describe any weaknesses suggests to the interviewer that you lack self-awareness or are a bit egotistical – are you really saying that you are completely perfect at everything that you do?

Pick a couple of minor weaknesses that are of little relevance to the job. For example, if the job involves a lot of contact with customers and colleagues, then you can say that you get bored when you have to spend a lot of time working on your own. Or if the job offers you a lot of independence and flexibility, you may argue that one of your weaknesses is that you get very frustrated when you are micro-managed.

When discussing your weaknesses, always talk about how you compensate for them, too. Describe the actions or steps that you take to ensure that your weaknesses don't affect your performance at work.

Consider this example of a weakness and how a candidate compensates for it:

My natural tendency is to make up my mind very quickly – and in the past this has got me into trouble. But I have come to realise that speed is not always appropriate so I always remind myself that I may need to collect more information and weigh up the pros and cons. Nowadays, if I am at all uncertain about a decision, I will seek input from colleagues.

What motivates you?

Employers are looking for people who are keen to make a difference to their organisation. So if you aren't terribly motivated by work and the only thing that keeps you going is the thought of leaving your workplace at the end of the day, keep that to yourself.

One trick is to say that you are motivated when you get to use the kinds of skills that the employer is looking for. For instance, if the employer requires someone with customer service skills, then – hey presto – it may be wise to say something along the lines of: *I really enjoy spending time with people and get a buzz out of dealing with customers and sorting out their problems. I hate it when I feel that I'm not doing my best on behalf of customers.* Yes, it sounds a bit cheesy, but if you say it with sincerity, it can nail you the job (if you're struggling with sincerity in interviews, Romilla Ready and Kate Burton's *Neuro-linguistic Programming For Dummies* (Wiley) helps you through by thinking positive).

Other good answers include:

- ✔ **Recognition:** While many interviewers consider it gauche to say that you are motivated by money, you can say that you like to have your good work recognised by your boss, peers, or clients.

- ✔ **Making a difference:** Especially in the charity or non-profit sector, saying that you are motivated by the pursuit of the organisation's goals is a good idea.

- ✔ **Challenge:** Another good answer is to say that you enjoy getting fully caught up in solving problems and getting to the bottom of difficult situations.

- ✔ **Self-development:** Employers like candidates who want to further their own learning and development. Do bear in mind the nature of the role that you are applying for, though. A management training scheme is likely to provide you with much more by way of development opportunities than, say, an office data entry job.

✔ **Money:** Only when going for a sales job should you talk about the fact that you are motivated by financial reward. In fact, many sales people are suspicious of candidates who say that they are not motivated by money and the luxuries that money can allow you to buy.

Don't just memorise one of these answers by heart. Take a moment to figure out what really motivates you – you'll sound much more genuine.

What are you passionate about?

This question is just a variant on *What motivates you?* However, the key to answering a question about passion is ensuring that your body language demonstrates not just enthusiasm but real passion. We remember observing interviews for a job as an assistant fashion buyer at a large high-street fashion retailer. All the candidates had fashion degrees and were equally knowledgeable. But the candidate who got the offer was the one whose eyes and face lit up when she talked about her passion for clothing and design and fabrics and trends and all things to do with fashion.

If being honest, a lot of people would struggle to find something to be really 'passionate' about at work. So you may be tempted to talk about a passion outside of work – perhaps a sporting interest or a community project. But if you do mention an outside interest, it allows the interviewers to wonder whether you'll be able to bring all your energies to work. So try to keep your answers within the world of work.

What are your biggest achievements?

An interviewer may ask for just one achievement or a handful – so give this question some thought beforehand. Wherever possible, keep most of your achievements work-related and focus on the benefits that you achieved for other people, such as:

✔ Increased customer or client satisfaction

✔ Greater revenues or profit

✔ A bigger slice of market share

✔ The elimination of inefficiencies or errors

✔ Cost reduction

✔ Improved relationship morale within the team or with other stakeholders

✔ Enhanced reputation of your employer

For example, an IT manager may say:

*We were asked by our head office in the US to upgrade all of our staff's comput-
ers to a new software package. We have over 600 computers across three locations in the UK and it was imperative that we handled the migration within the
space of a few days to ensure that there would be no compatibility issues. This
was back in March, which is traditionally a really busy time of year for our company. I had to attend a lot of meetings with senior managers to persuade them
that it was important. And I had to co-ordinate the efforts of my team to ensure
that all of the computers were upgraded within those few days. It took a lot of
planning and hard work, but I was really proud of the fact that we managed the
migration and had only a few minor problems – and no complaints from the
staff.*

Don't just talk about what the achievement was – you also need to say why it
was an achievement. Clearly demonstrate to the interviewer exactly what
you did to make your action an achievement.

If an interviewer asks you specifically to talk about an achievement outside of
work, always relate it back to the kinds of skills or characteristics that would
make you a good addition to the team. And don't just assume that the link is
obvious – explain the link to the interviewer. For example, passing a piano
exam is evidence of your ability to focus on achieving goals that you set for
yourself. Perhaps a sporting triumph is evidence of your commitment and
dedication to improving your health. Or raising money for a charity is evidence of your ability to work with a team to a deadline.

Book III

**Succeeding
at
Interviews**

What are you most proud of?

This is simply a variation of the question *What are your achievements?* The
trap here is for unwary candidates who may gush about their family or
accomplishments outside of work. While you may be terribly proud of your
children or your relationship or having lost weight or given up smoking, try
to use a work-related achievement.

Don't exaggerate your achievements. If you were involved in only a small way
in a much bigger team, then a skilled interviewer may be able to see through
you. Rack your brain and always pick examples where you honestly did make
a significant contribution.

What is your greatest failure?

Ooh, this is a nasty question. The interviewer is setting you a big trap to fall
into. The way to fend off this question is by saying that you don't think that
you have ever had a 'greatest failure'.

However, saying that you've never failed is not a good enough answer on its own. So go on to talk about some minor failure that you have experienced – perhaps a particular project that did not go well or a piece of work that was not up to your usual high standards.

Try to find an example of a situation that went badly due to unforeseen circumstances. Never blame anyone else for the failure – as an interviewer can label you as someone who shirks responsibility and seeks to point the finger at other people. And try to finish off your anecdote by talking about the lesson you took from it.

Honesty is a good trait, but too much honesty can be your downfall when answering this question! If you believe that you have been guilty of a major failure – even if it was only through bad luck or circumstance – try to play it down.

Do you have any regrets?

Regret is a very strong, emotionally laden word. Again, the trap here is for unwary candidates to end up confessing major misgivings about their lives.

Unskilled interviewers often ask closed questions. But even though answering with a simple *yes* or *no* is technically correct, avoid doing so as you'll lose out on an opportunity to sell yourself.

One way to avoid the trap would be to say something like: *Sure, I have made mistakes, but I don't think that I have any real regrets. I believe that I've learnt from every situation that I've been in. And those situations and my choices in those situations have made me the person that I am.*

Alternatively, you can admit to wondering what may have happened if you had made a different decision at some time in your career. But always assert at the end of your tale that your decision was the right one to have made at the time. For example:

We had an offer from a big American conglomerate to buy our business a few years ago. But the negotiations fell through because the conglomerate was not willing to pay us fairly for our business. As it turned out, the bottom fell out of the market and the value of our shares fell. But there was no way that we could have foreseen that terrorist attacks would cause a slump in the economy. So at the time it had been the right decision.

Why should we hire you?

This question is often used to bring an interview to a close, so treat it as your opportunity to sell yourself boldly to the interviewers. A good answer may match three or four of your key skills and characteristics to the job. For example:

Your advert said that you were looking for someone who is highly numerate, has good teamworking and presentation skills, and a willingness to work hard. I hope that my experience as a financial analyst at Transworld Bank shows that I'm good with numbers. Both of the jobs I've held so far have required me to work often long hours in a close-knit team and it's something that I very much enjoy. And my boss singled out my presentation skills in my last appraisal. So I think that I am a very strong candidate.

If you want to add the icing to the cake, you can go on to mention how much you want the job. Try a bit of subtle flattery in talking about the reputation or standing of the company. Or mention some other positive reasons you want to work for the company, such as the quality of their training scheme or the fact that the business is successful and growing.

Your body language and tone of voice are doubly important when answering this key question. Make sure that you exude confidence and enthusiasm as you list the key skills and characteristics that make you the right person for the job. If confidence isn't currently one of your strongest traits, take a look at Kate Burton and Brinley Platt's *Building Confidence For Dummies* (Wiley) for good advice.

Book III

Succeeding at Interviews

Talking about Basic Job Skills

No matter what job you are going for – a head teacher, a shop assistant, or a magazine editor – employers are looking for some fundamental skills. Being able to demonstrate that you are reliable, organised, and able to work under pressure – amongst other skills – are such prerequisites for any job that you must be ready to answer these questions.

Would you say that you're reliable?

As Homer Simpson would say: 'D'oh!' Only an idiot would say that they are not reliable. But rather than simply saying, *Yes, I am reliable*, the key here is to give an example or to explain why you think so.

Try to figure out what the interviewer really means by 'reliable'. If the job requires staff to clock in and clock out, then perhaps the interviewer means punctual and willing to work overtime. If the job requires a high level of responsibility, then maybe the interviewer means dependable.

Consider these example answers:

Yes, I am a very reliable person. I've never been late for work in the 18 months that I have worked at the Grantham factory and I'm happy to do overtime if we are falling behind on our deadlines.

Yes, I would say that I am very reliable. My boss knows that I'm the sort of person that he can leave to get on with an important task and I won't forget about it or quit until I have completed it.

What's your absenteeism/sickness record like?

Employers really worry that their staff may turn up late to work or take loads of days off sick. Hopefully, you can alleviate their concerns by saying: *I have a really good absenteeism record – I have only had X days off in the last few years*. The key is for 'X' to be less than a handful.

If you have taken quite a few days off from work, make sure that you can give a compelling reason why. But go on to stress that the reason has now gone away. For example:

I did have to take four weeks off from work because I tore a ligament when I slipped on an oil patch on the shop floor. But I've now fully recovered and have a clean bill of health so it will not pose any further problems in the future.

Never lie about your sickness record, as employers frequently check up on it. Job offers are often made *subject to reference* (checking out your employment history with former employers) and a lie at this stage can lead to the employer withdrawing their offer.

How would you describe your time management skills?

For most jobs, employers are looking for *time management skills* – the ability to distinguish between what needs to be done immediately and what can wait. Of course you need to say that you have good time management skills.

A good tactic is to say that you always prioritise the most important and urgent tasks to the top of the pile. When that doesn't work, say that you enlist colleagues to help or check whether the deadline can be moved. As a final option, you can say that you simply get on with the work and stay late to get everything done.

Go on to demonstrate your time management skills by giving an example of a time when you had to prioritise between different tasks.

As an example, just the other week I had a customer who wanted an emergency order dealt with immediately at the same time as my boss needed some financial data. There was no way I could have done both, so I asked a colleague to deal with the customer order while I put together the data that my boss needed.

Time management is ultimately the ability to distinguish between urgency and importance. *Urgency* describes whether a task needs to be done very soon or whether it can wait for a few hours or a few weeks. *Importance* describes the extent to which the task must be completed – some tasks are absolutely critical while others may be less crucial.

Are you an organised person?

Of course you are highly organised! Illustrate your organisational skills by talking about some of the methods or systems that you use to organise your work, such as:

- ✔ Making lists of tasks
- ✔ Keeping files and records on different projects
- ✔ Developing a routine or process
- ✔ Using tables, spreadsheets, computer programs, or even Gantt charts (but only talk about these if you genuinely have used them) to track progress on different pieces of work

Don't forget to prove that you really are organised by providing a short example about a project that you have organised or co-ordinated.

Be careful not to imply that you are so organised that you would find it difficult to function without your methods and ways of working. Sometimes the world of work throws up unexpected problems and situations that you just need to tackle spontaneously.

As a subsidiary question, an interviewer may ask you: *How tidy is your desk at work?* Such a question means that the interviewer probably believes that a tidy desk is a sign of a tidy mind – so full marks go to candidates who can describe an orderly workspace.

Book III

Succeeding at Interviews

Do you work well under pressure?

While the answer to this question is obviously yes, be careful not to exaggerate the extent to which you can cope with pressure. Try to relate your answer to the demands that the job is likely to make on you.

For example, if the job is likely to involve significant pressure, the following response may be fairly appropriate:

I positively thrive on pressure. My worst nightmare is a job that is entirely predictable and mundane. I really enjoy the fact that my job is different every day and you never know what new situations or challenges you may be facing.

If the job is more gently paced, saying that you love working under pressure may raise doubts in an interviewer's mind as to whether you would be bored by the job. So try an answer along the lines of:

I can cope with occasional bursts of having to work under pressure – for example, for the final couple of days every month it always gets a bit frantic. But for the most part, I enjoy the fact that this is a job that I can really learn and understand in detail and get good at.

If you need to demonstrate beyond a shadow of a doubt that you excel under pressure, use the acronym CAR (see the sidebar 'Driving towards great examples' at the start of this chapter) to provide an example. Make sure that the result at the end of your story is a positive one!

Would you say that you're creative?

An interviewer may ask if you are creative or innovative – and for all practical purposes, you can treat these as the same question. Your answer to this question depends on the nature of the job you are being interviewed for. If you're applying for a job requiring high levels of artistic ability and visual creativity (such as a graphic designer or an advertising executive), then say yes and have ready a portfolio with at least a couple of examples of how you have demonstrated your creativity.

Bear in mind that employers are looking for not just creative ideas, but actual tangible products, designs, and inventions. So make sure that your examples describe how you turned an idea in your head into a solution that benefited your team or organisation.

If you're not applying for a job that demands high levels of creativity and you feel that creativity really is not one of your strong points, then this is one occasion when you should feel comfortable being honest in saying so. But go on to stress some of your other key strengths and qualities.

If the job is a managerial one, you can get away with saying that creativity is not one of your key strengths. We have heard a number of managers impress interviewers by saying that while creativity is not one of their key strengths, they try to create an atmosphere in their teams that encourages creativity through brainstorming, running workshops and away days, and supporting the ideas that members of the team have.

Would you say you're good with detail?

For the majority of candidates, the answer to this question should be a yes. Of course employers don't want to take slipshod people on board.

If the job requires highly detailed work, give a simple example of how you ensure that your work is of a consistently high quality:

In my job it's really important to get all of the numbers right, so I always double check the data after I have entered it. And I'm glad to say that in my two years in the job so far, no one has ever found an error in my calculations.

The exception to this general rule is managers. For managers in middling to senior roles, employers often expect them to pay attention to the big picture rather than getting too bogged down in detail. So if you already manage a medium to large team of people – say at least a couple of dozen or more people – then you can get away with saying:

I have to admit that detail isn't one of my strong points. I try to keep focused on the big picture. However, I always make sure that I have good people in my team who can handle the detail.

How do you respond to change?

Interviewers do not want to end up hiring an inflexible and unadaptable employee. I'm sure you know the type – the grumpy person who complains about how things are 'nowadays' and constantly reminisces about the 'good old days' before such and such a change.

Book III

Succeeding at Interviews

The world of work is changing quickly – with factors at play such as globalisation, mergers and acquisitions, change programmes, and efficiency drives. Talking about how you have coped with one of these changes will illustrate your ability to deal with change.

Make sure that you can show that you're willing to adapt to new circumstances, maybe along the lines of:

A couple of people left our team in the space of just a week, which meant that we were heavily understaffed for a period of over a month. The rest of the team had to readjust our shifts to ensure that the helpdesk remained manned at all times. I volunteered for a few additional shifts because I knew that our customers would otherwise have no one to sort out their problems.

Another tactic showing that you not only cope with change, but excel at it, is talking about how you have helped others through change. Perhaps you had colleagues who were uncertain of a new rota, but you talked them round. Or you volunteered to work on a project team, committee, or task force responsible for some part of the change process. Either of these examples demonstrates that you are not only reactively able to cope with change, but can proactively contribute to it.

How are you with new technology?

A variation on questioning your ability to cope with change, this question about technology tends to get asked more of older candidates. If you think about it, new technology is being introduced all the time – from new computers and laptops to mobile phones and electronic key cards. Worrisome employers don't want to hire people who struggle to master even the very basics of how to use them.

Give as concrete an example as possible of getting to grips with some new facet of technology that has been introduced into your workplace:

We used to use transparent acetates and old-fashioned overhead projectors for teaching seminars. But the university decided to introduce laptops and projectors and asked us all to prepare our materials using PowerPoint. I'm pleased to say that after attending the briefing sessions on how to use the new technology, I've become a real fan of this new way of working.

What software packages are you familiar with?

If you are going for a role where software packages are important, then it's usually a good idea to list them somewhere on your CV. If an employer then asks you about your level of proficiency with different packages, make sure that you can give examples of what feats you can perform on each. For example:

I'm responsible for creating the monthly department newsletter, which usually means using that package to format and tabulate other people's contributions. I also have to import images and create detailed proposal documents for my manager. And I can merge lists of contacts with letter templates to create marketing mailshots.

 Even the most seasoned of executives is usually assumed to have a passing knowledge of how to use a computer. Partners in top City law firms and senior managers with budgets of hundreds of millions of pounds are expected to read and send their own e-mails and type a few words into a document. So if you can't do at least these two basic tasks, make sure you find someone to teach you how!

 If you really don't know anything about computers, then try to go on a training course or get a colleague or friend to teach you how to use the basics of the Microsoft Office package. Microsoft is by far the most popular software developer in the workplace, so is a good one to start with.

Book III

Succeeding at Interviews

How would you rate yourself as . . .?

An interviewer can ask you to rate yourself on a number of criteria – such as your skills as a leader, a team player, a teacher, or a researcher. Obviously, you need to begin by saying that you are a good leader, team player, or whatever. Don't let modesty get in the way of selling yourself – you can bet that other candidates are making all sorts of wild claims about how great they are.

To back up your claim, do go on to tell a short anecdote or cite an example as to why you think you rate yourself so highly. If you have won any awards or ever received any commendations or positive feedback from colleagues or customers, then this may be the time to mention it.

If an interviewer asks for a numerical rating, avoid giving yourself a score of 10/10. Trying to claim that you are perfect will come across as incredibly bigheaded. A score of 8/10 is more reasonable. Go on to say something like: *I believe that I'm very good at X, but there is always more to learn.* This response shows an ounce of humility and willingness to improve even further – good traits to have in an employee.

Overcoming Interviewers' Common Worries

Because employers are a worrisome lot, you have the task of convincing them you have no characteristics that should cause them undue concern. Sure, their job advert focuses on the positive qualities they're looking for in their candidate of choice, but be aware that employers are apt to think about the negative characteristics, as well. After all, I'm sure you know plenty of people who have bad tempers, who are difficult to manage and shy away from hard work, are boring to be around, and so on. In this section, we focus on how you can convince interviewers you have none of these negative characteristics.

What makes you lose your temper?

If you can truthfully say that you never lose your temper at work, then by all means say so. Explain to the interviewer exactly how or why you manage to keep your temper at bay when you're at work. For example:

I'm not the kind of person who ever gets angry at work. Anger just isn't productive and even in a crisis it's more important to figure out what can be done to sort out the situation than to shout and scream and point the finger of blame at people.

If you do occasionally lose your temper, word your response as carefully as possible:

I guess that sometimes I do let my frustration show. For example, when colleagues promise to do something and then let me down at the last moment, I have been known to have a few terse words with them.

How do you respond to authority?

No one wants to take on an argumentative employee who's resistant to authority. But your answer to this question – or its variant *How well do you take direction?* – may depend on the nature of the organisation.

In traditional and hierarchical organisations where employees are expected to know their place and defer to people more senior, show your keen appreciation of the need to defer to authority in your answer:

I respect authority and enjoy having a straightforward reporting relationship where my boss gives me guidelines on what I can or cannot do. In my current job, I know exactly what decisions I can make. For bigger decisions or larger items of spend, I always check with my supervisor. If I were to be taken on in this role, I would like to sit down with my manager as soon as possible to establish how best to work together.

If you think that your interview is with a progressive organisation, position yourself as a more freethinking candidate:

I have the utmost respect for authority, but I'm not the kind of person who will mindlessly do everything that my manager tells me. If I don't understand something or think that a decision isn't in the best interests of the team, I'll ask questions until I'm satisfied with my manager's response. But ultimately if I feel that management has listened to my questions or objections, then I have to respect their decision and get on with it.

Book III

Succeeding at Interviews

How do you deal with disappointment?

Being able to deal with setbacks and disappointment is a really important quality. Life (and work) doesn't always go the way you want it to, and candidates who admit to giving up immediately are frankly a pain to work with! Employers want people who live by the adage 'If at first you don't succeed, try, try again.'

Of course I don't enjoy being disappointed, but rather than dwell on the past I try to focus on the future. As such, I always try to make the best of any situation. If I feel that I can do anything to better the situation, then I try to do it. But if it looks as if the chance has gone, then I try to see what I can learn from it.

If you can, give an example of a situation when an initial rejection or rebuttal actually spurred you on to make a greater effort or take further steps that eventually led to success.

When I first wanted to work in music production, I sent off my CV to more than 80 companies and didn't get an interview from a single one. But I knew that I really wanted to work in the industry so I took my CV round to some of their offices and literally knocked on companies' doors. I physically visited 30 or 40 companies and got offered a week's unpaid work experience at one of them, and at the end of the week they offered me a job.

How do you cope with job stress?

The interviewer isn't asking you *whether* you can cope with stressful situations at work, but *how* you cope with them. Engaging in sports or exercise is probably the most socially acceptable way of letting off steam:

No matter how bad the day I've had – perhaps it's due to a difficult case or just too much to do – when I get home, I get changed and go for a 20-minute jog. Whenever I do that, I can literally feel the tension leaving my body.

Other ways of unwinding may include:

- Socialising with friends or colleagues.
- Cooking dinner for friends.
- Talking about a day's stressful activities with a friend or partner at home.
- Engaging in relaxing activities such meditation, yoga, or having a bath with scented oils.

Think about how your chosen method of unwinding may be viewed by the interviewers. An activity that seems completely acceptable in one organisational culture may be frowned upon in another. For example, interviewers at an investment bank or a fashion house are more likely to view having a drink in a favourable light, while they may be less impressed with people who go home to meditate. If you want to get maximum brownie points, emphasise any common interests you have with the interviewers or the people who typically work in their organisation.

What's your attitude to taking risks?

The key to answering this question is to think about the employer's likely attitude to risks. After all, would you want to put your life in the hands of a surgeon or airline pilot who admits to living on the edge? As such, industries such as manufacturing, oil and gas, airlines, and the health professions are probably very conservative about risk-taking because of the very real possibility of physical injury or death. Here's an example of an answer that fits well in the oil industry:

I'm a strong believer in never having to take risks. Ours is a difficult job and it's imperative that everyone has had a full health and safety briefing. I always assign two people to check that the equipment is sound before we proceed with the drilling.

Other companies may actively encourage their employees to take calculated risks if they feel that the downside is very much outweighed by the possible upside – and at the end of the day, they may only be risking a small chunk of their budget rather than loss of life or limb!

When talking about your attitude to risk, bear in mind that a world of difference exists between a calculated risk and a complete shot in the dark:

I don't mind taking risks if I feel that I have done whatever I can to establish the pros and cons. At the end of the day, most business decisions are slightly uncertain, but if the financial projections don't look too bad and my gut feeling is good, then I'll take a chance. Generally, my instincts have been sound and the majority of our projects make money.

Ours is a work hard, play hard culture – how do you feel about that?

Book III

Succeeding at Interviews

Employers like to hire in their own image. You've probably heard of the *Old Boys' Network* – chaps from stuffy schools and colleges hiring other chaps who went to the same schools and colleges. But even if the interviewers didn't go to a prestigious school, they still like to hire people who are like them.

If an employer describes the company culture, then obviously say that you think you'd fit into that culture really well. If you'd be happy working and playing hard – which probably means working a 12-hour day and then going out drinking with your colleagues – then tell the interviewers exactly that.

If you really don't feel that way, this probably isn't the right job for you. And admitting that you don't feel that way will almost certainly count against your candidacy.

Tell me something interesting about yourself

Hmm, this is a tricky one because the interviewer wants someone who has something to talk about outside of work. And this is a perfectly understandable question, too – would you want to work with someone who had nothing to talk about apart from work?

Do you have a skill or talent that you can talk about? Perhaps you have an unusual hobby or interest. Or maybe you have achieved something remarkable. What you talk about almost doesn't matter, so long as you can talk about something outside of the workplace.

Consider these genuine examples that I've heard:

- A call centre supervisor said that she was taking dance classes and her ambition was to be able to do the splits.

- A management consultant revealed that he used to be an aerobics instructor when he was at university.

- A primary school teacher mentioned that he had a turntable at home and spent occasional weekends DJ-ing at local nightclubs.

Be careful about trying to be funny. Humour is really difficult to judge – especially when you don't know people very well. Innuendoes can go down like a ton of bricks while an ironic statement may get taken at face value. For example, we once met an interviewer who thought a candidate was being deadly serious when he joked that he was wearing his girlfriend's underwear! So try to think of an interesting fact about yourself rather than answering this question in a flippant fashion.

What would you say your Unique Selling Point is?

A *Unique Selling Point* (USP) is a bit of marketing jargon. The interviewer is asking what makes you unique and why you stand out from the other candidates. As you can never know exactly what skills and experiences the other candidates have, talk about how you differ from (and are a better candidate than) your *peers* (people that you know at your own level in your industry). Or you can argue that your combination of skills and characteristics makes you unique.

Consider a couple of examples:

- *I've been working as a beauty consultant for a few years now. But without wanting to sound too bigheaded, I've noticed that I tend to pick up information about new products a lot more quickly than just about any other consultant I've worked with. And that enables me to sell the products much more successfully.*

- *What hopefully makes me unique is the fact that I have bundles of enthusiasm and a real ambition to progress. I am ever so keen to get on and build a career in this industry, and I think that you would find it difficult to find someone who has my energy and willingness to work hard.*

Seeing Yourself As Others See You

A common tactic employers draw upon is to ask you how different people may rate or describe you. The knack in answering this question is to talk up the positive remarks that others may say or have said about you while playing down some of the negative comments.

Don't lie. If everyone you work with says that you are really bad at a particular skill, avoid mentioning that skill. Remember that employers frequently check references as a condition of offering you a job. A reference that describes you as the complete opposite of how you have described yourself can be a real deal breaker.

What would your boss say about you?

A good answer alludes to some of the skills or qualities that the interviewers are looking for. Your cause won't be helped if your boss thought you were great at analysing quantitative data on your own if the job requires someone who can work on qualitative data in a team.

Treat this question as if the interviewers had asked you the question: *What would your boss say are your good points?* – there's no point in emphasising your weaknesses unless the interviewers specifically ask for them.

She would say that I'm someone who is totally reliable and a safe pair of hands for any difficult work that she might need doing. She also asks me to deputise for her in committee meetings.

If you are too extravagant in your claims as to how good your boss thought you were, the interviewers are more likely to ask you to justify your assertions with an example or two.

In your last appraisal, what was said about your performance?

Unfortunately, appraisals often have the tendency of focusing more on development areas and weaknesses than what you are good at, but your answer to this question should focus on your achievements rather than your failings.

I was pleased that my manager said that I had made significant progress toward becoming an area manager. I had succeeded in restoring good relationships with our suppliers and putting in place new service level agreements with them.

Book III

Succeeding at Interviews

Our performance is also rated across five key skill categories and I was pleased that I was rated as 'above average' on four of them, and 'exceptional' on one.

Another common variant on this question is: *What goals did your boss set for you in your last appraisal?* If this question is asked, describe the goals briefly, but then spend most of the time talking about the actions or steps that you have been taking (or intend to take) to reach those goals.

My boss thought that I should aim to boost my department's staff satisfaction score from its current 75% to 80%. I now plan to have a number of away days for the entire team to discuss our quarterly targets and how best to achieve them. And I am putting in place a coaching programme to ensure that the junior managers are spending at least an hour a week talking to each of their direct reports about the issues affecting them.

How do you think you can improve on your performance?

This question often follows, *In your last appraisal, what was said about your performance?* (see the preceding section for advice on how to answer that question). The interviewer is now asking you specifically about any areas for development or improvement.

Talk about not only why you failed to reach some of your targets but also what you have since planned to do to reach them in the future. And, if possible, talk about what benefits you are seeing as a result of your new approach.

My manager felt that while I'm very good at getting my work done, I need to be a bit more strategic in my outlook. He said that I have a tendency to focus on my own immediate piece of work, but not to look at the bigger picture. Since then I have been making a concerted effort to talk to the rest of the team more frequently to ensure that my own work ties more closely into the overall project's objectives. It has already helped us to spot some potential problems and deal with them before they affect the quality of our output.

What would your colleagues say about you?

This question is a common alternative to *What would your boss say about you?* (a question covered earlier in this chapter). While your boss may say that you are better than others in the team at certain skills, your team mates are unlikely to use the same sort of language.

Think about the contribution that you make to the team. What is it that you can always be relied upon to do? Or what sorts of problems or issues do your colleagues tend to come to you with? Make sure that your answer marks you out as an invaluable part of the team:

✔ *I think they would say that I tend to play the devil's advocate. I'm the kind of person who can see the problems with an idea or argument quite quickly. That doesn't mean that I'll automatically be negative about an idea, but it does mean that I can ask the right questions and point out the flaw so that we can think about how to make the idea more workable instead.*

✔ *My colleagues tend to see me as the person that they can come and talk to when they're feeling down. If they're having a bad day, they know that I lend a sympathetic ear. Sometimes they just take the opportunity to vent their frustrations and let off steam. But sometimes they are stumped by a problem and I tend to be quite good at seeing how they might deal with a situation.*

How would your team describe you?

This question only applies if you manage or are sometimes responsible for a team of more junior people. You're being asked to rate your own ability as a leader, manager, or supervisor.

Book III

Succeeding at Interviews

I think my team would say that I'm a fair and open manager. I try to get to know what sort of work they enjoy and what they are good or bad at. I try to give them work that they will find challenging but at the same time enjoyable. Once I've set my team a piece of work, I try to avoid checking up on them too much. At the same time, I have an 'open door' policy so that they can come to me with any problems whenever they need to.

Other key words used to describe desirable management styles include 'empowering' and 'democratic'.

How do you think your friends would describe you?

Your friends are unlikely to comment on your work skills. So focus more on the qualities and characteristics that make you a good person to know. Good qualities to mention include:

✔ A friendly and outgoing nature

✔ Sense of humour

✔ Reliability or loyalty

✔ Tact and ability to keep confidences

✔ Persistence, ambition, or determination

✔ Willingness to get up after being knocked down

My friends would say that I'm quite ambitious. I'm the kind of person who sets goals and then sets out to achieve them – for example, I didn't want to get too much into debt while at university so kept looking until I found a part-time job that I could juggle at the same time as my studies. But while I'm ambitious, I don't take myself too seriously. I'm good fun to be around and have a strongly ironic sense of humour.

Pick traits or attributes relevant for the job. For example, if applying for a job as a receptionist at a doctor's surgery, saying that your friends would say that you have a great sense of humour and are a constant practical joker may be less helpful than the fact they find you tactful and a pillar of strength when they are feeling unhappy.

Everyone has some kind of fault – what would other people say your faults are?

In this question, 'other people' can refer to your colleagues, your friends, or your team. If you have answered any of the previous handful of questions by describing the good stuff about yourself (as you should always do), a particularly canny interviewer then tends to follow up by asking about some of the bad stuff, too. However, the word 'fault' is quite strong – it suggests that you have a major flaw in your character. So beat the interviewers at their own game by preparing a story about a minor failing instead.

When talking about any faults, weaknesses, or areas for improvement, it's critical that you talk about the steps or actions that you take to limit or compensate for them, as shown in the following examples:

✔ *Of course I'm not perfect. I know that I can get very enthusiastic about new ideas and can come across to some people as a bit impatient. It's just that I get too keen about a project that I think has real benefits. So nowadays I try to keep in mind that I need to slow down to avoid bulldozing others.*

✔ *When I'm under pressure, I know that I can get a little uncommunicative. If I've got too much to do, I like to get my head down and get on with it. So on those rare occasions, people have said that I'm not my usually fun self. But when I've got the work out of the way, I quickly snap out of it.*

Discussing Your People Skills

If employers had to pick the most important category of skills in choosing between candidates, they'd probably pick interpersonal skills. Unless you are working in a sealed room without even a telephone in it (which is a highly unlikely situation – how many jobs can you name that don't involve any interaction whatsoever with other human beings?), you'll need good interpersonal skills to deal with colleagues, clients and customers, and suppliers.

In particular roles, such as sales, you may need highly developed pitching and negotiation skills. But the questions in this section are relevant to just about everyone.

Do you prefer to work on your own or in a team?

Team working skills are highly prized in most organisations. At the same time though, don't imply that you are completely hopeless and unable to concentrate when a task requires you to work independently of others.

This question has no single right answer. Your approach to the question depends on the nature of the job. Take a few seconds to think about how much time the job would require you to spend working in a team versus working on your own.

If, for example, the job requires you to work almost constantly in a team, an answer such as the following may be appropriate:

I can work on my own, but to be honest I get the biggest buzz from working in a fast-paced team. I like having people around me constantly to bounce ideas off. When there are lots of creative people around you, it doesn't feel like work to me.

If a job requires extensive periods of working independently but also intense bursts of working in a team, try:

To be honest I get my best work done when I can sit quietly and think on my own – so that's why I'm attracted to this job because you're offering the successful candidate the opportunity to work from home for up to three days a week. However, I couldn't work from home all week because I'd miss the human contact – so again this job is attractive because I would get the opportunity to share ideas with the rest of the team on those days in the office.

Book III

Succeeding at Interviews

Belbin's team types

Dr Meredith Belbin established that most people tend to fall into one of nine types when contributing to a team. Very briefly, these types are:

✔ **Plant:** A person who comes up with ideas. Others tend to view them as creative and imaginative.

✔ **Co-ordinator:** A chairperson who is good at getting others involved and organised.

✔ **Monitor Evaluator:** A sharp mind, this person is good at seeing the flaws and faults in others' arguments.

✔ **Completer Finisher:** A conscientious person who is good at attending to detail and meeting deadlines.

✔ **Implementer:** A person who is good at turning vague ideas into practical actions.

✔ **Resource Investigator:** A sociable person with a good network of contacts who uses that network to discuss and explore ideas.

✔ **Shaper:** A driven person who has the determination to overcome obstacles.

✔ **Team worker:** A co-operative person who is good at listening and enjoys getting on with the work that they are given.

✔ **Specialist:** Often a single-minded person who provides expertise or knowledge that others do not have.

These team type descriptors are quite widespread in business. But if you want to refer to your team type, first ensure that the interviewer is familiar with the typology by asking, *Are you familiar with Belbin's team types?* before launching into a description of where you believe you fit in.

Make sure that you are very familiar with your team type before trying to talk about it. Nothing is worse than a candidate who tries to talk about Belbin only for the interviewer to find out that they don't really know anything about the strengths and weaknesses associated with that type.

In reality, very few people can be labelled as one of the nine types all the time – people tend to shift between two or three types depending on the situation and their mood. But the typology serves as a useful framework for discussing differences in behaviour. If you want to read more on the topic, then simply type 'Belbin team types' into an Internet search engine.

We all have a team role – what would you say your role tends to be?

Are you a leader or a follower? Are you the person who comes up with the ideas or the person who can more easily see the flaws in other people's ideas? Do you tend to look at the long-term possibilities of an idea or are you more attuned to any immediate practical applications? Whatever the case, make sure that you can say that you have something of value to add to a team.

As with most interview questions, no single right answer exists. Relate your answer to the nature of the job. For example, if you are applying for a supervisory or managerial job, talk about the fact that others tend to defer to you and that you enjoy being in charge. Or if interviewed for a technical role, talk about occasions when you have introduced your specialist knowledge into team discussions.

These team-related examples give you some ideas:

✔ *I tend to be an optimist and motivator within the team. While I admit that I may not be the most creative person in the team, I can spot a good idea when I hear it and I do my best to get everybody talking about it. And after a team meeting, I can be relied upon to follow up on the idea, do a bit of research on it, and canvass opinion across the rest of the organisation before the next team meeting.*

✔ *I'm incredibly flexible when it comes to working in teams and one of the things that I most enjoy about my current job is the fact that I don't have a fixed role. I think I'd get bored if I was always doing the same thing in the team. But the fact that we are constantly shifting roles on different projects means that I get a lot of variety. And this is one of the features that attracts me to this role with you.*

If you want to get more technical about your role in a team, refer to your *team type descriptor*. See the sidebar 'Belbin's team types' for more information.

Book III

Succeeding at Interviews

Do you have good presentation skills?

Be careful of falling into the trap of saying that you are fantastic at absolutely everything. If good presentation skills are one of the key handful of skills necessary for the job, then of course you need to talk up your ability. But if you would only need to give presentations occasionally, be more measured in your response.

Some people are good at standing up and talking to a large audience on the spur of the moment with no preparation; others need to prepare their PowerPoint demonstration, write their speech, and rehearse it. Which approach do you need to be good at in the job that you're applying for?

Compare the following two examples relating to different jobs:

✔ *Standing up and giving presentations is something that I really enjoy and I've had a lot of practice at it, so yes, I think I have excellent presentation skills. I do lots of different presentations from standing up in team meetings and giving a brief summary on my week's work to writing out a speech for an hour-long keynote presentation at a legal conference last month, which they actually filmed and put onto a DVD for the delegates.*

> ✔ *I would say that I have quite solid presentation skills. We pick a teacher every week to give a seminar to the whole college. When it's my turn, I always spend a couple of evenings creating a PowerPoint presentation and writing bullet points onto pieces of card. Doing that preparation means that I can get my point across in a clear and effective way.*

The first example is more appropriate for someone who needs to do a lot of public speaking while the second example is better for someone who only needs to stand up in public occasionally.

For help with public speaking and presentation skills, turn to Book IV.

How would you rate your customer service skills?

The key to success in dealing with customers is having good listening skills and being able to grit your teeth and stay calm no matter how angry or unpleasant customers are. Make sure that you mention these qualities when constructing your answer. And don't forget to give a solid example of putting your customer service skills into action.

I think I have very good customer skills because I always put myself in their shoes and think how I would like to be treated if I were a customer. Just last week, I had a customer who came into the store wanting to buy one of the new season's skirts in her size. But we didn't have a size 14 on the sales floor and I couldn't find one in the storeroom. I suggested that she try one of the other stores in the city. I called a couple of the other branches and found one that had a size 14 in stock and told them to put it to one side for her. But she was a tourist and didn't know how to get from our store to the other location so I went out with her to the street to hail her a cab to take her there.

 One of the best examples to give is dealing with an initially angry or unhappy customer's complaint and ending up with a happy or even delighted customer. Or think about a time when you went out of your way to satisfy a customer's requests even though it was not necessarily your job to do so. Don't give an example that involves having to refer a customer to your manager or another department as it demonstrates to the interviewer that you are the type of person who shirks their problems. Similarly, don't let your story end up with the customer storming off because you couldn't resolve the situation for them.

 If meeting customers on a daily basis, you need to show that you are using these skills all the time. Make sure that you pick a recent example from the last couple of weeks or months. Going any further back in time may suggest to the interviewers that you only choose to use your customer service skills on special occasions!

How are you at handling conflict?

This is a trick question, because simply wading in and saying that you are very good at handling conflict may imply that you get into lots of arguments and disagreements with other people. Unless you are applying to be an armed peacekeeper, a more sensible tactic may be to start off by saying that you don't tend to get into many conflict situations.

Most people tend to be fairly bad at dealing with conflict. Some people are too aggressive and get others' backs up while others are too passive and back down when they should be standing up for their rights. A good balance between the two is to be able to explain that you try to assert yourself on key points but remain flexible on others.

When I'm dealing with customers, I realise that it's my job to take some of the flak when they are unhappy. If you try to argue back with them, that will only escalate the situation, so I always apologise on behalf of the company and try to find out what went wrong. I find that if you are sincere enough in your apology and explain that you are going to do your best to try to sort the situation out, the customer quickly calms down.

We need someone who is tactful and diplomatic – how does that profile fit you?

Are you the kind of person who can tell a white lie or bite their lip in order to spare someone's feelings? Or are you the kind of person who would just blurt out, *Yes, that dress does make you look fat.* While most organisations would be disappointed with people who tell lies or don't speak their mind all the time, they do want employees to be able to choose the right time and place to speak up.

I'm very diplomatic because I understand that speaking your mind may not always be the best course of action. Sometimes you need to think about the right time and place to make certain comments. For instance, when you want to criticise someone, I think you should always do it one-to-one and in private rather than openly, in front of other people.

An interviewer may ask if you have ever lied at work. Be careful when answering, as different organisations have different views on the extent to which it is appropriate or acceptable to hide the truth. For example, most businesses would say that lying to customers outside of the company is more acceptable than lying to colleagues within the company. Only a fine line separates a white lie from an outright falsification, so think through your answer carefully.

How do you take personal criticism?

A person who can't take personal criticism is a pain to work with. No one wants to work with someone who automatically takes offence at the slightest suggestion that her work is not perfect. And, no one likes a person whose bottom lip starts to wobble because he perceives criticism as an attack on his self-esteem. Here's a good response:

I welcome constructive criticism if I think that it is justified. If I think that my manager has a valid point, then I take it on board and think about how to improve my performance the next time that situation crops up. But if I don't think that it is fair, then I will keep asking questions until I understand where my manager's coming from. And if I don't agree with all of their points or feel that they have got the wrong end of the stick, then I try to explain my point of view.

Be careful not to give the interviewers the impression that you are a complete doormat. A world of a difference exists between listening to fair and constructive criticism and paying attention to all manner of criticism whether it is warranted or not.

Chapter 5

Getting to Grips with Questions about Your Work

In This Chapter

▶ Talking about your current and previous jobs

▶ Discussing your current or previous employer

*T*he most commonly asked questions in a job interview are about the past, present, and future of your career. Interviewers want to examine the relevance of your previous roles in relation to the vacancy they're seeking to fill. Interviewers also want to understand why you are looking to leave (or have already left) your current employer and join their company. And they want to see if you have thought through what you want from the rest of your career.

In this chapter, we help you talk up your career history and explain what you want from not only your next job but also the rest of your working life.

Responding to Questions about Your Work

Your CV (refer to Book II for more on this) is only a brief summary of your entire career and cannot possibly capture all the activities that you actually did in each of your previous jobs. And most interviewers would rather 'hear it from the horse's mouth' than read the details – so be sure to memorise your career history and be ready to talk through each of the jobs on your CV.

Relate all your answers to the kinds of skills and characteristics that the interviewers are looking for in the role you're being interviewed for. Don't simply rehearse the same answers for all the different interviews that you go to, as different organisations may want slightly different skills.

What does your day-to-day job involve?

Don't get bogged down in describing all the details of your current job. If you list every single action or duty that you have, you will quickly bore the interviewer. The way to shine when answering this question is to focus on three, four – or at most five – key areas of responsibility that you think the interviewers may be looking for.

> ✔ *I am responsible for all our company's graphic design needs. In practice, this breaks down into three main areas. The first is to produce the monthly newsletter that goes out to all our customers. So I have to chase different departments to write the sections of the newsletter and then assemble them in an attractive format. Secondly, I work with the marketing team when they want to design new logos to accompany new products. And thirdly, I'm responsible for ensuring that all the correspondence that goes out to customers is consistent with our brand by checking up on employees at all levels of the company and educating them about our standard document formats.*

> ✔ *As a senior associate, I run a team of six lawyers in the corporate law practice working directly with the partner. I am responsible for the day-to-day management of the lawyers, which includes managing their workload, ensuring that their work is of a high quality, and coaching and developing them so that they can take on work of an increasingly more difficult nature. I also act as a liaison between the firm and the client, making sure that the client is happy. But most importantly I'm looking out for opportunities to deepen the client relationship so that the client will use us for other transactions.*

Prepare an answer to explain the day-to-day workings of all your jobs to date, not just your last one. An interviewer can conceivably go on to ask: *What did your other jobs entail?* or *Please tell me about the main duties that you performed in each of your jobs*.

How did you get your last job?

You often hear people saying that job hunting is a job in itself. Answering this question is an opportunity for you to show your tenacity in chasing down a job. If you went through a lengthy and difficult selection process, you may win a few extra points for explaining the steps that you had to go through to get the job.

Last year our company announced that it was restructuring the company and creating six new regional manager positions. All the 300 or so existing area

*managers were invited to apply, which involved completing a ten-page applica-
tion form and submitting various letters of reference. I believe that about 200 of
us applied for the new positions. I put in my application and was invited to
attend an assessment centre in which we had to complete a battery of psychometric tests. We were also interviewed by a psychologist and had to give a presentation to one of the regional directors. The successful applicants were then
invited to a second-round panel interview, which consisted of the three regional
directors, a finance representative, and the director of human resources. At the end
of a rather gruelling two-hour interview, I was successful in securing the position.*

If applying for a position requiring a lot of networking on the job – such as in
sales or business development – you may again win Brownie points by talking
about how you networked your way into the job.

*I had been reading the appointments sections of newspapers for a while to see if
any opportunities existed in my field, but hadn't seen any for ages. So I started
ringing people I knew and explained that I was looking to move out of the finance
sector and into consumer goods. I didn't ask them for a job, but asked if they
knew any people who could talk to me about the consumer goods industry. It
took quite a while and a lot of phone calls and meetings, but eventually I found
my way to the managing director of my current employer who was willing to
give someone like me a chance.*

What do you like about your current job?

Even though the perks of the job may really be your favourite bit – such as a
subsidised canteen, six weeks annual holiday, and an easy-going boss – a
good answer focuses on the fact that your current job gives you the opportunity to exercise certain skills. A *great* answer would focus on how you exercise skills that are uncannily similar to the ones mentioned in the job advert.

> ✔ *I like the fact that I'm helping line managers to make decisions that can
> have a very large impact on the success or failure of the company. Of
> course I spend some of my time analysing the weekly financial perfor-
> mance of individual departments. But once I have those numbers, I can get
> out and spend time helping the line managers to make decisions about
> how to allocate their budgets and spend their time. And the fact that I'm
> working with non-accountants to help them understand the principles of
> financial management is probably the most satisfying part of my job.*

> ✔ *What I enjoy most about my job is that each day can be very different. One
> day I can be carrying out safety checks and inspections on the machines
> and equipment. The next, I could be installing or upgrading electrical cir-
> cuits. Or I could be working with the managers to develop improvements to
> the maintenance procedures.*

Book III

**Succeeding
at
Interviews**

What do you dislike about your work?

An interviewer may find it hard to swallow if you claim that you enjoy every single aspect of your work. Everyone has minor dislikes or frustrations with their work and you need to be ready to talk about some of them. Your tactic can be to talk about factors outside of your control – for example, unwieldy organisational procedures to follow or inefficient systems that do not allow you to work as productively as you would like to. Using this tactic may be a good idea if you are fairly certain that the situation is different in the interviewers' organisation.

You don't want to sound permanently unhappy in your job, or you can come across as a grumpy individual that the interviewers would be better off rejecting. Be very careful to make it clear to the interviewers that you rarely feel frustrated or irritated by these factors.

In my current role, I have to travel to all the branches in the entire north of England, so I spend about four days out of five on the road. I used to enjoy it but now the appeal is starting to wear off and I have increasingly been thinking about taking a head office role. One of the attractions of coming here today is that I would be based in the Leeds office at least three days a week.

When asked about what you dislike in your job, you may want to talk about a necessary evil that your job entails, such as the need to complete an incessant amount of paperwork. But be careful to ensure that paperwork (or any other element of a job) isn't going to be a key part of the job before talking about how much you dislike it!

I don't think there is anything in particular that I really dislike in my job. I enjoy meeting suppliers and building the relationships between our company and each of theirs. I guess if I had to think of something, then it's the paperwork that I have to complete once I get back to the office. But I realise that the documentation is important and once I've got it done, I can focus on the tasks that I enjoy more.

How is your performance measured?

Although this question asks you to talk about the way in which your performance is measured, what the interviewer is really interested in is the extent to which you fall behind, meet, or exceed your targets or objectives.

Most people have targets or objectives set on an annual or perhaps quarterly basis. If you are not familiar with your goals, dig out your last appraisal in order to prepare the answer to this question. In some jobs, such as a call centre operator or a retail sales assistant, you may even have daily targets to meet. But interviewers are not interested in your performance on a day-to-day basis; your performance over a longer period of time such as a month or a quarter is what really matters.

My performance is measured against about a dozen criteria, but I have two main objectives that make up over 70 per cent of whether I get an end-of-year bonus or not. One objective is my management of a cost budget and the other is the extent to which I minimise manufacturing downtime. In the first quarter of the year, I'm ahead of both targets by between three to four per cent.

If you are falling behind with any of your targets or objectives, make sure that you have good reasons to explain why.

I have three main objectives for the year. The first is to generate £100,000 worth of new business. The second is to deliver £180,000 of consulting work in a year. And the third is to accrue a certain number of personal development points by reading books, attending workshops, and finding out about competitors' activities. In the first half of the year, I achieved 113 per cent of my consulting delivery target. I'm also ahead of the game in terms of my personal development points. However, I've only managed to generate 85 per cent of my new business target – but that's mainly because I've been so busy doing consultancy work that I haven't had the chance to attend many conferences and to network.

Many managers are measured against a balanced business scorecard, comprising elements such as financial performance, customer satisfaction, staff satisfaction, and innovation. If you're measured in this way, make sure you can describe your performance against target for all the major elements of your job. And if you're not meeting your target in any particular area, you can bet that the interviewer will want to talk about it in more detail – so be ready with some answers.

What have you learned in each of your previous jobs?

This question can be taken in two different ways. The interviewer may be asking, *What skills have you learned in each of your previous jobs?* or *What lessons have you learned in each of your previous jobs?* Rather than making an assumption, clarify what information the interviewer is seeking. So begin by asking: *Would you rather I talk about the skills I picked up in each of my jobs or the lessons that I learned?*

If the interviewer is interested in skills rather than lessons, talk about a transferable skill you picked up in each job relevant to the job you're applying for:

Going back to the beginning, Robinson and Partners was my first job, so I learnt a lot about working on projects, setting goals, and working to deadlines. At Recruitment Solutions, I got the opportunity to hone my client-handling skills because I was working with a wide range of companies, from small companies to large employers. In my current role, I am supervising two trainees, so I've become very good at delegating work clearly and then coaching and explaining when they have any problems.

Here's an example of a response if the interviewer is more interested in your philosophical take on your career:

In my job at Mail Express, I learnt that you can't let people down. When you say you're going to do something, then you just have to get on with it and do it. There was one occasion when I stayed in the office until after midnight because I didn't want to disappoint the marketing team. In my current role, I've learnt about the importance of office politics. I've observed plenty of occasions when people's ideas have been shot down not because they were bad ideas, but because the people suggesting them were insufficiently friendly with the managing director.

When you ask whether the interviewers are more interested in the skills you acquired or the lessons you learned, they can easily say *Both*! So be ready to give a full response to the question.

Why did you leave each previous employer?

If the interviewers are asking you this question, then they may have a concern that you are the kind of person who flits from one company to the next. If the company were to offer you a job, are you likely to join them for good or get bored and move on after only a couple of months? The interviewers may have this concern if they read on your CV that you've had a number of jobs but stayed in each of them for less than 18 months or so.

In reality, people leave one company to join another for all sorts of reasons. But some reasons are more acceptable in the eyes of interviewers than others. Try to focus on the positive reasons that led you to move to a new company rather than dwell overly on the negative aspects of the job that made you want to leave your last one.

Some of the most acceptable reasons for leaving include:

- ✔ **Seeking greater responsibility:** *I enjoyed my time there, but after only a year, the other teachers were telling me what a fantastic job I was doing and that they wished I was head of department. Unfortunately the incumbent was showing no signs of wanting to leave, so I realised I would need to find a new school if I wanted to progress.*

- ✔ **Wanting more of a challenge:** *I was managing a number of mid-sized accounts at that company and quickly got to grips with the role. Within a year, I realised that I was ready for more of a challenge to keep me interested and on my toes, so I moved companies. I'm still managing similarly-sized accounts, but they tend to be more complex in nature.*

- ✔ **Searching for greater security:** *I had joined that business believing it was a stable place to work. Unfortunately it went through a couple of rounds of redundancy and I didn't feel that it was offering me an environment in which I could do my best work, so I was looking to join a more established and stable company.*

- ✔ **Seeking full-time employment:** *I was originally hired to provide maternity cover for six months. The other executive decided to take another three months off and was willing to do a job share with me when she returned, but I'm now looking for a full-time job in which I can fully immerse myself.*

- ✔ **Wanting to develop yourself:** *My goal has always been to move into general management. In my previous roles I was getting a lot of experience of managing the cost side of the equation, but I was lacking the experience of managing the revenue side. So I deliberately sought out a move into sales and marketing by joining that next company.*

Finish off with a statement to assure the interviewers that you are now ready to settle down into a career with a single employer:

I realise that I have moved around a couple of times in my career already. But all those moves have helped me to develop particular skills. I am now ready to stay with one employer so long as they are able to offer me good development opportunities.

Are you a good manager?

I'm sure you realise that answering anything other than 'yes' to this question is foolish if you're applying for a managerial role. But rather than just saying 'yes', make sure you explain in a couple of sentences why you think you're a good manager.

Book III

Succeeding at Interviews

For example, you can mention three or four of the key skills that you exercise as a manager. The following list may help you:

- ✔ Delegating work, supervising it, and checking for mistakes.
- ✔ Coaching, developing, or mentoring members of your team.
- ✔ Creating a vision or business strategy for your department or business unit.
- ✔ Working with the management team or board on issues affecting the whole organisation.
- ✔ Inspiring or motivating your team to achieve results.
- ✔ Shaping the atmosphere or culture within your team or department.

Vary the extent to which you talk up your experience and skill in the job depending on the seniority of the role and the responsibility that goes with it.

For a very senior role, focus on the more strategic side of management:

Yes, I think that my team would say that I am a good manager. Having such a large team, I rely on my direct reports to manage the department on a day-to-day basis. My role is to coach my direct reports and hopefully help them to progress to larger roles elsewhere in the business. The majority of my time is spent interfacing with other departments and working with the rest of the management team on the strategic management of the overall business.

If you have only had limited supervisory experience, give a more measured response:

Yes, I'm a good manager because I try to understand what the members of my team are good or not so good at. That understanding allows me to delegate work that plays to each individual's strengths.

Sidestepping Questions about Your Current Company

Interviewers can be quite nosy; they often like to have a poke around and find out a bit about the company that you are (or have been) working for. Just as the presenter Loyd Grossman used to ask in that TV programme

Through the Keyhole 'What kind of a person lives in a house like this?', the interviewers want to understand 'What kind of a person works in a company like this?'.

How you talk about your current company often reflects on what the interviewers think of you. No company is perfect, but if you bad-mouth your current employer too much, the interviewers may start to wonder if it really is such a terrible place to work – or is it just that you are a terribly negative person or a person who is terribly difficult to please?

Exercise discretion when talking about your current employer, especially if the company by which you are being interviewed is a competitor to your current company. Giving away confidential information not only can land you in hot water with your current employer, but also raises concerns in the interviewers' minds that you may one day be equally disloyal in a future job interview when talking about their company.

How would you describe your current company?

While bad-mouthing your current company too much makes you sound like a terminally miserable individual, talking in overly glowing terms about the company simply won't ring true either. If your current company really is such a fantastic place to work, why are you leaving?

Try to mention twice as many good points as bad points when describing your current employer. And finish off your response by referring to specific aspects of the interviewers' organisation that you find attractive.

Here are some examples of responses that meet the two-thirds to one-third rule:

> ✔ *It's a good place to work. The directors are very transparent in their decision making, so we all feel very involved in the direction of the company and the decisions that are made. We also have quite a cohesive team so we're friends as well as colleagues and we make the effort to go out for lunch or a drink a couple of times a month. The only down side is that the company hasn't grown much in the last couple of years, which means that there has been almost no opportunity for promotion. And that's the main reason that I'm looking to join a growing business such as yours.*

> ✔ *The company is growing fairly quickly and as such it's an exciting place to work because we have so many new projects to work on. The company*

Book III

Succeeding at Interviews

prides itself on its culture of focusing on results rather than how we work. So we dress casually in the office and the managers let us work from home as often as we like so long as it doesn't affect our ability to do the work. The only reason I'm looking to leave is because the company has a policy that means that I can't transfer from my current role into an account executive role. Obviously, your company is rather more progressive in that respect, which brings me here today.

How would you rate your current boss?

Although you may get away with pointing out negative aspects of your current company, you'll be treading on far more dangerous ground in disparaging your boss. In any situation involving differences of opinion, two sides exist to the story. By talking about the failings of your current boss, the interviewers may wonder if some of the fault actually lies with you.

Always be positive about your current manager's abilities, and keep any sinister thoughts to yourself!

- ✔ *I have a good boss at the moment. He gives me a lot of latitude in how I do my work. We meet for a couple of hours about once a week to tackle any problems that I raise. And he trusts me completely, so it's refreshing not to be micro-managed at all. All in all, he's a good manager to work for.*

- ✔ *I would rate my boss quite highly. I think that she has really taken the time to understand what I want out of my career and has given tasks that help me to achieve my goal of moving into a customer-facing role. And she was very understanding when my son was involved in a car accident last year and I needed to take quite a few days off to help with his convalescence.*

Don't make your current boss sound *too* fantastic. If one of the interviewers is your prospective future boss, they may start to feel insecure!

What's your boss's biggest failing?

If the interviewers specifically ask you to criticise your boss, try to deflect the question by emphasising only their good qualities.

To be honest, I don't think my manager has any major failings. She has a lot of experience in the field so I'm always surprised by how much I keep learning from her. And she has a very dry sense of humour that makes her good fun to be around.

If the interviewers continue to push you to point out a failing or fault in your current boss, then allow yourself to point out some relatively minor issues.

> ✔ *I still find it difficult to think of anything that's a real failing. I suppose this is more of a minor quibble. My manager tends to be incredibly busy and spends quite a lot of time out of the office, which means that it can be quite difficult to get paperwork signed off when I need to get authorisation to spend on a large item. But I really don't want to blow it out of all proportion as he has lots of good points that I've already mentioned.*

> ✔ *It's really difficult to think of much to complain about. But if I'm being really picky I guess he can be a bit forgetful at times. He's forgotten times and dates of meetings on a couple of occasions. But it doesn't happen often and nowadays I always take the precaution of copying e-mails in to his personal assistant so that she can discretely manage his schedule.*

Why do you want to leave your current company?

Just as you need to emphasise the positive qualities of jobs that you moved to when answering *Why did you leave each previous employer?* (refer to this section earlier in the chapter for tackling that question), you need to avoid whingeing about the negative aspects of your current employment situation such as dull colleagues or a hopeless boss. Focus instead on the positive qualities of the company that is interviewing you.

It's not that I want to leave my current company so much as wanting to join yours. I enjoy my current work and have some great colleagues and I'm sure that I'll keep in touch with quite a few of them after I leave. But what I hope to gain from joining your organisation is the greater involvement in international projects that I've not had so far in my career.

What is your current notice period?

This is a mostly factual question. Read your employment contract before the interview to ensure that you give the right answer and don't raise a potential employer's hopes by telling them your notice period is only a month if you are really tied in for three months!

Book III

Succeeding at Interviews

Don't forget to take into account any leave days that you may have accrued. If the employer is looking to fill a vacancy urgently, then being able to join even a few days earlier may swing the decision in your favour. On the other hand, if you do have any holidays planned that you are unwilling to change, do mention them.

My notice period is four weeks. But I have five days' annual leave that I have yet to take. So in theory I could hand in my notice and start with a new company within three weeks.

In a few very competitive industries and certain highly-paid jobs, employers sometimes put employees on *gardening leave* when they give notice. The employers no longer want the employees in their workplace (possibly building up ideas or contacts to take to a new job) so they send them on a period of paid absence. Do mention if this may be the case for you.

Technically, my contract says that I have to give three months' notice. But when other analysts have handed in their notice in our department, the bank has always just paid them off and asked them to leave immediately. The only slight wrinkle is that I have just arranged to take my kids to Disneyland in two weeks' time, so I wouldn't be able to start until I return in three weeks.

May we approach your referees?

Consider asking interviewers to hold off from checking your references until you have received a definite offer of a job. You don't want to irritate your referees by bombarding them with requests for references from too many companies.

If you are still in employment and any of your referees work at your company, you may be worried about the prospect of alerting them to the fact that you're looking for a job. If you explain your situation in the following way, you'll probably find that most interviewers are very understanding:

I'd be happy for you to check my references eventually and I'm sure that they will confirm everything that I've been saying about myself in this interview. But would you mind waiting until you've decided to make me a firm offer? I'd rather not draw their attention to the fact that I'm looking elsewhere for a job.

If you have already left an employer, then your answer can be an unmitigated yes:

Please do approach my referees. The contact details for my last boss and the operations director are at the bottom of my CV. I'm sure that they will say pretty much the same thing about me as I've been telling you.

Most employers make job offers contingent on receiving satisfactory references. So when you receive such an offer, talk to your referee to make sure that what you have told your new employer corresponds with what your referee is going to tell them.

Book III

Succeeding at Interviews

Chapter 6

Talking about Why You Want a New Job

*I*nterviewers understandably want to find out why you want to work in their industry and, more specifically, why you want to work for them as opposed to one of their competitors.

In this chapter, we give you advice on how to impress interviewers with your knowledge of their company and how to talk about what you are looking for in your new job with them.

Answering Questions about the Employer

When employers are looking for the perfect person for the job, they often comment that a lot of candidates tend to have fairly similar skills and experience. So interviewers ask questions to figure out how much you know about their organisation and the job on offer. After all, if someone were applying to work with you, wouldn't you want to know why?

Make sure to visit the interviewing company's Web site and read all the literature available to you about the company and the role. And if the organisation is a big one, check the *Financial Times* or the business sections of quality national newspapers to see if any recent developments have hit the headlines.

If the company has branches, showrooms, restaurants, or shops, visit them at least a couple of times to get a feel for the company – interviewers take a dim view of candidates who don't.

What do you know about our company?

While this is a very open-ended question, treat it as if the interviewers have asked you to repeat back to them a couple of positive points attracting you to the company. Even if you have come across some information about a crisis or failure in the company, avoid mentioning it unless the interviewers specifically ask you about it.

Engage in some subtle flattery about the interviewers' company. The interviewers probably enjoy working there, and they want to know that you will too. Slip in some mentions of how you know what you know about the company: Good phrases include *I saw on your Web site*, *I read in the Financial Times*, *I gathered from your annual report*, and so on.

Take a look at these example responses:

✔ *I know that you are a growing organisation with a turnover of around £70 million last year and that you were awarded the Chemical Engineering Federation's Award for Innovation two years ago. I read in your annual report that you are increasingly moving into injection moulded plastics, which I believe will be a growth area given the trend for car manufacturers to use it in their assembly processes.*

✔ *I've been living in the area for a few years now and used to go into your restaurant on the high street. I have always been impressed by the quality of the food and the fact that the menu changes every month to incorporate produce that is in season. The waiting staff has without exception been attentive and friendly too. So when I heard that you were opening another restaurant and were recruiting, it was really a no-brainer to apply to work for you.*

✔ *I used to work as an in-house lawyer and our head of department always used to say that if she had the budget, she would be using your firm. I read on your Web site that you have recently opened an office in Amsterdam and are opening another early next year in Prague in line with the managing partner's vision of creating a truly European firm. And if I'm honest, that kind of growth and opportunity is very attractive.*

✔ *I appreciate the fact that you use only organic, natural ingredients in your skincare products. I also read on your Web site that you have ambitious growth plans and that the board is unwilling to sell out to a large multinational business because they are worried that they may dilute the original philosophy of the company's founders to use natural ingredients and recipes that have been handed down the generations.*

Don't think that you can get away without doing your research just because a company is not a large business that gets discussed in the newspapers. Just about every company has some kind of brochure that they send out to customers interested in their services or products. If applying for a job, ring up and be honest – tell them that you have an interview with them and ask if it's okay to get some of their materials.

How much do you know about this position?

Before you go for the interview, practise saying out loud the key responsibilities of the job. This is a critically important question and you do not want to have to utter any *erms* or *ums* when answering it.

Try these responses on for size:

> ✔ *I gather that it is a full-time position working in either the Fulham or Ealing health clubs. The main responsibility is educating gym users and ensuring that they are using the equipment safely. And if they want a personal training plan, to sit down with them, understand their goals, and structure a workout schedule for them. At the same time, the job's not just about safety and training but also about building a rapport with gym users so that they grow accustomed to visiting the gym and are therefore more likely to renew their memberships when they expire.*

> ✔ *The successful applicant will work directly with the purchasing director. The biggest part of the role will be to provide administrative support to the director as well as the two purchasing managers, which may include anything from arranging travel and overnight stays for them to handling incoming phone calls and formatting the occasional document.*

Book III

Succeeding at Interviews

Many organisations send out a job description if you ask for it. Or a job description may be downloadable from the jobs section of their Web site. Even if the organisation does not provide you with a full job description, read the job advert thoroughly to ensure that you memorise the main responsibilities and duties associated with the job. If applying for a job through a recruitment agency, make sure you get as much detailed information from the agency about the job as possible.

How would you rate our products/ services/Web site?

Don't automatically assume that you must flatter the interviewers by making implausibly positive remarks about their products, services, or Web site. If the fact that these aspects are flawed or missing some key element in some way is common knowledge, then the interviewers may appreciate your insight.

Use the *2:1 rule* when discussing the company's products and services. Doing so means making at least two positive comments about the company's product before mentioning one negative comment. For example:

I think your clothing range is fantastic – otherwise I wouldn't be applying to work here. The women's basics are extremely good value and it always surprises me how quickly you get catwalk trends into your shops. The smarter clothes are also very impressive – I've spotted that a few other shops on the high street are following your lead in having a more tailored jacket shape this season. I guess the only gap is a men's range, but I've read rumours in the trade press that you are thinking of launching one next year.

Do your research before the interview in order to answer this question successfully. If the company has a tangible product, get your hands on it beforehand so that you can experience it for yourself.

If applying for a role involving you using or selling the company's products or services, make sure that you are extremely familiar with them. If applying for a support role – for example in finance, human resources, or the legal team – you can get away with a more passing familiarity with the products or services.

What is it that attracts you to our company?

This question is very similar to *What do you know about our company?* (detailed earlier in this chapter). Think about how the organisation likes to portray itself to the outside world and answer this question by listing two or three qualities or characteristics that attract you to it, specifically explaining why each of those qualities are of interest to you.

Ramping up for a revamp

If you're being hired to revamp part of the company – for example, the role is specifically to do with turning around the business – then feel free to constructively criticise the company.

I think the products used to be leaders in the field about three or four years ago. But some of

the discount retailers have really brought the quality of their products up to scratch, which has left some of your products looking a little tired. But the situation's not irrecoverable as I think customers still have a great affinity for the brand.

🖊 *You have a great reputation in the marketplace and it's extremely important for me to be working for a market leader. Your two-month training programme would be an excellent springboard for my career, too.*

🖊 *The school has an excellent reputation in the county for helping its students to achieve top exam grades. You also have some of the best facilities and resources. More than that, I've been very impressed by some of the other teachers that I met last week – they all seemed relaxed, friendly, and very supportive.*

To really impress the interviewers, have a few more qualities or characteristics up your sleeve that attract you to the company. When you have told the interviewers your top two or three reasons, state: *I could go on with more reasons if you would like?*

Book III

Succeeding at Interviews

How would you rate us against our competitors?

Most interviewers want to hear that they rate very highly against their competitors. Of course, this question assumes that you know not only quite a bit about the interviewers' company but also have at least a passing familiarity with their main competitors.

Talk up some of the positive ways in which this company compares with its competitors. Even if the company is not the largest, it may be the fastest growing. Perhaps the company has some highly rated products or the best training programme. Just make sure you have something positive to say!

You have a fantastic reputation. You grew by 9 per cent last year, which was nearly twice that of any other publisher. And you're the market leader in the health and fitness and youth magazine segments, which are both predicted to be major growth areas in the medium term.

What do you think our unique selling point is?

Most organisations believe that they are better than their competitors or unique in some respect. A *unique selling point* is pretty much what it says – the reason why a company stands out as different to its competitors. If asked this question, tell the interviewers what they want to hear.

I believe you're still the only company that produces its drinks using only entirely fresh ingredients, while all of the other fruit drink makers use at least some fruit from concentrate.

Your research should uncover some hints as to how the company sees itself. Look for how the company describes itself and try to paraphrase some of these back at the interviewers.

Even if you can't unearth any features that are entirely unique to this one organisation, you can argue that the combination of two or three aspects makes it unique.

Your bank offers some of the best value products on the high street while at the same time offering customers the ability to ring up their local branch rather than be put through to a faceless call centre.

Do you have any concerns about our organisation?

Even if you do have some concerns, your safest bet is to keep these to yourself for the moment. Wait until you have been offered a job to ask the questions that you really want answered. If asked this question during the initial interview, use the opportunity to reiterate one or two reasons why you want to work for this company:

Not at all. I like what I've seen and heard so far. In particular, I didn't realise that the fast-track promotion scheme was being made available to all of the team leaders. So that would be a real bonus for me.

The only exception to this rule would be if some piece of news or a rumour has been widely reported in the trade press or newspapers:

If you were in charge of our company, what would you do differently?

This question tends to be asked of managerial rather than entry-level candidates, and isn't a question to regularly expect to come up against. But the way to answer this really tough question successfully is to compliment the company and then to offer only limited and constructive criticism. Don't take this question as an invitation to pass judgement on how poorly the whole organisation is run! And don't just say *nothing* when asked if you'd run anything differently within the company. The interviewers are looking for an intelligent opinion rather than outright flattery.

Nearly everything does sound great about your company. But I have to say that the recent departure of your finance director and the subsequent drop in your share price did leave me wondering about the financial stability of the business. Rumour has it that you will need to make mass redundancies to achieve your end-of-year target. How may that affect the team that I would be joining?

Answering Questions about What You're Looking For

Book III

Succeeding at Interviews

Interviewers almost always want to know why you are looking to leave your current employer and why you may want to join their organisation. You should also be ready to answer questions about what you are looking for and what other companies you may be applying to.

Why are you looking to leave your current company?

This question is very similar to *Why did you leave each previous company?* (covered in Book III, Chapter 5).

You win more brownie points by talking about why you want to join the interviewers' organisation than by whingeing about what is wrong with your current employer.

Try one of these sample answers on for size:

✔ *I don't really want to leave as I've got some good friends there. But I think that I have learned as much as I can. In order to push myself, I need to work for a larger business that will offer me a greater diversity of personnel and training issues.*

✔ *The situation is not so much that I want to leave my current hospital as I want to join your department. In order to reach my goal of becoming a certified physiotherapist, I need to get more experience of working with patients with sports injuries, which I would be able to get with you.*

If your current job isn't challenging you, what could you do to change it?

So many candidates talk about wanting to move jobs because their current one 'isn't challenging enough' that this reason has become a bit of a cliché. In asking this question, the interviewers want to know if you simply moan about not being challenged enough in your current job or whether you ever try to change the nature of your role.

The ideal response is to state that you tried to pursue more interesting work but found that the organisation's rules or perhaps your boss would not let you.

I did ask my boss if I could sit in on more of the production team's meetings and he was receptive to the idea. But HR said that some of the production team may take offence because they are a higher grade than I am, so they asked me to stop attending. I thought it was fairly outrageous, but that's the company's policy.

Don't lie! If you never took any action to try to change your current job, then don't say that you did. Instead, try an answer like this one:

I suppose I could ask my boss if I could transfer into the compliance team. I haven't to date because my boss has been under a lot of pressure recently, as the team has been one member short. I thought that I should wait until they filled the vacancy, but to be honest six months have passed and there's still no sign of the position being filled.

Why do you want to work in this industry?

Before you blurt out the real reasons why you want to work in the interviewers' industry, do think about the socially acceptable reasons for doing so. For example, saying that you want to work in television production because *It sounds glamorous and well paid* won't go down as well as saying *Every day is different and you have an instrumental role in communicating interesting ideas to a wide audience.*

Respond to this question by emphasising your skills and strengths. Here's another example to base your own on:

I've always wanted to work in the not-for-profit sector because I feel that it's important to be giving something back to the community and society as a whole rather than only making profit for shareholders. The people that I've talked to so far all seem to have a real desire and passion to make a difference, and I really want to be surrounded by people like that rather than people who work only to earn a living.

If moving from one industry into a new one, have two or three reasons why you are making the move. You may want to compare and contrast your old industry with your new one, too.

In the insurance sector, people tend to be pigeonholed depending on what they've done before. From my reading and discussions with people in the consumer goods sector, I get the impression that a lot more flexibility exists in how teams work together and the way that people are allowed to carve out their own careers depending on where they want to go in the future.

Who else are you applying to?

In the dim and distant past, applying to multiple employers may have been taken as a sign of disloyalty. But in today's job market, responding that you have applied to a number of companies shouldn't be a problem. You want your response to indicate that you are actively looking – but you don't necessarily need to name the other employers or go into specifics.

Feel free to say that you have applied for the same role in different companies. But saying that you have applied for many different roles is almost certain to be read as a sign of indecision about what you really want from your career.

See if you can adapt one of these example answers to suit your situation:

> ✔ *I've applied to the other large accountancy firms as well. I've decided that I want to train as an auditor, but I want to work for a nationwide firm rather than a local or even medium-sized firm.*

Book III

Succeeding at Interviews

✔ *I've applied to a range of companies who are all willing to support employ-ees in achieving the national certificate in IT skills. I've applied to a couple of businesses in the Bromley area as well as the local council. But I have to say that my preference would be to work for a small company such as yours where I could get to know the rest of the team.*

How does this job compare with others you're looking at?

This question is often an obvious follow up to *Who else are you applying to?* (dealt with in the previous section). A good answer must explain to the inter-viewers why you think that this job is better than the others you're consider-ing. Draw upon your research on the company's nature and offerings for an ideal response.

In reality, the differences between competitors in the same sector may be very slight to people outside of that industry. But you can bet that those dif-ferences seem very pronounced to those who work in that industry, so make sure that you understand them.

Have a look at these good responses:

✔ *It's difficult to distinguish between the different jobs because this is the first interview that I have attended. But you have been very friendly yet chal-lenging today. And the fact that your recruitment team responded so quickly probably says something about the efficiency and professionalism of the rest of the organisation, too.*

✔ *The day-to-day job isn't in itself that different from the other hospitality jobs. What is different, though, is that you are a part of a much larger group, which would give me greater options for career progression in the medium-to-long term.*

✔ *Given that you won a national award for your graduate training scheme last year, I'd be silly to want to work anywhere else.*

Have you received any job offers so far?

Interviewers often think that candidates who have received job offers from elsewhere – particularly from their competitors – are probably more desir-able than ones who have not. The ideal response talks about other offers that you have received.

Yes, I've received an offer from Alliance Ventures for the same role. But my gut instinct is that the culture here would suit me much more. While the people here obviously work hard, I get the feeling that you don't take yourselves quite so seriously as they do at Alliance.

Don't lie if you haven't received any offers, though! If the interviewers start to ask more questions about your other offers, you'll almost certainly get caught out! If you haven't received any offers, just be honest and say that you have yet to receive any.

No, I haven't yet. But this is only the second interview that I have attended so far and I have at least two more interviews in the next few weeks.

How would you describe your dream job?

This is a trick question. The interviewers are surreptitiously trying to sound out how much you want to work in the position that is on offer. The interviewers will reject you if you describe a job that is too far removed from what is on offer. Respond to this question by mentioning as many positive aspects of this job as you can.

Think about the specific job you're applying for. What are the positive aspects of this job that make you want to work for this company?

Book III

Succeeding at Interviews

✔ *I've always wanted to work in sales. I enjoy the process of researching customers and pursuing them until I can close a deal. I can't really imagine working in any other function.*

✔ *My long-term, dream job is to become a finance manager. So what I hope to get out of this job is a solid training, plus support and sponsorship for me to complete my accountancy exams.*

✔ *What I'm looking for is a job that will provide me with some career opportunities. I've had a couple of jobs in the last few years, but I want to settle down with one company that will provide me with good training and hopefully opportunities to develop myself.*

Don't talk about your fantasy job – perhaps transatlantic journeys in first class, mingling with celebrities, and earning pots of cash for very little work (admit it . . . you want to be a footballer). Talk about realistic aspects of your 'dream' job, such as good training, promotion prospects, a sociable team, and so on.

Who would your ideal employer be?

Be careful of this trick question. You can get into hot water if you name an organisation too different from the one interviewing you. The interviewers obviously want to hire someone who wants to work for them; they won't want to hire someone who is considering their organisation only as a second choice. However, don't lie. Unless the interviewers' organisation genuinely is your ideal employer, don't say that it is. Instead, focus on some of the attributes about this organisation that do attract you.

Consider these two answers:

- ✔ *I want to work for a large employer that is truly international in scope. Getting a good training programme is obviously very important. And I want the opportunity further down the line – perhaps three or five years in the future – to be able to transfer to an overseas office.*

- ✔ *My ideal employer would be based in the Oxford area. It would be a small firm of surveyors because I want to get to know a team well. And it would specialise in commercial and industrial rather than residential projects because that is where my interest lies. So your firm fits all three of those criteria for me.*

Evaluating Your Fit with the Organisation

Candidates often have unrealistic expectations that the grass really will be greener on the other side of the fence. However, interviewers know that the upside of moving to their company may also be accompanied by possible downsides such as minor problems readjusting to new team mates and a new culture – and what they want to know is whether you realise that too.

What do you think you can bring to the team?

Treat this question as if the interviewer is asking you to name two or three skills and qualities that they want and you have. Make sure that you tailor your response to how you would use those skills and qualities in the team environment.

Even if you have already answered questions about your skills and experience, interviewers rarely tire of hearing the same message.

> ✔ *What I can bring to the team begins with my research credentials and track record of adding value through both qualitative and quantitative research. I'm also the sort of person who doesn't give up easily when faced with a challenge. In fact, I positively enjoy having new problems to crack. All in all, I think I'd be a real asset to the team.*

> ✔ *I've been told that I'm a good person to have on the team because I'm willing to give of myself. I actively enjoy coaching and enthusing others about the work because it's a job that I'm enormously passionate about.*

If the interviewers want you to talk in more detail about what you can bring to their company, think back to some of the answers you have prepared in response to questions asking you to talk about yourself (refer to Book III, Chapter 4).

We are a diverse company – how will you cope with that?

By *diversity*, employers are usually referring to the fact that their company encourages employees regardless of their gender, age, race, religion, or sexual orientation. A good answer is to say that you would have no problem with this situation because your current employer is also very diverse.

I'm glad to hear that your company is very diverse because our company is too. Thinking about our department alone, we have more female managers than male managers. The department head is ten years younger than I am. And I'm pretty sure that most minorities and other cultures are very well represented too.

If you have not worked in a very diverse company, you can try to argue that you would very much like to join this particular company precisely because of its diversity.

Your company's diversity is one of the factors that leads me to want to work for you. I have to admit that our small company does tend to be a bit white, middle class, and male and I think that's a real shame as we probably don't employ the best talent that we could.

What kind of manager would you like to work for?

The interviewers want to see how you may fit into their particular organisation, so no single 'right' answer applies to all interviewers. You need to figure out the kind of culture and style of manager that you may end up with in this company.

Consider these two example responses:

- ✔ *I'd like to work for a manager who is supportive of me and my career goals. I've reached the stage now where I'm good at my job but I want to advance to the next level. So I hope that my manager will be brave enough to give me big projects and challenging work that keep me interested.*

- ✔ *I enjoy working for supervisors who are very clear in communicating exactly what they want from the rest of the team. I've observed teams having problems when it hasn't been clear who was supposed to be doing what.*

How long do you plan to stay in this job?

One of the biggest concerns employers have is recruiting a candidate who decides to leave after only a handful of months. Especially if an employer is planning to invest time and money in training you, they probably want you to stay for a period of at least three or four years. Make it clear that you are looking to develop your career within a single organisation – theirs.

Saying that you want to change roles in less than a couple of years is okay so long as you make it clear that you want to stay with the one employer.

I can see myself staying with you for the foreseeable future – certainly for at least three or five years. As I've explained though, I don't see myself staying in the role of internal compliance for more than nine months to a year. I see it as a stepping stone to achieving a regional management position either in the UK or the rest of Europe.

If you've jumped around a lot of jobs, try to reassure the interviewers that you are now looking for career stability. Perhaps mitigating circumstances (such as family circumstances) led to you changing jobs in the past. So be sure to set the interviewers' minds at ease that, should you be offered the job, you will not leave within just a few months.

Why should we hire you?

This question sounds quite intimidating and the interviewers can often sound as if they doubt your ability. But answering this question successfully only requires you to summarise the most important skills and qualities that you have and the employer is looking for.

I have already mentioned the skills that I believe I have in terms of growing existing accounts and winning new ones. I also have an extensive network of contacts throughout the industry, which allows me to keep abreast of ideas and developments in the field. In addition to that, I'm determined to become a partner in a business within the next 18 months so you know that I'll be dedicated and hard working in order to achieve that.

Where do you see yourself in five years' time?

We have heard so many candidates stumble at this hurdle because they have not prepared an answer to it! The truth is that you probably don't know what you want to be doing in five years' time – but you can't say that to interviewers as they may take it as a sign of lack of forethought.

TIP

Five years is conceivably long enough to say that you want to be doing something outside of the company – such as setting up your own business. But the safer bet is to say that you are looking for some form of career progression within the company.

Given that your company has just announced plans to open a third office in the Oxfordshire region, I assume that there will be opportunities for progression within the business. Within a couple of years I hope to be promoted to an assistant merchandiser and then sometime after that to a merchandising manager. So I could easily see myself working for you in five or even more years' time.

When would you be available to start?

Don't count your chickens before they're hatched! The interviewers are not necessarily saying that they want you to start with them immediately. Treat this question as if the interviewers are asking you about your notice period (see Book III, Chapter 5).

Deflecting Questions about Money

People don't like to talk about money. Just as most people think asking their mates how much they're earning is a bit rude, interviewers and candidates tend to skirt around the issue too.

A lot of employers give an indication of the salary on offer in their job advert. But plenty of employers try to attract as many candidates as possible with vague statements such as 'competitive salary' or 'highly attractive package'.

The golden rule is to delay talking about money for as long as you can. In the early rounds of the interview process, the balance of power lies with the interviewers. But once the interviewers have made you an offer, the balance of power swings in your favour – only then try to negotiate over pay.

How much are you earning at the moment?

This is a fairly straightforward factual question. Answer the question by telling the interviewers exactly how much you are currently earning.

Don't price yourself out of the market by implying the interviewer must automatically match your salary. You may want so say something like: *My salary is only one part of the equation. What is most important to me is finding the right role that will challenge and develop me.* You may currently be earning more than the interviewers are expecting to pay, but they may conceivably raise their offer if you're the right person for the job.

Bear in mind the relative scarcity in the market of people with your skills and experience. For example, fewer executives with ten years' experience of running an advertising agency are out there than advertising trainees with only a year's experience. The more certain you are that your skills are in short supply, the more bullish you can probably afford to be with your answers.

Consider the following two example responses:

> ✔ *I'm earning £18,500 with up to a 10 per cent bonus plus benefits at the moment. However, as I said earlier, I'm more interested in finding the right organisation that will help me to achieve my long-term career goal of becoming a store manager than earning a few pounds more at this moment in time.*

> ✔ *My basic salary is £85,000 and I'm entitled to a bonus and profit share,
> which could be as much as £40,000 this year. But I'd rather not get bogged
> down in talk about money because I think we should probably spend this
> initial discussion establishing whether I'm the right candidate to turn
> around your business.*

How important is money to you?

Most employers like to believe that they hire people who would continue to
work for them even if they won the Lottery.

Consider these two good responses:

> ✔ *Of course I need to earn enough to live on, but money isn't a major factor
> in deciding where I should work. It's more important for me to work for a
> business that has a solid reputation and good prospects for development
> and progression.*

> ✔ *Money isn't important in its own right. It's more important to me that I'm
> doing a good job and receiving recognition for my hard work and achieve-
> ments. I suppose that my salary and bonus are financial indicators of how
> well the business thinks I'm doing. If I'm doing a good job, I want the busi-
> ness to recognise that by awarding me a fair bonus.*

The main exception to the rule is sales people, employers of whom are sometimes sceptical of candidates who do not think that money is terribly important. Below is a good response for this situation:

*I must admit that I want the things in life that money can buy – such as a big
house, a plasma television, a fantastic car, and two or three holidays a year. But
I realise that you don't get anything for nothing, so I'm prepared to work incredibly hard to get what I want out of life.*

Book III

**Succeeding
at
Interviews**

*How much do you think
you are worth in a job?*

If the organisation has yet to make you a firm offer, resist the temptation to
reply to this question with too specific a number. Your best bet is to dodge
the question by saying that finding the right job and organisation to work for
is more important than getting a big wad of cash (even if that isn't necessarily true!).

Read up on job adverts and talk to headhunters, recruitment agencies, and other people in your profession and industry to get a rough idea of your worth in case the interviewers press you for a more specific figure.

Having looked at other similar opportunities, it seems that managers with my kind of background and experience are being made offers in the region of £30,000 to £35,000. But, as I said earlier, my primary consideration is finding the right company to join.

What would you consider adequate remuneration for this role?

Even though the question sounds like a request for a precise number, the same rule applies as for any other question regarding pay: Unless you have already received a firm offer, avoid pricing yourself out of the market by stating a number that may be too high for the company to afford.

Avoid the tawdry topic of money by reiterating that finding a job that allows you to develop your skills and further your career ambitions is your primary goal.

Obviously I'm looking for more than I am currently earning. But that's not the only factor that will decide my next career move. I'm more anxious to ensure that I feel I can add real value and that the management team will take my ideas and opinions seriously.

Sales people are the exception to the rule. Sales people are typically very motivated by money and interviewers expect sales people to want to talk about money.

At the moment I'm on a basic salary of £12,000. For the first £100,000 of sales that I generate, I earn a 6 per cent commission. For anything over that, I earn 8 per cent commission. So I'd need an offer that could beat that.

I'm afraid you're a bit expensive for us

Perhaps you've told the interviewers exactly how much you are earning and they reply with this statement. Don't be despondent, however. Employers usually have some discretion to offer a bigger pay package for the right candidate. Don't give the interviewers a disgusted look and abandon the interview. Do your best to convince the interviewers that you are the strongest candidate. And once they have selected you over all the other candidates, you may find that they can boost the overall offer.

Even though an employer may not be able to beat what you are currently earning, try negotiating a deal that is better for you in the medium-to-long term. For example, you may be able to ask for a deferred pay rise, share options, or a bonus based on performance.

Just because I earn a little bit more than you are currently willing to pay doesn't mean that I'm no longer interested in this opportunity. I'm intrigued to find out more about why this vacancy has arisen, and perhaps we can work something out if I am the right candidate for you.

What would you like to be earning in two years' time?

If you answer with too high a number, the interviewers may think that you have unrealistic expectations about the job. But if you answer with too low a number, you may unwittingly commit yourself to receiving unreasonably low pay rises for the foreseeable future!

Try to avoid answering with numbers at all. Focus on what you want in terms of career progression and job satisfaction.

I'd like to be earning more, but the precise number isn't that crucial to me. My primary aim is to progress in my career. My understanding from your Web site is that good assistant managers can feasibly be promoted to general managers within 18 months to two years.

Interviewers can ask you about every conceivable time frame. So be ready to talk about how much you may want to be earning (and where you want to be in terms of career progression and job satisfaction) in three, four, five, and more years.

Four years is quite a long time away, but I hope to have made significant progress in my career and be on course to becoming a fully-fledged resort manager. I really don't have that much of an idea of the earning potential as I'm much more focused on furthering my skills and getting international work experience under my belt.

Book III

Succeeding at Interviews

Chapter 7

Thriving Under the Pressure Interview

· ·

In This Chapter

▶ Getting to grips with pressure interviewing

▶ Keeping calm in the face of an interview onslaught

▶ Working out answers to common pressure questions

▶ Handling other odd questions

▶ Coming up with something to say to any question

· ·

All interviewers can be mean. But certain interviewers take their mean-ness even further, subscribing to a school of interviewing that believes that candidates should be put under extreme pressure to see how the candidate fares. These guys really want to make you squirm.

Interviewers with this outlook see it as a way of testing how you may cope with unexpected situations and stress on the job. What would you do if you went to a meeting with an unhappy customer screaming abuse at you? What if a colleague burst into your office saying that a warehouse fire has destroyed all your stock? Or what if aliens have abducted half of the team but you still need to get the project completed by midday? Okay, the latter isn't terribly likely to happen. But you get the idea – these interviewers want to see whether you would crack under the strain or cope with confidence.

The problem with pressure interviewers is, you never know when you may meet one. These people look just like any other interviewers and they may even start off being all smiley and ask you some nice easy questions. Suddenly the questions and the tone of the interview may change. This chapter is about preparing for the commonest pressure questions. And because you can never prepare for every single question that you're likely to be asked, We finish off by discussing some ways to deflect all manner of odd and uncomfortable questions.

Maintaining Your Composure

Pressure interviewing is designed to throw you off balance. The interviewer may hope that the sheer strangeness of the question puts you at a loss for words. Or the interviewer may pose a very straightforward question but ask it in a decidedly negative or condescending tone in the hopes of eliciting some kind of emotional reaction – perhaps a moment of hesitation and indecision, or a touch of annoyance. The key to dealing with pressure interviewing is to always keep calm. *Who would you rather meet – Albert Einstein or Michael Jackson?* Well, in response to this question, I'd be tempted to quip back *Michael Jackson because Einstein's corpse would probably smell quite badly.* But being flippant in an interview will win you no points. Even if the question sounds completely ridiculous – which many of them are – you must follow the interviewer's lead and answer it as if it were a perfectly natural question.

Another common tactic used by pressure interviewers is to make negative statements about you and see how you react. The interviewers may shake their heads and say: *I just don't think you're emotionally tough enough for the job.* Now, some candidates may sit there and think, oh well, that's my chance gone. But a good candidate in this situation shows their backbone by asking, *Why do you think that?* or perhaps *I'm surprised you say that. I know that I'm tough enough and I'll give you an example of when I demonstrated my emotional toughness. . .*

No matter how stupid or odd a question or statement, don't let your puzzlement or irritation show. Keep a neutral expression on your face at all times. Perhaps nod sagely as you think about the answer, and then deliver your response with a completely straight face. Save your amazement and incredulity at these interviewers' questions for when you meet your friends in the pub at the weekend.

Responding to Leading Questions

The commonest pressure questions try to put you on the spot by implying – or perhaps saying outright – something negative about you, leaving you to fight your way uphill to impress the interviewers by countering their insinuations.

To really stand head and shoulders above the other candidates, try to get some of your personality across. Interviewing well isn't just about answering the questions in a technically proficient manner. If you come across as coldly professional and competent, that impression will win you no favours. Try to seem likeable and human – as well as professional and competent, of course.

All of us have personality defects – what is yours?

This is a strongly-worded question and a cunning trap, implying that *every-one* has a personality flaw of some type. Weaker candidates can fall into this trap by exposing some serious failing about themselves. But the cunning response is to deflect the question and actually treat this question as if you have been asked to talk about a minor weakness of yours.

Never talk about any negative characteristics of yourself without also going on to talk about how you compensate for them. So do talk about a minor weakness, but immediately go on to tell the interviewer how you monitor and control that weakness, preventing it becoming an issue at work.

I wouldn't say that I have any personality defects – it's a very strong word. But of course I have areas in which I'm not as strong as others. For example my nat-ural tendency in my personal life is to be quite spontaneous and relaxed about what tasks I need to do and how I run my social life. But I realise that I can't allow myself to become disorganised at work so I always make the effort to spend a few minutes every day thinking about the key tasks I need to achieve and making a list. This allows me to focus on what I need to do and to prioritise how to spend my time.

The candidate here has managed to respond to a potentially leading and very negative question in a positive way.

Why did you not achieve more in your last job?

Another strongly-worded question, this implies that you should apologise for not having become the Chief Executive already. Some candidates may get flustered and start making excuses about what has held them back. Instead, prepare a response to this question that shows what you *are* proud of.

Book III

Succeeding at Interviews

Talk in a confident manner about the reasons why you are very happy with your career progression so far and either tell the interviewers about what you have learned or reiterate some of your main career achievements:

> ✔ *I'm actually very happy with my career progression so far. Even though I still have the same job title, I have actually learnt a huge amount. When I started the job as an Assistant Buyer two years ago, I had no experience of buying whatsoever. Whereas now when my manager is away on holiday, she allows me to represent our department at client meetings – so I feel that I have gained a lot in skills, experience, and client credibility. I'm now ready for the next step in my career, which is what brings me here today.*

> ✔ *I don't see achievement purely in terms of promotions and rising up the hierarchy. It has always been more important for me to enjoy the job and feel that I am learning new skills. I was asked to apply for a promotion but that would have meant that I'd be managing a team of trainers rather than doing hands-on training, so I turned it down.*

If your CV makes it obvious that you really could have achieved more, then you may need to make that admission. But go on to explain exactly why you have been caught in that rut. I've heard candidates use perfectly respectable reasons such as:

> ✔ An illness in the family – which can include yourself.

> ✔ Long-term disability of a child or family member.

> ✔ Needing to stay in a geographic area in order to keep a child at school during their GCSEs or A Levels.

> ✔ Other personal circumstances such as wanting to focus on bringing up a child or having to deal with a tricky divorce.

But go on to explain how those circumstances have changed. Then stress that you are now up for a new challenge and want to kick your career into a higher gear again.

Even though this question is designed to put you on a back foot, be sure to resist the temptation to fabricate a sad story if it isn't true. Remember that employers often check references and are likely to find you out.

How would you respond if I said that you're not the best candidate we've seen today?

An interviewer may ask this question with a hint of a sneer in their tone of voice to see how you cope with disappointment. But you know better than to show any such negative emotion. So instead show your mettle by asking the interviewer: *I'd be very surprised to hear that and I'm very interested to know why you think that. Can you tell me why you think I'm not the best candidate?*

Keep your tone of voice very warm when you ask the interviewer why they think you may not be the best candidate – otherwise, you can risk coming across as abrasive.

Hopefully the interviewer will then give you a couple of reasons that you can counter. For example, if the interviewer says, *I don't think you have enough experience of negotiating deals with suppliers* or *I think you are somewhat lacking in the maturity needed for this role*, then you can tell them your best example of negotiating a deal or a story that illustrates how you dealt with a tricky situation with confidence and maturity.

If the interviewer refuses to give you reasons why they think you are not the strongest candidate they've seen, go on to reiterate some of your key qualities:

Obviously I can't say that I am the very best candidate, as I've not met the other candidates. But what I do know is that I am incredibly determined in my work. I've decided that I want to work in this industry and I'm willing to put in long hours and do whatever it takes to get the job done and build a career in fashion. And my career track record so far should show you that I always achieve what I put my mind to.

How would you rate me as an interviewer?

It *nearly* goes without saying that you should not criticise your interviewer even if you think they *are* disorganised or incompetent. However, neither should you fall into the trap of fawning insincerely and by lavishing too many compliments on the interviewer.

Depending on the style of the interview, choose a response such as:

- ✔ *I'd say that you are quite a tough interviewer and have asked some very challenging questions that have really forced me to think about how I would deal with different situations. But I would add that being tough on candidates is only fair, as it is a tough job and you want to get an idea of how I would be able to cope with real pressure.*

- ✔ *I think that you have been a very fair and professional interviewer so far – you have tried to establish a rapport and put me at ease so that I can talk in a relaxed fashion about my skills and experience.*

If you must criticise the interviewer, say that the interview has been very good so far, but that you hope to be given the chance to ask the interviewer some questions about the company and why the interviewer enjoys working there.

What keeps you up at night?

Asking what keeps you up at night is a negative question, implying that you should reveal some deep-seated worries. Describing your worries will almost certainly be taken as a sign of weakness. So your correct answer here is to say that nothing – or almost nothing – keeps you up in a work context.

I can honestly say that nothing keeps me up at night. My job is very important to me, but I always make sure that I do the very best that I can to handle a situation. If a difficult situation or lengthy project needs a lot of work, then I make sure that I make a list at the end of one day so that I can get straight into tackling the most urgent issues the next day. Once I know that I have done the very best that I can, I find that there is nothing to be gained by worrying unduly about something and letting it interfere with my sleep.

If the interviewer continues to pressurise you and says that *something* must keep you up at night, then you may concede by giving an example (briefly) of a work issue that has had you slightly worried in the past.

I sometimes get nervous before big presentations. But when I know that a big presentation is coming up, I take plenty of time to prepare my slides and rehearse my material. I still wouldn't say that a presentation has given me any sleepless nights, but I certainly do wake up in the morning very aware that I need to do some more hard work that day to prepare for it.

Why do you think you are better than the other candidates?

Interviewers asking you this question are trying to lure you into talking about yourself in overly positive and glowing terms.

In most interviews, you won't get to meet the other candidates. Even if you do meet them, you're more likely to exchange nervous smiles and have a polite chat while sitting in reception than to have an in-depth discussion with the other candidates about their skills and experience. So it would be unfathomably arrogant of you to mouth off about why you are better than people that you have no right to comment on.

Demonstrate an ounce of humility by refusing to compare yourself to people that you can't possibly comment on. Snide comments about other candidates only show you up in a poor light. Instead, stick to talking about your own key qualities.

I don't think I can honestly say that I am better than the other candidates because I have never met them. All I can do is tell you again about my key qualities and why I think I'd be great in this job. I've been told by people that I'm articulate and hard working. I also hope that I've demonstrated my determination and passion for getting into this industry. Hopefully my personality and sense of humour have come across as well. And so all I can do is trust you to make the right decision.

When talking about qualities such as passion, personality, and sense of humour, your facial expression and body language are just as important as conveying a sense of those qualities. Just saying the words with a lifeless face and slumped posture sends out all the wrong signals!

Even if you're applying for an internal post and do know the other candidates, resist the temptation to snipe about them. Pointing out their flaws and weaknesses may reflect badly on you. So stick to your guns and focus on your personal achievement instead.

Responding to Closed Questions

Book III

Succeeding at Interviews

Closed questions such as *Do you take work home with you at weekends?* can technically be answered with just a 'yes' or a 'no'. But you know better than to answer in that way. You also need to explain your reasons why. In fact, it sometimes matters less whether you actually say yes or no than giving a compelling reason why you answered yes or no.

But sometimes neither the 'yes' nor 'no' response is appropriate. On occasion you may need to hedge your bets a little by saying 'it depends', and then go on to explain why you may need to change your behaviour depending on different circumstances.

Do you like regular hours and routine working patterns?

The 'right' answer to this question can very well be a 'yes' or a 'no' depending on the circumstances. For example, if you're applying for work as an ambulance driver, then you are probably going to be working shifts and sometimes crazy hours, meriting one response. But taking on part-time work as part of a job-share may mean that the hours will be very carefully determined weeks in advance.

Look at the job advertisement to get an idea of what the 'right' answer to this question may be. If the description of the job stresses words such as 'flexibility', 'some travel may be expected', 'variety', and 'shift working', then it's likely that the interviewer is looking for you to say that you don't like regular hours and a routine working pattern.

Consider the following two very different responses to the question:

✔ *No, because I'd hate to have a job that involved coming into the office at nine o'clock, having an hour's lunch, and then leaving at five thirty every single day. It would bore me rigid, which is exactly why I'm interested in the nature of this job – I like the fact that I could be called upon at short notice to work in different parts of the country and to work either at our branches or a customer's offices. It's the variety that will keep me on my toes.*

✔ *Yes. Having a regular working pattern is precisely what I'm looking for. When I saw your advert in the paper looking for someone to work Mondays to Thursdays, I thought that it would suit me perfectly. My daughter has just started at a pre-school group that runs four days a week, so it would give me Fridays off to spend with her. But at the same time, the regularity will give me an opportunity to learn a job and get good at it.*

Do you mind paperwork?

Again, the 'right' answer depends on the nature of the job. But the word 'paperwork' implies bureaucratic shuffling rather than productive work. So even if you do enjoy paperwork, think of another way to put it. For example:

I wouldn't say that I enjoy all paperwork. But I do enjoy being thorough in processing documents. If the contracts aren't signed, then the business could lose a lot of money, so one of the reasons why I'm attracted to this job is that I have a lot of responsibility in ensuring that all of the documentation is correct and up-to-date, and that the right people have access to it in a speedy fashion.

Office-based jobs such as office manager, clerk, personal assistant, or in fact any junior job are likely to involve a fair chunk of paperwork. So prepare your response to the question accordingly.

If applying for a job as a sales person or a consultant, however, you'd expect most of your time to be spent face-to-face with customers or clients. So you may say:

I can't say that I'm the biggest fan of paperwork and I'd much rather be out on the road meeting customers and suppliers. But I realise that it needs doing – otherwise the rest of the team back in the office wouldn't know what orders have been placed. So I make an effort to get all of my paperwork done at the end of the day. With every job goes some elements that are less enjoyable, but it doesn't make them any less important or essential.

If the post is managerial, with people in your team or perhaps a secretary to support you, then it can be acceptable to say that while you personally don't enjoy paperwork, you always ensure that you have competent people around you who can do it.

Have you ever broken the rules to get a job done?

The trap in this question is that a 'yes' answer can label you as a maverick rule breaker, while a categorical 'no' can make you come across as an inflexible worker.

A big difference exists between breaking a rule occasionally to achieve a benefit for your organisation and flagrantly breaking rules because you find them restrictive.

When answering this question, explain that you broke a rule only because you had to react quickly to a situation that would otherwise have meant that your employer would have lost out. Adding that you 'technically' may have broken the rules but that others in the team agreed that it was the right course of action, can be a good idea too.

I have broken the rules, but only because it would otherwise have cost our company thousands of pounds. We were on a deadline to get hundreds of brochures printed and delivered to a customer by Friday afternoon. I'm supposed to get my boss to sign off on spend of over £500, but she fell ill suddenly a few days before the deadline. So I went ahead and ordered the printing and got the brochures delivered to the customer because it was what we had discussed doing any way. When my boss got back, she agreed that it had been the right thing to do. So while I have on occasion technically broken the rules, I only did it because I had the interests of the business in mind.

Book III

Succeeding at Interviews

Do you take work home with you at weekends?

Answering that you don't take work home at weekends can make you appear inflexible; answering that you do take work home can make you sound ineffective during the week. So answer this question by finding a happy medium between the two options.

I rarely find that I need to take work home with me at the weekend. I make a habit of doing as much as I can in the office and I find that it's easier to work when you have your colleagues available to discuss ideas with. Having said that, though, at busy times of the year – for example at year end – I do find myself working all hours to get everything done before the auditors come in.

In answering this question, think about the nature of the industry that you want to work in. If it is commonly known that successful people in this type of job often take work home with them, then you may have to let the interviewer know that you are willing to do so as well.

Do you have any doubts about your ability to do the job?

Employers are looking for confident workers who can get on with the job at hand. I've never seen a job description where they are looking for insecurity as a desirable trait! So even if you are seeking a much bigger promotion and do secretly harbour some doubts, let your response show off your more confident side. Be careful, however, not to sound arrogant by demeaning the job and making it sound as if you think you can do it in your sleep.

If you think that the interviewer has some doubts about your ability, try to second-guess what they may be worried about and go on to reassure them that the job is within your abilities.

I know that this is a significant leap for me to take on managerial responsibility, but I've actually been readying myself for it for about a year now. Even though I have not formally had a team to manage before, I have deputised for my manager on a number of occasions when she has been on holiday or out of the office. So I have actually run the rest of the team of four people for up to a week at a time and delegated to them, checked their work, and made sure that they were happy.

Don't you think you are overqualified for this job?

The interviewer may be worried that the job is too easy for you and that you may quickly get bored of it and want to move on. If you don't think that you are overqualified, then you can ask: *It's interesting that you see me as overqualified. What is it exactly that makes you think that?* You can then counter any objections or worries that the interviewer may have.

But if you think that you actually probably are overqualified, make sure that you have other compelling reasons to explain why you will stick at the job. For example, you can talk about wanting a better work/life balance or wanting to join a smaller company where you have more say in the direction of the business.

Example answers include:

> ✔ *I realise that I've been managing a team of sales people in my last two roles. But what I've come to notice more recently is that I actually enjoy dealing with customers much more than I do managing the team. You could say that I have too much experience, but for me, this is much more about finding a role that I really enjoy rather than doing the one that looks better on my CV and pays more.*

> ✔ *I've spent most of the last three years travelling extensively and the truth is that I miss my family. My children are growing up very quickly and I don't want to miss it. Don't get me wrong as I still really enjoy my job, but I need to find something that will give me a bit more stability.*

Book III

Succeeding at Interviews

Would you have any problems relocating?

Book III, Chapter 1 deals with the importance of reading the original job advertisement and other literature when researching and preparing for an interview – so make sure that you don't get caught out by this question.

If relocation was never mentioned, then ask why this question has come up. But never say that you are unwilling to move as it may close the door on the job entirely.

You can then choose from one of the following lines of response:

✔ *I understand that I'll be based in this office until the end of the year, but that you are thinking of relocating to amalgamate with some of the other functions down in Basingstoke. That's a big plus when it comes to this job as my partner has just accepted a job in the south-east of England and that's one of the reasons that has prompted me to look for a new job.*

✔ *I'm sorry, but I didn't realise that relocation was a possibility. I didn't see any mention of it in the job advert or anything on your Web site. But relocation isn't out of the question as what I've heard so far about this unique role makes it sound ideal for me. Could you tell me a bit more about the proposed relocation please?*

Do you mind travelling?

Just like the last question about relocation, you should already know whether much travel is associated with the job before you step into the interview room.

You can then tailor your response as appropriate:

✔ *I get a real buzz out of travel. There are some people who moan about having to travel, but it's not a chore for me as I really enjoy driving/flying/ taking trains.*

✔ *I don't mind having to travel occasionally with work. For example I had to travel with the Marketing Director a couple of times a year and spent a couple of nights each time in Manchester and Edinburgh. But am I right to think that this job will primarily be based in this office?*

Talking about Changes of Direction in Your CV

Employers are often scared of taking risks. For this reason, they usually prefer to take on candidates who have run-of-the-mill backgrounds – people who have worked their way up in the one industry. For many employers, candidates with an unusual background scare employers a little.

If you have a career including any significant changes of direction, work hard to convince the interviewers that you really are the best person for the job.

Why have you changed jobs so many times?

The interviewers are probably implying that if you've switched jobs frequently in the past, are you likely to move on from theirs sometime soon as well? Whatever reasons you give for your changing jobs in the past, aim to assure the interviewers that your circumstances have now completely changed.

To add the icing to the cake, finish your response with a compelling reason why you intend to make this next career move your last one – for quite a few years anyway.

After citing your reasons, offer a finishing statement along the lines of:

My work has always been a big part of who I am. And having researched your company and customers and having met a few of you now, I think this could be a place where I could learn and grow in a role.

Avoid blaming job moves on interpersonal difficulties. Mentioning this reason once may be acceptable, but mentioning it more times signals to interviewers that you're difficult to manage.

Take a look at these two examples:

- *I really enjoy the job, but haven't had much luck finding an employer that fits me. My first company suffered financial problems and made several of us redundant. I left the next company because they wouldn't support me in my professional exams. My next employer got taken over and a round of redundancies occurred. And in my current organisation, I feel like an insignificant cog in a massive machine given their huge size. What I want to do is find a medium-sized business, like yours, which is small enough for me to get to know the whole team well, but at the same time large enough to offer me some variety in my work.*

- *I moved around a couple of times because I was essentially pretty immature and wasn't very focused on my career. In my early twenties I didn't have much direction. But that drifting is all in the past – I got married a couple of years ago and have very different priorities now. As you can see, I've been with my current employer for nearly two years and am only considering your company because you are offering more responsibility in the role.*

In the first example, the candidate gives a compelling reason (wanting to move into a medium-sized business) for wanting to move this one last time. In the second example, the candidate uses marriage as a way of drawing a line between a flighty past and a career-oriented future.

Book III

Succeeding at Interviews

Getting the right experience

Changing careers can be a bit of a chicken and egg situation. Employers won't take a risk on you because you don't have the right skills and experience; at the same time, you can't get the right skills and experience because no one gives you the chance!

Voluntary work is one of the best ways to develop your skills and experience. Volunteering for a few evenings or weekends a month can often be a stepping-stone to getting the job that you ultimately want.

Approach organisations such as:

✔ Charities, welfare groups, local schools, and homes for the sick or elderly.

✔ Hospitals or hospital radio stations.

✔ Environmental and conservation groups.

✔ Political parties, arts centres, and churches.

Volunteers can get involved in all manner of activities, from fund-raising to working in a charity shop, handling back office paperwork to working on projects in the community. You can get more information about volunteering from Web sites, including:

✔ www.volunteering.org.uk

✔ www.csv.org.uk

✔ www.vso.org.uk

You may find it difficult to talk about why you moved from job to job, as any reasons can sound a little negative. So conveying your passion for the job is doubly important.

Given your background, why have you decided to change career?

Are you an accountant who wants to become a teacher, an IT engineer who wants to become a gym instructor, or a surveyor who now wants to train as a physiotherapist? Whatever your choice, work hard to convince the interviewer to take you on at the start of a drastic career change.

Mention some of your transferable skills from your previous roles or your more relevant experience and relate them to your new chosen career. If you're lacking relevant skills to talk about, see the sidebar 'Getting the right experience' for ideas to help you out.

> ✔ *Realising what I really wanted to do took me a while. I've been flitting around between various corporate jobs for seven years now and I've certainly enjoyed most of them. But I've come to the realisation that I definitely don't want to be confined to an office. Then I hit upon the idea of nursing – a profession that allows me plenty of people contact outside of an*

office environment. In the last year, I've been doing some voluntary work on Saturday mornings at a local hospice and that experience has totally cemented the idea that I want to take up nursing as a vocation.

✔ *I started working in hospitality in various hotel and restaurant jobs. But then I wanted to travel so went to work for an airline. Now I've decided that I want a stable career that doesn't involve shifts. Little opportunity exists for career progression in hospitality or the airlines. For this reason, I'm looking to join your organisation – because you're offering a training programme plus a more stable working environment that will enable me to grow and progress in a career. However, all of my roles have involved considerable customer contact, so I have a good understanding of what makes people tick and how to deal with them, which I think is essential in working for a bank.*

Do you want to change career because you are disillusioned with your current one?

This is a negatively phrased question. The interviewers are implying that you are running away from your current or last career rather than looking to change into a new career for positive reasons.

Avoid going into detail about the reasons you are disillusioned with your current or last career. Focus instead on the positive reasons that attract you to your new career. No one likes a moaner!

Yes, I have been feeling less motivated about my current role. But I've been giving the issue a lot of thought and have decided that this change of career is right for me. Just like a lot of other people, I ended up in my current career rather than planned it. Now, however, I am making a conscious plan. This job is right for me because I think consultancy will give me exposure to a wide range of businesses across industry sectors. In addition, the projects will tend to be shorter and more challenging – so a steeper learning curve will exist and I'll learn more as a result.

To what extent are your personal circumstances impacting upon your desire to change career?

Perhaps you mentioned earlier in your interview that you're moving in with your partner, having children, or getting divorced. If the interviewers are asking you this question, they may be worried that your desire to change career is because you are looking for an easier life or because you're running away from your old life.

Book III

Succeeding at Interviews

Avoid getting into detail about your personal life. Instead, reassure the interviewers that your sitting in this interview is a reasoned and rational decision on your part.

Note that in both of these two example responses, the candidates tell the interviewers that they have rationally evaluated the impact of their personal lives on their work:

> ✔ *I can honestly say that starting a family has very little to do with my desire to change careers. In fact, doing this job will mean taking a cut in my salary – at a time when the additional family member means that we'll need more money. But I just can't give up this opportunity to move into a creative field.*
>
> ✔ *Perhaps getting divorced has made me look at all aspects of my life again. But I've been very careful to separate the emotional changes in my life from the rational decisions that I need to make about my career.*

Only allow yourself to talk about your personal circumstances if they directly relate to your new career.

I'd say that my personal circumstances are very relevant to my choice to train as an acupuncturist. I was in such a poor state of health before I started seeing an acupuncturist myself. I was totally amazed at the improvement in wellbeing that I experienced in only six sessions. So I began looking into Chinese medicine and alternative health models. I've been reading extensively around the topic for some time now. But what sealed this choice of career for me was meeting different practising acupuncturists and getting a feel for how they spend their time and how rewarding they find it.

How do we know that you'll stick with this change of direction?

This is a perfectly valid question. If you're dissatisfied with what you've been doing up until now, how do the interviewers know that you won't get dissatisfied with this new career too?

Try to convince the interviewers that this is what you want to do by talking about the time, effort, and money you have invested in researching and educating yourself about your new career.

Don't forget that interviewers are not only evaluating *what* you say but also *how* you say it. If you don't sound enthusiastic and passionate about your new career choice, why should the interviewers believe you?

The following examples demonstrate your research (in the first example), and your passion (in the second):

✔ *I'm going to stick with a career this time because I've always had a passion for property. I read about property trends in the papers and on Web sites and talk about property with friends. Over the last few months, I've also sought out different estate agents to find out the precise ins and outs of the job. I feel that I have an excellent appreciation of the realities of the job. I understand that the hours can be very long and that my pay will be almost totally dependent on my performance, but those details don't put me off – in fact I feel even more determined to work in the industry.*

✔ *All of my jobs so far have helped me understand what I enjoy about working life. I started in finance but found that I didn't get enough people contact. I moved into human resources but felt my organisation wasn't taking our department seriously enough, so I switched to sales admin. Through working with the sales people and getting to know them and learn exactly what they do, I realised that I wanted to work in sales too. This job has the perfect combination of features for me – I enjoy being with people, and using my brain to figure out how to influence them. I can guarantee you that this is the job I have always been looking for.*

How do you feel about starting at the bottom again?

Don't reply to this question by just saying that starting over at the bottom isn't an issue. You need to demonstrate to the interviewers that you have given this situation some thought.

I think I'm going to enjoy the situation actually. I'd be a fool to expect to come into your industry without any relevant experience. I know that the first six months is filled mainly with running errands and doing other people's administration. But the whole point of being a runner is to absorb information and learn, and that's exactly what I'll be doing for the first year.

How will you cope working with peers who are ten years younger than you?

This question is a variation on the preceding one, 'How do you feel about having to start at the bottom again?'. You need to convince the interviewers that this concern is not an issue.

Book III

Succeeding at Interviews

Getting an insight into your new career

Changing career can be incredibly daunting. Talking to people who are already in your dream job is one of the best ways to find out whether your new career is really going to suit you.

If you don't know anyone who works in your chosen field, then ask round. Talk to your friends and family – do they know anyone who is in your dream job?

Once you find a contact, arrange a chat over coffee – and of course you buy!

Good questions to ask people already in the job include:

✔ What do they do on a day-to-day, hour-by-hour basis? What do they most enjoy about their work? What are the worst or most boring aspects of the job?

✔ What career paths exist in the industry? Do people in the profession tend to be self-employed or set up their own business? Or do they join small, medium, or large organisations?

✔ What training did they require? What exams or other forms of assessment did they have to complete? How expensive was the course?

If you have any younger peers or perhaps a younger manager in your current job, mention this in support of your answer that this issue won't be a problem for you.

I don't think it will be an issue at all. In my current job, a few of the managers at my level are a good few years younger than me anyway and we all get on very well. And the fact that I'll be working with lots of enthusiastic younger people will keep me on my toes.

How will you cope with the drop in salary that changing career necessitates?

In answering this question, you need to convince the interviewers that you have weighed up the pros and cons – and decided that the pros ultimately outweigh the cons.

I've given a lot of thought to this issue. But I've wanted a job in this field for so many years now that I must simply cut back to make this work. I've already calculated exactly how much I need to live on and where I can save. But in the longer term, my firm intention is to work my way up in this industry, so earning the entry-level salary for the rest of my life is unlikely.

If you have a partner at home who's willing to shoulder some of your financial commitments, then do tell the interviewers.

Although an interviewer should not ask about your home or personal life, you may choose to bring it up yourself if you think that doing so is an asset in the interview. Strictly speaking, the interviewers shouldn't ask you further questions about your partner. But in reality their curiosity may get the better of them. So do be ready to answer a few conversational questions about your partner if you mention them first!

What would you do if you were unable to secure a job in this profession?

This question is a test of how much you want to change careers and enter the interviewers' profession. Are you completely dedicated to this one profession?

Get across the fact that you are only looking for jobs in this particular field.

I'd be devastated if I couldn't work in this profession as I've set my heart on doing so. But to be honest, I'm not considering the possibility of failure at the moment. Your company is obviously one of the top-rated organisations in this field. But if I fail to impress you, I will continue to apply for jobs with some of the lesser-known organisations.

Fending Off Weird and Wonderful Questions

Certain interviewers like to think of themselves as pop psychologists. These people may have read an article once or know someone who knows someone who is a psychologist – and they now believe that certain questions can allow them to peel aside your defences and delve into your personality.

Now, the truth of the matter is that the following questions would never be asked by anyone who has even a half-decent understanding of psychology. But as this is an interview and there are certain rules to abide by, you must simply grit your teeth and smile sweetly in the face of these truly, outstandingly bizarre questions.

Be careful not to sound too rehearsed when responding to the following questions. The idea in a pressure interview is to come across as cool and collected, but not as if you have memorised your answers off by heart. If you answer straightaway without any hesitation at all, then the interviewers may see through you. So make sure that you at least pretend to give each question a moment's thought!

Book III

Succeeding at Interviews

See this pencil I'm holding? Sell it to me

You may expect this question to be asked of people going into sales, but in fact it tends to be asked mainly when interviewers want to put non-sales people under pressure. The interviewers are trying to frighten you with a seemingly odd request.

You can potentially be asked to sell just about anything in sight, from a notebook to the desk at which the interviewers are sitting.

Sales people have to be good mannered, polite, and enthusiastic. Make sure that your tone of voice, facial expressions, and body language display those qualities in answering this question. Passing this question is not just a case of saying the right words – it is just as important for you to appear as if you believe in the words, too.

A good tack may be to follow four simple steps to selling anything:

1. Ask the interviewer some questions to establish his need for the item. For example if you are asked to sell a potted plant: *Do you already own any potted plants? Would you like to own any more?* The interviewer is bound to say no to your questions, which leads onto the next step.

2. Talk about the features and qualities of the item. Describe the shape and texture of the leaves; tell the interviewer about the number of flowers and their colour.

3. Next focus on the benefits of the item. For example, a potted plant may make the room seem greener and more pleasant to work in. It can also relax people who come into the room and make them feel more at home. Plants also generate oxygen and remove stale carbon dioxide.

4. Finally, make a strong statement to finish, such as: *In summary, I think it's a great plant and I'd be delighted to have one of these at home. Would you like one?*

If you follow those steps, your eloquence should suitably impress the interviewer.

Who was your favourite teacher?

Even though the question is asking you to name your favourite teacher, make sure that you are able to explain why he or she was your favourite too. Finish off your answer by reinforcing some quality that you currently possess as a result of your favourite teacher.

A couple of examples:

> ✔ *Miss Ellwood taught me English until I was 13 years of age. And what has really stayed with me is the way she brought the characters in books to life. She really instilled in me the importance of reading – not just for learning but also for pleasure. So nowadays I make sure that I read a couple of management or business biography books to round out my knowledge.*

> ✔ *Mr Jackson taught me A Level chemistry. What I liked about his style was that he always made us aware of the fact that what we were learning for our exams was not always the whole truth – that it was a simplified version of what scientists currently understood about chemistry. So it was his teaching style that really filled me with the desire to go on to university to study chemistry and begin a career in science.*

If you were an animal, what would you be?

This question definitely falls into the category of silly pop psychology questions. But remember that you can't tell an interviewer that a question is stupid! The interviewer is wondering how you see yourself. So be sure to pick an animal with suitably positive characteristics.

REMEMBER

There's no definitive right answer for choosing what sort of animal you'd be. But lions, tigers, and eagles are generally thought to possess more noble qualities than snakes, weasels, and pigs!

Keep your answer short and sweet in the hope that the interviewer will go on to ask you a more sensible question:

> ✔ *I'd say I was like a wolf because I'm canny and can smell a good story – which isn't a bad quality in a journalist.*

> ✔ *I'm like an elephant because I can shoulder a large burden. I can take on lots of work, but also take on the emotional burden of stressed team mates too.*

If you were a cartoon character, who would you be?

Just like the previous question about animals, this is a ridiculous question. But grin and bear it. It almost doesn't matter what character you choose so long as you explain it by talking about some positive, job-related characteristics:

Book III

Succeeding at Interviews

> ✔ *I'm like Hercules in that Disney film. I'm strong and confident – very little gets me down.*
>
> ✔ *If I had to pick one, I guess I'm like Bugs Bunny. He never gets taken for a ride and always has the last laugh!*

Tell me a story

The pitfall to avoid in answering this question is telling a random story not involving yourself or telling a story that does not sell your career achievements.

The best answer is to talk about your career:

I graduated in 1993 and I've had a variety of roles since then. I started working in a call centre but quickly decided that I wanted a job that allowed me more face-to-face customer contact, so I moved into the hotel industry. I started in a small local chain but got promoted quickly up to desk supervisor and then four years ago to hotel general manager. But I think that I've learned everything that I can from managing that small hotel. And as there have been no opportunities within the company to transfer to another hotel, that's what brings me to this interview today.

Ensure that the interviewer wants to hear this tale by checking first: *Is it okay if I tell you the story of my career?* If the interviewer stops you and insists that you tell the story of your life outside of work, try to squeeze in a couple of facts about your career too:

I was born in Sheffield and grew up there but went to university in Southampton and graduated in 1993. My first job was working in a call centre but then I decided that I wanted to move into a job with more face-to-face contact. In my spare time I'm a keen amateur photographer and a bit of a tennis fanatic. I'm now a general manager managing a hotel with about 120 staff but on the look-out for a bigger hotel to run.

This question is *not* an invitation to tell the interviewer about your entire life in excruciatingly boring detail from the day you were born. Summarise key facts and keep your response under two or three minutes at the very most.

Who do you most admire and why?

Think back to the list of skills that this particular interviewer's organisation is looking for. If they have mentioned financial acumen as a key skill, then talk about a role model who has demonstrated financial acumen. If the employer is on the lookout for tenacity, then pick someone to talk about who has demonstrated determination in his or her life. Some examples:

✔ *I really admire Sir Terry Leahy, the Chief Executive of Tesco. He has single-handedly turned around what used to be an ailing supermarket into one of the world's dominant forces in retail. He has engineered the company's expansion into non-food sectors and pushed revenues, profits, and shareholder return up. I aspire to be as good as he is.*

✔ *The Sales Director where I used to work was a really great role model. She had two children so always tried to get away by 5.30pm every evening. But she was able to work at such a pace and get such a huge amount done that leaving on time was never an issue. She was incredibly focused and had an amazing ability to prioritise – and I hope that I've picked up some of those traits from her.*

Don't just pick one example of someone you admire for every single interview that you go for. Think through a different answer for every single organisation. Different organisations look for different skills, so your response must reflect that.

If you could meet anyone living or dead, who would it be and why?

Again, as with the question about describing someone that you admire, try to pick someone who has qualities or characteristics that put them (and you) in good stead for the job that you are being interviewed for.

If you have already picked one business leader for your question about who you admire, make sure you have a different leader for this question.

I'd like to meet the first Chief Executive of the National Council for Voluntary Organisations to ask him what made him so passionate about wanting to promote the voluntary organisation sector. Our job of getting people to donate money to charitable causes is becoming increasingly harder work, and I'm sure that he would be an inspirational person to meet.

Be careful of picking politicians unless you are 100 per cent sure of the interviewers' political allegiances. Just as the adage warns you to steer clear of politics and religion at dinner parties, picking a politician from the wrong party can have immediately disastrous consequences for your chances of getting the job!

Book III

Succeeding at Interviews

What is your greatest fear?

Knowing exactly what kind of fear the interviewer is trying to get at is difficult. Ask a question to check before you jump in with the wrong sort of response: *Do you mean a professional fear or a personal fear?* If the interviewer leaves the choice up to you, then talk about a professional fear.

This is quite a negative question. Try to turn the question to your advantage. End your response on a high note by talking up some positive quality about yourself.

Some example responses:

- ✔ *I wouldn't say that I have any fears as such – it's a very strong term. But I do worry occasionally and take very seriously the threat that Internet-based retailers pose for our industry. To me, that means that I must make even greater efforts to make sure that the customers visiting our shops can get a positive customer experience that will keep them coming back to us rather than buying from the Internet.*

- ✔ *Personally, I worry for the future of my children. Growing up nowadays seems to be filled with so many more perils than when we were growing up 30 years ago. But I do the best that I can – I try to instil good values in my children and make sure that they eat well, and I play with them and get them to exercise. It's all a good parent can do.*

Saying Something Is Better Than Saying Nothing

No matter how much preparation you do, you're never going to be able to predict and prepare for every single question that you can come across. And eventually you may get asked a question that you just don't have an answer for.

Now, you may be tempted to apologise and say, *I don't know*. But you may as well just say, *I'm stupid and I can't think of an answer. I'm a rubbish candidate. Throw my CV into the bin now!*

Playing for time

If you can't think of an answer within the first few seconds, then your first tactic may be to play for time to allow you to think about the question a bit more. But don't just sit there saying nothing.

Silence during an interview can be either perfectly acceptable or excruciatingly painful. If you tell the interviewers that you need a few moments to think about the question, they'll give you a bit of space – but if you don't, they'll start to worry for you – and that is never a good impression to leave them with.

If you don't understand the question, you can perhaps ask for more clarification. Try one of the following:

- ✔ *That's a tough one. I'll need to think about it for a moment.*

- ✔ *That's a really good question. I'm sure there's a really good answer to it, but I'm afraid that you've got me there. Could we perhaps move on and maybe come back to it in a bit?*

- ✔ *You'll have to excuse me but I'm not entirely sure I understand the question. Could you rephrase it for me please?*

- ✔ *I'm not familiar with that particular term. Could you just explain that to me please?*

Book III

Succeeding at Interviews

Making a last ditch effort

If you really can't think of how to answer a question, you may be forced to admit it. But if at all possible, try talking up some positive quality about yourself or give a related example to illustrate your skill in a similar area:

- ✔ *I have to admit that I've never had to deal with that area of responsibility in my current role. However, I'd be very keen to take it on as a responsibility and in fact that's one of the reasons why I'm so excited about the possibility of working for you.*

- ✔ *I'm sorry but I haven't used that particular software package before. However, I do learn incredibly quickly. For instance, last year I had never used the XYZ package but effectively taught myself how to use it from scratch in about four weeks.*

- ✔ *I've never been in that precise situation myself with a customer. But something similar did once happen with a colleague. For example. . . .*

Even more bizarre questions

Some interviewers pride themselves on devising fiendish new questions to goad candidates with. Some more genuine questions that I've heard interviewers ask candidates include:

✔ What five famous people would you invite to a dinner party and why?

✔ Why are manhole covers round?

✔ Define true happiness.

✔ Would you rather be famous or powerful?

✔ Do you think the government should increase the national minimum wage or not?

Have a go at answering these questions. The reason the interviewer is asking these questions is to catch you off guard. Even if you don't know the answer, you still have to come up with something convincing. So how would you respond to these off-beat questions?

Chapter 8

Handling Hypothetical and Analytical Questions

. . . .

In This Chapter

▶ Judging the best response to give to hypothetical questions

▶ Talking about key concepts

▶ Finding the solution to numerical questions

. . . .

*W*hile interviewers are interested in your past and the skills that you can bring to the job, they also want to know how well you may fit into their organisation. Having certain skills is all very well, but can you exercise them in any situation? So interviewers may ask hypothetical questions to gauge how you would deal with situations that they can foresee happening. If you're being interviewed for a management position, interviewers may also ask you to define key management concepts to see if you think along the same lines as they do.

If you are being interviewed for a job that requires a fair degree of ability with numbers, be ready to show you can analyse simple numerical problems and give the interviewer an answer. More often than not, interviewers expect you to handle these problems in your head rather than by using a calculator or even a pen and paper.

In this chapter, we discuss ways to deal with some of the most common hypothetical questions, and questions requiring definitions of management concepts. And we round off by giving you some examples of the most common numerical questions that interviewers are likely to pose.

Responding to Hypothetical Questions

Hypothetical questions almost always have the word 'would' in them. Look out for phrases such as *How would you. . . ?* or *What would you . . .?* Another common tactic is to ask, *If . . . blah blah blah. What would you do?*

Don't assume that a single right answer exists. Interviewers in a small, cost-conscious business may be looking for a very different answer to interviewers in a large, growing, and very successful company. Do your research and devise responses to the following hypothetical questions for each interview that you go to.

The secret to handling hypothetical questions is telling the interviewers what you think they want to hear – which may sometimes be different from what you would actually do.

What would you do if your boss asked you to do something that went against your principles?

Most people would probably answer this question by saying that it depends on what your boss had asked you to do. But 'it depends' is not a satisfactory answer. Tell the interviewers what they probably want to hear – that you would act in the best interests of the organisation.

This is a hypothetical situation. Even if in reality you are prepared to stand up for your principles, the interviewers would probably rather know that you would do what is best for their organisation.

The first thing to do is to weigh up the request against the values and rules of the organisation. If my boss has asked me to do something that is in line with those values but just goes against my personal values, I would have to do it anyway – because it is for the good of the organisation. However, if my boss has asked me to do something that is not in keeping with the organisation's values, then I would question it.

What would you do if you disagreed with a decision taken by your manager?

This is a similar question to the one above, so a similar tactic is probably a safe bet. Emphasise that you would try to discuss the decision with your manager first.

In preparing a response to this question, think about the nature of the interviewers' organisation. Do you think they would consider it most important to obey your manager? Or would they want you to act in the best interests of the organisation?

Contrast these two responses:

> ✔ *How I behave would depend on why I disagreed with the decision. For example, if I thought that the decision was not in the best interests of the organisation, then I would raise the issue with my manager and try to convince him or her of my arguments. If my manager listens to me and understands my reasons, but still wants to go ahead with his or her decision, then I would have to abide by it.*

> ✔ *If I thought that a decision would go against the interests of our organisation and our customers, then I would have to challenge my manager on the issue. If my manager did not see reason, then I may talk to a colleague and get a second opinion. If, on discussion, we felt that the decision was completely inappropriate – perhaps because it would damage the organisation or harm our relationships with customers – then I would have to escalate the issue and perhaps raise my concerns with my manager's manager.*

The second answer is more appropriate for situations in which you think your manager is clearly wrong. The first answer may be more appropriate if the decision is merely about a difference of opinion.

Book III

Succeeding at Interviews

What would you do if your child were suddenly taken ill?

This question is rather unfair – potentially illegal – especially as it tends to be aimed at women with children rather than men. As such, you may be technically within your rights to refuse to answer it. However, refusing to answer it can make you appear unnecessarily testy or aggressive. So try to keep any irritation in check.

Remember that this question relates to a purely hypothetical situation. In reality you may want to drop everything and head home to look after your child. But that answer won't get you the job.

Nurseries and day centres typically ask parents to remove their children if they have any illnesses that can infect other children. A good response to this question is saying that you have other people to look after your child if necessary.

> ✔ *My son is at a full-time nursery. But in case of medical emergencies, they have the contact details of my mother as well as my partner's parents. So one set of his grandparents would be more than happy to look after him. And certainly my parents nursed me and my siblings through everything from the measles to chickenpox.*

> ✔ *I have a very good nanny who looks after the children. So I'm sure that she would be able to cope with any minor medical emergencies – certainly most common childhood ailments and even a broken bone. It would have to be a very major emergency for me to have to go home – and I don't foresee that happening.*

Would you rather be a big fish in a small pond or a small fish in a big pond?

The 'right' answer to this question depends entirely on the size of the company that you are applying for. Read the organisation's literature carefully to work out how many people are employed – is it counted in dozens, hundreds, or thousands?

Interviewers can also ask you much more direct questions such as: *Why would you want to work for a small organisation like ours?* or *Why are you looking to join a large company when all of your experience so far has been with smaller ones?*

Compare or contrast your past experience of working in larger or smaller firms to what's on offer in each particular interview.

Take a look at these two different responses:

> ✔ *I'd much rather be a big fish in a small pond. Working in my current firm, with nearly 800 other lawyers, I feel that I have very little impact on the overall running of the business. I want to join a firm in which I can get to know the team better and feel that I am having more of a say in shaping its future.*

> ✔ *I'm looking to jump into a bigger pond. One of the main reasons I'm look-ing to join your organisation is that so far I have only worked for small companies. Joining a large business will give me exposure to larger and more complex projects across a number of offices and locations. Working in a large organisation will also give me a greater understanding of more sophisticated, leading-edge processes, too.*

If you spotted a colleague doing something unethical, what would you do?

In most instances, in response to this question the interviewers want you to say that you would take a course of action to intervene or report the person as appropriate. If there are certain 'right' ways of acting in your particular industry – for example, the legal and medical professions have very clear guidelines on how to deal with such individuals – then make sure your answer includes these.

I would get in touch with the human resources department to speak about the matter. I would try to discuss the issue confidentially and without mentioning the individual's name. If it became clear that his behaviour was definitely unethical, then I would report the issue to my line manager.

If you have dealt with this situation before, give this as an example. Examples are more credible than merely saying what you *would* do in this situation.

Book III

Succeeding at Interviews

What would you do if a colleague came to you in tears?

Empathy and consideration for others are important qualities in employees. The worst thing in a crisis situation is having a colleague point the finger of blame or simply say *I told you so.*

Show the interviewers you have good listening skills and can offer not only practical assistance but also a shoulder to cry on.

I'd take my colleague aside – perhaps to an unoccupied office – and try to find out what had upset them. But to start with, the colleague probably doesn't want to be bombarded with questions, so I'd try to be sympathetic. Once they have calmed down, I would try to find out what the matter was. Then I would look for

*ways to help – such as taking on some of their work, talking to a difficult cus-
tomer, or getting another colleague involved. But throughout, I'd focus on being
sympathetic and reassuring.*

How would you react if your boss said that you needed to come into the office for the entire weekend?

In practice, you may be a bit disgruntled about working at the weekend. But
your response to this question needs to demonstrate your flexibility and
commitment to the job.

*Obviously, working at the weekend is not a situation that I hope will happen
very often. But I'd have no problem with it. In fact, one of the reasons I'm looking to change jobs is because I'm starting to feel that my current role isn't suffi-
ciently challenging – I'm being under-utilised. So in fact it may be a nice change
to have too much work to do!*

Talking about how you *would* react is all very well, but also try to give the
interviewers an example of when you had to work outside your contracted
hours.

Working hours are becoming an increasingly difficult area of working life.
If you need some help in finding out what's legal and what's not, read Liz
Barclay's *Small Business Employment Law For Dummies* (Wiley).

What would you say if I were to offer you this job right now?

The 'right' answer depends on how much the interviewers expect you to
know about the job. For example, if you have been headhunted for a specific
role and know relatively little about a post, then you can say:

*Well, it sounds very interesting so far. But before accepting the job, I'd need to
spend a bit more time researching the business and reading up on your products
and the challenges ahead of you. Ideally I'd like to meet a few more of the team
to find out whether we'd get on together. But so far it all sounds very promising.*

If, however, the interviewers provide you with plenty of information about
their organisation, the role, the salary and benefits, and you still want the job,
then a better answer is to declare your enthusiasm:

I would say yes immediately. I've done a lot of reading about your organisation and I think that your positioning with regards to your competitors is fascinating. I also like the fact that this interview has been quite relaxed yet challenging. For me, that's a sign that this is the right place for me to work.

Defining Key Concepts

A little knowledge can be a dangerous thing. Sometimes interviewers who have read a management textbook or two may want to know whether you have the same level of insight into models and concepts as they do.

How would you define team work?

In asking this question, the interviewers want to know whether you can put the needs of the team ahead of your own needs.

Two common variations on this question are: *What makes for good team work?* and *How would you define co-operation?*

I would define team work as the ability for a group of individuals working together to accomplish more than they could accomplish individually. In practical terms, this means that individuals must be willing to put the needs of the team above their own needs at times.

Book III

Succeeding at Interviews

Be ready to give an example of a time you demonstrated good teamworking skills, as the interviewers can easily follow up this question by asking: *And can you tell us about a time when you demonstrated your teamworking skills?*

What makes for a good working environment?

Answering this question requires a good idea of the kind of culture that typifies this industry or even this specific company. For example, interviewers in a public sector organisation may be looking for an answer that mentions the need to follow established rules, while a pharmaceutical company may expect candidates to talk about the need for people to have a thirst for knowledge.

Good research pays off in answering this type of question. Read widely to get an idea of the culture and kind of team environment within the interviewers' organisation. If, however, you're not sure of the working culture, talk briefly about some general features that all organisations aspire to:

I think it's really important for everyone to feel that they can express their opinions openly. Managers must be willing to listen to ideas and encourage everyone to pull together in the best interests of the team.

How would you define leadership?

Hundreds of definitions of leadership exist, so feel free to adopt one you already know. However, how you respond to this question may depend on the nature of the organisation interviewing you.

For example, a traditional organisation may expect an answer along these lines:

Leadership is about communicating the goals of the organisation to the team and then delegating tasks to appropriate members of the team, checking up on their work, and ensuring that they're making progress.

Alternatively, a more progressive organisation may want to hear about terms such as 'vision' and 'empowerment':

Leadership is about involving stakeholders to create a shared vision, and then motivating and empowering the team so that they want to achieve that vision. Good leadership is about getting to understand the strengths, weaknesses, and needs of individual members of the team and being able to coach and develop them so that they can tackle progressively greater problems and opportunities.

Dealing Effectively with Numerical Challenges

Employers often complain that employees lack ability with numbers. Most employees rely on calculators, cash tills, and computers for the most simple of numerical tasks. But what happens if you input the data wrongly and get a key decimal point in the wrong place? Or what if the cash till breaks down? The interviewers want to know whether you can cope without the benefit of technology.

How many bottles of carbonated water are consumed daily in California?

On the face of it, this question seems impossible to answer. How the heck should you know how many bottles are consumed daily in Britain – let alone California?

But the interviewers are not looking for a correct answer. They may not even know the precise answer themselves! Instead, what the interviewers are looking for is whether you can take a problem and, using reasonable assumptions and some mental arithmetic, come up with a sensible estimate.

A correct answer to numerical hypothetical questions rarely exists. Extrapolate from information that you do possess to calculate your estimate. As you may imagine, management consulting firms and investment banks, in particular, like to use these sorts of 'guesstimate' questions.

The answer to this question may go along these lines:

I've read somewhere that if California were a country in its own right, it would be something like the sixth or seventh largest country in the world. On the other hand, it's not as densely populated as most European countries, so I'd hazard a guess that it has only a tenth of the population of the UK or France, so it would have around five million people living there.

Thinking about the people that I know, I'd say that a lot of middle class people are drinking bottled water – so maybe one in three people in the UK drinks a bottle of water a day. But the question was about carbonated water. As most people seem to drink still water rather than fizzy, I'd estimate that only one in four bottles of water are carbonated. So that means that around one in twelve people in the UK drinks a bottle of carbonated water daily.

But people in California are reputedly much more health-conscious than those in the UK. So let's say twice as many people there drink bottled water. So that makes one in six people in California. So one in six out of five million people – that's, um . . . Well, one in five would be one million. So one in six is going to be around 850,000 people. So the answer is around 850,000 bottles of carbonated water a day.

In this example and those following, whether the number is 'correct' or not isn't the point. Rather, the assumptions, estimates, and mental calculations must seem reasonable – and these are more interesting to the interviewers than the actual answer itself.

Book III

Succeeding at Interviews

Talk out loud as you work out your answer. The interviewers don't want you to sit in silence calculating the answer and then simply say '60,000 bottles a day' at the end – they want to hear your chain of thought.

How many cars does Pakistan have?

This is another 'guesstimate' question. Again, the interviewers are interested in your line of reasoning. You may start this challenge by working out the population of Pakistan based on your general knowledge of the world, and then try to estimate how many people will own cars.

Remember, to talk through your assumptions out loud.

I think I read that India is the second largest country in the world, with a population of around 800 million people. From maps that I've seen of that part of the world, Pakistan is roughly a fifth or sixth of its size. Assuming it has a similar population density to India, let's call that 150 million people in Pakistan.

Now, large parts of the population are very poor, so won't have a car. I'd assume that around 90 per cent of the population are too poor to own a car. So that leaves 15 million people as potential car owners. Let's assume that each family only has one car.

In the UK, the typical family consists of two parents and 2.4 children. But in Asia, grandparents tend to live with families. And Asian countries have a higher birth rate, so let's call that three children. Assuming that there are seven or eight people in the average Pakistani family, that's 15 million divided by seven or eight which is . . . around two million cars?

I have a dinosaur on an island – how many sheep would I need on the island to feed it in perpetuity?

This is yet another 'guesstimate' question – although it is dressed up as a more complex problem. As dinosaurs died out millions of years before sheep lived on the planet, there really is no right answer to this question! Again, you need to make a number of reasonable assumptions and then arrive at an answer. By the way, we have heard an interviewer at a top investment bank ask candidates this question – we're not making it up!

So the question is basically how many sheep would I need on the island in order for them to be able to breed enough to feed the dinosaur. Okay, let's assume that a meat-eating dinosaur needs to eat hundreds of kilograms of flesh every day – so let's call it 20 sheep every single day. Multiplying that number by 365 equals about 7000 sheep every year.

Now let's think about the rate at which sheep can breed. One ram can impregnate many dozens of female sheep, so let's assume that the population is 99 per cent female. I assume that there's plenty of green grass on the island and perfect breeding conditions. One sheep can produce several lambs at a go and let's assume that they all make it to adulthood because of those perfect conditions. So if each sheep is producing on average four lambs every year, then you would basically need 7000 divided by four sheep on the island, which equals approximately 1700 sheep to give birth and not be eaten.

So you'd need 7000 sheep in the first year, who would all get eaten. And you'd need another 1700 sheep to produce the next year's lot of sheep. So you would need approximately 8700 sheep to begin with.

Now, the assumptions made above may be a bit flaky and there is actually a precise mathematical formula you can apply to questions about perpetuities. But the interviewers are not looking for mathematical formulae – they're looking for the ability to make assumptions and apply rough rules.

Book III

Succeeding at Interviews

If you are unsure about your ability to work through analytical problems, then practise them with a friend or ideally another job seeker. Take it in turns to devise simple questions such as the ones in this section to quiz each other.

I'd like you to multiply 8 by 9 and then take 13 away from the result

This question is a straightforward numerical challenge. Unlike the previous 'guesstimate' questions in this section, a right answer exists. 8 multiplied by 9 is, of course, 72. Taking 13 away from 72 gives you 59. But the challenge is whether you can do that calculation in your head – and quickly.

If applying for a job that involves numbers – anything from working as an analyst to working behind a bar or in a shop – practising your multiplication tables and mental arithmetic helps.

To prepare for such an interview, have a go at calculating the answers to the following sums – without using a calculator or even pen and paper of course!

> ✔ *What is 12 plus 36 plus 17?*
>
> ✔ *A pint of beer costs £1.23 in my pub. How much will a round of four pints cost?*
>
> ✔ *As quickly as possible, what is 6 times 8?*
>
> ✔ *I am expecting 60 guests in my restaurant tonight. Assuming that each person eats one-fifth of a cake, how many cakes will I need to buy?*
>
> ✔ *A customer buys some goods in our shop costing £11.16. She gives you a £50 note. How much change will you give her back?*
>
> ✔ *A customer says that your colleague has short-changed him. He was expecting 64p back but actually received 37p. How much would you need to give him back?*

You get the idea. If you don't feel comfortable doing these sums, make up some of your own and practise doing them in your head.

Don't worry if your times tables and mental arithmetic are a bit rusty at first. Practising daily soon gets you up to speed at this skill again.

Chapter 9

Succeeding at Competency-Based Interviewing

*C*ompetency-based interviewing is simply a technique that interviewers use to scrutinise your previous experience to find out whether you have the relevant skills they really need for the job.

Psychologists have discovered that one of the best predictors of whether job candidates will be successful in a job is the past experience they have. Just think about the situation for a moment: If you were looking for a negotiator, wouldn't you rather employ someone who had experience of negotiating deals than someone who can only talk about how she *would* or *may* negotiate? Or if you were looking for a data analyst, wouldn't you feel more confident hiring someone who can talk you through analytical problems he had dealt with in the past than someone who says that he could probably pick it up?

Competencies are just management-speak for 'the skills and behaviours that determine success at work'. So the interviewers look for you to describe the skills you used and how you actually behaved in different work situations.

Discovering the Rules of the Game

The key to excelling at competency-based questions is to always respond by talking about a specific incident in the past that you dealt with. Don't answer by talking about how you *would* handle a situation. And don't talk about how you *generally* handled those kinds of situations in the past.

Talk about a single incident that happened to you. Be ready to relate specific details and even names of other people who were involved, approximate dates, and the locations if necessary.

Also, be ready to talk about your example in a lot of detail. The interviewers will likely bombard you with dozens of questions to find out what the situation was, who was involved, what you did and why you did it, how other people reacted, what you said or did next, how other people changed their reactions, and so on.

A lot of candidates exaggerate their experience to some degree. But the whole point of competency-based interviewing is to catch out liars. Just as the police question suspected criminals, the interviewers fire multiple questions at you in quick succession to get at the truth. You are much more likely to trip yourself up by lying.

Spotting competency-based questions

Competency-based questions often do not sound like questions at all. While most interview questions start with questioning words such as *what*, *when*, *how*, and *why*, competency-based questions tend to sound more like requests.

You can spot competency-based questions because the interviewers instruct you to tell them about particular situations or to give specific examples. Look out for language such as:

- ✔ 'Give me an example of a time when you. . .'
- ✔ 'Tell me about an occasion when you. . .'
- ✔ 'Talk me through a situation that you have been in when. . .'
- ✔ 'Can you tell me about an instance in which you. . .'

If you hear language like this, the interviewer is almost certain to want a specific example that you have experienced.

Dealing with skilled competency-based interviewers

If an interviewer asks you an initial question and then continues to ask perhaps three or four further questions, you know that you are in safe hands because this is the sign of a very competent and well-skilled interviewer. The sidebar 'Competency-based interviewing at its best' shows an example of the sort of interview you should hope to find yourself in. The interviewer is likely to have been trained in the skills of competency-based interviewing – in other words, how to dig the information out of you. Simply follow the interviewer's lead and describe how you handled that specific situation.

Competency-based interviewing at its best

Here's a worked example of a good competency-based interviewer speaking to a candidate. As you can see, a skilled interviewer asks as many questions as necessary to establish exactly what happened and how you resolved a situation.

Interviewer: *Tell me about the last time you faced a problem and how you tackled it.*

Candidate: *This was about two months ago. As I mentioned earlier, I work in a team of five accountants reporting to the accounts manager. We discovered that a computer virus had corrupted most of the reports that we had to hand in at the end of the month. And so we had about three days to do over a week's worth of work.*

Interviewer: *Going back to the beginning, how did you first discover the virus problem?*

Candidate: *It wasn't me who discovered it. Our accounts clerk found the problem and shouted it around the room. She was panicking and getting really stressed out. And the first thing I did when I saw this was to sit her down and get her to tell the rest of us exactly what the problem was.*

Interviewer: *So what happened next?*

Candidate: *I suggested that we check whether we had viable back-ups but unfortunately the virus had infiltrated our system before the weekly back-up had been done.*

Interviewer: *So what did you do next?*

Candidate: *We brainstormed ideas and decided to get help from the finance department of another business unit. Doing so wasn't standard practice, but I suggested the idea to my*

boss, who agreed it was the right thing to do. And so we ended up getting all of the accounts completed by the end of the month.

Interviewer: *Sorry, can I go back in time a little bit. You said 'we'. What was your role in that brainstorming process?*

Candidate: *I say 'we', but it was my suggestion to initiate a brainstorm. I laid down some rules for the brainstorm – that we would come up with as many ideas as possible before critiquing them.*

Interviewer: *What other options did you come up with and how did you decide to get help from the other finance department?*

Candidate: *The main other option was to hire temporary staff to help us with processing the data. But that would have cost over £1000. Someone else in the team then joked that it was a shame we couldn't get the accounts team based at our other office to help us and I thought it was a good idea. No one had done it before, but I thought it may be worth giving a go, so I said that I would suggest the proposed solution to my boss.*

Interviewer: *And how did your boss respond to the idea?*

Candidate: *He didn't like the suggestion initially. But I showed him the cost analysis of how expensive it would be to get temporary staff in. And I said that I had already checked that our other office wasn't busy. So eventually he let me bring their team to our office for a few days.*

Interviewer: *Thank you. Let's move on to the next question now. . .*

Competency-based interviewing at its worst

Just as some interviewers are great at asking competency-based questions, others are less skilled. If you find yourself in this situation, follow the lead of the candidate in the following example to help you get your point across.

Interviewer: *Tell me about the last time you helped out a colleague.*

Candidate: *This happened a couple of weeks ago. I noticed that one of my colleagues, John, was just sitting there with his head in his hands. He was just staring at his computer screen but not actually doing any work. So I thought I'd help him out.*

Interviewer: *Thank you. Moving on to the next question. . .*

Candidate: *Actually, can I just add something to that last question about my colleague? I hadn't initially realised what the problem was, so I took*

him to the canteen and sat him down. He was really down but eventually with a bit of listening, I found out that he'd just heard that he'd lost his biggest customer to a competitor. So he was really worried that he was going to be fired. To cut the rest of the story short, I suggested that he warn our boss that he was going to miss his target for the month. And then I worked with him to create an action plan to find a new customer, which we managed to do over the course of a few months.

In this example, the candidate gives additional information to demonstrate a number of further skills. First, that the candidate possessed empathy and sensitivity. Second, that the candidate was able to make useful suggestions. Third, that the candidate was able to support a colleague in creating an action plan.

Be sure to read the following section, 'Dealing with unskilled competency-based interviewers' in case you find yourself dealing with an interviewer who isn't skilled in this technique.

Always talk about what you did in the first person singular by saying *I did*, *I spoke*, *I suggested*, and so on. Avoid describing what *we* did too much. After all, whom are you trying to get a new job for – you or your entire team?

Dealing with unskilled competency-based interviewers

Although many interviewers are skilled at asking competency-based questions, many other interviewers merely dabble in the technique. They ask an initial question but then fail to ask any supplementary questions or only ask one or two follow-up questions. The danger is that if you don't tell the interviewers what they need to know, they may score you down for not possessing the right skills. So the challenge in this situation is for you to answer the questions that they should be – but aren't – asking.

You can spot unskilled interviewers by counting the number of follow-up questions that they ask. If interviewers ask less than two further questions, then you may need to give more lengthy responses than you had to with skilled competency-based interviewers, (see the sidebar 'Competency-based interviewing at its worst').

If you're not satisfied that the interviewer knows enough about the skills that you used in a particular situation, you may even need to politely interrupt him and provide him with an additional few sentences to describe exactly what you did in a given situation.

Identifying Likely Questions

You may be a bit disheartened by the need to prepare for so many different competency-based questions. In an actual interview, however, some of the questions covered in this chapter may simply never apply to you. The type of questions asked depend on the sort of job that you're going for. And, in practice, you can actually anticipate many of the questions that the interviewers are likely to ask you.

Take a look at the original job advert for the interview you're attending and try to pull out the main skills and qualities that the interviewers are looking for.

Consider the excerpt from a job advert, shown in Figure 9-1, where I've underlined the job's main skills and qualities. From this advert, expect to have questions about all the underlined skills, such as:

- ✔ *Tell us about a time that you dealt with a difficult customer.*
- ✔ *Give us an example of a time when you negotiated something with a customer or colleague.*
- ✔ *Can you give us an example of an occasion when you have been knocked back, but then had to motivate yourself again?*
- ✔ *Tell us about an instance when you had to be flexible at work.*
- ✔ *Can you tell me about an occasion when you had to organise a project?*

Book III

Succeeding at Interviews

Figure 9-1:
Highlighting
the key
skills in a
job advert.

> **XYZ Company**
>
> We're looking for people to join our team as Client Liaison Officers (CLOs). CLO candidates must have excellent <u>customer service skills</u>, as you will be dealing with customers face-to-face and on the telephone on a daily basis. You must also have good <u>negotiation skills</u>. In addition, you should be <u>self-motivated</u>, <u>flexible</u>, and able to <u>organise your own workload</u>.

Or consider the excerpt from a job advert shown in Figure 9-2. Again, the four key competencies are underlined. So be sure to prepare for questions such as:

- ✔ *Tell us about a team that you have led.*
- ✔ *Talk me through how you have coached or developed a member of your team.*
- ✔ *Can you talk me through a time that you had to think strategically in terms of running your team?*
- ✔ *Tell me about a time when you improved the profitability of your team or division.*

Figure 9-2:
More
qualities to
pick out in a
job advert.

> **We want you!**
>
> JKL International seeks a new regional manager to <u>lead a team</u> of more than 100 staff spread across three branches. You must be excited by <u>coaching and developing</u> your team and see yourself as a manager with the ability to <u>think strategically</u> and <u>improve the profitability</u> of the region.

Always talk about specific examples. Be ready to explain a situation, the task you were faced with, the actions you took, and the result that you achieved.

Questions about Your Thinking and Planning Skills

Interviewers often break down competencies into different categories. And interviewers often put great emphasis on recruiting employees with judgement and decision-making, organizing, and planning skills.

You're okay to take a few moments to think of an example to competency-based questions. If you haven't prepared a good example beforehand, just say: *That's a tough question, can I think about it for a few moments?* Don't panic!

Tell me about a significant project that you managed

When asked about a significant project that you've managed, be aware that the interviewers are not only interested in what the project was, but also in how you organised it and made it happen. In answering this question, make sure that you tell the interviewers how you planned the project and then subsequently delivered it.

Have a personal example to talk about. Be ready to talk about when you managed a project, what the project was, why you were given the piece of work initially, and what actions you took in order to make it a success.

A junior candidate may talk about a less significant project, such as:

I was asked to organise the Christmas party for our 25 staff and given a budget of £50 per head. I started by sending out an e-mail to everyone in the office to check whether they preferred to have the party on a Friday night after work or on a Saturday, and the majority favoured Saturday. I then rang up nearby hotels to find out costs. Most were quite expensive but I found three or four that were within our budget. I asked them to fax over menus and I looked on their Web sites to check the quality of the hotels. I eventually found two hotels that fit our criteria so I went to visit them both. I thought that one seemed a grander venue so negotiated a deal with them. Then nearer the time, I sent out invitations and handled people's requests for vegetarian options. The party was a big success and my boss was really pleased.

Book III

Succeeding at Interviews

Now give me an example of a project that went wrong

In an interview, be ready to talk about projects that didn't turn out so well, along with those that did. Whenever you tell an interviewer about a situation that you handled well – such as in answering 'Tell me about a significant project that you managed' (see the preceding section) – you may also get asked about a situation that didn't work out so well.

Consider this answer:

About three months ago, our sales director asked me to arrange a breakfast meeting for a dozen clients served by our Manchester office. I began by checking with our sales team when would be a good date to run the breakfast meeting and we chose a date in 8 weeks' time. I then looked up on our system to find out our largest clients. Then I rang up our clients to invite them to the breakfast meeting. I also wrote out a script so that I could get across the key points of why they should turn up to the meeting. Doing so took me around three days, but ultimately I got 15 clients to sign up. I figured that even with a few cancellations, we would still end up with 12 people turning up on the day itself. The organisation of the event went swimmingly until the day itself. That was the day back in January when we had all that snow, so 12 clients cancelled and only three turned up. Of course, the event was a waste of money, but there was nothing that any of us could have done differently.

Talking about failure is okay as long as you can show that you did everything in your power to attempt to deal with a situation, but that it failed because of circumstances out of your control.

Make sure that you can explain any lessons that you learned from a project or piece of work that went wrong.

Give me an example of a difficult decision that you have made

Be ready to talk about a difficult decision you've had to make and why it was difficult. For example, was the decision tough because you had to deal with many sources of information and the right choice was unclear? Or was the decision tricky because of the emotional impact or consequences on yourself or other people? This example demonstrates what we mean:

I was asked by my manager at head office to review options for cutting costs in my office by £85,000 per year. I knew that it was going to be a painful process and I didn't want my staff to worry unduly so I took my three supervisors and our finance manager for an away-day session on a Saturday afternoon. We decided that we could trim some costs – such as payment of overtime, training budgets, and staff entertainment – by a bit. But I realised that we really needed to make a handful of redundancies to meet the target. I asked my finance manager to do a cost-benefit analysis of which staff would need to go. The following week, when she came back with her recommendations, I sent a copy to my area manager. Once my manager approved the finance manager's recommendations, I discussed the final decision with my supervisors. And then I asked for those four employees to come into my office one at a time so I could tell them face-to-face. Of course, these employees were upset, but I assured them that the decision wasn't personal and that we would give them good references. Making these people redundant was one of the toughest decisions I've ever had to make, but it was the only option given what our head office was asking us to do.

Interviewers are much more interested in work decisions than personal ones. Avoid talking about personal decisions such as whether to move house, start a family, or get divorced.

Interviewers like to hear about any analytical techniques you used or even just brainstorming ideas weighing up pros and cons.

Talk to me about a mistake you made and what you did to rectify it

When asked about a mistake, pick a work-related mistake you made, and then focus your attention on describing the actions you took to resolve the situation. For example:

I've been part of the team manning the IT helpdesk for six months now and this incident happened about a month after I started. One of the team was on maternity leave and another was off sick, so I allowed a junior trainee to fill in for two shifts a week. Unfortunately, a couple of people in the company rang me up to complain that they had been given bad advice that had made their computers freeze up. So, of course, I had to apologise profusely to these colleagues and sort out their problem. Then I had to take the trainee aside and explain the error he'd made. I made sure to explain that the mistake wasn't his fault as it had been my decision to put someone unqualified on the helpdesk. Making sure the

Book III

Succeeding at Interviews

trainee understood the correct way of handling that problem was more important than shouting at him.

Saying that you have never made a mistake makes you appear defensive. Don't fall into this trap.

Questions about Leading and Managing

If applying for a job that involves managing or supervising any employees, you're likely to be asked about your experiences of being in charge of others.

At one time, managers used to use a style of management known as *command and control* – bossing the team around, checking up on them, and punishing them when they didn't get the work done properly. However, most modern organisations are looking for more empowering managers who can motivate and support rather than bark orders and chastise.

Tell me about a time you inspired a team

You may think that you have never 'inspired' anyone. But try to think of an occasion when you motivated or encouraged others – even if it was just one person.

Check out this for an answer:

The management team had decided to restructure the business for the second time in 18 months and everyone was feeling negative about the prospect of yet more upheaval. I decided that we needed to inject some spirit into the team, so I set up a competition. We took a Friday afternoon off from our normal work and I told everyone that I would be splitting them into three teams to compete in coming up with novel ideas for servicing our customers in the wake of the restructure. Whichever team devised the best ideas for how to improve our performance would win a case of wine. They came up with some really good ideas and we had a lot of fun. Afterwards, the team was a lot more energised than they would have been if I hadn't initiated the team competition event.

You can talk about inspiring others in the light of bad news such as a restructuring or redundancies. Or you can talk about inspiring people after receiving good news, such as a business opportunity that you motivated your team to strive for.

Talk me through how you coached or developed a team member

Employers want to hire people who can help others to improve their skills. Make sure that you can share an example that shows the interviewers how you took time to understand a member of your team's weaknesses and then set about tackling those weaknesses together.

Here's a good example:

When I joined my current company, I was asked to manage an existing team of sales people. One of them wasn't hitting his sales targets and my manager said that we may need to let him go. I decided to give him a last chance, so sat him down and we talked about his performance. He said that he was fine in making presentations to clients, but wasn't very good at negotiating deals with them – and that's why he wasn't hitting his targets. I offered to help and did a couple of customer roleplays with him so that I could evaluate what he was doing. Next, I gave him advice on what he could be doing better. Once I thought he had the hang of useful techniques, I shadowed him on a couple of customer negotiations. I'm pleased to say that this person really improved and two months later reached his sales targets.

Coaching typically involves face-to-face discussions, but can also include tools such as shadowing and sending people on training courses.

Tell me about an occasion when you had to deal with a difficult team member

If you possibly can, aim to talk about an occasion when you dealt with a difficult member of the team and turned them around – perhaps through coaching and development – into a productive member of the team.

This example explains a tricky situation in a positive way:

I noticed a few months ago that a bit of conflict existed in our team of technicians in the lab. I talked to each of them individually and the opinion seemed to be that one of them, Mel, was shirking some of her workload. I took Mel out for lunch and asked if everything was okay. She said that everything was fine, so I then had to tell her that I thought the team were experiencing some problems. She got angry and told me to leave her alone, so I did. But after a couple of weeks, I received a complaint about her work again. So I took her aside for a second time and we discussed the problem. She still did not recognise that a problem existed, so I told her that I would allocate work to her on a daily basis. She wasn't happy with my suggestion at first but eventually she came to accept it and the problem appears to have gone away.

If the interviewers have already asked you for an example of someone that you have coached, talk about someone you had to have hard words with or even discipline.

Questions about Your People and Customer Skills

Even if you're not applying for a job as a manager of any sort, you still need to demonstrate your skills in handling other people. Employers need to know that handling situations ranging from influencing, persuading, and selling, to dealing with difficult colleagues and customers isn't a problem for you.

When talking about how you dealt with another person, remember to mention the full range of communication methods you used from face-to-face meetings through to telephone conversations, e-mail, and even faxes and letters.

Tell me about a time that you persuaded someone to change their mind

Explain to the interviewers a situation when a person – such as a colleague, a customer, your boss, or perhaps a supplier – initially disagreed with your point of view. Then tell them exactly what you said or did to bring the other person round to your viewpoint.

Our department was badly understaffed and a couple of us in the team tried to persuade our editor that we needed to take on a junior staff writer. Jackie, the editor, was against the idea because she said that we didn't have the budget. I knew that she would never listen to a member of her team, so I mentioned the idea to one of the other editors and persuaded this other editor to talk to Jackie. The other editor managed to persuade Jackie because Jackie tends to respect her peers more than her team.

Another common variant on this question is for interviewers to ask: *Can you give me an example of a time that you had to adapt your communication style to meet someone else's needs?* Your response would still follow the approach taken in this example.

Talk to me about a difficult colleague you've worked with

Talk about how you turned an initially bad relationship into a more amicable one. Organisations want employees who can use their communication skills to foster effective working relationships – by asking tactful questions, listening, demonstrating empathy, and being assertive when necessary.

Here's an example of a suitable answer:

Four other administrators work in our office and the most senior of them has always had a bit of a temper. Even trivial matters annoy him and he tends to blame others for his own mistakes. I've tried to have a decent discussion with him about his work or projects that have gone wrong, but he refuses to accept responsibility. His attitude was beginning to affect the quality of our work, so eventually I decided to talk to our manager. I explained to the manager that I didn't want to get this administrator into trouble, but that his behaviour was affecting our work. My manager had a few words with him, and this other administrator has been a lot better since then.

If you can't honestly talk about having turned a relationship around, then make sure that you can at least demonstrate how you managed to work effectively with a difficult colleague.

Have you ever had to give someone negative feedback at work? How did it go?

This question is very similar to *Talk to me about a difficult colleague you've worked with* (dealt with in the preceding section). However, in answering this question, you must demonstrate that you gave the colleague a piece of advice that changed their subsequent behaviour.

Book III

Succeeding at Interviews

This response does just that:

We work in an open plan office and focusing on your work when other people are talking loudly on the phone or to each other can be quite difficult. One of my colleagues has a loud voice and tends to laugh quite loudly too. He also bellows on the phone and given that his job is to call clients, it was really getting on the nerves of the rest of the team. So one day I took him out for a coffee and said really politely that he had a very loud voice and that it was annoying quite a few of us. He was really mortified and said he didn't realise he was being such a nuisance. Since then he has made a huge effort to keep his voice down.

A good management adage is to 'praise publicly, criticise privately'. So the best time to give negative feedback is always in a one-to-one discussion rather than an open confrontation.

Tell me about a time you used your personal network to business advantage

Interviewers are most likely to ask this question when the job involves selling or business development. But networking is also a useful skill in many jobs for keeping tabs on what competitors are up to and finding out what customers want.

Here's an example showing how you've networked successfully:

My job is to set up service contracts with corporate clients and it helps to have a good network. I used my personal network last week, actually – I was putting together a proposal for one client and did not know how low I should price our offering in order to win the bid. Luckily, the operations director of the organisation seeking the quote used to work at another company with whom I've done business, so I gave him a ring. He hinted that the purchasing director was more interested in the quality of service than price. So I really focused on quality in our presentation and as a result we've been short listed for the next round of bidding.

Tell me about a time you sold something to a customer

Interviewers usually ask this question of candidates applying for sales jobs. If you have never sold a product or service to an external customer, then talk about when you sold an idea to an internal customer (a colleague).

Remember that a 'sale' doesn't necessarily need to be anything too grand:

When I was at university, I had a part-time job in a women's clothing shop. I remember one time when a woman came in wanting a summer dress for a wedding reception she was going to. She tried on several dresses but didn't like any of them. I chatted to her about the wedding and asked what other people would be wearing. She said that everyone else would probably be wearing summer dresses so I suggested to her that she buck the trend by buying a blouse and skirt combination. She loved the idea and spent over £200 on a complete outfit.

Effective selling is not only about *pushing* products on customers by telling them about features and benefits. Effective selling is also about top salespeople talking about the need for *pulling* customers into buying the product by asking questions and establishing what customers like and need.

Give me an example of a time you exceeded a customer's expectations

Organisations assume that you can meet a customer's expectations in terms of being polite and delivering what they expect. But what they really want is candidates who exceed expectations and delight customers. In fact, a lot of organisations use the slightly cheesy term *customer delight* to describe what they're hoping to achieve.

This example demonstrates great customer service:

We had a really big printing job on recently. The customer had asked for the materials to be ready for them to pick up on Friday afternoon, but they rang to say that they were running late. Unfortunately, our shop was due to close at 5 p.m. and the customer was worried about getting to us on time. I suggested arranging a courier to deliver the materials and the customer thought it was a great idea. But because it was such a big job, I knew that the cost of a courier was relatively small – so I said that I'd also send the courier free of charge. The customer was absolutely over the moon and has been using us ever since.

If you can, tell the interviewers that you took the initiative to do something out of the ordinary.

Do tell the interviewers if you received a letter of thanks from a customer, praise from your manager, or repeat business as a result of your initiative.

Book III

Succeeding at Interviews

Questions about Your Personal Effectiveness

One key group of competencies focuses on employees' ability to motivate and develop themselves. When you face setbacks, you need to be able to get up and get on with the job. And when you spot a weakness – perhaps an area of skill, knowledge, or even a personality trait – in yourself, you need to be able to work on that weakness and better yourself. The questions in this section are geared toward helping you prepare answers for personal questions.

Tell me about a time that you failed to achieve your goals

Don't say that you have never failed to achieve your goals because it just sounds unbelievable. Your best bet is to describe a situation when you did not achieve everything that you set out to do – a partial failure rather than a complete failure:

Every month I assemble a report for our area manager. I have to get information from four departments and write an introduction and executive summary for the whole report. Two months ago, I e-mailed each of the department heads and asked them to write the couple of pages that I needed and told them when I would need the information. Three departments gave me the information on time, but one did not. I chased him by e-mail and phone, but he didn't respond. So I went to this department head's office in person, but he said that he had been too busy and that the earliest he could get the information together would be two days after my deadline for the report. However, I persuaded him to spend just ten minutes with me telling me most of what I needed to know so that I could write his section of the report. I managed to cobble something together, but everyone knew that that section of the report was not as strong. I did everything that I could, but I'm afraid that I didn't produce as good a report as I normally do.

With negatively phrased questions such as this, try to illustrate how you did everything possible, but failed because of circumstances out of your control.

A common variation on this question is: *Talk to me about an occasion you failed to meet a deadline.* Again, the best strategy is to talk about just missing a deadline because of extremely unusual circumstances.

How did you respond to the last piece of criticism you received?

Candidates who say that they don't listen to constructive criticism may as well say that they're going to be difficult to manage – can you imagine having someone working for you who won't listen to your constructive criticism? This question is related to 'How do you take personal criticism?' (see Book III, Chapter 4).

Try working out a response similar to this example:

Perhaps three or four months ago, my boss said that I didn't always have very good listening skills. I think that I always do listen when I'm in meetings, so I was a bit taken aback. I asked her what she meant and after a bit of thought she said that on occasion she'd seen me not looking at the person speaking or even engaging in doodling on my notepad. I accepted the feedback – I do have a tendency to doodle when I'm bored. And even when I'm actually listening, I don't always look at the person who's talking. But I've taken both bits of criticism on board and make an effort to not only listen, but to look as if I'm listening too.

If you don't accept feedback automatically, you need to say so and then be sure to explain that you challenge and ask questions to make sure that the feedback is justified.

Book III

Succeeding at Interviews

Give me an example of how you have developed yourself

When outlining ways that you've developed yourself, make sure to indicate that you were aware of a development need and then took steps to meet that need. For example, simply talking about courses that your manager insisted you go on doesn't show your own personal enthusiasm for professional development!

Mention a development need that arose in your last appraisal. Alternatively, think about the skill areas where you used to be – but are no longer – weak.

Here are two examples of ways in which you, as a candidate, can say that you've developed yourself:

✔ *In my last performance evaluation, my manager suggested that I needed to become more familiar with the basics of employment law to add more value to the line managers that I support. So I researched appropriate courses and how much they cost. I made a proposal to my manager and he signed off for me to attend a two-day workshop on the topic back in November. Since then, I've become much more comfortable discussing with line managers the rules and potential problems associated with hiring and firing decisions.*

✔ *I've worked quite hard on developing my sales skills. I've always had good customer skills, but until recently had never had to sell to customers. When I first started working in my current job, I didn't really understand that we would have sales targets to reach and I struggled to achieve them. So I watched some of the good sales assistants and tried to pick up on some of the techniques and phrases they used. Over the last year or so, I have been working hard at improving my sales skills and I've been meeting my targets for the last three months.*

Don't forget to talk in the first person when describing what happened. Use phrases such as *I did . . .* or *I decided to . . .* rather than *My manager told me to . . .*

Chapter 10

Taking Control in Unusual Situations

*T*he traditional interview involves one or two interviewers and you, perhaps across a desk or a table in an office. However, all sorts of other types of interview can be offered to you. In this chapter, we cover some of the other situations and devious challenges that interviewers can use to test and evaluate candidates.

Dealing with Panel Interviews

In a panel interview, you may find yourself confronted with a row of up to eight or ten interviewers. Panel interviews are particularly popular in the public sector and for more senior roles.

To pass panel interviews with flying colours, follow these tips:

✔ **Follow the lead of the interviewers.** If faced with many interviewers, you may not be offered the chance to shake hands and say hello to each of them. In some cases, not all the interviewers even introduce themselves.

✔ **Maintain eye contact mainly with the person on the panel who asks you each question.** Do look occasionally at the other panel members when answering the question, but for the most part maintain eye contact with the person who actually asked you it.

> ✔ **Don't let yourself be put off by a panel.** The questions fly at you from all corners, but take your time to answer each at your own pace.
>
> ✔ **Prepare for panel interview questions as you would any other type of interview.**

Never assume that any of the panel members are unimportant. A common ruse used by interviewers is to pretend that one of them is merely a note taker.

Handling Hi-Tech Interviews

Employers know that technology can drastically reduce the costs of recruitment. Especially when you or the interviewers are busy, they may want to conduct an initial interview by telephone or via video conferencing. The interviewers may then invite a shortlist of candidates to a second round, face-to-face interview.

Hanging on the telephone

Telephone interviews are tricky because establishing rapport or conveying your enthusiasm for the job without the face-to-face element of most interviews is difficult. However, you can create a positive impression on the phone if you always:

- ✔ Eliminate background noises.
- ✔ Smile when speaking.
- ✔ Use verbal cues (such as *I see* and *That's interesting*) instead of nodding and eye contact.
- ✔ Have copies of your CV or application form in front of you.
- ✔ Thank the interviewer at the end.

Make sure you get the interviewer's name and contact details and consider sending a thank you e-mail or letter afterwards to maximise your chances of getting the job.

Handling video conferencing and Webcams with finesse

Video conferencing tends to be restricted to high-level appointments, but a growing number of employers are exploiting Webcam technology to conduct first interviews over the Internet.

Follow this advice to help your hi-tech interview run smoothly:

- ✔ Dress smartly.
- ✔ Avoid wearing too much white (beware screen glare!).
- ✔ Check your Webcam settings.
- ✔ Speak more slowly than normal (watch out for time lags).
- ✔ Avoid using hand gestures (they blur on screen).

If you experience any technical problems – such as not being able to see or hear the interviewers clearly – speak up immediately! Don't expect the problem to go away of its own accord.

Getting Ready for Psychometric Tests

Two broad categories of psychometric test exist. *Aptitude tests* have right and wrong answers – these most commonly measure skills such as numeracy, verbal reasoning, and spatial awareness. *Personality tests* measure your preferences in certain situations and you don't have to worry about 'right' or 'wrong' answers, because they don't exist.

Passing aptitude tests

Aptitude tests are daunting if you haven't done them before. When you're invited to an interview, find out if you must complete one of these tests.

By far the commonest aptitude tests measure verbal reasoning and numeracy skills. Some employers may also devise their own tests for spatial reasoning – for example, if you're applying for a job as an engineer.

Almost all aptitude tests are timed. Read the instructions carefully to see how much time you have for the entire test. If you find you're struggling with a single question for more than a couple of minutes, move on to the next question to avoid dropping too many points.

Every time you encounter a different aptitude test, read the instructions carefully. Precisely how much time do you have for the questionnaire? And exactly how should you respond? For example, some tests ask you to circle the correct response; others ask you to underline the correct response or fill in a small circle. A few tests ask you to select more than one answer per question. *Never* make any assumptions about the instructions – read them carefully.

Book III

Succeeding at Interviews

Completing personality questionnaires

Personality tests assess how you typically respond to different situations. Would you rate yourself as a tough or fairly sensitive person? Would you say that you tend to be very talkative or a bit quiet at work?

Personality tests are not usually timed. But the best way to complete them is to read through the questions and jot down your response fairly quickly. The more you mull over the responses, the more likely you are to confuse yourself.

Be careful not to try to second-guess the aim behind the personality test. Many candidates think that they should answer as if they are more extroverted and outgoing than they actually are. But sometimes an employer may be looking to reject candidates who are *too* extroverted in case they get bored of the job quickly.

Succeeding at Assessment Centres

Organisations that use competency-based interviews often invite candidates to *assessment centres*. At these events, the people scrutinising you are often called *assessors* rather than interviewers. The assessors don't simply ask candidates to talk about their skills – they want to observe those skills in action.

That an assessment centre is a real place – such as a specially designed building for putting candidates through their paces – is a common misconception. But the term actually means a collection of different techniques for scrutinising how candidates perform in different situations. Assessment centres can be held at a variety of locations, from the organisation's own offices to a hotel or conference centre.

Passing in-trays

In-tray tests are designed to simulate a day in the office and to test your ability to assimilate and prioritise information.

An in-tray usually consists of a collection of paperwork such as letters, reports, and printouts. Usually, some of the items are very important while many others may have been put in to distract you. They may be based on an entirely fictitious business or they may be made-up items concerning a real business.

Some modern organisations may even simulate a real day in the office by providing you with a computer and a telephone. You may have to type up a report or send e-mails to colleagues and customers while taking phone calls – the whole experience can be quite tough if you're not ready for it!

Read the instructions carefully and identify the key points. Too many candidates go wrong simply by misreading what they're supposed to do.

Follow these tips to do well at in-trays:

- ✔ **Look for themes:** Always begin by skim-reading all the items to get a sense of any overarching topics that may link individual items.

- ✔ **Identify key issues:** Prioritise the crucial items that need handling.

- ✔ **Prioritise your actions:** Develop a rough idea in your head as to a ranking for issues within the in-tray. Tackle the ones at the top of your list first.

- ✔ **Differentiate between action and further investigation:** Although you may be expected to take action on certain urgent and critical issues, the assessors may be looking for good candidates to notice that certain issues require further investigation before a course of action can be decided upon.

Look for guidelines within the in-tray documents as to the team or organisation's priorities. These guidelines are typically written by your line manager or a more senior manager (such as the managing director, chairperson, or CEO). These guidelines can be labelled *key initiatives*, *vision/value statements*, *company imperatives*, and so on. Show the assessors that you take into account organisational rules by ensuring that all your proposed actions align with these guidelines.

Book III

Succeeding at Interviews

Excelling at group exercises

The assessors may gather a group of candidates – usually some number between three and eight people – together and ask you all to discuss a topic or engage in a task while they observe you. The key in these exercises is to demonstrate that you're confident, but not arrogant, and that you can be a team player without dominating the discussion or being rude.

Group exercises can vary enormously, but some popular ones include:

- ✔ Discussing a topic in the news.
- ✔ Constructing a tower out of children's play bricks.
- ✔ Evaluating a business idea and coming up with recommendations for taking it further.

Be sure to read the instructions carefully, picking up on the precise nature of the task or topic of conversation.

Here are some tips for handling group exercises:

- ✔ Encourage others to speak.
- ✔ Watch your body language.
- ✔ Build on others' suggestions.
- ✔ Demonstrate your enthusiasm.

Being a star in role play simulations

The assessors may ask you to role play a scenario similar to the job you're applying for. For example, if applying for a managerial position, they may ask you to discipline an actor pretending to be an unruly member of your team.

Bear in mind that the organisation has probably invested a lot of time and money in designing the simulation and training managers or even bringing in consultants to run it. So make sure that you behave as if the situation was serious. If you say that you 'don't like role plays' or don't play along, expect to be marked down automatically.

The key in role plays is to think about the nature of the job that you're applying for. Decide upon the required skills and try to demonstrate them throughout. For example, if you're applying for a customer service job that requires tact and diplomacy, make sure that you behave tactfully and diplomatically when talking to other candidates in a group exercise.

Role play simulations test not only what you say but also how you say it. Make sure that your body language is consistent with what you are talking about – for example, demonstrating empathy or enthusiasm in your facial expressions, tone of voice, and use of hands.

Role play simulations vary enormously from job to job and organisation to organisation. However, here are some common tasks:

- ✔ Meeting an angry customer.
- ✔ Selling products or services to a new client.
- ✔ Disciplining a member of your team.

Be yourself. Candidates often go wrong when they attempt to second-guess what the assessors are looking for. Just behave as if you were actually facing these situations. Don't try to be someone that you're not.

Book IV
Delivering Perfect Presentations

In this book . . .

As they say in the scouts, be prepared! Knowing how to prepare for and deliver a winning presentation is the name of the game in this book. Here we help you to get clued up on body language, structuring your presentation, and give you lots of tips on how to make your delivery a success.

Here are the contents of Book IV at a glance:

Chapter 1

Organising Your Presentation

In This Chapter
▶ Choosing material for your presentation
▶ Selecting the best way to organise your material
▶ Making an outline that works for you
▶ Dealing with the limitations of time
▶ Figuring out how to organise your presentation

The standard advice for organising a presentation or speech is: Tell the audience what you're going to say, then tell them, and then tell them what you've told them. We've heard many consultants offer this advice to their clients, look meaningfully into their eyes like they've just delivered some great insight, and then wait to be hailed as geniuses. But the problem with the tell-tell-tell formula is that it doesn't really tell you anything. (How's that for irony?) This advice is like telling someone that you build a ship by assembling a load of material so that it will float while you're in it. Okay, great. But how do you do that?

This chapter provides a detailed look at how to organise a presentation. We tell you everything from how to decide what to tell an audience, to how to arrange what you tell an audience, to how much to tell an audience. Actually, this is a tell-all chapter.

Selecting Material to Include

Before you can organise your presentation, you must first choose the material for it. But your real task is deciding what *not* to use. No matter what your topic, you'll always be able to find a lot more material than you'll have time to discuss. And, more importantly, audiences have a limit to how much material they can absorb. Here are a few guidelines to keep in mind when choosing what material to include:

- ✔ **Select a variety of material.** You know the expression 'variety is the spice of life'? Applied to speeches, it means using a mix of types of material – anecdotes, statistics, examples, quotes, and so on. A variety of material makes your speech more interesting. It also increases the chance that each member of your audience will find something appealing.

- ✔ **Keep your audience in mind.** Choose material that your audience will understand and find interesting. The question isn't what you know about the topic. It's what does the audience need to know in order to make your presentation a success.

- ✔ **Carry a spare – always.** Keep some material in reserve – an extra example, statistic, or anecdote. You never know when you'll need it, especially in a Q&A session following the talk.

Following Patterns of Organisation

Imagine that someone hands you a piece of paper that says 'm', 'd', 'u', 'y', 'm'. It doesn't seem to mean much. (Unless the letters are supposed to be an eye test.) Now assume that the person hands you the paper with the letters arranged as 'd', 'u', 'm', 'm', 'y'. Is your reaction a little different? Congratulations, you've recognised a pattern.

Patterns play a critical role in how we assign meaning and how we interpret messages. You could read a lot of perceptual psychology theory to figure out this stuff, but we'll let you off the hook and skip it. Suffice it to say that human beings have a natural tendency to organise information into patterns. The way we shape those patterns determines much of the outcome of our communications with each other. So, the patterns you put into your presentation play a vital role in how well your audience understands what you're communicating.

Sticking to two key rules

If you want the pattern to strengthen your presentation as much as possible, abide by the following two rules.

Make the pattern obvious

Have you ever seen those pictures that are all little dots? You know, the ones that you can't tell what the picture is supposed to be until you hold it close to your face? And then you're supposed to be able to see an image? Yes, the dots form a pattern because some people see the image, but the pattern really isn't obvious – at least to us and many other people who have never perceived the image.

Keep this fact in mind when you put together a presentation. You don't want a 'little dot' pattern that won't be recognised by everybody. You want a pattern that your whole audience can perceive. Your presentation isn't an intelligence test. You don't want to find out whether your audience is smart enough to discover your hidden structure. You want to make sure that your pattern is obvious so that your audience can perceive it – easily. Your pattern can never be too obvious.

Choose an appropriate pattern

Consider your topic and audience when choosing a pattern. What pattern will best help get your message across? For example, if you're talking about the history of a boundary dispute in your neighbourhood, a chronological pattern probably makes more sense than a theory/practice pattern. (See the section 'Checking out commonly used patterns', later in this chapter, for more information on types of patterns you can use.)

Checking out commonly used patterns

Although patterns are infinite in variety, certain ones appear over and over again. Here are a few of the most common patterns for presentations:

- ✔ **Problem/solution:** State a problem and offer a solution. For example, your presentation to a school's board of governors criticises the poor physical condition of the school. You then talk about a property scheme that could alleviate some of the financial pressures. What you emphasise depends on what the audience members already know. Do you need to make them aware of the problem or do they already know about it? Are there competing solutions? And so on.

- ✔ **Chronological:** If you plan to speak about a series of events (the history of accidents at that corner where you want a stop sign), organising your speech in a past/present/future pattern makes it easy to follow.

Book IV

Delivering Perfect Presentations

✔ **Physical location:** You may want to use this pattern if you're talking about things that occur at various locations. If you plan on giving the company orientation speech to new employees, you can divide the talk by floors (first floor, second floor, third floor), buildings (Building A, B, and C), or other physical areas (European operations, North American operations, Asian operations).

✔ **Extended metaphor or analogy:** This pattern uses a comparison of two items as a way of organising the entire presentation and is commonly used in speeches given by teachers or trainers. 'Today I'll talk about how giving a presentation is like the flight of an airplane. We'll talk about the takeoff, the landing, the flight, the passengers, and the control tower. The takeoff is the introduction . . .'

✔ **Cause/effect:** You state a cause and then identify its effect. This pattern is common in scientific presentations but it also works well for identifying where fault may lie. 'The southern region decided to listen to some management consultant this quarter. So it instituted new procedures, bought new expense-reporting software, and made a commitment to innovative sales methods. As a result, its gross sales declined by 50 per cent, and its margins shrank by 10 per cent.' (But the consultant had record profits.)

✔ **Divide a quote:** Each word of a quote becomes a section of the speech. Clergy often use this technique in sermons. 'The Bible says, "Wisdom is better than rubies". What does this really mean? Let's start with wisdom. Is it just your IQ? No. Most of us know people who have a high IQ who aren't very wise.' This technique is also frequently used by motivational speakers and sales trainers.

✔ **Divide a word:** Pick a word and build your speech around each letter of the word. 'Today, I'm going to talk about "LOVE". "L" stands for laughter. Laughter is very important in our lives because . . .' This pattern is popular with clergy, inspirational speakers, and consultants.

✔ **Theory/practice:** Start by explaining what you thought would happen – the theory. Then describe the actions taken and what actually happened – the practice. You can use this pattern when talking about something that didn't turn out as planned by explaining the big gap between theory and practice.

✔ **Topic pattern:** This is a free-form pattern that can be used for any type of speech. You divide your topic into logical segments based on your own instinct, judgement, and common sense. For example, you may use this pattern in a presentation on the topic of humour. The segments are: Why humour is a powerful communication tool, how to make a point with humour, and simple types of non-joke humour anyone can use. This easy-to-follow pattern makes sense for the material.

Packaging and bundling

One of the most powerful ways to organise information is in the form of a numerical list. For example, you can say, 'I have some good ideas'. Or you can say, 'I have four good ideas. The first is . . .' The number makes the statement much stronger. Because the audience tends to keep track of numbers, using them grabs their attention, keeps their attention, and helps them follow along and understand what you say.

You can use this technique to organise your entire presentation, such as 'Ten Ways to Increase Productivity'. Or you can use it for individual segments, such as, 'We've talked about the importance of humour, how to write a joke, and how to tell a joke. Now let's talk about six simple types of humour that don't require comic delivery.'

Don't go overboard – keep your lists short. If you make the list too long, you can actually lose the audience. Suppose your boss walked into a meeting and said, 'I've found 50 ways to raise revenue. The first is . . .' How would you feel after you realised he was going to discuss every one of them?

Creating Your Outline

An outline is a blueprint for your talk. It lets you see what points you're making, how they're related to each other, and whether they're arranged in a proper order. A good outline shows you how to construct a good speech. And like a blueprint for a building, an outline for a talk can take many shapes and forms.

Figuring out when to start your outline

You have two basic choices regarding when to make an outline: Make the outline before you've written your presentation or after you've written it. People disagree on which way is best. But here's the secret. The best way is the one that works for you. Consider the differences between writing the outline before or after you write the text of your presentation, and then decide which approach works best for you:

> ✔ **Before you write the presentation:** With this approach, you focus on your purpose and identify the ideas that will achieve that purpose. Then you turn the ideas into major and minor points and fit them into

Book IV

Delivering Perfect Presentations

an outline structure. Only then, when you can see exactly what you'll say, do you begin to flesh it out. This is an absolutely logical way to proceed. If the outline makes sense, it helps ensure that the content of your presentation will make sense.

✔ **After you write the presentation:** Alternatively, you may just plunge right into developing your material word for word. You could think about the order in which you'd tell it to a friend, as well as what examples you'd use. Then write the outline after the presentation is written. This approach enables you to discover any flaws in your presentation's structure so that you can rewrite where appropriate.

Deciding the number of points to include

The number of points in an outline should reflect the number of points in your presentation. So you need to decide how many points to divide your material into. To make the best decision, follow these guidelines:

✔ **Decide what the audience needs to know.** Determine which points are absolutely essential for you to include in your message. And we mean *absolutely* essential, as in, if one of these points were omitted, your speech couldn't succeed.

✔ **Avoid putting in too much information.** Many people try to pack too much information into a single speech. But a limit exists as to how much an audience member can absorb. Figuring out how much is too much may sound tricky but the following two guidelines can make the process easier on you:

 • **Use no more than seven main points.** People disagree over the maximum number of points that you should have in a talk, but the highest number that we've found works in practice is around seven. Less is usually better. The amount of time you have to speak is also a critical factor. Many experts suggest three major points for a half-hour talk.

 • **Reorganise to reduce the number of points.** You've gone through your material and found 15 main points that are absolutely essential. Don't even think about doing your speech that way. First, make sure that you really can't lose a few of them. Second, reorganise the points so that they're included under fewer headings. Think of 5 to 7 major points under which your 15 points can be subcategorised.

Timing

Most people associate *timing* with how to tell a joke. But by timing, we mean how much time it takes to deliver the talk you've written. Does it fit the time slot you've been given? Check out the following sections to find out the important concepts of timing.

Setting the length of your speech

William Gladstone once observed that a speech need not be eternal to be immortal. His point is well taken: Longer doesn't mean better or more meaningful in the world of presenting and speaking in public. Waffle on for too long and you'll simply bore your audience. Follow these guidelines to make sure you set an appropriate length of time for your presentation:

✔ **Don't feel obligated to fill your entire time slot.** Use your common sense. You shouldn't stretch your speech to fill an hour-long time slot if you can get the job done in just 45 or 50 minutes. Your speech can end up sounding disorganised, and your points can get hard to follow when you throw in extra information just to cover another 15 minutes. On the other hand, one of us recently spoke at a conference where another speaker, who was slotted for a one-hour speech, completed his talk in ten minutes. As you can imagine, the conference organisers were less than thrilled.

Although concluding early can thrill your audience, concluding late can have the opposite effect. Even running on by just an extra five minutes could make the audience impatient and possibly angry. Your audience members are busy, and they don't appreciate a speaker putting them behind schedule. They expect you to be done on time, so don't disappoint them.

✔ **Twenty minutes is a good length.** If you can choose how long you'll speak, pick 20 minutes. This gives you long enough to cover a lot of information thoroughly, let the audience get to know you, and make a good impression. And the time's short enough to do all that before the audience's attention span reaches its outer limit.

Polishing your timing

Einstein's theory of relativity may say that time and distance are identical, but many public speakers apparently disagree. They just can't go the distance in the time they've been allotted. You certainly don't want to join that group. So check out the following tips to ensure that you and your audience finish at the same time:

✔ **Estimate the time from the length of your script:** As a rule of thumb, one double-spaced page of 10-point type equals two minutes of speaking time. So preparing a standard 20-minute talk is like writing a 10-page essay. (Keep that in mind when the person inviting you to speak says it will be easy to do.)

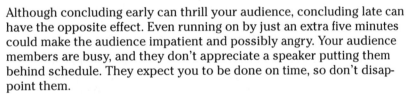

Book IV

Delivering Perfect Presentations

✔ **Convert practice time into a realistic estimate:** Many speakers practise their speech aloud to get an idea of how long it will take to deliver. But be careful: For every minute that you practise your speech alone, it'll take you about a third longer when you speak in front of people. We tend to slow down because we wait for feedback and have to focus on making eye contact with the audience as well as presenting our materials. So a 30-minute talk could take 40 minutes. The duration of your presentation may increase by as much as 50 per cent when you speak to an audience of several hundred people. And if you're frightened when you face an audience, you may speak faster than you did while practising.

✔ **Make an adjustment for humour:** If you use humour in your talk and it's effective, part of your speaking time may be consumed by audience laughter and applause. Don't forget to account for that time, especially for large audiences numbering in the hundreds of people. With a large group, some of the group may get the joke straight away. Others may get it a little later. And the third group laugh simply because everyone else is laughing. So if your material is genuinely funny, be prepared to allow extra time for the waves of laughter or applause.

✔ **Be prepared to cut:** You were told that you'd have 30 minutes to speak. But the meeting doesn't go as planned and the organiser says you have only 15 minutes. What do you do? Of course the biggest mistake would be to try to cram your half-hour's worth of material into 15 minutes. Talking loudly and faster doesn't work! You will leave your audience with the impression that you are a bit manic. Perhaps worse, nothing will sink in.

✔ **Don't cut the conclusion:** When you need to cut part of your presentation, don't cut the conclusion. Your speech is like the flight of a plane, and the passengers are your audience. When you forgo the conclusion, you're attempting a crash landing. If you've been told in advance that your time will be shortened, cut material from the body of your talk. Eliminate some examples or even a main point if necessary. What if you need to cut while you're speaking and you're rapidly running out of time? Find a logical place to stop and sum up what you've already said. Even better, have a conclusion that you can go into from any point in your talk.

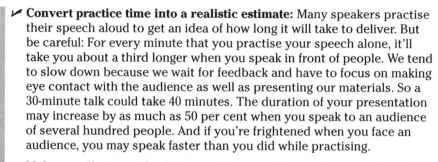

Organising Your Presentation Effectively

As many ways to organise presentations and speeches exist as there are people giving them. But one of the simplest and most effective is to use cards, as follows:

1. **Write ideas on cards.** Begin by writing down each idea you have on a separate card. Write on only one side of the card to leave lots of room for editing. Say you're writing a presentation about training courses at work. One card may say, 'Get graph from human resources on uptake of current courses'. You may scribble 'comments from trainers' and 'list of currently available courses' on other cards. By the time you're done, you may have dozens of cards.

2. **Pile the cards into patterns.** So now you have a couple of dozen cards full of ideas. What next? Spread them on a big table or the floor and look for patterns. Try to group them into piles. For example, one pile may be 'benefits of the current training programme', while another may be 'downsides of the current training programme'.

3. **Sequence the cards in each pile.** Say you end up having six or seven cards in each pile. Keep rearranging the cards within a particular pile until you have a good flow between the cards. In doing so, you may find a gap in the sequence – say that cards 1, 2, and 3 work well but card 4 doesn't fit and needs rewriting before it flows into card 5. Another tip is to number the cards. Doing so helps you keep track of them much more easily. Perhaps label the piles A, B, C, and so on, and then number the cards 1, 2, 3 within each pile so they'll be A1, A2, A3, B1, B2, B3. This system doesn't mean A goes first, just that all the cards in that pile go together.

4. **Sequence the piles of cards.** Look at what you've got and see which pile is logical for starting your talk. Then look for the second, third, and so forth, until all the cards are in the best order.

Short takes on long speeches

The long-winded speaker has inspired plenty of one-liners regarding the subject of public speaking. Here's a small sample:

✔ Many a public speaker who rises to the occasion stands too long.

✔ No speech is all bad if it's short.

✔ The longest word in the English language is 'And now a word from our guest of honour'.

✔ If the speaker won't boil it down, the audience must sweat it out.

✔ An after-dinner speech is like a headache – always too long, never too short.

✔ Having a train of thought is alright if you also have a terminal.

✔ Second wind: What a speaker acquires when he says, 'In conclusion.'

✔ A speech is like a love affair – any fool can start one, but it takes a lot of skill to end one.

Relating to Your Audience

Establishing rapport with your audience is your primary goal – a feeling of mutual warmth and a sense that you're on the same wavelength. The following sections present a few ways to achieve that goal.

Putting yourself in the shoes of your audience

Imagine that you're one of the members of the audience. What do they already know? What might they be interested in? Putting your audience at the heart of what you do – considering their needs and interests ahead of your own – is a great way to make them relate to you. In the following sections, we discuss some brilliant techniques for working out what your audience needs from you.

Discussing the world from the audience's point of view

Let the audience know that you can see the world or issue their way. Look for common experiences that both you and the audience share. For example, if your job has ever encompassed any of the duties of your audience, you could describe work situations that create a rapport and allow you to see the world from your audience's point of view. Or describe frustrating universal experiences such as traffic jams or dealing with faceless helplines.

People like to hear data related to what they do. So if you don't have an experience to share, you can substitute a study. But first acknowledge that you don't have the experience – or you'll lose credibility.

Making personal experiences universal

Although an audience wants to hear about a speaker's personal experience, using 'I' all the time can turn them off. You can end up sounding like a raging egomaniac. So go ahead and describe that experience – just find and emphasise the universal aspects of your personal experience. This advice applies to anyone using any kind of personal material — see the examples below:

- ✔ **Example 1:** 'You know, I used to be a plumber. Let me tell you about the time I flushed a fish down the toilet and it got blocked up.'

- ✔ **Example 2:** 'Did you ever have a job that you really hated but you couldn't quit because you needed the money? I used to be a plumber. And I couldn't quit because I needed the money. Let me tell you about what happened when a fish ended up getting flushed down a toilet and blocking it up.'

In the second example, the plumber tells the same story but the audience relates to him differently. Now he's not just a plumber talking about plumbing. He's a person who had a humorous experience with a lousy job – something everyone can understand.

Customising your remarks

Customising grabs the audience's attention and gets the audience involved in your speech. Tailoring your speech or presentation to a particular gathering makes the speaker a bit of an insider and lets the audience know that you went to the trouble of learning about them. And the good news is, a little (and we mean very little) customisation goes a long way. We've given speeches where we made half a dozen references geared specifically to a particular audience and were showered with praise afterwards for the research we did to learn about the group. Make comments – humorous comments, praise, or just simple observations – about local businesses, the people you're speaking to, an organisation's history, or local news, events, or customs.

Use your imagination and consider what may impress you if an outsider referred to it.

Don't be offensive! If you're going to use a name of someone in or related to the group, clear it with a senior person at the organisation first. If you plan on poking fun at anything else local, discuss it with someone first to avoid inadvertently offending someone in the audience.

Pushing their buttons

Purposely work in a reference to a hot topic – a source of minor controversy with the audience. Find an issue that affects the entire audience, not one that only affects key players and that no one else would understand. In addition, make sure that the issue isn't too controversial to mention – your contact will probably be reliable here.

One of the simplest ways to find a hot topic is to ask your contact whether any recent or pending legislation or initiatives will negatively affect the audience. When the answer is yes, you have your issue.

Acknowledging what the audience is feeling

If you're speaking under any special circumstances, acknowledge those circumstances. Is the audience sweltering in a hot, stuffy room? Would the audience prefer to be anywhere but listening to you? Has the audience made certain assumptions about you? Get the issue out in the open or it will remain a barrier between you and your audience.

Book IV

Delivering Perfect Presentations

Identifying and addressing audience subgroups

Keep in mind that an audience may be made up of numerous subgroups – each with its own special needs and agendas. To create rapport with your entire audience, you need to include something for each of them.

Highlighting the benefits of what you've got to say

Make sure that the audience knows what they're going to get out of your speech. Identify and emphasise the benefits early in your talk and issue frequent reminders.

Chapter 2

Writing the Presentation

* *

In This Chapter

▶ Beginning your talk

▶ Using logical and emotional appeals

▶ Integrating stories, quotes, and statistics

▶ Supporting your ideas with definitions, analogies, and examples

▶ Managing transitions

▶ Concluding in style

* *

After you have a topic and an outline, you only have the skeleton of your presentation figured out. You still have to create a beginning, middle, and end by adding support to the outline you've created. Although searching for various forms of support for every point you plan to make sounds like a lot of sweat, you can consider this chapter the equivalent of a protein shake for presentation writing. We show you the proper techniques to ensure that you create the content to back up your points and build the presentation of your dreams.

Creating the Perfect Introduction

A journey of a thousand miles begins with a single step. That statement also applies to presentations — a talk of any length begins with the introduction. The following sections cover the steps that you must take in making this first leg of your journey.

Answering audience questions

The audience has several questions that they want answered within the first few minutes of your talk. Think of the questions journalists ask to report a story: Who, what, when, where, why, and how. Your audience wants to know those same things. So be sure to answer the following questions in your introduction:

✔ Who are you? (Do you have any experience or credentials?)

✔ What are you going to talk about?

✔ When will you be through?

✔ Where is this talk going? (Is there some sort of agenda, organisation, or structure?)

✔ Why should I listen? (Really a 'what' question – what's in it for me?)

✔ How are you going to make this interesting?

Including necessary background

If the audience needs certain information in order to understand what you'll be talking about, give it to them in the introduction. If your talk won't make sense unless audience members know the definition of a certain term or they're aware of a certain fact, tell them. Also, you may need to provide background about why you *won't* be covering a particular subject or subtopic – especially if the audience expects you to address it.

Using greetings and acknowledgements

Many speakers open talks with endless greetings and acknowledgements to the sponsoring organisation and key members of the audience. Boring! No one wants to hear you list the names of every dignitary on the dais. All right, sometimes you have to name names, but you don't have to do it as your opening line. If you must acknowledge a load of people, do it as the second item in your introduction – not the first.

Making your introduction the right length

The introduction should be no more than 10 to 15 per cent of your presentation. And it shouldn't be more than 4 or 5 minutes at the very most. Remember you're there to talk about your topic and not about you (unless you have been invited to talk about yourself, of course.) So avoid making the audience yawn – don't take forever.

Writing out your introduction

Write out your entire introduction word for word. Don't worry that you're just supposed to use key words or sentence fragments when writing the body of your presentation, or that a fully scripted presentation may sound strained. The introduction is an exception, and writing it out actually provides the following benefits to your presentation:

 ✔ **You can edit it into its best form.** If you just make a note that you're going to tell a certain story in the introduction, you don't write out or practise the story. You figure you already know it. Then when you tell it, you end up rambling; you don't economise words; and the story doesn't achieve its maximum impact.

 ✔ **You can deliver a successful intro even if you're anxious.** The introduction is the most anxiety-producing section of your presentation in terms of delivery. Stage fright is at its peak. If you get really nervous and your introduction is just a few key words, you may not even remember what they represent. Writing out the introduction word for word helps ensure that you'll carry it off successfully even if you suffer from a case of the jitters.

The introduction is the first part of your talk, but ideally you should write it last. Why? Because this section's an introduction. You need to know what you're introducing. After you write the body of your presentation and your conclusion, then you've got something to introduce.

Using the show biz formula

In planning your introduction, recalling the show biz formula never hurts: Strong opening, strong close, weak stuff in the middle. Your introduction is the strong opening. Your conclusion is the strong close. Those are the two parts of your presentation that have the most impact on how the audience remembers your performance. So make sure your introduction *is* strong.

Book IV

Delivering Perfect Presentations

Avoiding common mistakes

Sometimes what you don't say in your introduction is even more important than what you do say. Avoid starting on the wrong foot – especially if that foot is inserted in your mouth. Here are some common mistakes to avoid:

✔ **Saying 'Before I begin. . . .'** This is a patently absurd phrase. It's like airline personnel who ask if anyone needs to preboard the plane. You *can't* preboard. After you start going on the plane, you *are* boarding. And as soon as you say, 'Before I begin', you've begun. If you want to make some comments before you get into the body of your presentation, try 'Before I get into the meat of my presentation . . .' or 'Before we get stuck into the topic, I'd like to say . . .'.

✔ **Getting the names wrong.** If you're acknowledging people, organisations, or places, such as towns or cities, make sure that you know their names and pronounce them correctly. No one likes to be called by the wrong name. Messing up names makes you look very unprepared, lowers your credibility, and makes the audience wonder what else you're going to screw up.

✔ **Admitting that you'd rather be anywhere else.** If we're in your audience, our immediate response is: 'So get out of here.' Yes, you may be in a position where you're giving a presentation that you don't want to give, but don't whine to the audience. No one wants to hear you moaning, and doing so doesn't help. You still have to give the presentation, and you just seem like a big baby.

✔ **Admitting that you're not prepared.** Doing so is insulting to your audience. If you're not prepared, why are you speaking? No one wants to waste time listening to someone who isn't prepared. Although this is common sense, a lot of speakers make this mistake. Why? They're really making excuses in advance. They know they're not prepared. They know their presentation will go down horribly, and they want the audience to know that they're really not a terrible speaker – they're just not prepared. The logic seems to be that if you alert the audience in advance that you know your presentation is going to be rubbish, somehow that improves your image. Wrong. You just seem like an idiotfor being unprepared. If you're not prepared and you're going to speak anyway, just do it.

✔ **Admitting that you've given the identical presentation a million times for other audiences.** Even if your audience knows this fact, don't rub their faces in it. Every group likes to feel unique. Let your audience operate under the illusion that you prepared the talk especially for them. And if you're smart, you'll throw in just a couple of customised references to promote this illusion.

✔ **Using offensive humour.** A lot of speakers still labour under the myth that you've got to open with a joke. You don't. But if you do use this technique, don't tell a racist, ethnic, sexist, or off-colour joke. No faster way exists to turn off an audience.

- **Announcing that you had a ghostwriter.** Admitting this fact is like a magician showing how the tricks are done. Your audience likes to think they are hearing from you. Let them think so. Remember, a 'ghostwriter' is supposed to be invisible – you know, like a ghost.

- **Apologising.** Unless you accidentally activate the emergency sprinkler system, shut off the power for the room, or knock the podium off the stage, *never begin by apologising*. Apologising sets a horrible tone for audience expectations – they expect something bad. Why else would you be apologising? Plus, an apology draws attention to something the audience may not otherwise notice. If you don't start by apologising for your presentation, the audience may actually think what your saying is good. And if they don't think your presentation's good? You can always apologise later.

Getting Started in Fifteen Fabulous Ways

No matter how the introduction begins, the effect that every speaker desires is the same – to knock the socks off the audience. You want your audience to focus their full attention on you and have them hanging on your every word. The big question is, how do you accomplish this feat? Well, no magic formula exists but there *are* lots of ways to begin. On the next several pages is a list of ideas just to get you started. And hopefully these ideas may even inspire you to create your own unique introduction.

Breaking the ice

Presenters can introduce themselves in all sorts of weird and whacky ways. We've heard of a speaker who brings in an ice cube, puts it on a table, takes his shoe off, and smashes it onto the ice. Of course, he then goes on to say: 'Now that we've broken the ice, we can talk about . . .'

A music therapist of our acquaintance often starts by asking her audience to hum with her. Apparently, humming opens up the airways and gets people breathing more deeply, injecting a blast of oxygen into their systems and waking them up.

We even know of a professor who sings his introductions.

All of these techniques work very well for their audiences. But think very carefully before deciding to use an unusual introduction to your presentation. What you think is funny and attention-grabbing may just seem odd and inappropriate to the wrong audience.

Using a quotation

Quotations make good openings for several reasons: They're easy to find; they're easy to tie into your topic; and, if chosen appropriately, they make you sound smart. Whether funny or serious, they get the audience's attention.

You'll find plenty of books stuffed full of quotations. But a good place to start may be to check out a free Web site: www.quotationspage.com. You'll find quotations from all of the usual suspects, from Shakespeare to Winston Churchill, Aristotle and Oscar Wilde.

Using a rhetorical question

Asking questions is an effective way of introducing a topic. A *rhetorical question* is one that you ask but don't actually want the audience to shout out answers to. But, by giving them pause for thought, a rhetorical question involves the audience as they mentally answer.

For example, a speaker talking about the provision of health services in the developing world may ask: 'When you're thirsty, how far do you go to get a drink? Maybe you go to the kitchen tap or to the fridge for a can of your favourite soft drink. But imagine living in the developing world and having to treck a mile each way every time you want a drink. How would that make you feel?'

Using a story or anecdote

Everyone loves stories – especially if they're real, personal, and relevant.

If you're presenting on a topic, you probably have a wealth of experience about it. So take a moment to consider the right story to share with others. Remember that your own story or anecdote can appeal either to the logical or emotional needs of your audience.

Using a startling statistic

We have some good news and some bad news about statistics. The bad news is statistics tend to put people to sleep. The good news is that dramatic, carefully chosen statistics keep people *from* going to sleep. They serve as a wake-up call. A startling statistic is particularly effective in an introduction.

A good resource for statistics is the National Statistics Web site: www. statistics.gov.uk. This site is packed with statistics covering Britain's economy, population, and society at both the national and local level – both in summary and detailed form. For example, you'll find statistics about births and deaths, economic performance of businesses, and how much people spent in shops last year. And this information's all published free of charge.

Using a startling fact

An interesting or startling fact always provides a good way to start a presentation. If you find the fact fascinating, chances are so will your audience. Counter-intuitive facts are always thought-provoking, too.

Say you're giving a talk about exercise and weight loss. One interesting fact is that people who embark on a new programme of exercise sometimes actually put on weight to begin with – because they are gaining muscle and losing fat. Muscle is a lot denser than fat, so people can actually shrink in waist size but go up in weight. This kind of slightly unexpected fact can kick off a presentation or talk very effectively.

Using a historical event

A historical event that relates to your topic is always a good way to begin a presentation. Historical references make you look smart and put your topic in perspective.

For example, say that you're giving a talk on the topic of apathy and the importance of voting in elections. Here are some interesting historical events that were determined by just a single vote:

- More than a 1,000 years ago in Greece, an entire meeting of the Church Synod was devoted to one question: Is a woman a human being or an animal? The issue was finally settled by one vote, and the consensus was that women do indeed belong to the human race.

- In 1776, the nascent United States of America decided by just one vote to adopt English as its national language instead of German.

- In 1923, just one vote was enough to elect the leader of a new political party in Munich. His name was Adolf Hitler.

The Internet is a great source of free historical information. For both medieval and modern British history, try the digital library at British History Online: www.british-history.ac.uk.

Using something that happened today

Any fact about the date you're speaking on can be used to open your presentation. Is it a holiday? Is it a famous person's birthday? Is it the day the light bulb was invented? This device is closely related to the historical event opening, but is not identical. You're not looking for an historic event related to your topic. You're just looking for some kind of event that occurred on this date. (When you find the event, then you relate it to your topic.)

A good place to mine for information is the 'This Day In History' section of the History Channel Web site: www.historychannel.com. For example, picking April Fool's Day, the Web site tells us that the Royal Air Force was formed with the amalgamation of the Royal Flying Corps (RFC) and the Royal Naval Air Service (RNAS).

Using the title of your presentation

Many speakers use the title of their presentation as part of their introduction. For example, you may be giving a political talk entitled 'Little Trouble in Big China'. You could try to weave the title of your presentation into your introduction in the following way:

There's a film called Big Trouble in Little China, but I'm here to talk about Little Trouble in Big China. Or at least that's the Chinese government's version, as they censor much of what goes out. So it seems that there is Little Trouble in Big China.

Provoking your audience

Want to get your audience's attention? Get them riled up about something as soon as you start speaking.

Here's how James P Grant, the late Executive Director of the United Nations Children's Fund (UNICEF), used a provoking opening at an international development conference: *'Permit me to begin with a few friendly provocations: First, I would suggest that nobody – not the West, not the United States, nobody – "won the Cold War".'*

Showing your knowledge of your audience

An audience is always complimented if you know something about them. This tactic shows that you made an effort to learn about the audience members. The perfect place to display this knowledge is in your introduction.

For example, if you're speaking at a local school, you may mention the time of year (such as start of term, end of term, impending exams, and so on). Or if you're speaking to a charity, you may refer to when they received their charter or to some snippet of information you gleaned from their Web site.

Referring to your audience immediately makes them appreciate that you've taken the time to research them rather than just delivered a standard talk or presentation.

Developing a common bond

Showing that you have something in common with the audience is always a good tactic.

For example, if you're speaking to a group of businesspeople, do you have any family members or friends that you could refer to?

My brother-in-law is an accountant. And when I first met him he went to great pains to tell me how his job isn't at all boring. And when he began to explain that his job isn't about counting beans but actually investigating how businesses make and lose money, well, I was hooked.

Emphasising the subject's importance

Of course, the topic should be of interest to the audience. But saying that something is important and explaining why gets immediate attention.

Say you're presenting at a medical conference on the topic of diseases in developing countries:

I'd like to remind you of the importance of this issue. This is human history in the making. We have the power to eliminate tuberculosis in sub-Saharan Africa. Just think how monumental that might be – for children growing up in 10 years' time to not have to worry about catching a disease that has been all but wiped out in the Western world.

Book IV

Delivering Perfect Presentations

Referring to the occasion

Want an easy way to begin? Just remind the audience of why you're speaking – the occasion that has brought you all together. And refer to the emotions or thoughts that may be going through the audience members' heads.

A scientist speaking at a climate change conference may refer specifically to the audience and other delegates:

I think there are mixed emotions in the room. There is a genuine sense of excitement that we are all gathered here today to share our latest findings about climate change and its impact on our ecologies. But there's also a palpable sense of trepidation in the room too, as we all recognise that we are on the brink of multiple, and possibly irreversible, ecological catastrophes.

Relating your presentation to previous presentations

If you're not the first speaker of the day, you can begin by telling the audience how your presentation relates to what they've already heard. Doing so helps the audience to see the big picture and how the different speakers' topics are related.

Of course, using this tactic means getting to know beforehand what your fellow speakers are going to talk about. Otherwise you may have to come up with something on the spot – and you need a lot of practice of standing up in front of audiences to develop that skill.

A useful tool is to talk about some aspect of a previous presenter's talk that you found 'interesting'. For example: 'What was most interesting to me about the preceding sessions we've had so far today was that we hear remarkably similar things from our clients here at ABC Bank. In fact, I'd go on to say that . . .'

Finding Solid Forms of Support

This section isn't about tights and hosiery. Support refers to the items you use to prove and illustrate your points – the basic material that makes up your speech – stories, quotes, and statistics.

Because your support is the basic material for your speech, what kind you use, as well as how you use it, is very important. Three basic rules regarding forms of support are:

✔ **Make sure that your support really supports something.** Don't throw in quotes, statistics, and stories just to show off or beef up the length of your talk. Use them only to prove, clarify, or illustrate a point.

✔ **Use a variety of support.** Different people respond to different types of information. Some people like statistics; others like quotes and stories.

✔ **Remember that less is more.** Using one dramatic statistic gets more attention than three boring statistics. One great example makes more of an impact than two so-so examples.

Mastering the art of storytelling

Throughout history, people have passed down customs, ideas, and information by telling stories. We seem to be hardwired to recognise and respond to this type of communication, which is why stories are so powerful when used in a talk.

Anyone can use a story, but using a *good* story and using it effectively sets you apart from the average speaker. Here are a handful of guidelines we've gathered together to give you some ways to use stories effectively in your presentations:

✔ **Tell stories for a purpose:** You should have a reason for telling a story. And the reason – a lesson, moral, or objective – should be obvious to the audience. Telling pointless stories is one of the quickest ways to turn off an audience. (Just think of how you feel when Auntie Jane corners you at Christmas after knocking back a few too many sherries.)

✔ **Tell personal stories:** You know how much you like to hear stories about yourself or people you know. So just think of all the attention your presentation could receive if you use stories about yourself or people familiar to your audience. Personal stories interest an audience much more than just plain facts.

If you don't have many personal stories or stories about real individuals to tell, you can still add personal stories to your talk. You can either use hypothetical stories or interview other people and tell their stories. Other people's stories are so simple to find and are such a great source of material that you shouldn't overlook them, although many speakers do. Audience members will also tell you stories after your speech.

Book IV

Delivering Perfect Presentations

Collect the more relevant and interesting of these – don't forget to ask permission to use them, of course.

✔ **Tell success stories:** Nothing succeeds like success, and that includes success stories. Think of the stories that you liked as a child. Most of them ended with the words 'happily ever after'. Those words are the sign of a success story. People like to hear stories about how an idea or action worked out successfully.

✔ **Try out stories first:** The first time you tell a particular story shouldn't be when you're standing at a podium addressing your audience. You need to know how the story works – what kind of response it gets from others. So try stories out first on your friends, neighbours, colleagues, and anyone willing to listen. Their responses – body language, facial expressions, laughter, and other verbal and nonverbal responses – give you an idea of how to tweak the content, delivery, or timing of your story. The story should get better every time you tell it, and by the time you use the story in a speech, you should have a polished gem.

✔ **Develop more powerful stories:** You can make your stories more effective if you understand exactly how and why they affect an audience. To accomplish this task, ask yourself (and answer) the following questions:

- What's the objective, moral, lesson, punch line, or purpose of the story?

- What's the plain-English synopsis of what you're trying to get across?

- What are the beginning, the middle, and the end?

- Does the story have a people focus? Who are the main characters in the story? Why are they interesting?

- What is the sequence of events that makes the story work? Are there some facts or data that should be put into the story? Does the story as you currently tell it have too many facts and too much data? Do they really help the story or hurt it?

- What are the human factors in the story that make it interesting?

Making an impact with quotations

Quotes get immediate attention – especially when they're attached to a famous name. In today's sound-bite society, quotes provide a great way to make a strong impression in the minds of audience members, if you know how to use them effectively. Improve the quality of your presentation by following these guidelines the next time you include a quote in your speech:

✔ **Relate the quote to a point:** A quote should be used to make a point otherwise it's irrelevant – no matter how funny or insightful it is. Sometimes you may find a great quote that just doesn't fit, and you can't make it fit without reworking a great deal of your talk. Just accept the fact that the quote doesn't fit, and save it for your next talk.

Using quotes that have nothing to do with your topic can make you sound like a namedropper. The audience can tell when you're trying to appear smart by dropping names in your speech. Throwing around phrases, such as 'As Albert Einstein once said. . . .' or 'According to Socrates. . . .' sounds forced. While you're trying to sound smart, using such quotes often has the opposite effect.

✔ **Use a variety of sources:** Unless you're doing a tribute to a particular celebrity, no one wants to hear endless quotes from a single source. That type of repetition gets boring fast. If you're only going to quote the Dalai Lama, then why didn't you just get the Dalai Lama to give your speech? Mix it up a bit. Go ahead and quote the Dalai Lama, but quote Aristotle, Confucius, and Doctor Who, too.

✔ **Keep it brief:** You don't want to lose the conversational quality of your presentation, and a long quote starts to sound like you're reading it, even if you're not. Shorten lengthy quotes and tell the audience that you're paraphrasing. Just say, 'To paraphrase Mr Whoever', then say the shortened quote.

✔ **Use a simple attribution:** Just say, 'Mr So-And-So once said . . .' and give the quote, or give the quote and then say who said it. You can sound a bit ridiculous if you say 'quote . . . unquote' unless you're doing a dramatic reading from a court transcript.

✔ **Cite a surprising source:** You can bolster support for your argument in a powerful way by using quotes from an unlikely source. It's so unexpected for a Labour politician to support his position by quoting a Conservative, or a trade union leader to advance her cause by quoting management, or a Sunday morning vicar to prove his point by quoting the song lyrics of a boy band. Such startling contrasts always get attention and can be very effective.

✔ **Hedge your bets whenever you're in doubt:** If you're not sure who said the line that you're quoting, you don't have to delete the quote from your speech – you just have to know how to cover yourself. Simply say, 'I believe it was Mr Famous Name who once said. . . .' or use the great cover phrase, 'As an old philosopher once said. . . '. After all, everyone is a philosopher of one sort or another. So if you find out that the line came from Donald Duck, you can still argue that he was being philosophical.

Doing it by numbers

Benjamin Disraeli, one of our more notable Prime Ministers, famously once said, 'There are three kinds of lies: lies, damned lies, and statistics.' He may have overstated the case, but not by much. Statistics enable you to slice up reality in a way that suits your perspective.

Statistics and numerical data can provide some of the most influential support in your entire speech, but they commonly lose their impact because speakers use them ineffectively. Get your numbers to register on your audience's bottom line by checking out these suggestions:

- ✔ **Give your audience time to digest:** Most people can't process numbers as rapidly as they can process other types of information, so don't drown your audience in numerical data. Give your listeners time to digest each statistic; don't just spew numbers at them. If you don't space statistics out, the audience will – space out, that is. (An exception to this rule involves *startling* statistics; see the later bullet point in this list for a discussion of this exception.)

- ✔ **Round off numbers:** If you're telling aerospace engineers how to build a more efficient jet engine, then by all means, use exact numbers. But if exact numbers aren't critical to your subject matter or to your audience, give everyone a break – round them off. Your listeners don't need to know that the candidate you backed won with 59.8 per cent of the vote. Just say 60 per cent.

- ✔ **Use a credible source:** A statistic is only as impressive as its source. Did you get your numbers from the *Financial Times* or the *News of the World*? A big difference lies between the two.

    What many people don't realise is that the *Financial Times* may not always be the more credible source. Credibility depends on your audience. You may be speaking to people who read the *News of the World* religiously and distrust the *Financial Times*, categorising it as a tool of the rich. Only your audience can bestow credibility upon a source. Keep that point in mind when you select your statistics.

- ✔ **Repeat key numbers:** If you want people to hear and remember an important statistic, say it more than once. Just think of the audience as a person you've wanted to date and who has just asked for your number. You wouldn't just say it once, would you?

- ✔ **Use startling statistics:** The big exception to the general rule that statistics are boring is the *startling* statistic. This term refers to numerical data that's so surprising that it just grabs your attention. A startling statistic is inherently interesting.

For example, if you were giving a speech about the need for more recycling, you might start by using this statistic from the `recycle-more.co.uk` campaign: In 2000, people in the UK bought 5 billion aluminium drinks cans. Apparently only 42 per cent of them were recycled. So 2,900,000,000 cans were thrown away, which is approximately 7,495,000 cans a day or over 331,000 cans every hour of every single day!

✔ **Relate the numbers to your audience:** Numbers are abstract concepts, and if you want to make an impact, you have to make the audience relate to the numbers you plan to discuss. To make numerical data more concrete, try the following techniques:

- **Put statistics into familiar terms:** Discuss numbers in a way that people can understand. Explain numbers in terms that have real meaning for your audience.

  For example, in the recycling example, the average household uses 3.2kg of aluminium cans a year – about 208 cans. Ask your audience to imagine 208 cans piled up on their kitchen table. Or, even better, bring in a pile of 208 cans to present them with a very real scene of what those statistics mean in practice.

- **Create a picture:** Transform your numbers into a concrete image so your audience can see the statistic. Paint a picture for them.

  Regarding the recycling of aluminium cans, the `recycle-more.co.uk` Web site tells us that if all the aluminium cans recycled in the UK last year were laid end to end, they would stretch from John O'Groats to Land's End 140 times. That fact should give your audience pause for thought.

- **Use analogies:** Turn your abstract statistics into easy-to-visualise images.

  In Britain, as in most of the Western world, the aging population is a crucial issue. Young people aren't having as many babies as they did a few decades ago. Which means that in the future fewer workers will exist to pay for the pensions of the elderly. Right now it requires around four workers to pay the pension of each elderly person. But in a few years' time, as the whole population becomes increasingly older, there'll only be two workers available to pay for that pension. And all the while the cost of that pension keeps swelling up like a balloon. By the time the people currently leaving school are ready for retirement, that pension cost balloon may just well have burst.

- **Create visual aids:** If you have a great deal of numerical data in your presentation, consider putting it into a visual format – using computer technology, slides, or overheads of charts or graphs. If your audience members can see the data, they'll find it much easier to digest.

Clearing the air with definitions

If someone offered you a new job and said that they would pay you a 'huge' salary, you'd be pretty excited, wouldn't you? But the canny part of you might want to ask 'how huge exactly?' Because what an employer defines as 'huge' might not be what you define as huge. And, in the same way, audiences don't always define words in the same way that you might.

If you don't want to risk confusing or annoying your audience, make sure that you're all speaking the same language. The following list shows you a few ways to use definitions in a speech to prevent misunderstandings:

- ✔ **Use the dictionary definition:** The simplest way to define a term is to look it up in a dictionary and use the definition in your presentation. For example, if you're going to talk about ethics, then you might lead off by saying,

    'The *Oxford English Dictionary* defines ethics as the science of morals in human conduct.'

- ✔ **Use your personal definition:** If you don't like the dictionary definition, then give the meaning of the term as you define it.

    For example, the *Oxford English Dictionary* defines quality as 'the degree of excellence of a thing'. However, you might say,

    'How do I define *quality* in a news report or analysis? My measure is summed up in three words: *Accuracy*, *objectivity*, and *responsibility*.'

When a word is emotionally charged, some members of your audience may misinterpret your remarks unless you clearly explain *your* use of the term. For example, you may be talking about money. You could say that 'money is evil' and go on to say that the pursuit of money for its own sake can lead people down a path toward greed and selfishness. Or you could say that 'money is good' because it allows those people who have it to support those who do not. So always explain why you are taking a particular stance on an issue.

Unlocking concepts with analogies

An analogy is a comparison that highlights similarities (and differences) between two objects or concepts. An analogy provides one of the fundamental ways that we gain new knowledge. An analogy allows us to explain the unknown in terms of the known. When a toddler asks, 'What's heaven?' and you answer, 'It's like school, but there's only playtime and no homework', you're using an analogy.

Analogies are particularly well suited to presentations that teach, train, or educate an audience – any talk in which you're explaining something. They also provide an opportunity to add a touch of humour. For example, you're giving a talk about lack of leadership and might say, 'Leadership is like the Loch Ness Monster. You hear about it a lot, but no one sees it very often.' And then pause to wait for the laughs!

Getting heard with examples

Two of the most frequently used words in the world are 'for example'. We use these words to illustrate what we're talking about, which is why examples are probably the most common devices for supporting ideas and assertions.

You can use two types of examples in your speech: real and hypothetical. You base a real example on fact. You base a hypothetical example on imagination – the data's made up.

Real examples tend to be more powerful than hypothetical examples because they're, well, real. The example's something that actually exists that you can point to. Hypothetical examples are always subject to the criticism that they're not real. However, they can be very effective in presentations that involve philosophy, law, or theoretical concepts.

Regardless of whether you use real or hypothetical examples, if you want to get maximum mileage from them, don't ignore positive examples. Too often, speakers tell you what you shouldn't do, but they never say what you should do. So don't fall into this trap yourself. You can take a specific example and talk about how it went wrong and how it may have been handled differently. But if you're going to give just one side of the example, talk about the right behaviour and allude to the wrong one – and not the other way around. Don't leave the audience hanging.

Making Transitions

Transitions may be the most overlooked part of any presentation; yet they're one of the most important. Transitions are how you get from one point in your presentation to another. They don't involve dramatic rhetorical devices like the introduction or conclusion. They don't offer fascinating information or anecdotes like the body of the presentation. Transitions are still crucial, though – they're the glue that holds your whole presentation together.

Figuring out how to use transitions

Even if your presentation has the world's greatest introduction, body, and conclusion, you still have to get from one to the other. Step forward transitions. They connect the various parts of your presentation, and they flesh out its organisation. Transitions let your audience know when you're moving from one idea to another and how all your ideas fit together.

Most people know that transitions have two traditional functions:

- To lead from one section or idea to another.
- To provide internal summaries that let the audience know where they're at, where they've been, and where they're going in regard to the presentation.

But transitions can also be used to gain and hold audience attention.

Managing the transition mission

Transitions have a lot of work to do – especially for such an overlooked part of a presentation. The following are three important tasks that transitions can perform.

Leading from one idea to another

The primary role of the transition is to lead your listeners from one idea to another.

Perhaps the most important transition is the one between the introduction and the body of your talk. In our airplane model, this point is when the plane pulls out of the takeoff pattern and settles into cruising mode. Turbulence here can make the passengers very nervous. They want to know that the plane is heading in the right direction and that you'll provide a smooth flight all the way.

But the transitions between major points are also crucial. Speakers often get it wrong here. For example, you're sitting in the audience listening to a presentation and the speaker is talking about the monetary policy of Bolivia.

But the next thing you know, the speaker is discussing a labour shortage in Eastern Europe. How did you get from Bolivia to Eastern Europe? Probably without a transition.

Fortunately, a simple way exists to handle the transition between the introduction and body of your presentation, as well as the transitions between main points. Here's the secret: Organise your presentation around a number of points and state that number in your introduction. Then the transitions are a breeze. 'Today I will be speaking about the three reasons for the coming worldwide economic depression. First is the monetary policy of Bolivia. . . . The second reason we are headed for a worldwide depression is the labour shortage in Eastern Europe. . . . Third. . . .' This process is transition by numbers, and it works.

The numbering technique can also be used to make transitions to and between subpoints. 'First is the monetary policy of Bolivia. There are two aspects to Bolivian policy that are troubling. . . .'

One more important transition exists: that between the body of your presentation and the conclusion. And this transition's very easy to handle. Sometimes you can just say 'In conclusion' and it works. But remember that this transition must alert the audience that you're going into your close. Use expressions such as: 'What can we learn from all this?', 'Let me leave you with one final thought', 'Now, in my three remaining minutes, let me remind you of what we've discussed'. Make the transition sound as though you're going to wind down and wrap up.

Summarising

The second traditional function of transitions (see the earlier section 'Leading from one idea to another' for the first) is to provide internal summaries – short announcements that let the audience know where they've been, where they are, and where they're going. The need for these summaries is frequently dismissed by inexperienced speakers who feel that they're too repetitive – that they're just filler. Well, yes and no. Internal summaries *are* repetitive, but they're *not* filler. They play a vital role in any presentation, especially those longer than a few minutes.

In understanding a presentation, speakers have a distinct advantage over the audience – they know what they're trying to say. Speakers know exactly what their message is, how it's structured, and all its points and subpoints. In writing the presentation, speakers have an opportunity to read their message many times. Audiences don't have that luxury. They only hear the presentation once – as it's given. They can't put the presentation in reverse, play it again, and freeze-frame the parts they didn't catch.

Book IV

Delivering Perfect Presentations

Here are a few tips about using internal summaries:

- ✔ An internal summary should succinctly state what you just covered and announce where you are in the presentation.

- ✔ Use an internal summary every time you move from one major point in your talk to another major point.

- ✔ Internal summaries can also be used when moving from subpoint to subpoint.

- ✔ The longer your presentation, the more internal summaries you need.

Getting attention

Transitions can also be used to gain attention. Although they're not traditionally used for this purpose, no reason exists why they shouldn't be. Under a more traditional view, transitions can serve as internal summaries telling your audience where they've been, where they are, and where they're going. The *where they're going* part raises interesting possibilities for gaining attention.

When you tell your audience where they're going, why not make it exciting? Instead of just restating the structure of your talk in a straightforward, matter-of-fact manner, why not try to inject a little something different into the proceedings? Use a *teaser*. A teaser is the short blurb you hear on some radio and television programmes just before they go to a commercial break. For example, 'Coming up in the next half of our show: our househunters discover that their property isn't all they thought it was' or 'A politician who *kept* a promise – right after these announcements'. The teaser is designed specifically to get your attention and keep you from changing the channel.

You can use the teaser technique to make your internal summaries excite the audience members about what lies ahead in your presentation. Give them some great coming attractions that keep them glued to their seats. How do you do that? Think about why the audience should even listen to your talk. What's in it for them? As you write your transitions about what's coming up, frame them in terms of audience benefits.

Avoiding common transition mistakes

Transitions form the glue that holds a presentation together. Unfortunately, many speakers become unglued trying to insert transitions properly. Avoid the following mistakes.

Too few

Not having enough transitions in your presentation is the biggest mistake. Having more can't hurt because you can never make your presentation too clear to your audience. You've been living with your presentation for quite a while. You're intimately familiar with the content; your audience isn't. The more guidance you can give the audience about how your presentation's structured and where it's going, the better.

Too brief

If the transition is too brief, your audience can easily miss it. Missing it may have the same effect as having no transition at all. The most common, and overused, brief transition is 'and'. We've heard talks that used 'and' almost exclusively as a transition and the effect is almost comical. The presentation sounds like a load of disjointed ideas tacked together – 'and' is the tack. 'In addition' is a close runner-up.

Too similar

Variety is the spice of life – and it also works wonders with transitions. Don't use the same couple of transitional phrases over and over again. Doing so gets boring. Use an assortment of transitions: 'Now let's take a look at . . .', 'In addition . . .', 'The next point is . . .', 'For example . . .', and 'By that I mean . . .'. Endless possibilities exist.

Spicing Up Your Speech with Classic Rhetorical Devices

If you had a dispute in ancient Greece, you faced both good and bad news. The good news: Lawyers weren't invented. The bad news: You had to argue your own case. The ancient Greeks developed all sorts of rhetorical devices to improve their speeches – because they wanted to win.

This section presents a few of the classic devices. And don't worry, they still work today. Anyone from six-year-olds to lawyers to professional speakers still use these techniques, and use them effectively.

Book IV

Delivering Perfect Presentations

Hyperbole

Hyperbole is a fancy word for exaggeration. People use hyperbole instinctively in everyday conversation: 'I was waiting a year for you to get off the phone.' 'It's about a million miles from here to Hong Kong.' Hyperbole's a wonderful device for emphasising a point in a speech or presentation. Here's an example from a comedian describing his early days:

> One of the first clubs I performed at was a small, dark place. It was so dark I could barely see the three people in the room – the two in the front row listening to me and the guy in the back row developing film.

Allusion

An *allusion* is a reference to a person, object, or event from the Bible, mythology, or literature. Here are a couple of examples:

- ✔ Allowing children to drink alcohol from the age of 16 would be like opening a Pandora's box of trouble ranging from early liver damage to alcoholism.
- ✔ Every organisation has an Achilles' heel – a weakness that we can exploit. We just need to find out what it is.

Alliteration

Alliteration refers to a phrase in which the words begin with the same sound. For example, the phrase 'salacious, sleazy scandal' uses the repetition of the 's' at the beginning of each word to create a memorable sound.

You can also use alliteration to make the title of your talk more memorable. For example, the title 'Persecuted People in Politics' may be easier to recall than 'Persecuted Individuals and Government'.

Metaphor

A *metaphor* is a short, implied comparison that transfers the properties of one item to another. A classic example comes from Martin Luther King's 'I Have a Dream' speech in which he talks about: '. . . the manacles of segregation and the chain of discrimination.'

The metaphor can add a poetic quality to your speech while still allowing you to make a point. Say you want to talk about the devastation caused by a natural disaster. Rather than referring to the hurricane, you can dress it up in a metaphor: 'An invisible hand decimated the village.'

Simile

A *simile* is like a metaphor except that you make a directly stated comparison of one thing to another. (A simile usually uses the words 'like' or 'as' to make the comparison.)

Say, for example, a politician is talking about the need to control unscrupulous financial advisors: 'You have a massive influx of inexperienced investors, and a real potential for conflicts of interest – it's like dry kindling and a match. And it's something I want to avoid as I've seen too many people's life savings go up in smoke.'

Comedy writer Ben Elton uses a pattern whereby he confounds our expectations of a simile: 'In my hallway, there sat a big square box, which was exactly like . . . a big, square box.' The audience is then surprised by the unexpected.

Rhetorical question

A *rhetorical question* refers to a question that the speaker asks for effect. The audience isn't expected to answer. Rhetorical questions are designed to focus attention on the subject of the question. This device is often used in introductions, conclusions, or transitions.

For example, say you want to highlight the plight of abandoned dogs:

> How would you feel if you were thrown out onto the street? Would you enjoy being cold and lonely? Would you enjoy scrabbling around in dustbins for a bite to eat? Would you be content and happy? Would you?

The rule of three

The *rule of three* refers to the technique of grouping together three words, phrases, or sentences. For some reason, a grouping of three items makes a powerful impression on the human mind. (Don't ask us why. Just trust us that it does.)

Some of the most famous passages from the world's greatest oratory have used this technique:

- ✔ 'I came. I saw. I conquered.' (Julius Caesar)
- ✔ '. . . government of the people, by the people, for the people. . . .' (Abraham Lincoln)

Business speakers frequently use this technique. The beauty of the rule of three is that it can work its magic on any topic – no matter how commonplace or mundane. Just take a few minutes to think about your subject. You can always come up with three items to group together. Are you talking about a new accounting procedure that must be followed by all employees? It affects managers, hourly staff, and temps. Is your subject quality management? It starts with awareness, training, and commitment.

Repetition

Repetition refers to repeating a group of words in an identical rhythm. This device draws attention to the phrase and can even be used to pull a whole speech together. Martin Luther King's 'I Have a Dream' speech is a classic example. Dr King repeated the phrase 'I have a dream' throughout his entire speech.

But repetition doesn't have to run throughout an entire presentation. You can use the technique to dramatise one section, or even one sentence, of your talk. The following example uses repetition to stress the effects of global warming on our children's future:

> It's our children who will suffer if we don't do something about global warming. It's our children who will see the seas rise and overwhelm their homes. It's our children who will ask us why we did nothing.

So repetition is a dramatic way to create a rhythm, to make a point, or to show your style. Repetition's a dramatic way to be dramatic.

Creating the Perfect Conclusion

Remember the ending to every fairy tale you've ever heard? 'And then they lived happily ever after.' Your presentation may not have much in common with a fairy tale, but you can create a similarly perfect ending for it. The following sections give you some simple rules.

Cueing the audience in advance

The audience likes you to let them know in advance that you plan on concluding. Tell them when you're getting *close* to your conclusion. 'Turning now to my final point' and 'I'll give two more examples before I wrap up' are types of statements that give the audience confidence that you'll reach your final destination – soon. These statements also help the audience formulate an estimated time of arrival.

Making it sound like a conclusion

People expect a conclusion to sound a certain way – like a conclusion. Audiences tend to become upset if you think you're finished but they don't. So make the wrap-up obvious. Use phrases such as 'in conclusion', 'to conclude', or 'in closing'. Such phrases are always good starting points – for ending.

Finding the right length

The conclusion should usually be about 5 to 10 per cent of your speech. Your summation can be too short, but a much more common mistake is making it too long. Don't go on forever. Sum up and sit down.

Writing it out

Two reasons exist for writing out your conclusion. First, doing so combats stage fright. The period when you're concluding is the second most jittery time for speakers. (The most likely time for stage fright to strike is when you begin.) If you write out the conclusion, you don't have to worry about forgetting it. Second, and more important, if you write out the conclusion, you know when to conclude. A written summation's an insurance policy to protect you from rambling.

Making the last words memorable

The last few lines of your conclusion are the most important. So make them memorable. Go for an emotional connection with the audience members. Make them laugh. Make them think. Make them stand up and applaud.

Here's a simple formula for setting up your final line: Just say, 'I have one final thought that I want to leave you with.' (An alternative is, 'If you remember just one thing I've said today, remember this . . . .') Then give your audience a heck of a thought. Word that concluding thought strongly and make it relevant – to your talk and your audience.

Announcing your availability

No matter what the circumstances of your speaking engagement, always make time to answer questions after you're finished. Announce your availability during the conclusion.

Imagine you're in the audience. You hear a talk that you think is absolutely terrific. When the presentation's finished, you go to talk with the speaker, and he gives you the brush off. Blimey. First, you feel stupid. Then you get angry. And then you change your opinion of the presenter and the presentation, right? Now you think the speaker is an idiot, and the talk wasn't so great after all. So don't be an idiot. Be kind to your fans. And don't forget – the fact that you're finished speaking doesn't mean that you're done quite yet.

Avoiding common mistakes

Sometimes what you don't say in your conclusion is even more important than what you do say. Avoid the following common mistakes:

- ✔ **Going over your time limit.** Make the conclusion coincide with the end of your allotted time. If you want to be perceived as a genius, finish five minutes early, but don't go on for longer than expected. An old joke on the lecture circuit defines a 'second wind' as what a speaker gets after he or she says, 'In conclusion'. Don't let that happen to you. It's not pretty.

- ✔ **Rambling.** Reviewing the points you've already made should be done in a brief and orderly manner – preferably in the order you discussed them. Make the conclusion easy to follow. Stick to your plan.

- ✔ **Adding new points at the end.** The conclusion is a time to review what you've already said – not make another speech. Introducing new ideas in the conclusion means that you haven't properly fitted them into the overall framework of your presentation, which in turn means that these ideas will have less impact. The audience will have to figure out where they belong. And actually – the audience will just want to go home.

- ✔ **Saying you forgot to mention something.** Doing so makes you look disorganised, and the audience worries that you'll make another speech. One solution is: If the point is really important, boil it down to a very succinct statement. Then, after you've summarised the points you've already made, say you want to leave the audience members with one final thought. Then give them the point you forgot to mention. If you had already planned to leave them with a different final thought, don't worry. Just say you want to leave them with two final thoughts. First give the point you forgot and then give the final thought you had planned. (Yes, this is an exception to the rule against adding new points at the end.)

Wrapping Up in Style

Psychologists have found that audiences tend to remember introductions and conclusions more strongly than what is said in the middle of a presentation. Assuming you've started with a strong introduction, don't let yourself down with a flaccid conclusion.

Referring back to the opening

If one of the functions of the conclusion is to provide closure, then referring back to your introduction is a great way to do it. You use the conclusion to return to remarks you made in your introduction. If you asked a question in your opening, you answer it in the conclusion. If you told a story, you refer to it again. This technique gives a wonderful sense of completeness to your presentation.

Using a quotation

You can never go wrong ending with an inspirational quotation related to your message. Just make sure your choice is not only inspired but also totally relevant.

Asking a question

Asking the right question can be a powerful way to end a presentation. Presumably the question implies an answer – the one you want the audience to reach.

Closed questions (those that can only be answered 'yes' or 'no') are good ways to finish off your talk. Then no one can fail to answer the question for themselves.

For example, say a doctor is talking about eating too much fat as a cause of heart disease. The doctor might finish by asking: 'Now that you've heard how we have to crack open a patient's rib cage, do you think you fancy having triple bypass surgery?'

Telling a story

You can choose from several types of stories: funny, shocking, moving, dramatic, educational, personal, fictional, biblical, or allegorical. Any one of them can be effective if appropriate for your topic and your audience.

Reciting a poem

If you recite a poem, make it short. Audiences switch off very quickly if you read more than half a dozen lines. The poem can be inspirational or funny, but it must, must, must tie into your talk. And because poetry is a pretty much neglected art form these days, you may want to get a second opinion. Share your poem with a friend or colleague and see if they get the link between it and your topic.

Telling the audience what to do

This type of ending is very specific. You conclude by telling the audience *exactly* what to do.

Say you're talking about fostering and adoption. After presenting the trials and tribulations involved in fostering and adopting, you might tell your audience exactly how they can do it: 'Find out more at the Barnardo's Web site. It's Barnardos.org.uk and there's a very clear link to the pages about fostering and adoption. So, again, that's Barnardo's, spelt b-a-r-n-a-r-d-o-s, dot org, dot uk. Just do it.'

Asking for help

Just ask for help. This technique's a simple but overlooked conclusion. Most people really do respond. If they've taken the time to come to listen to your talk (and assuming you carried it off with panache), then your audience are more than likely to help. So whether you are looking for volunteers to help with a fund-raising 'bring and buy' sale or for businesspeople to donate prizes for a raffle or volunteers to contribute to an organisational change programme, just ask. You may be surprised.

Chapter 3

Understanding Body Language

. . . .

. . . .

*P*ublic speakers should speak up so they can be heard, stand up so they can be seen, and shut up so they can be enjoyed. That advice may be harsh, but it does highlight a very important aspect of presenting and public speaking: Much of your talk's impact comes from how you look and sound.

Understanding Body Language

Body language refers to the messages you send through facial expression, posture, and gesture. One famous psychological study estimated that nearly 80 per cent of your impact is determined not by *what* you say but *how* you say it. Body language is a language that you already use every day, and most of the meanings are obvious. A smile indicates happiness. A frown signals disapproval. Leaning forward means active engagement in the discussion.

Not as obvious, though, is how *you* employ body language. Watching a videotape of yourself can reveal some amazing insights. Using this method is the quickest way to improve your body language – because the camera doesn't lie. It reveals movements and gestures that you may not know that you're making. Ask someone to videotape you giving a presentation or speech. Then watch the video with the sound off. Common sense tells you most of what you need to correct such as fidgeting with your hands, hunching your shoulders, or repeatedly touching your hair while speaking. Other things to keep in mind are facial expressions, posture, and gestures.

Sending a message with facial expressions

If the eyes are the windows to the soul, then the face is the front of the house. Its appearance says a lot. And how you make your face appear says a lot about your message.

The single most important facial expression is the smile. Simply smiling at an audience can create instant rapport anywhere in the world. A smile is universally understood. Unfortunately, many speakers – particularly business speakers – feel they must wear their 'business face' at all times. They're *serious* businesspeople. They have facts and figures. They have bottom-line responsibilities. If they smile, they might seem . . . human.

You don't need to smile all the time, though. You're not a walking advert for your dentist. In fact, inappropriate smiling can undermine your entire message. But the occasional smile will make your audience warm to you – so don't underestimate its power.

Use your face to accentuate key points. Act out what you're saying. Are you incredulous about a statistic you've just cited? Raise your eyebrows in disbelief. Are you briefing the audience on a strategy that you disagree with? Frown. Or stick your tongue out at them. (Just kidding. Actually, that action's highly offensive in some cultures. See the 'Going international' section, later in this chapter.)

Punctuating your presentation with posture

Your mother was right. You should always stand up straight – especially when you're giving a speech or presentation. An audience may think a speaker with sloppy posture is lazy, ill, or tired. Likewise, an audience thinks of a speaker with good posture as an upright, confident individual.

The following tips can help you maintain perfect posture:

- ✔ **Stand up straight with your feet slightly apart and your arms ready to gesture.** This is the basic, preferred posture for any presentation or speech.

- ✔ **If you must sit, lean slightly toward the audience.** Leaning forward shows that you're actively engaged with the audience. Leaning back signals retreat.

- ✔ **Lean on the podium only once in a while for effect.** Planting yourself on the podium makes you look weak.

✔ **Avoid standing with your hands on your hips.** You'll come across as a bossy PE teacher. Besides, doing so makes you look like you're leading a game of Simon Says. Instead, use your hands to make gestures that enhance your message. For example, if you have three key points, count them out on your fingers.

✔ **Avoid swaying back and forth.** Unless you're talking about how to use a metronome or discussing the finer points of seasickness, no one wants to watch you in motion. Swaying back and forth is very distracting. Keep your trunk stationary from the waist up.

✔ **Avoid standing with your arms folded across your chest.** You'll look like a thug from a gangster movie. What are you going to do? Beat up the audience? Besides, you should be using your arms to gesture and emphasise your points.

✔ **Avoid standing with your arms behind your back.** Doing so limits your ability to gesture. And if you clasp your hands together, it makes you look like you've been handcuffed and arrested. Let the audience see your hands as you use them to emphasise points in your presentation.

✔ **Avoid standing in the fig leaf position.** We diagnose this stance when a speaker holds both hands together over his or her crotch – like the fig leaves that Adam and Eve wore. If you're posing for a Renaissance-style painting of blushing modesty this position's fine, but it looks really stupid in any other circumstance. You look as though you want to hide something from your audience. Instead, use your hands to augment your message with gestures.

✔ **Avoid burying your hands in your pockets.** People will wonder what they're doing down there. Putting one hand in your pocket from time to time is fine. But don't leave it there. And make sure never to fiddle with loose change as it really annoys the audience. Having your hands in your pockets also prevents you from using them to gesture.

Giving the right message with gestures

A cynic once suggested that speakers who don't know what to do with their hands should try clamping them over their mouths. That suggestion, though mean-spirited, does highlight a common problem for speakers – what to do with your hands. You can't get around the fact that you have to do *something* with them. And your choice has important consequences for your speech.

Using gestures properly in a speech means breaking one of your mother's basic rules: You *don't* want to keep your hands to yourself. You want to share them with your audience. How do you do that? Just follow these simple guidelines and you'll do fine:

- ✔ **Create opportunities to use gestures.** If you're worried that gestures won't occur to you naturally, then plan your presentation so that you can include appropriate ones. Include a few items in your talk that beg for gestures. Talk about alternative courses of action, for example 'on the one hand . . . and on the other hand'. Talk about how large or small something is. Talk about how many points you'll make and hold up your fingers. (This technique works best if the number is ten or less.)

- ✔ **Vary your gestures.** If you make the same gestures repeatedly, you start to look like a robot. And the predictability lowers audience attention levels. Don't let your gestures fall into a pattern. Keep the audience guessing. Doing so keeps them watching. Check out your gesturing habits by videotaping yourself; hit play then fast forward. You can easily see where gestures are repetitive or overdone.

- ✔ **Put your hands in the steeple position.** Your hands really will take care of themselves as you speak. But if you insist on guidance, just put them together in front of you as if you're applauding. That's the steeple position. Now you don't keep your hands like that. The steeple position's just a rest stop. As you talk, your hands will naturally split apart from the steeple. Sometimes they split widely. Sometimes they split narrowly. The steeple position places your hands in a position where they'll move without your thinking about them. However, too many speakers keep their hands glued together in that position for much too long.

- ✔ **Make your gestures fit the space.** A common mistake speakers make is transferring gestures used in small, intimate settings to large, formal settings. For example, people at a cocktail party gesture by moving their arms from the elbow to the end of the hand. But if you're speaking to a large audience in a large space, you must adjust your gestures. You must open them up and make them larger. Are you going to emphasise a point? Move your arms from the *shoulders* to the ends of your hands instead of from the elbows.

- ✔ **Make bold gestures.** Your gestures should communicate confidence and authority. Tentative, half-hearted attempts at gesturing make you look weak and indecisive. Get your hands up. (No, we're not about to rob you.) You'll look more assured if your hands are higher than your elbows. Be bold. Don't use a finger if a fist is more dramatic. Watch politicians speaking in the House of Commons for inspiration.

- ✔ **Think about your gestures ahead of time, but don't memorise them.** Think about the gestures you'll use. Think about where they may fit into your presentation. But don't plan them your gestures out in specific detail. And don't memorise them. Memorised gestures are obvious to the audience and make you seem robotic.

✔ **Avoid these types of speakers:**

- **The banker:** They keep rattling coins in their pockets. They sound like a change machine. The sound is very distracting.

- **The optician:** They constantly adjust their glasses. They're on. They're off. They're slipping down their noses. Do everyone a favour and avoid touching your glasses – or get some contact lenses.

- **The tailor:** They fiddle with their clothing. The tie is a big object of affection for male speakers in this category. They twist it. And pinch it. And rub it. No one listens to the talk. We're all waiting to see if the speaker will choke himself.

- **The jeweller:** They fiddle with their jewellery. Necklaces are a big attraction for female speakers in this category. And you'll find ring twisters of both genders.

- **The lonely lover:** They hug themselves. This position looks really weird. They stand up in front of the audience and put their arms round themselves while they speak. They lose a lot of credibility.

- **The beggar:** They clasp their hands together and thrust them toward the audience as if they're begging for something. They probably are – a miracle.

- **The hygienist:** They keep rubbing their hands together like they're washing them. Doing so looks weird for a few reasons. There's no soap. No water. No sink. And a load of people called an audience is watching.

- **The toy maker:** They love to play with their little toys – pens, markers, pointers – whatever happens to be around. They turn them in their hands. They squeeze them. And they distract the audience.

- **The hair stylist:** They keep flicking, pulling, or rearranging their hair. Yes, the audience knows you've just got a nervous habit, but they still wonder when you last washed your hair.

Going international

As if standing up and giving a presentation or speech isn't already tough enough, it takes on a whole new level of difficulty when you address audiences from around the world. Cultural differences come into play. And navigating the proprieties of appropriate body language is as simple as walking through a minefield without a map.

To get through your presentation without causing offence, start by following one basic rule: Remember that body language isn't universal. So how do you know if your body language will be offensive?

Here are some general guidelines for using body language successfully when you speak around the globe:

- **Speaking to a northern European audience:** Northern European audiences prefer a formal style, and that preference is reflected in a low-key use of body language. North Europeans such as Germans and Scandinavians don't tend to like high-energy styles with emphatic gestures and lots of walking back and forth across the stage. They consider that type of delivery shallow and it lowers the speaker's credibility.

- **Speaking to a southern European audience:** Southern Europeans including the Spanish and Italians are a bit more relaxed than our northern European counterparts and much prefer a bit more energy and emphasis. So allow yourself some of the more expansive gestures and feel free to walk around the stage area a bit if you like.

- **Speaking to a North American audience:** North American audiences appreciate an animated style of delivery. So allow yourself to make bigger gestures and to be more passionate. And these audiences iare quite happy for presenters to stride all over the stage when speaking, too.

- **Speaking to an Asian audience:** Asian audiences are perhaps just a little bit more formal than the Brits, but generally the same rules apply. However, Asian audiences will be attentive and respectful even if the speaker isn't any good.

- **Speaking to a South American audience:** South American audiences like a speaker who is decisive. That means gestures and movement can be expansive and emphatic.

These general guidelines can help you plan a speech to international audiences, but the only way to be sure that specific gestures won't be offensive is to talk with people from that culture before you turn up. So make sure you ask your contact questions about what may be appropriate before you set off.

Making Eye Contact Count

At some point in many old tear-jerker romantic films, the heroine tells the hero (or vice versa) that she doesn't love him anymore. (Usually the villain has forced this situation upon them.) The violins rise up strongly on the soundtrack. The camera pans in for a close-up. Shock and disbelief register across the hero's face. And inevitably he utters this immortal line: 'Look me in the eye and say that.' The hero means that her words aren't true until she says them while making eye contact.

'If looks could kill.' We've all been glad they can't when we've been on the receiving end of this statement, but when you give a presentation or speech, looks *can* kill. Depending on what you do or don't look at, looks can kill your entire presentation. Use the following rules to prevent yourself from committing a criminal offence:

- ✔ **Look at individuals.** As you gaze around the room, make eye contact with as many individuals as possible. A common myth is to pick out a friendly face and look at it. That quickly seems weird. This poor person wonders why you're staring at him or her, and so does the rest of the audience. Look at a variety of individuals. Remember, you want to be a search light, not a laser beam.

- ✔ **Establish eye contact at the end of a thought.** Eye contact is most effective at this point. People will nod their heads under the pressure of your gaze, and their doing so is a big plus for you. Because of the structure of English sentences, the important information is usually in the second half of the sentence; so, making eye contact at the end of a thought emphasises the important part. By making eye contact in this way, you force people to nod when you make a point. That nodding doesn't automatically mean that they agree with you, but it subconsciously forces the audience in that direction.

- ✔ **Look at the audience, not everywhere else.** If you look out the window, so will your audience. This fact is also true for looking at the ceiling, the walls, or the floor. The audience plays follow the leader, and you're the leader. Look at them so they'll look at you.

- ✔ **Look at more than one spot.** Make sure that you establish eye contact with all parts of your audience. Cover the entire room. If you look straight ahead and never look toward the sides or if you look only at the people toward the front, you risk losing a major portion of your audience because everyone towards the side and in the back feels left out. No, you don't want your head to look like a machine gun pivoting back and forth as it sprays eye contact at the crowd. But you do want to keep your gaze rotating from one part of the audience to another.

- ✔ **Spend more time looking at the audience than your notes.** Some speakers get so hung up looking at their notes that they don't look at the people in front of them. Big mistake. The notes aren't going to applaud when you're done. And neither will the audience if you haven't looked at them. Ideally, you should rehearse your talk enough so that you don't

Book IV

Delivering Perfect Presentations

need to refer to your notes much at all. But if you must read from them, first make sure your notes are easy to read – large print, legible, only a few key words per card. Second, watch how TV news presenters read from their notes. They look down. They read the notes. They look up. They look into the camera. They tell you one thought. Then they repeat the process. Head up. Head down. Head up. Head down. (Just don't do it too fast or you'll look like a nodding dog on a car dashboard.)

✔ **Look at the noses of the audience if you're nervous, not over their heads.** A big myth of giving presentations is that gazing over the heads of your audience is okay. But people can tell if you're speaking to the clock on the back wall. And the smaller the audience, the more obvious this technique becomes. If you're too nervous to look in your audience's eyes, just look at the tips of their noses – it works.

Mastering Physical Positioning and Movement

Although you may have your intro down pat and think you're totally prepared to give your presentation, you may have forgotten that getting to and from the podium, as well as standing and moving when you're there have important consequences for your talk. So check out the tips we provide in the sections below to make sure your presentation gets started on the right foot.

Managing entrances and exits

Imagine your name being announced. You get up to move towards the podium and stumble. Your notes go flying and you knock a glass of water on to the stage. Not a good entrance. Not how you want your entrances, or exits, to be remembered.

Getting onstage with class

The beginning of a presentation or speech is its most critical part. Everyone knows that. But when does it begin? Does your presentation kick off when you start speaking? When you walk to the podium? When you enter the room?

We believe your presentation starts almost from the moment you leave home. The next few paragraphs walk you through how you should begin your presentation, starting from home.

After you leave your home, you never know when a member of your audience may see you. And if you're observed engaging in some questionable activity, your image may suffer. When you ascend the stage to speak, you want to project an aura of confidence and command. You want to be all-powerful. You don't want any audience members to recall that an hour ago they saw you eating a greasy burger on the steps of the conference centre or picking your teeth in the car park.

Get to the room early and make sure that the podium, microphone, and any audiovisual equipment are arranged properly. Pay particular attention to microphone cords and power cords. You don't want to open your talk by tripping and falling. If you're speaking on a stage, check where the steps up to it are located. Plan your route to the podium and practise it before your speech if possible.

While you're waiting to speak, listen attentively to any speakers preceding you. When you're introduced, rise confidently and walk assuredly to the podium. Shaking hands with the person who introduced you is optional. (Unless the person extends his or her hand!)

When you arrive at the podium, place your notes where you want them. Open them. Look out at the audience. Pause. Then give a fantastic presentation.

Getting offstage in style

Saying the last words of your speech is only the beginning of the end. You still have a lot to do. And that doesn't mean hurriedly gathering up your notes and getting out of there. First and foremost, you must bask in the thundering ovation that your audience will no doubt deliver. (If, for some unfathomable reason, they're not immediately forthcoming with applause, then you can give them a hint. If you're feeling brave, anyway. When a deafening roar of approval doesn't greet your closing, you could make a short bowing motion with your head and shoulders. The audience usually get the message.)

After you've accepted your ovation (and answered any questions), you must disconnect yourself from the microphone (if you were using a clip-on device). Many speakers forget this step, and it can be quite embarrassing. Even if you don't wear the mike into the toilet, everyone still hears you breathing, and you lose credibility.

After the microphone is detached, gather your speaking materials and depart from the podium in a confident manner. Stride purposefully back to your seat. Smile and acknowledge audience acclaim along the way. If you're followed by another speaker, become a model audience member. Wait expectantly for the speaker with your full attention directed at the podium.

Book IV

Delivering Perfect Presentations

Act this way even if you've just given the world's worst presentation. Amazingly, people will give you the reaction you ask for. If *you* act like the presentation was a success (even if it wasn't), a better than average chance exists that the audience will play along. Doing so makes *everybody* feel better.

You're never really finished until you've left the site of your presentation, you no longer have contact with any audience members (such as in a hotel bar after your talk), and you're home in bed.

Moving around

People have short attention spans today. And movement helps maintain audience attention. Of course, speakers who move endlessly and erratically will distract from their message. Follow these tips to have all the right moves:

- ✔ **Use up and down movements.** Find a reason to bend over close to the floor or reach up into the air. These movements – used very occasionally – can make you look more interesting to the audience.

- ✔ **Move purposefully.** Make every movement count. Whether you're gesturing, changing position, or walking from one location to another, the movement must support your message. Pacing is an example of *non*-purposeful movement that you should avoid.

- ✔ **Be aware of audience depth perception.** If you're speaking from a stage in a large room, moving left or right has much more impact than moving forward or back. (This phenomenon is created by depth perception. Don't ask us to explain it.) Remembering this effect is important because it goes against instinct. You may assume that moving towards or away from the audience has the bigger effect. It doesn't. A step forward or back doesn't have half the impact of a step left or right. Keep that in mind when you want to emphasise a point.

- ✔ **Move in an irregular pattern.** A major value of movement is that it helps maintain audience attention. But moving in a regular pattern has an opposite effect. The predictability of any regular pattern lulls the audience into a semi-hypnotic state (also known as sleep). You want to keep moving. Just make sure no one else knows where you're going.

- ✔ **Avoid making nervous movements.** Speakers who constantly pull at their hair, shift from foot to foot, play with their notes, scratch themselves, and adjust their clothes are very distracting. So avoid those types of nervous movements. Don't be a perpetual motion machine. You'll end up looking very nervous or as though you need the toilet. Either way, the audience won't focus on what you're saying.

Getting into the power position

For those of you dragging out a yoga mat now, when we say *power position* we're talking about the power position when you're speaking from a stage. To find this spot, divide the stage into a three by three, nine-square grid: back left, back centre, back right, left centre, centre centre, right centre, front right, front centre, front left. The power position is front centre.

But don't just stand in this position. Move into different squares as you speak. If you want a mechanical formula, find cues in your talk that suggest moves. 'I was in a cattle shop looking at bulls. And over on the right I saw (move to a square on the right) a beautiful set of china teacups. I took one to the proprietor (move into another square) and I said, "Is this the famous china in a bull shop?"' (Now you'd better move to a rear square because with puns like that, the audience may start throwing things.)

This process of moving from square to square is called making an active stage picture. Doing so ensures that you don't just stand in one place, and it makes you more interesting for the audience to watch. Just remember to return frequently to the power square.

Working from a podium

Many people believe that podiums act as a barrier between the speaker and the audience – that the speaker is 'hiding' behind the podium. So, many public speaking teachers, communication coaches, and other professional presenter types give this advice: Don't use a podium. Nowadays, presentations are as much about entertainment as information. And if you do use a podium, get out from behind it as often as possible.

However, if you feel nervous without a podium and you want to use one, then go ahead.

Two reasons exist why you may want to use a podium, and the first is common sense:

1. **If you're comfortable behind a podium and nervous in front of it, then stay behind it.** You'll give a better presentation. Getting out from behind the podium to 'eliminate a barrier with your audience' is pointless if doing so creates a bigger barrier – crippling nervousness (see Book IV, Chapter 4 for more on coping with nerves).

Book IV

Delivering Perfect Presentations

2. **Eye contact is more important than being able to see your body.** An audience's first connection with you is always with your facial expression and eye contact. So long as you're making good eye contact and using a range of appropriate facial expressions to animate your face, it doesn't matter if the audience can't see your body. However, stepping away from the podium occasionally (if you feel confident enough to do so) can be a good change for your audience.

Using the podium effectively

Just like anything else you do while giving your presentation, using a podium does have guidelines; check them out below:

- ✔ **Use the podium as a strategic tool.** The podium doesn't just have to be a place where you dump your notes and give your speech or presentation. The podium can play a much more active role in your talk. Timing is a perfect example. Say you ask your audience a rhetorical question and want them to ponder on the answer. Try turning your back on them and walking away for a few seconds. By the time you return to the podium, your audience should have had a few seconds to think about your question.

- ✔ **Look at your notes while you're moving behind the podium.** Want to disguise your reliance on notes? Look at your notes whenever you move. When you make a gesture, shift position, or turn your head, take a quick peek at your notes. Like a magician's hand, the audience will focus on your movement rather than what you're actually doing – reading.

- ✔ **Use a podium to 'hide' when appropriate.** Even if you don't like to stay behind a podium, sometimes you may need to draw audience attention to something other than yourself. Are you using PowerPoint slides, overheads, or a volunteer from the audience? Standing behind a podium makes perfect sense for these situations, especially if the podium is placed off to the side.

- ✔ **Avoid pressing or gripping the podium.** Using a podium is okay – but not as a crutch. Standing rigidly behind your podium is a sign that you're not as confident as the audience would like you to be.

  Gripping the podium for dear life is another common mistake – like you'll float away if you let go. Again, your behaviour's disconcerting for the audience, because clinging to the podium is an obvious indication of extreme nervousness. Instead of concentrating on what the speaker is saying, the audience is mentally placing bets on when he or she will pass out.

Paralanguage: What Your Voice Says about You

People don't just judge you by what you say – they also judge you by how you say it. Do you say the words loudly? Rapidly? Monotonously? Do you have an accent? Do you mispronounce words? All of these factors – *how* you say things, not *what* you say – are known as *paralanguage*.

Here are some tricks and tips for using your voice.

- **Warm up your voice.** You're about to speak. You're opening line is a gem. People will be quoting it for years. You're introduced. You get to the podium. You open your mouth to deliver your *bon mots* and . . . your voice cracks. So much for the brilliant opening. That's why you need to warm up your voice. Find an empty room or pop into the toilet before you speak and do some vocal exercises. Hum. Talk to yourself. Get your voice going. (But make sure that no one is in there with you. You *don't* want anyone in the audience to remember you as the person talking to themself in the loo.) *Singing For Dummies* by Pamelia S. Phillips (Wiley) has several excellent exercises for warming up your voice that work just as well for speaking as they do for singing.

- **Pronounce your words clearly.** You know that speaking with your mouth full isn't polite. Well, sounding like you're speaking with your mouth full isn't polite either – especially if you have an audience. It can be hard enough for one person to understand another even when they each know exactly what was said. Don't make communication even more difficult. Pronounce your words clearly.

- **Get rid of filler sounds and phrases.** Filler sounds and phrases take up space for no reason, sound stupid, and distract the audience from your message. Banish these words and phrases from your vocabulary: Like, you know, um, okay, ugh, ah, actually, interestingly enough.

- **Use vocal variety.** Monotony refers to more than just tone of voice. Yes, a monotonous voice may be the result of speaking in one tone. But it may also result from speaking at one rate of speed, in one volume, or in one pitch. If you're monotonous in any of those ways, you have a problem. If you're monotonous in all of those ways, the audience will fall asleep. The cure is vocal variety. Speed up to express excitement. Slow down if you need your audience to take heed of a warning message.

- **Use your voice for emphasis.** You can completely alter the meaning of a sentence simply by changing the words you emphasise. Say the

Book IV

Delivering Perfect Presentations

following line aloud and emphasise the word in italics. 'Are you talking to *me*?' 'Are *you* talking to me?' 'Are you *talking* to me?' Alright, enough with the Robert DeNiro impressions. You get the idea. Use vocal emphasis to reinforce the meanings you want to communicate.

✔ **Slow down after mistakes.** No one is perfect. Everyone makes mistakes. Inevitably, you'll mispronounce a word or stumble through a tongue-twisting phrase. The natural instinct is to speed up when you make a mistake. Don't. Doing so highlights your error and increases your chances for making additional errors. So slow down.

✔ **Use volume as a tool.** Volume is a powerful tool that you can easily manipulate. Changing your pitch or tone may be difficult, but anyone can speak more loudly or softly. Try dropping your voice to a conspiratorial whisper as if you're conveying a secret. Or try raising your voice when you are talking about how exciting a new opportunity could be. Doing so can have an amazing effect on an audience.

Many speakers think you should never speak softly. Wrong. Speaking softly can be incredibly effective. We've seen speakers whisper and draw in an entire audience. People lean forward in their seats. How can they hear? If you're speaking into a microphone, speaking softly doesn't matter. The whole point of using the microphone is that it allows you to speak in a full range of volumes.

Speaking at a high volume can also be used dramatically. If you're telling a tale of some struggle or argument, it may be appropriate to yell some of the dialogue. Just make sure you don't overdo it. You want to entertain your audience, not shock them into a stunned silence.

Any time you shift your volume, people will pay attention. Volume's an easy way to vary your speech pattern. So use it.

✔ **Use pauses.** A common mistake among inexperienced (and nervous) speakers is to speak without pausing. They just rush through their talks, one thought merging into another. The audience *listens* to a lot of words but don't *hear* a thing. They become clogged with information.

The pause is a vital part of the communication process. It leaves time for the meaning of what's been said to sink in. And a pause clears the way for the importance of what comes next. Also, pausing before a change of subject, major point, or interesting fact creates an impression of confidence. Pausing also highlights the point. Don't be afraid to use pauses.

Chapter 4

Overcoming Nerves

- -

In This Chapter

▶ Reducing mental anxiety with proven techniques

▶ Controlling the physical symptoms of stress

▶ Handling nervousness

▶ Using your nervousness

- -

*N*ervousness, stage fright, the jitters. The words themselves are enough to make you feel faint. Social scientists may have created other terms to describe nervousness – 'communication anxiety' or 'communication apprehension' – but whatever you want to call it, the symptoms are universally recognised. Your heart pounds. Your hands shake. Your forehead sweats. Your mouth goes dry. Your stomach lurches. And that reaction's just when you get asked to speak in public. You feel really bad when you actually have to give the presentation.

If you do experience a touch of nerves, congratulations; you're in the majority. According to one frequently cited survey, most people consider public speaking more frightening than death. And you're in good company – celebrities alleged to suffer from stage fright include veteran actors such as Laurence Olivier, Peter O'Toole, and Edward Woodward. Although you just have to accept that those feelings of nervousness may always be with you, we discuss some great techniques in this chapter so you can figure out how to control them and use them to your advantage.

Changing Your Perceptions

Teacher to pupil: 'Think positive.' Pupil to teacher: 'I am. I'm positive I'm going to fail.' This old joke highlights an important point – feeling nervous is a purely mental phenomenon. However, if nervousness can be caused mentally, it can be cured mentally. Just consider the way you look at things.

Realising how your audience really feels

Feeling nervous in front of others is a very egocentric affliction. *I'm* scared. *I'm* nervous. *I'm* going to pass out. Me. Me. Me. You may easily lose sight of your audience's interests, but the audience has as much at stake as you. You may suffer from *stage fright* but your audience may be more scared than you. They may suffer from *seat fright* – the fear of wasting time listening to a bad presentation. For you to succeed in giving a great presentation and controlling your fear, you need to know the following four things about your audience:

✔ **The audience wants you to succeed.** By showing up, members of your audience give you a tremendous vote of confidence. They don't want to spend their precious time to come and hear you fail. They want your presentation to be a success. Their success is linked to yours. When your talk is terrific, people in the audience feel good for having turned up.

✔ **You have knowledge that the audience wants.** You were asked to speak for a reason – probably because you have information that the audience desires. You're the expert. You have stories, learning, or data that the audience members are clamouring for. Even on the rare occasion that the audience knows more than you about your topic, you can still provide new information. Only *you* can provide your own unique insights. No one else knows *your* view and interpretation of the material. Think of yourself as sharing valuable knowledge and ideas with your audience.

✔ **The audience doesn't know that you're afraid.** Psychological research shows that the speaker and the audience have very different perceptions about stage fright. Often, an audience can't even detect anxiety in a speaker who claims to be extremely nervous. This situation is like the spot cream advert you see on TV. A typical teenager suffering from acne gets a pimple on his nose. He imagines the pimple is as big as a watermelon and that people are staring at it wherever he goes. Of course, no one even notices it. Nervousness works the same way. Stage fright is a mental pimple that seems a lot worse to you than to your audience.

Visualising success like a pro

The concept of visualisation is simple and straightforward. You just imagine yourself performing a task successfully. Top athletes and sports players use this training technique. They imagine themselves scoring goals, knocking the ball for a six, or getting that hole in one. These people imagine these activities in vivid detail and try to remember past successes and build them into the image.

Popular cures that don't fight fright

Throughout history, human maladies have inspired remedies that claimed fantastic curative powers but actually proved worthless. Snake oil for the common cold. Blood-sucking leeches for fevers. Ear plugs for political speeches. Naturally, a few 'cures' have been offered for stage fright. Here are two famous ones that don't work.

✔ **Imagining the audience naked:** This alleged cure for stage fright is probably as old as human speech itself. We can just see this advice being dispensed by one caveman to another: Caveman 1: 'Don't be nervous; just imagine that the audience is naked.' Caveman 2: 'But they are naked.'

✔ **Taking booze and pills.** Another folk remedy often suggested for nervousness is to have a stiff drink or down a Valium. Doing so is supposed to help you calm down. The problem is: They don't actually make you relaxed, they make you groggy. You feel sleepy and unable to string a coherent sentence together. And then when the effects do wear off, maybe halfway through your presentation, the nerves come back with a vengeance – turning your talk into a far worse nightmare than if you hadn't had that pint or pill.

Apply visualisation techniques to *your* presentation. Imagine yourself giving your talk. Your voice fills the room with wisdom. People in the audience hang on your every word. (If they lean any further forward, they'll fall out of their chairs.) They give you a standing ovation and rush the stage to carry you out on their shoulders.

But don't expect results immediately. Visualisation is like any technique – you get better at it the more you practise. So make sure that you take as many opportunities as you can to visualise success in the run-up to the big day.

Talking yourself into a great presentation

Your audience only has to hear you once. You have to hear yourself all the time, so the messages you send yourself are very important. We're talking about your *internal dialogue* – the little voice that says things to you in your head. When you repeat these messages over and over, you start to believe them. So you've got to be careful what you say. If you keep telling yourself that you'll ruin your presentation at a critical moment, you probably will.

Book IV

Delivering Perfect Presentations

Talking to yourself is the flip side of visualising success – not talking yourself into failure. But the technique involves more than that. Successful visualisation techniques apply to a specific task – like giving a presentation. Your internal dialogue has a much broader focus. It applies to *everything* you do.

So how can you keep the self-chatter positive? Follow these techniques recommended by top psychologists:

- **Dispute irrational thoughts.** Say that this thought pops into your head: 'If I stand in front of an audience, I'll forget everything I know about the topic.' You need to label it as an irrational thought and challenge it. You can challenge this thought by saying, 'I've never been in a situation in which I've forgotten everything. I've practised this talk six times – so I'm not likely to forget what I'm going to say.'

- **Use personal affirmations.** 'I'm the greatest speaker in the world.' 'My subject is fascinating and the audience will love it.' 'I'm an expert.' Yes, they're a little cheesy, but they build confidence. Just as negative thoughts can make you feel worse about yourself, positive thinking can create a relaxed and confident mood. The more you talk yourself into believing your personal affirmations, the less stress you'll encounter with your speech or presentation.

- **Imagine the worst-case scenario.** Face your fear directly. Think about the worst possible thing that could happen and realise that it's not that awful. If you make a mistake while you're speaking, you can correct it and continue. If the audience doesn't give you a standing ovation, they may still applaud. Even if the presentation is a total disaster, no one is going to die. A poor presentation isn't the end of the world. Get the situation in perspective.

Transforming Terror into Terrific

A man goes to the doctor for a check-up. He says, 'I look in the mirror and I'm a mess. My skin is sagging. I have blotches all over my face. My hair is falling out. What is it?' The doctor says, 'I don't know, but your eyesight is perfect.'

Unfortunately, a lot of other people have perfect eyesight, too – especially when it involves observing any physical signs that you may be nervous. But thankfully, eliminating or disguising the sweating and shaking isn't that hard.

Discovering stress-busting exercises

Even though stress is technically all in your head, its effects can be quite physical. So if you can't treat your mental state, treat your physical symptoms.

Breathing

Take a deep breath. Hold it. Hold it. Now let it out slowly. Good. Do it again. Breathe deeply and slowly. Really slowly. And keep it up. Don't you feel better already? Breathing slowly is one of the world's oldest techniques for relieving stress. You release carbon dioxide every time you exhale, which decreases the acidity of your blood and increases the flow of oxygen to your brain.

Stretching

Stretching is a great way to relieve muscle tension quickly, and it doesn't take long to do. Stretching for as little as 10 or 15 seconds can be beneficial. Now, you can't just do yoga in the middle of a banquet when you're the after-dinner speaker, but you can excuse yourself and do a few quick stretches in the toilet just a few minutes before you're due to start. Use the following exercises to get you past the finishing line:

- ✔ **Head rolls:** Slowly turn your head from side to side. That's the warm-up. Now move your head clockwise in a circle (look up, right, down, and left). Do this three times and then reverse the direction. You'll feel the tension flowing out of your neck.

- ✔ **Arm lifts:** Stretch your right arm up into the air as far as it will go. Hold it for a few seconds. Bring it back to your side. Now stretch your left arm up as far as it will go. Keep repeating the process. At school, your PE teacher probably made you do this exercise as a form of torture. Now you're going to do it for relief. It helps stretch out your back.

- ✔ **Jaw breakers:** Open your mouth as wide as possible (as if you're going to scream). Then close your mouth. Keep opening and closing your mouth. This exercise helps relieve tension in the jaw. You can also use your fingers to massage the muscle that connects the jaw and the rest of the head.

Book IV

Delivering Perfect Presentations

Moving around

Some speakers like to take a quick walk or jog on the spot to get rid of nervous energy. Are there stairs in the building where you'll speak? A few trips up and down some flights of stairs may be helpful, but don't overdo it. You don't want to be sweaty, tired, and out of breath by the time you go on.

Spotting the real secret: Don't look nervous

A little nervousness is good and a lot of nervousness is bad. So you should control your nervousness and keep it at an acceptable level. You can manage your nervousness by following all the standard techniques described in this chapter.

How nervous you are doesn't really matter – *as long as you appear calm*. All that counts is that the audience thinks you're confident. Try these tips and tricks for disguising some of the common signs of nerves:

- ✔ **Fidgeting:** Fidgeting is an announcement that you're anxious. Touching your face with your index finger or rubbing it under your nose or scratching above your lip or toying with any jewellery are all signs of nervousness. The solution: Keep your hands in front of you in the 'steeple position'. (See Book IV, Chapter 3 for a description of this position.) If you're using a lectern, place your hands on either side of it or on it as if you're playing the piano.

- ✔ **Pacing:** Pacing is another very visible sign of anxiety. The solution: Move closer to the audience and then stop for a moment. Then move somewhere else and stop.

- ✔ **Sweating:** How you handle the sweating is what counts. If you take a handkerchief, open it up and swipe at the sweat – you look like a nervous wreck. The solution: Never open the handkerchief. Keep it folded in a square. *Dab* at the sweat and then replace the handkerchief in your pocket. If you tend to sweat a lot, wear a t-shirt under your shirt to avoid visible staining.

- ✔ **Hands shaking:** Your hands shaking like a leaf is a pretty good indication of nerves. The solution: Use cards rather than sheets of paper for your notes. Paper, which is larger and weighs less than cards, makes your shakiness more apparent. Also, don't hold props or other items that show that your hands are shaking.

Preventing and Handling Nervousness

Don't be worried about feeling nervous when you're speaking. Just keep the following tips in mind and you'll be ready for anything.

Writing out your intro and conclusion

Nervousness is most intense before you begin speaking. So giving special attention to your introduction is important from a stage-fright perspective.

The introduction is the most anxiety-producing part of your presentation or speech. If you write out your introduction and practise it until you have it down pat, you reduce your anxiety.

Similar preparation should be given to the conclusion – often the second most anxiety-producing part of a presentation.

Anticipating problems and preparing solutions

Anticipate any problem that could arise and have a plan ready to deal with it. For example, whenever you stumble over a tongue-twisting name or phrase, you can have an all-purpose recovery line ready: 'Let me try that again – in English.'

What if you forget what point you were going to cover next? You can buy time by asking the audience a survey question that requires a show of hands. Or you can review what you've already covered. Or you can skip ahead to a different point.

Arriving early

Fear of the unknown probably produces more anxiety than any other cause. Until you get to the location where you're presenting, you face a lot of unknowns. Is the room set up correctly? Did they remember to give you an overhead projector? Plenty of little questions can add up to big sources of stress if you don't have answers for them.

You can get the answers simply by going to the room, so do it early. The earlier you arrive, the more time you have to correct any mistakes and the more time you have to calm down. You may also get a chance to meet members of the audience who arrive early, which can reduce stress by making the audience more familiar to you.

Book IV

Delivering Perfect Presentations

Dividing and conquering

Many speakers who suffer from nervousness claim that what triggers their fear is a large audience. A few people, no problem. A big group, forget it. To cope with a large crowd: Look at one face in the audience at a time – especially faces that appear interested in what you're saying. Keep coming back to these people. (Normally, a basic rule of eye contact is that you shouldn't stare at only a few people and we discuss that in Book IV, Chapter 3. But overcoming nervousness is the exception. If the only way you can prevent yourself from passing out is to look at only a few people, then do it.)

Not apologising for nervousness

Many speakers feel compelled to apologise for being nervous. Don't apologise for making a mistake. Just let it go. You don't want to draw additional attention to your nervousness.

Practising makes perfect – and confident

Familiarity breeds contempt, apparently. But the reverse is true for presentations and public speaking: Familiarity breeds confidence. Practising your presentation can help reduce nerves. Here are a few tips for rehearsing away your fears:

- **Rehearse out loud.** The only way that you can tell how your presentation will sound is to listen to it. *That means that you have to say it out loud.* Practise your talk in an empty office or at home and do it at the volume at which you need to speak. Don't just whisper it out loud. Practise projecting your voice at full volume so you become comfortable with saying the words out loud. Listening to the voice in your head or whispering it meekly don't count – those are not the voices that your audience will hear.

- **Simulate real conditions.** The more closely you can simulate actual speaking conditions in your rehearsals, the more confident you'll be for the actual event. Use the actual notes that you'll use when you present. Use the actual clothes that you'll wear. (At least wear them in your dress rehearsal. That's why dress rehearsals are called dress rehearsals.) Will you be using a handheld microphone for your talk? When you practise at home, use a hairbrush to simulate the microphone so you can get some practice at keeping it close to your mouth at all times.

- **Time it.** Time your presentation. Do it while you're rehearsing in front of an audience. (Audience reactions can affect the length of your talk.) Time your entire presentation. Doing so is the only way to determine whether your talk will fit its assigned time slot. And having that knowledge can relieve a lot of anxiety.

- **Rehearse questions and answers.** If you'll have a question-and-answer period after your presentation, being prepared for it is essential for reducing anxiety. Anticipate questions that you may receive. Rehearse your answers.

Chapter 5

Handling Questions
from the Audience

. . . .

In This Chapter

▶ Checking out some basic guidelines

▶ Designing a perfect answer

▶ Answering questions with six techniques

▶ Discovering how to handle hostile questions

. . . .

Aprofessor travelled from university to university speaking about quantum physics. One day his chauffeur said, 'Professor, I've heard your lecture so many times I could give it myself.' The professor said, 'Fine. Give it tonight.' When they got to the university, the chauffeur was introduced as the professor. The chauffeur delivered the lecture, and nobody knew the difference. Afterward, someone in the audience asked a long question about Boolean algebra and quantum mechanics. The chauffeur didn't miss a beat. He said, 'I can't believe you asked that question. It's so simple, I'm going to let my chauffeur answer it.'

Unfortunately, most people don't have a chauffeur who can answer tough questions. So you have to drive yourself through the maze known as the question-and-answer session. Many speakers let their guard down during this session. Doing so's a big mistake. Even if you gave a great presentation, a poor performance during the question and answer (Q&A) session can totally change the audience's perceptions of you and your topic. Equally, if your presentation was mediocre, a strong performance during the Q&A can leave the audience with a very positive impression. So, read the rest of this chapter to make sure you give a great performance during the Q&A (but read the rest of this book to make sure the rest of your presentation is a hit, too!)

Discovering the Basics

To give a sparkling performance during a question and answer session, stack the odds in your favour by following a few basic rules.

Anticipate questions

The secret to giving brilliant answers is knowing the questions in advance. In some circles, this ability is called clairvoyance. (In a school exam, it's called cheating.) In our system, knowing the questions is called anticipation. You anticipate what you'll be asked.

Just use your common sense to anticipate questions. Think about your presentation and your audience. Then generate a list of every possible question that the audience may ask. Don't pull any punches. Think of the toughest questions that may come up. Then ask your colleagues or friends to think of the toughest questions they can devise, too.

After you've compiled a comprehensive list of questions, prepare an answer for each one. Practise saying your answers out loud until you feel comfortable with them. With a little on-the-spot tweaking, they may also help you answer questions that you didn't anticipate.

Answer questions at the end

Taking questions *after* you've made your presentation is generally better than while you're giving it. If you take questions during your talk, it distracts both you and the audience, it makes your presentation harder to follow, and it can ruin your rhythm. (Someone asking a question just as you're building to the climax of your most dramatic story is always thrilling.) Unless you're a very confident presenter, tell the audience at the beginning that you'll take questions at the end.

Don't let a few people dominate

Every so often, you get an audience from which one or two people ask questions – endlessly. The moment you finish answering their first questions, they're asking others. Whatever their motivation, your job is not to play 20 questions with them. You want to have a conversation with the *entire* audience, not just one or two members of it.

Try to take questions from as many different audience members as time permits. Don't let a couple of people ask all the questions, unless they're the only ones with questions. Doing so just frustrates everyone else whose hand is raised, wanting to ask you something. Eventually such audience members just give up.

Be fair. Don't favour one section of the room over another. The best approach is to try to call on people in the order in which they raised their hands. Don't give in to bullies who don't wait their turn and instead shout out questions. Shouting out is the oral equivalent of jumping a queue, and is definitely not fair to the people who have been patiently waiting for you to call on them.

Establish the ground rules early. When you open the session up for questions, tell the audience that everyone will initially be limited to a single question. Then if time permits, you'll take a second round of questions.

Encourage questioners to ask questions, not to give speeches

You just asked for questions. Despite the fact that you're standing at a podium and you've just given a lengthy presentation, someone in the audience is bound to want to give a presentation-length speech, too. One of these people exists in every crowd, and your job is to make sure they don't launch into a speech.

You're the speaker. You opened up the session for questions – not speeches. When one of these people starts giving a speech, you must cut it off. How do you do it? Try gently interrupting the person and suggest a question: 'So what you're really asking is. . . .' (If the reply is, 'No, that's not what I'm asking,' then immediately say, 'Could you state your question, please?')

Listen to the question

If you want to be successful in a question and answer session, then you need to listen. We mean *really* listen: Go below the surface of the words used by the questioner; read between the lines; watch the body language; and listen to the tone of voice. Doing so enables you to identify what the questioner is really asking. Yes, intensely listening is exhausting (and you still have to look fresh and dapper), but your answers will be infinitely better if you really listen to every question.

Book IV

Delivering Perfect Presentations

Repeat the question

Not repeating the question you've been asked is an enormous mistake. Nothing is more frustrating than giving a brilliant answer to a question that wasn't asked.

Three major reasons exist why you should *always* repeat the question:

- ✔ You make sure that everyone in the audience heard the question.
- ✔ You make sure that *you* heard the question correctly.
- ✔ You buy yourself some time to think about your answer. (If you want even more time, rephrase the question slightly and say, 'Is that the essence of what you're asking?')

If a question is lengthy or confusing, don't repeat it word for word. Rephrase it so that you make it concise and understandable.

Don't guess

If you don't know the answer to a question, never guess. *Never.* Doing so's a one-way ticket to zero credibility. Once in a while you may get lucky, beat the odds, and bluff the audience. But most of the time, someone will call your bluff. Then you have a big problem. First, you'll be exposed as not knowing the answer you claim to know. More important, the audience wonders if you bluffed about anything else.

If you don't know the answer to a question, admit it. Then take one, some, or all of the following actions:

- ✔ Ask if anyone in the audience can answer the question.
- ✔ Suggest a resource where the questioner can find the answer.
- ✔ Offer to discover the answer yourself and get it to the questioner.

Remember, nobody knows everything!

End the Q&A strongly

The Q&A session is your last chance to influence audience opinion – of your topic, your ideas, and you. So you want a strong ending. Keep these two things in mind:

✔ **End the session on a high note.** Don't wait for audience questions to die off and say, 'Well, I guess that's it.' You'll look weak and not in control.

✔ **Make sure the last question you get is one that you can answer.** Don't say, 'We only have time for one more question.' It may be a question you can't answer or handle well. Again, answering poorly will make you look weak.

After you've answered a reasonable number of questions, start looking for an opportunity to end the session. Wait till you get a question that you answer brilliantly. Then announce that time has run out. Of course, you'll be happy to stick around and speak with anyone who still has a question.

What if you don't get any questions that you can answer brilliantly? Don't worry. Just make the last question one that you ask yourself. 'Thank you. We've run out of time. Well, actually you're probably still wondering about [fill in your question].' Then give your brilliant answer.

One more word (actually four) about ending the Q&A session: End it on time. Some audience members come solely for your presentation and may need to leave. They don't care about the Q&A. (Or they don't care about the questions being asked.) So stick to the schedule. You can make yourself available afterward for anyone who wants to keep the discussion going.

Coming Up with a Perfect Answer

Apparently experts are people who know all the right answers – if they're asked the right questions. Unfortunately, your audience may not always ask the right questions. This section presents some ways to make sure your answers will be expert, no matter what you're asked.

Treating the questioner properly

Questioners may be rude, obnoxious, opinionated, egomaniacal, inane, obtuse, antagonistic, befuddled, illiterate, or incomprehensible. You still have to treat them nicely. Why? Because they're members of the audience, and the audience identifies with them – at least initially. Use these suggestions for dealing with someone who asks you a question:

✔ **Assist a nervous questioner.** Some audience members who ask questions may suffer from a touch of nervousness themselves. These people want to ask their question so much that they try to ignore their pounding hearts, sweaty palms, and stomach cramps. As they ask their questions, they try to forget that all eyes in the room are on them, but ignoring this situation is often difficult. So anxious audience members having trouble getting out their questions isn't unusual. They'll stammer and stutter, they'll lose their train of thought, and they'll make the rest of the audience extremely uncomfortable. Help these people out. Finish asking their questions for them if you can. Otherwise, offer some gentle encouragement. By breaking in and speaking yourself, you give nervous questioners time to collect themselves. They'll be grateful. And so will everyone else.

✔ **Wait for the questioner to finish.** Unless the questioners are rambling or they're nervous and need help, let them finish asking their questions. Too many speakers jump in before the question is fully stated. They *think* they know what the question is, and they start giving an answer. They look very foolish when the questioner interrupts saying, 'That's not what I was asking.' Only interrupt the questioner if they're using the opportunity to give a little speech of their own.

✔ **Recognise the questioner by name.** If you know the name of the person asking the question, use it. Doing so has a powerful effect on the audience. It makes you seem much more knowledgeable and in control. And the people whose names you say always appreciate the recognition.

✔ **Compliment the questioner, if appropriate.** If the question is particularly interesting or intelligent, saying so is okay. But be specific and say why. Some communication gurus advise never to say, 'Good question' because doing so implies that the other questions weren't. To avoid offending anyone, say, 'That's an especially interesting question because. . . .' This statement implies that the other questions were also interesting – a compliment. Phrasing your response that way also eliminates all the value judgements attached to the word 'good'.

✔ **Treat the questioner with dignity.** Yes, the question may be inane or even stupid. But you don't want to be the one to point it out. No matter how idiotic the query, treat the questioner with dignity. If you imply that the question was stupid, you make yourself look bad, generate sympathy for the questioner, and discourage anyone else from asking questions.

✔ **Look fascinated as they ask their questions.** For a questioner to rise out of the anonymity of the audience to ask a question can take a lot of guts, so don't discourage questioners by looking bored or condescending while they're speaking. Even if you think the question is silly, look fascinated. Give each questioner your full attention. Make eye contact. Lean forward. Nod while they are speaking to show that you're listening. Show that your most important priority is listening to the question.

Nothing is more insulting or dispiriting than a speaker who looks around the audience for the next question while the current question is being asked. And not only the questioner is offended. The whole audience picks up on the negative nonverbal message.

✔ **Stay calm and in control.** No matter how offensive the question or questioner, don't attack them. Use diplomacy and finesse to dispose of such annoyances. If the questioner is a major annoyance, the audience will recognise it. Don't become an annoyance yourself by getting defensive. The questioner wants to provoke you. Don't take the bait.

Designing your answer

You never know exactly how to answer until you receive the question, but knowing that isn't really helpful if you're trying to prepare in advance. The following general guidelines can help you formulate your answers:

✔ **Keep it brief.** Your answer should be a simple, succinct response to the question asked. Too many speakers use their answer as an excuse to give a second presentation. Give everyone a break. If the audience wanted an encore, it would have asked for one. And remember, many members of the audience may not even be interested in the question you're answering. They may be waiting to hear the next question – or ask one.

✔ **Refer back to your presentation.** Tying your answers back to your talk reinforces the points you made earlier. This tactic also makes you seem omniscient. (You somehow foresaw these questions and planted the seeds of their answers in your presentation.)

✔ **Define the terms under discussion.** Say someone asks if you think the middle class deserves a tax cut. You say, 'Yes.' The questioner immediately disagrees by arguing that giving a tax break to the middle class is unfair. After a ten-minute debate, everyone realises that no real disagreement exists. You don't think any family making more than £100,000 deserves a tax break, and neither does the questioner, but you define such families as 'rich'. The questioner defines them as 'middle class'. Make sure that everyone is on the same wavelength. Define the terms of what you're talking about up front.

✔ **Refer to your experience.** Referring to your personal and professional experience in your answer isn't bragging. That experience is one of the reasons you've been invited to present and part of what makes you an expert. The audience *wants* to hear about your experience. Just don't do it for every single question.

✔ **Point out misconceptions stated by the questioner and firmly state your position.** Never let a questioner define your position. An alarm should go off when you hear a questioner say something like, 'Well, based on your talk, it's obvious that you think. . . .' Typically, what the questioner says you think, *isn't* what you think at all. Don't let anyone put words in your mouth. If this situation occurs, address the problem immediately – as soon as the questioner finishes asking the question.

✔ **Dispute the questioner's facts or stats if you disagree.** Don't get locked into the questioner's facts or premises. If the questioner makes assumptions with which you disagree, politely say so. If you dispute the questioner's statistics, say so. Don't build a nice answer on a faulty question. Start by dismantling the question.

✔ **Be honest.** Don't make promises you won't keep. Don't say that anyone can call you at your office to ask questions if you know you won't take their calls. Don't say you'll find out the answer to a question if you know you won't. Don't offer to send information to someone if you know you'll never get around to it.

✔ **You can politely decline to answer a question.** But don't evade questions by acting like you're answering them. You're not obligated to answer every question. (You're *really not* under interrogation although a Q&A may sometimes seem that way.) But if you evade questions, you lose credibility. Doing so looks like you're ducking the issues. If you don't want to answer a question, say so firmly and politely. State the reasons why and move on to the next question.

✔ **Raise all of your points in your presentation, rather than hoping to be asked a particular question.** Leaving important points out of your presentation because you want to save them for the Q&A session is dangerous. If no one asks the right questions, you may never get a chance to make those points.

Delivering your answer

Having the perfect answer doesn't mean much if you can't deliver it effectively. But don't worry. The following simple rules ensure that your response will be – well, perfect.

✔ **Have the appropriate attitude.** Match your demeanour to the substance of the question and your answer. If someone is confused, be understanding. If someone is blatantly offensive, be forceful and disapproving (without counterattacking). If someone is seeking information, be professorial. Never lose control of yourself. Never be discourteous.

> ✔ **Look at the entire audience.** Don't limit eye contact to the questioner. Start off by looking at the questioner, but as you give your answer, direct your eye contact to the entire audience. You're speaking to everyone – not just the questioner.
>
> ✔ **Avoid being smug.** This attitude doesn't win any accolades from the audience, and it just creates a barrier. Being smug can also backfire in a big way: The audience starts rooting for you to screw up. The first time you fumble an answer – even if you're just mis-stating an insignificant detail – smugness comes back to haunt you.

Using Question-Handling Techniques

How do you become an expert in deftly fielding questions? Practice. Practise what? The following six basic techniques can help you build your question-handling skills.

Reversing the question

Someone in your audience may ask you a question for the express purpose of putting you on the spot. No sweat. Just reverse it. For example, the questioner makes a big show of appearing bored and asks, 'What time are we going to take a break?' Don't get defensive. Just respond, 'What time would you like to take a break?' This process is mental judo. You use the weight of the questioner's own question against them.

Redirecting the question

Someone asks a question. You don't have the faintest idea how to answer it. What can you do? Get the audience involved. Redirect the question to the entire group. Say, 'That's an interesting question. Does anyone have any thoughts on the subject?' Or, 'Does anyone have any experience with that situation?' The audience is a great resource; take advantage of it.

Book IV

Delivering Perfect Presentations

Rephrasing the question

'Last week's news that your chief executive will stand trial for bribing a minister has finally revealed how your parasitic company got government approval for a drug that's already killed 200 people. Will you now issue a recall to remove it from the market?' Hmmm. Are you really supposed to repeat this question for the audience? Of course, the questioner is pretending to ask a question but is really making an attack. So don't repeat back the question. In fact, you never want to repeat a question that presents a problem – doing so is embarrassing, difficult, hard to follow, whatever. So, although you shouldn't repeat the question word for word, you should rephrase it to your advantage. 'The question is about how we will convert our concern for public safety into action. Here are the steps we are taking to protect the public. . . .'

Keep in mind that a question can be a problem just because the questioner has worded it in an obtuse manner. 'In your opinion, will the actions of the Bank of England to control inflation through monetary policy, combined with global financial trends – particularly the devaluation of the Euro – result in economic forces that validate or prove wrong the City bulls in the short term?' Huh? Rephrase the question so that the audience can understand it (assuming *you* can understand it). Such a response may be, 'If I understand correctly, the question is whether the stock market will go up or down in the next few months.'

Exposing a hidden agenda

Sometimes a question contains a hidden (or not so hidden) agenda. It may be a loaded question. It may be some other type of trick question. It may be a question containing an accusation – 'How could anyone in good conscience possibly suggest cutting funds for the nursing department?' No matter the method, the question contains a 'hook'. The questioner wants to provoke a certain answer so that he or she can argue with it. The question is just a setup for a fight.

Don't fall for this trap. Instead of launching into an answer, acknowledge your suspicions. With responses, such as 'Do you have some thoughts on that?' or 'It sounds like you're expecting me to give you a certain answer. What is it you're trying to get me to say?' Politely expose the hidden agenda and get the questioner to speak about it first.

Putting the question in context

'Isn't it true that you were in Mr Smith's bedroom the night he was found stabbed to death in his bed?' This is known as a loaded question. The question is framed in a way that makes the audience members jump to very specific conclusions that make you look bad. Your response has to broaden their frames of reference. You have to provide the missing information that 'unloads' the question. 'Well, yes, as a police photographer, I did take pictures of the crime scene a few hours after Mr Smith died. That's why I was in his bedroom the night he was stabbed to death.' The meaning of any words or behaviours can be distorted if they're taken out of context. Giving a context to any question that needs one is up to you.

Building a bridge

Watch a politician evade a question in the following example. 'Minister Blowhard, are you going to vote against a tax increase?' 'Well sir, you want to know if I'm going to vote against a tax increase. What you're really asking is how can we get more money into the pockets of more hard-working people. Let me tell you about my 12-step plan for reviving the economy. . . .'

The minister has built a bridge. He's constructed a phrase that allows him to move from a question he wants to ignore to a topic he wants to address. In this case, the bridge is, 'What you're really asking is. . . .' You can use lots of bridges of this sort, for example:

- ✔ 'It makes much more sense to talk about . . .'

- ✔ 'The real issue is . . .'

- ✔ 'The essential question is . . .'

- ✔ 'What you should be asking is . . .'

- ✔ 'If you look at the big picture, your question becomes . . .'

Use a bridge to move a short distance away from a question you dislike, rather than to evade it completely. You lose credibility when you evade a question. You have to give the appearance of at least attempting to answer.

Handling Hostile Questions

The prospect of dealing with hostile questions is a huge fear facing many speakers and presenters. Stop worrying. You can use tried-and-tested techniques for handling this problem. In fact, a little advance planning can significantly reduce your chance of receiving these pesky questions altogether.

Identifying hostile questions

Don't put a chip on your shoulder and assume that anyone who disagrees with you is hostile. Even people who disagree can have a legitimate question. They don't necessarily want to argue with you. They may just want information.

However, if someone asks you a false assumption question they are being hostile. ('Do you think you'll get 10 or 20 years for income tax evasion?' and 'Isn't this an amazing achievement – for a woman?') You can safely assume these questioners are out to get you.

Heading them off at the pass

The simplest way to handle hostile questions is to not get any. Unfortunately, we can't guarantee that you won't, but these techniques can help you minimise the number you do receive:

- ✔ **The inoculation:** Can you anticipate specific hostile questions that you'll receive? Then raise them and answer them during your presentation. By beating your enemies to it, you leave them with nothing to ask you.

- ✔ **The admission:** Admit at the outset of the Q&A session that you're not the world authority on everything. Set audience expectations properly regarding the extent and areas of your expertise. Tell the audience what you don't know. This technique helps defuse potential hostility and disappointment resulting from your inability to answer specific questions.

- ✔ **The revelation:** At the outset of the Q&A session, announce that the people who ask questions must begin by identifying themselves. They must reveal their name, organisation, and anything else you want to require. Having to reveal this information is a major barrier to hostile questioners. They don't like losing the cloak of audience anonymity. Acting like an idiot, being hostile, and getting confrontational with the speaker is much easier if no one knows who you are.

Dealing with hostile questions

Receiving a hostile question is like being tossed a bomb. You need to know how to defuse it before it blows up in your face. Use the following tactics:

✔ **Empathise with the questioner.** Start by recognising that the questioner is upset and emphasise that you *understand* his or her point of view even if you don't agree with it. Make sure you communicate that you bear no personal animosity toward the questioner. Your disagreement is solely about the issue in question. 'I can see that you feel strongly about this issue, and I understand where you're coming from. Let me give you a few more facts that may affect your opinion. . . .'

✔ **Establish common ground.** Find an area where you and the questioner can agree and build your answer from there. 'Then we agree that the budget will have to be limited to 75 per cent of what we spent last year. We just differ on how to allocate the money. . . .' If you're really stuck for finding common ground, the all-purpose (albeit somewhat weak) response that works for any hostile question is: 'Well, at least we agree that this is a controversial issue. . . .'

✔ **Put the question in neutral.** If you get a question loaded with emotionally charged words or phrases, rephrase the question in neutral terms. (See the 'Rephrasing the question' section, earlier in this chapter.)

✔ **Be very specific.** Talk about specific facts and figures. Be concrete. The more you get into theory, speculation, and opinion, the more opportunity you provide for disagreement. You want to limit the opportunities for arguments.

✔ **Ask why they're asking.** What if you're on the receiving end of a loaded question or any other blatantly hostile query? Don't even bother giving an answer. Just say, 'May I ask, why did you ask that?' Doing so can go a long way to defusing the situation. The questioner, often embarrassed that you spotted the trap, may withdraw or modify the question. (See the 'Exposing a hidden agenda section, earlier in this chapter.)

✔ **Elude the hostile questioners.** Don't allow continued follow-up questions from people who just want to interrogate you in a hostile manner. No reason exists for it. You should be giving everyone in the audience a chance to ask questions. Just tell them that other people would like a turn to ask questions. You can also say that you'll be happy to discuss their concerns at the conclusion of the Q&A session.

Book IV

Delivering Perfect Presentations

Index

Notes

Notes

Notes

Notes

Notes

Notes

FOR DUMMIES®

Do Anything. Just Add Dummies

PROPERTY

UK editions

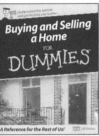

978-0-7645-7027-8

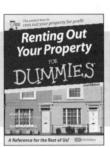

978-0-470-02921-3

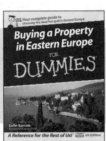

978-0-7645-7047-6

PERSONAL FINANCE

978-0-7645-7023-0

978-0-470-51510-5

978-0-470-05815-2

BUSINESS

978-0-7645-7018-6

978-0-7645-7056-8

978-0-7645-7026-1

Answering Tough Interview
Questions For Dummies
(978-0-470-01903-0)

Being the Best Man
For Dummies
(978-0-470-02657-1)

Body Language FD
(978-0-470-51291-3)

British History
For Dummies
(978-0-470-03536-8)

Buying a Home on a Budget
For Dummies
(978-0-7645-7035-3)

Buying a Property in Spain
For Dummies
(978-0-470-51235-77)

Cognitive Behavioural Therapy
For Dummies
(978-0-470-01838-5)

Cricket For Dummies
(978-0-470-03454-5)

CVs For Dummies
(978-0-7645-7017-9)

Detox For Dummies
(978-0-470-01908-5)

Diabetes For Dummies
(978-0-470-05810-7)

Divorce For Dummies
(978-0-7645-7030-8)

DJing For Dummies
(978-0-470-03275-6)

eBay.co.uk For Dummies
(978-0-7645-7059-9)

Economics For Dummies
(978-0-470-05795-7)

English Grammar For Dummies
(978-0-470-05752-0)

Gardening For Dummies
(978-0-470-01843-9)

Genealogy Online
For Dummies
(978-0-7645-7061-2)

Green Living For Dummies
(978-0-470-06038-4)

Hypnotherapy For Dummies
(978-0-470-01930-6)

Life Coaching For Dummies
(978-0-470-03135-3)

Neuro-linguistic Programming
For Dummies
(978-0-7645-7028-5)

Parenting For Dummies
(978-0-470-02714-1)

Personal Developmet
All-In-One For Dummies
(978-0-470-51501-3)

Pregnancy For Dummies
(978-0-7645-7042-1)

Retiring Wealthy For Dummies
(978-0-470-02632-8)

Self Build and Renovation
For Dummies
(978-0-470-02586-4)

Selling For Dummies
(978-0-470-51259-3)

Sorting Out Your Finances
For Dummies
(978-0-7645-7039-1)

Starting a Business on
eBay.co.uk For Dummies
(978-0-470-02666-3)

Starting and Running an Online
Business For Dummies
(978-0-470-05768-1)

The Romans For Dummies
(978-0-470-03077-6)

UK Law and Your Rights
For Dummies
(978-0-470-02796-7)

Writing a Novel & Getting
Published For Dummies
(978-0-470-05910-4)

Available wherever books are sold. For more information or to order direct go to www.wiley.com or call 0800 243407 (Non UK call +44 1243 843296)

FOR DUMMIES®

Do Anything. Just Add Dummies

HOBBIES

978-0-7645-5232-8

978-0-7645-5395-0

978-0-7645-5476-6

Also available:

Art For Dummies
(978-0-7645-5104-8)

Aromatherapy For Dummies
(978-0-7645-5171-0)

Bridge For Dummies
(978-0-471-92426-5)

Card Games For Dummies
(978-0-7645-9910-1)

Chess For Dummies
(978-0-7645-8404-6)

Improving Your Memory
For Dummies
(978-0-7645-5435-3)

Massage For Dummies
(978-0-7645-5172-7)

Meditation For Dummies
(978-0-471-77774-8)

Photography For Dummies
(978-0-7645-4116-2)

Quilting For Dummies
(978-0-7645-9799-2)

EDUCATION

978-0-7645-5434-6

978-0-7645-5581-7

978-0-7645-5422-3

Also available:

Algebra For Dummies
(978-0-7645-5325-7)

Astronomy For Dummies
(978-0-7645-8465-7)

Buddhism For Dummies
(978-0-7645-5359-2)

Calculus For Dummies
(978-0-7645-2498-1)

Cooking Basics For Dummies
(978-0-7645-7206-7)

Forensics For Dummies
(978-0-7645-5580-0)

Islam For Dummies
(978-0-7645-5503-9)

Philosophy For Dummies
(978-0-7645-5153-6)

Religion For Dummies
(978-0-7645-5264-9)

Trigonometry For Dummies
(978-0-7645-6903-6)

PETS

978-0-470-03717-1

978-0-7645-8418-3

978-0-7645-5275-5

Also available:

Labrador Retrievers
For Dummies
(978-0-7645-5281-6)

Aquariums For Dummies
(978-0-7645-5156-7)

Birds For Dummies
(978-0-7645-5139-0)

Dogs For Dummies
(978-0-7645-5274-8)

Ferrets For Dummies
(978-0-7645-5259-5)

Golden Retrievers
For Dummies
(978-0-7645-5267-0)

Horses For Dummies
(978-0-7645-9797-8)

Jack Russell Terriers
For Dummies
(978-0-7645-5268-7)

Puppies Raising & Training
Diary For Dummies
(978-0-7645-0876-9)

FOR DUMMIES®

The easy way to get more done and have more fun

LANGUAGES

Spanish
FOR DUMMIES

A Reference for the Rest of Us!

978-0-7645-5193-2

French
FOR DUMMIES

A Reference for the Rest of Us!

978-0-7645-5193-2

Italian
FOR DUMMIES

A Reference for the Rest of Us!

978-0-7645-5196-3

Also available:

Chinese For Dummies
(978-0-471-78897-3)

Chinese Phrases
For Dummies
(978-0-7645-8477-0)

French Phrases For Dummies
(978-0-7645-7202-9)

German For Dummies
(978-0-7645-5195-6)

Italian Phrases For Dummies
(978-0-7645-7203-6)

Japanese For Dummies
(978-0-7645-5429-2)

Latin For Dummies
(978-0-7645-5431-5)

Spanish Phrases
For Dummies
(978-0-7645-7204-3)

Spanish Verbs For Dummies
(978-0-471-76872-2)

Hebrew For Dummies
(978-0-7645-5489-6)

MUSIC AND FILM

Guitar
FOR DUMMIES

A Reference for the Rest of Us!

978-0-7645-9904-0

Filmmaking
FOR DUMMIES

A Reference for the Rest of Us!

978-0-7645-2476-9

Piano
FOR DUMMIES

A Reference for the Rest of Us!

978-0-7645-5105-5

Also available:

Bass Guitar For Dummies
(978-0-7645-2487-5)

Blues For Dummies
(978-0-7645-5080-5)

Classical Music For Dummies
(978-0-7645-5009-6)

Drums For Dummies
(978-0-471-79411-0)

Jazz For Dummies
(978-0-471-76844-9)

Opera For Dummies
(978-0-7645-5010-2)

Rock Guitar For Dummies
(978-0-7645-5356-1)

Screenwriting For Dummies
(978-0-7645-5486-5)

Songwriting For Dummies
(978-0-7645-5404-9)

Singing For Dummies
(978-0-7645-2475-2)

HEALTH, SPORTS & FITNESS

Fitness
FOR DUMMIES

A Reference for the Rest of Us!

978-0-7645-7851-9

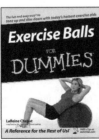

Exercise Balls
FOR DUMMIES

A Reference for the Rest of Us!

978-0-7645-5623-4

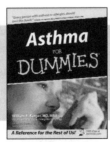

Asthma
FOR DUMMIES

A Reference for the Rest of Us!

978-0-7645-4233-6

Also available:

Controlling Cholesterol
For Dummies
(978-0-7645-5440-7)

Diabetes For Dummies
(978-0-470-05810-7)

High Blood Pressure
For Dummies
(978-0-7645-5424-7)

Martial Arts For Dummies
(978-0-7645-5358-5)

Menopause FD
(978-0-470-061008)

Pilates For Dummies
(978-0-7645-5397-4)

Weight Training
For Dummies
(978-0-471-76845-6)

Yoga For Dummies
(978-0-7645-5117-8)

Available wherever books are sold. For more information or to order direct go to www.wiley.com or call 0800 243407 (Non UK call +44 1243 843296)